DESIGN AND ANALYSIS of ALGORITHMS

DESIGN AND ANALYSIS of ALGORITHMS

Jitendra Singh

KHANNA BOOK PUBLISHING CO. (P) LTD.
DELHI

Design & Analysis of Algorithms
Jatinder Singh

ISBN: 978-93-80016-71-9

Published by:
Khanna Book Publishing Co. (P) Ltd.
4C/4344, Ansari Road, Darya Ganj, New Delhi-110 002
Phone: 011-23244448 Telefax: 011-23244447
E-mail: contact@khannabooks.com
Website: www.khannabooks.com

Regd. Off: 1694-95, 1st Floor, Nai Sarak, Delhi-110006 (India)
Phone: 011-23283211 Telefax: 011-23256658

Printed in India by:
S.P.S. Printers & Binders, Delhi

CONTENTS

CHAPTER 1: DATA STRUCTURE BASICS

CHAPTER 2: ANALYSIS OF ALGORITHMS

UNIT 2

UNIT 4

UNIT 5

UNIT 1

ALGORITHM ANALYSIS AND DESIGN FUNDAMENTALS

CHAPTER 1

UNIT 1

DATA STRUCTURE BASICS

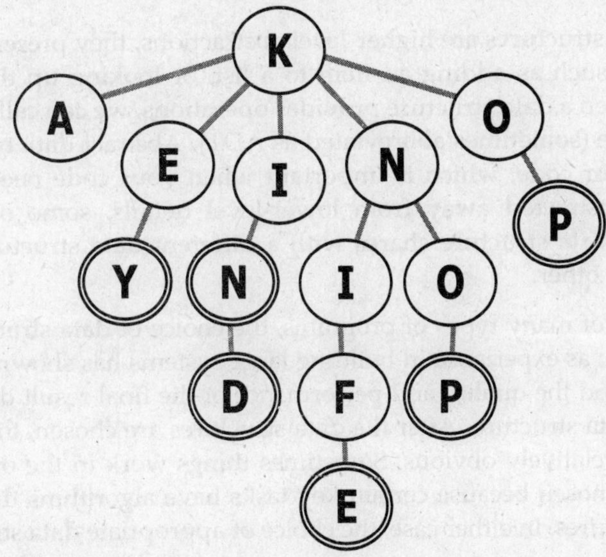

1.1 INTRODUCTION

A data structure is a way of storing data in a computer so that it can be used efficiently. A data structure is a collection of data organized in some fashion.

Data Structure = Organized Data + Allowed Operations

Often a carefully chosen data structure will allow a more efficient algorithm to be used. The choice of the data structure often begins from the choice of an abstract data structure. A well-designed data structure allows a variety of critical operations to be performed, using as little resources, both execution time and memory space, as possible.

Different kinds of data structures are suited to different kinds of applications, and some are highly sp‹cialized to certain tasks. For example, B-trees are particularly well-suited for implementation of databases, while routing tables rely on networks of machines to function.

Data structures are not really algorithms that you can find and plug into your application. Instead, they are the fundamental constructs for you to build your program around. Becoming fluent in what data structures can do for you is essential to get full value from them.

Data structures are abstractions we use to manage large amounts of information and the relationships different pieces of information have with each other. Sometimes we use data structures to allow us to do more: for example, to accomplish fast searching or sorting of data. Other times, we use data structures so that we can do less: for example, the concept of the stack is a limited form of a more general data structure. These limitations provide us with guarantees that allow us to reason about our programs more easily. Data structures also provide guarantees about algorithmic complexity -- choosing an appropriate data structure for a job is crucial to writing good software.

Because data structures are higher-level abstractions, they present to us operations on groups of data, such as adding an item to a list, or looking up the highest-priority item in a queue. When a data structure provides operations, we can call the data structure an abstract data type (sometimes abbreviated as ADT). Abstract data types can minimize dependencies in your code, which is important when your code needs to be changed. Because you are abstracted away from lower-level details, some of the higher-level commonalities one data structure shares with a different data structure can be used to replace one with the other.

In the design of many types of programs, the choice of data structures is a primary design consideration, as experience in building large systems has shown that the difficulty of implementation and the quality and performance of the final result depends heavily on choosing the best data structure. After the data structures are chosen, the algorithms to be used often become relatively obvious. Sometimes things work in the opposite direction - data structures are chosen because certain key tasks have algorithms that work best with particular data structures. In either case, the choice of appropriate data structures is crucial.

Simple Data structure can be used as building blocks of complex data structure, Array is type of Data structure using which we can build more complex data structure.

1.2 TYPES OF DATA STRUCTURE

Data structure can be classified into three different types.

1. Linear & Non-linear: which means the data stored in a sequence is called Linear, other is Non-linear (array is Linear & Tree is non-linear).

2. Homogeneous & Hetrogeneous: Which means the data structure, which contains single type of data, is known as Homogeneous & other Hetrogeneous.

3. Static and Dynamic: This is means the allocation of memory, either static or Dynamic. The allocation of memory is static if it is allocated in advance and dynamic if it is allocated at run time.

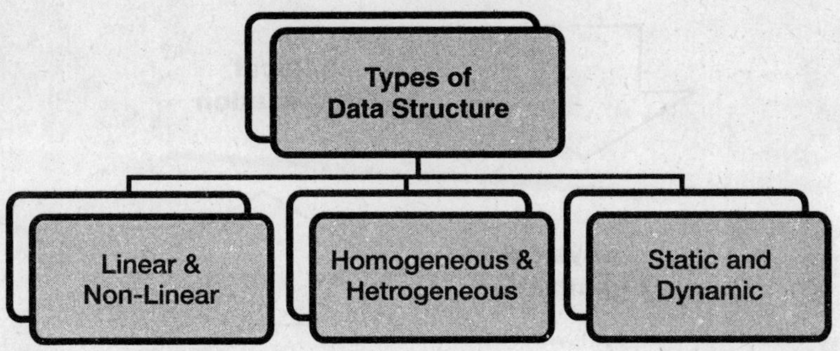

1.3 ELEMENTARY DATA ORGANIZATION

While a composite data item is defined in terms of its components, an elementary data item is defined in terms of its exact real-world meaning. That can be expressed in carefully worded text:

Date Hired: The most recent date upon which the employee reported for work; i.e. the date from which the current or former employee was continuously on our staff.

or as a simple formula
Vacation days due = Current vacation days earned + Carryover vacation days Current vacation days used

Attributes of Numeric Data Items

If the elementary data item is numeric(for example), then the definition should specify these attributes:

- Unit of measure (Note that the developers are not constrained to use this for the internal representation.)
- Range – minimum and maximum permitted values in the stated unit of measure (Some old fashioned representation-based tools ask for "number of positions".)
- Precision (or accuracy) – the smallest significant magnitude in the stated unit of measure
- scale (float or fixed)

Logical or Physical Organization

There is one important distinction that must be made at the outset when discussing file structures. And that is the difference between the logical and physical organization of the data. On the whole file structure will specify the logical structure of the data, that is the relationships that will exist between data items independently of the way in which these relationships may actually be realised within any computer. It is this logical aspect that we will concentrate on. The physical organization is much more concerned with optimizing the use of the storage medium when a particular logical structure is stored on, or in it.

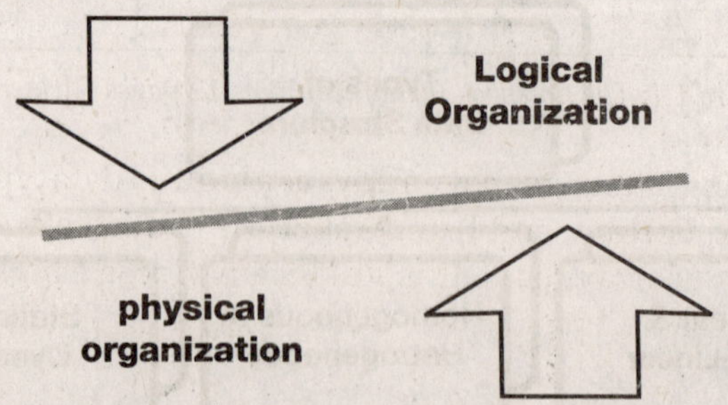

Typically for every unit of physical store there will be a number of units of the logical structure (probably records) to be stored in it. For example, if we were to store a tree structure on a magnetic disk, the physical organization would be concerned with the best way of packing the nodes of the tree on the disk given the access characteristics of the disk. The work on data bases has been very much concerned with a concept called data independence. The aim of this work is to enable programs to be written independently of the logical structure of the data they would interact with. The independence takes the following form, should the file structure overnight be changed from an inverted to a serial file the program should remain unaffected. This independence is achieved by interposing a data model between the user and the data base. The user sees the data model rather than the data base, and all his programs communicate with the model. The user therefore has no interest in the structure of the file.

1.4 VARIOUS DATA STRUCTURES

The various data structures are discussed as follows:

1.4.1 Arrays

In computer programming, an **array**, also known as a vector or list, is one of the simplest data structures. Arrays hold equally-sized data elements, generally of the same data type. Individual elements are accessed by index using a consecutive range of integers, as opposed to an associative array. Some arrays are multi-dimensional, meaning they are indexed by a fixed number of integers, for example by a tuple of four integers. Generally, one- and two-dimensional arrays are the most common.

Array is a **finite, ordered set of homogeneous** elements stored in a **contiguous** memory location. Arrays can be traversed either in Row major or Column Major order. A Sparse array is which contains a relatively number of **Zero** elements.

The concept of an array can be daunting to the uninitiated, but it is really quite simple. Think of a notebook with pages numbered 1 through 12. Each page may or may not contain information on it. The notebook is an *array* of pages. Each page is an *element* of the array 'notebook'. Programmatically, you would retrieve information from a page by referring to its number or *subscript*, i.e., notebook(4) would refer to the contents of page 4 of the array notebook.

1	2	2	...	...	10	11	12

Figure 1.1: The notebook (array) contains 12 pages (elements)

Most programming languages have arrays as a built-in data type. Some programming languages (such as APL, Fortran, and J) generalize the available operations and functions to work transparently cver arrays as well as scalars, providing a higher-level manipulation than most other languages, which require loops over all the individual members of the arrays

1.4.2 Linked Lists

A **linked list** is one of the fundamental data structures used in computer programming. It consists of a sequence of nodes, each containing arbitrary data fields and one or two references ("links") pointing to the next and/or previous nodes. A linked list is a self-referential datatype because it contains a pointer or link to another data of the same type. Linked lists permit insertion and removal of nodes at any point in the list in constant time, but do not allow random access. Several different types of linked list exist: singly-linked lists, doubly-linked lists, and circularly-linked lists.

Linked lists can be implemented in most languages. Languages such as Lisp and Scheme have the data structure built in, along with operations to access the linked list. Procedural languages such as C, C++, and Java typically rely on mutable references to create linked lists

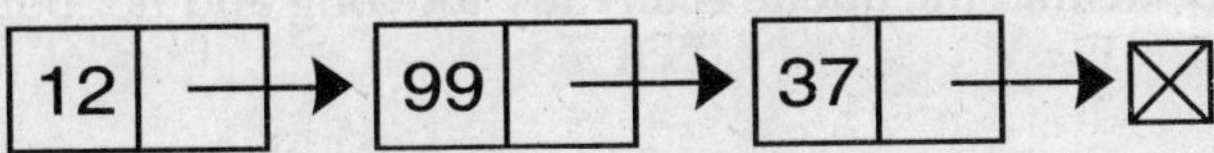

Figure 1.2: Single Linked-List

1.4.3 Stacks

A stack is a collection of items in which only the most recently added item may be removed. The latest added item is at the top. Basic operations are push and pop. Often top and isEmpty are available, too. Also known as "last-in, first-out" or LIFO.

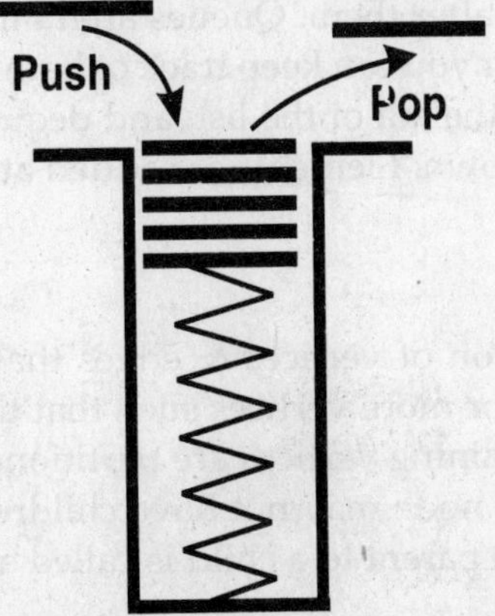

Figure 1.3: Stack

Stacks are a specific kind of linked list. They are referred to as LIFO or Last In First Out. Stacks have specific adds and removes called push and pop. Pushing nodes onto stacks is easily done by adding to the front of the list. Popping is simply removing from the front of the list. It would be wise to give return values when pushing and popping from stacks. For example, pop can return the struct that was popped.

4.4.4 Queues

A queue is a basic data structure that is used throughout programming. You can think of it as a line in a grocery store. The first one in the line is the first one to be served. A queue is also called a FIFO (First In First Out) to demonstrate the way it accesses data in providing services to people, and in computer science, transport and operations research a queue is a First-In-First-Out (FIFO) process – the first element in the queue will be the first one out. This is equivalent to the requirement that whenever an element is added, all elements that were added before have to be removed before the new element can be removed.

One characteristic of a queue is that it does not have a specific capacity. Regardless of how many elements are already contained, a new element can always be added. It can also be empty, at which point removing an element will be impossible until a new element has been added again.A practical implementation of a queue of course does have some capacity limit, that depends on the concrete situation it is used in. For a data structure the executing computer will eventually run out of memory, thus limiting the queue size. For a waiting queue of people, eventually there might not be enough space to squeeze into, or people might decide that the queue is already too long and not bother adding themselves to it

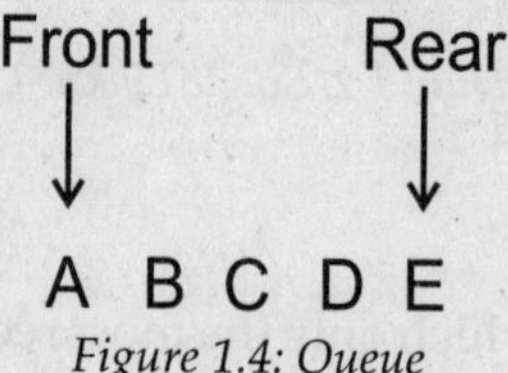

Figure 1.4: Queue

Think of a typical (non-priority) printer queue: The first jobs submitted are printed before jobs that are submitted after them. Queues aren't more difficult to implement than stacks. By creating a tail pointer you can keep track of both the front and the tail ends of the list. So you can enqueue onto the tail of the list, and dequeue from the front of the list. In figure 1.4 a simple queue is shown. Elements are added at read, while deleted at front.

1.4.5 Trees

A tree is a non-empty collection of vertices & edges that satisfies certain requirements. A Tree is a finite set of a zero or more vertices such that there is one specially designated vertex called root and the remaining vertices are partitioned into a collection of sub-trees, each of which is also a tree. A node may not have children, such node is known as **Leaf (terminal node)**. The line from parent to a child is called a branch or an edge. Children to same parent are called siblings.

A **Binary Tree** is a tree that is either empty or consists of a root node & two disjoint trees called left & right sub-tree. 2-tree or strict binary tree, is a binary tree, which either contains no children or two disjoint children.

A tree is often used to represent a *hierarchy* . This is because the relationships between the items in the hierarchy suggest the branches of a botanical tree. For example, a tree-like *organization chart* is often used to represent the lines of responsibility in a business as shown in Figure 1.5. The president of the company is shown at the top of the tree and the vice-president is indicated below her. Under the vice-presidents we find the managers and below the managers the rest of the clerks. Each clerk reports to a manager, each manager reports to a vice-president, and each vice-president reports to the president.

It just takes a little imagination to see the tree in Figure 1.5. Of course, the tree is upside-down. However, this is the usual way the data structure is drawn. The president is called the *root* of the tree and the clerks are the *leaves*.

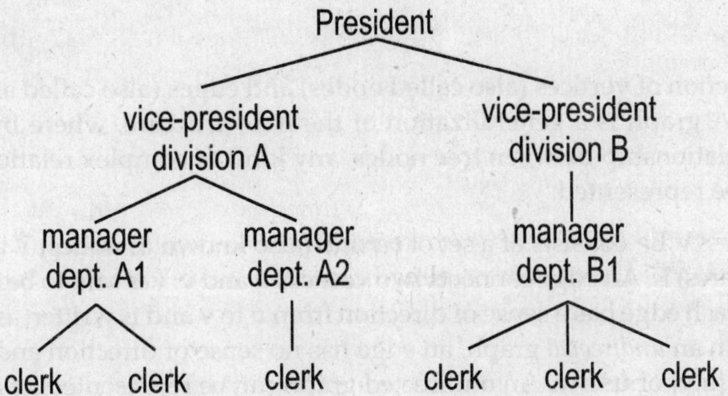

Figure 1.5: *Representing a Hierarchy using a Tree*

A tree is extremely useful for certain kinds of computations. For example, suppose we wish to determine the total salaries paid to employees by division or by department. The total of the salaries in division A can be found by computing the sum of the salaries paid in departments A1 and A2 plus the salary of the vice-president of division A. Similarly, the total of the salaries paid in department A1 is the sum of the salaries of the manager of department A1 and of the two clerks below her. Clearly, in order to compute all the totals, it is necessary to consider the salary of every employee. Therefore, an implementation of this computation must *visit* all the employees in the tree. An algorithm that systematically *visits* all the items in a tree is called a *tree traversal.*

1.4.6 Heaps

A Heap data structure is a binary tree with the following properties:

- Complete Binary tree - It is a **complete binary tree**; that is, each level of the tree is completely filled, except possibly the bottom level. At this level, it is filled from left to right.
- Heap Order – It satisfies the heap-order property: The data item stored in each node is greater than or equal to the data items stored in its children.

It is implemented as an array where each node in the tree corresponds to an element of the array.

Examples:

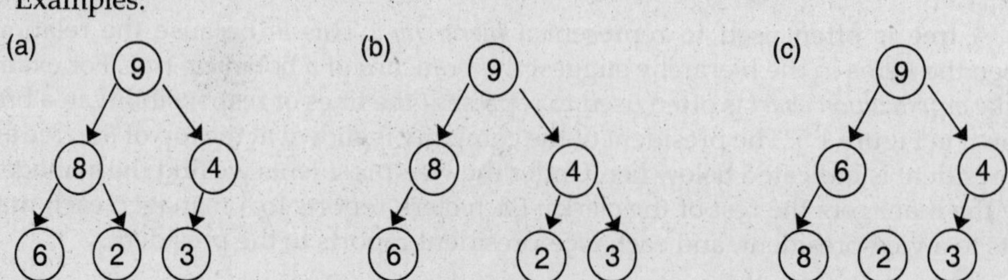

Figure 1.6: *In the above examples* **only (a) is a heap**. *(b) is not a heap as it is not complete and (c) is complete but does not satisfy the second property defined for heaps.*

1.4.7 Graph

Graph is a collection of vertices (also called nodes) and edges (also called arcs) that connect these vertices. A graph is a generalization of the tree structure, where instead of a strict parent/child relationship between tree nodes, any kind of complex relationships between the nodes can be represented.

Graph G=<V,E> consists of a set of *vertices* (also known as nodes) V and a set of *edges* (also known as arcs) E. An edge connects two vertices u and v; v is said to be *adjacent* to u. In a *directed* graph, each edge has a sense of direction from u to v and is written as an ordered pair <u,v> or u->v. In an *undirected* graph, an edge has no sense of direction and is written as an unordered pair {u,v} or u<->v. An undirected graph can be represented by a directed graph if every undirected edge {u,v} is represented by two directed edges <u,v> and <v,u>.

The number of edges with one endpoint on a given vertex is called that vertex's degree. In a directed graph, the number of edges that point to a given vertex is called its in-degree, and the number that point from it is called its out-degree. Often, we may want to be able to distinguish between different nodes and edges. We can associate labels with either. We call such a graph labeled

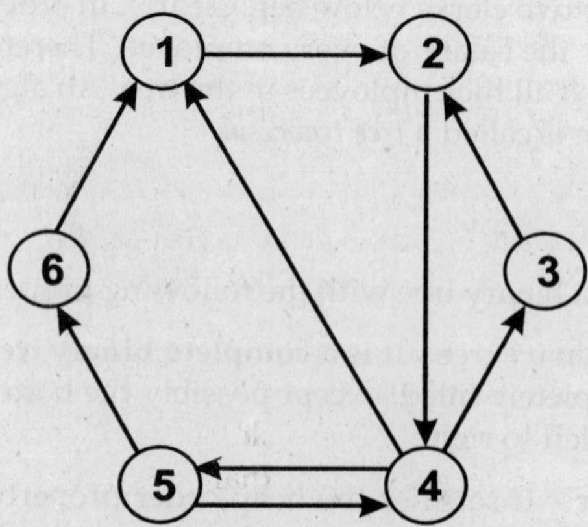

Figure 1.7: Directed Graph

UNIT I

1.4.8 Hash tables

The basic idea of a hash table is that each item that might be stored in the table has a natural location in the table. This natural location can be computed as a function of the item itself. When searching for an item, it is not necessary to go through all the possible locations in the table; instead, you can go directly to the natural location of the item. The function that computes the natural location of an item in a hash table is called a hash function. A hash table is in fact an array, so a location in a hash table is specified by an integer index. When a hash table is used to implement sets, the hash function takes a possible element of the set and returns an integer value that specifies the index in the array where that element should be stored.

The obvious problem that arises is that an array is a finite data structure with a relatively small number of locations. On the other hand, the number of different values that are candidates for storage in the table is typically very large or even (as in the case of strings) infinite. This means that it is not possible to assign a different hash code to each possible value. When we try to store two values that have the same hash code in a hash table, the result is what we call a collision. That is, a collision occurs when two items that we want to store in a hash table both have the same natural location in the table.

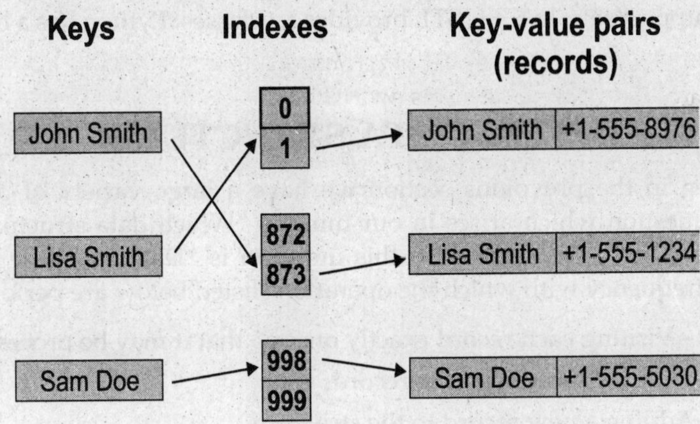

Figure 1.8: A small phone book as a hash table.

Hash tables are often used to implement associative arrays, sets and caches. Like arrays, hash tables provide constant-time O(1) lookup on average, regardless of the number of items in the table. However, the rare worst-case lookup time can be as bad as O(n). Compared to other associative array data structures, hash tables are most useful when large numbers of records of data are to be stored.

Hash tables store data in pseudo-random locations, so accessing the data in a sorted manner is a very time consuming operation. Other data structures such as self-balancing binary search trees generally operate more slowly (since their lookup time is O(log n)) and are rather more complex to implement than hash tables but maintain a sorted data structure at all times.

1.4.9 Sets

A **set** is a collection of certain values without any particular order. It corresponds with the mathematical concept of set, but with the restriction that it has to be finite. Disregarding sequence, it is the same as a list. A set can be seen as an associative array where the value of each key-value pair is ignored.

Sets can be implemented using various data structures. Ideal set data structures make it efficient to check if an object is in the set, as well as enabling other useful operations such as iterating through all the objects in the set, performing a union or intersection of two sets, or taking the complement of a set in some limited domain. Popular methods include arrays (in particular bit arrays), hash tables, and any sort of tree structure. A Bloom map implements a set probabilistically, using a very compact representation but risking a small chance of false positives on queries. Any associative array data structure can be used to implement a set by letting the set of keys be the elements of the set and ignoring the values.

However, very few of these data structures support set operations such as union or intersection efficiently. For these operations, more specialized set data structures exist. One of the earliest languages to support sets was Pascal; many languages now include it, whether in the core language or in a standard library. Java programming language offers Set interface to support sets. In C++, STL provides set classes. Python has a builtin set type, but no set literal

1.5 OPERATIONS ON DATA STRUCTURE

As we have seen in the prevoious section we have a large variety of data structures availiable. The question which arises in our mind is "Which data structure to use for a particular application?". The answer to this question is "Data structure is choosen by considering the frequency with which the operations listed below are performed":

1.5.1 Traversing – Visiting each record exactly once so that it may be processed.

1.5.2 Searching – Finding location of the record.

1.5.3 Insertion – Adding a new record to the structure.

1.5.4 Deletion – Deleting a record from the structure.

1.5.5 Sorting – Arranging records in some logical order.

1.5.6 Merging – Combining records in two different sorted files into a single sorted file.

So, If the travering operation is performed more frequently than other operations, we may prefer arrays over trees as arrays are linear data structure while trees not.

1.6 ALGORITHM COMPLEXITY

What is an algorithm and why do we want to analyze one? And the answer to this question is An **Algorithm is** a process or set of rules used for calculation or problem-solving, esp. with a computer. Algorithm can be given in many ways. For example, it can be written down in English (or French, or any other ``natural'' language). However, we are interested in algorithms, which have been precisely specified using an appropriate mathematical formalism--such as a programming language.

Algorithms are the ideas behind computer programs. An algorithm is the thing which stays the same whether the program is in Pascal or is in BASIC. To be interesting, an algorithm has to solve a general, specified problem. An algorithmic problem is specified by describing the set of instances it must work on and what desired properties the output must have, for example

Problem: Find the greatest common divisor (GCD) of two integers, m and n. *Euclid's Algorithm*:

while m is greater than zero:
If n is greater than m, swap m and n.
Subtract n from m.
n is the GCD

The complexity of an algorithm is a function g(n) that gives the upper bound of the number of operation (or running time) performed by an algorithm when the input size is n. There are two interpretations of upper bound.

(i) ***Worst-case Complexity:***

The running time for any given size input will be lower than the upper bound except possibly for some values of the input where the maximum is reached.

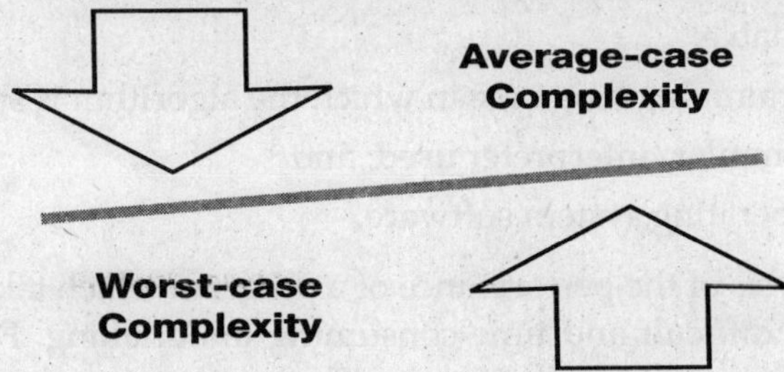

(ii) ***Average-case Complexity:***

The running time for any given size input will be the average number of operations over all problem instances for a given size.

Because, it is quite difficult to estimate the statistical behavior of the input, most of the time we content ourselves to a worst case behavior. Most of the time, the complexity of g(n) is approximated by its family O(f(n)) where f(n) is one of the following functions. n (linear complexity), log n (logarithmic complexity), n^a where a≥2 (polynomial complexity), a^n (exponential complexity).

Given such an expression of an algorithm, what can we do with it? Well, obviously we can run the program and observe its behavior. This is not likely to be very useful or informative in the general case. If we run a particular program on a particular computer with a particular set of inputs, then all know is the behavior of the program in a single instance. Such knowledge is anecdotal and we must be careful when drawing conclusions based upon anecdotal evidence.

In order to learn more about an algorithm, we can ``analyze'' it. By this we mean to study the specification of the algorithm and to draw conclusions about how the implementation of that algorithm--the program--will perform in general. But what can we analyze? We can determine the running time of a program as a function of its inputs;

- determine the total or maximum memory space needed for program data;
- determine the total size of the program code;
- determine whether the program correctly computes the desired result;
- determine the complexity of the program--e.g., how easy is it to read, understand, and modify; and,
- determine the robustness of the program--e.g., how well does it deal with unexpected or erroneous inputs?

In this text, we are concerned primarily with the running time. We also consider the memory space needed to execute the program. There are many factors that affect the running time of a program. Among these are the algorithm itself, the input data, and the computer system used to run the program. The performance of a computer is determined by the hardware:

- processor used (type and speed),
  - memory available (cache and RAM), and
  - disk available;
  - the programming language in which the algorithm is specified;
- the language compiler/interpreter used; and
- the computer operating system software.

A detailed analysis of the performance of a program which takes all of these factors into account is a very difficult and time-consuming undertaking. Furthermore, such an analysis is not likely to have lasting significance. The rapid pace of change in the underlying technologies means that results of such analyses are not likely to be applicable to the next generation of hardware and software.

1.6.1 Big O notation (Upper Bound)

A theoretical measure of the execution of an *algorithm*, usually the time or memory needed, given the problem size n, which is usually the number of items. Informally, saying some equation f(n) = O(g(n)) means it is less than some constant multiple of g(n). The notation is read, "f of n is big oh of g of n".

Formal Definition: f(n) = O(g(n)) means there are positive constants c and k, such that $0 \le f(n) \le cg(n)$ for all $n \ge k$. The values of c and k must be fixed for the function f and must not depend on n. **Also known as** O.

1.6.2 Ω-Notation (Lower Bound)

A theoretical measure of the execution of an *algorithm*, usually the time or memory needed, given the problem size n, which is usually the number of items. Informally, saying some equation $f(n) = \Omega(g(n))$ means it is more than some constant multiple of g(n).

Formal Definition: $f(n) = \Omega(g(n))$ means there are positive constants c and k, such that $0 \le cg(n) \le f(n)$ for all $n \ge k$. The values of c and k must be fixed for the function f and must not depend on n. **Also known as** omega.

1.6.3 Θ-Notation (Same order)

A theoretical measure of the execution of an *algorithm*, usually the time or memory needed, given the problem size n, which is usually the number of items. Informally, saying some equation $f(n) = \Theta(g(n))$ means it is within a constant multiple of g(n). The equation is read, "f of n is theta g of n".

Formal Definition: $f(n) = \Theta(g(n))$ means there are positive constants c_1, c_2, and k, such that $0 \le c_1g(n) \le f(n) \le c_2g(n)$ for all $n \ge k$. The values of c_1, c_2, and k must be fixed for the function f and must not depend on n. **Also known as** theta

As an example, $n^2 + 3n + 4$ is $O(n^2)$, since $n^2 + 3n + 4 < 2n^2$ for all $n > 10$. Strictly speaking, $3n + 4$ is $O(n^2)$, too, but big-O notation is often misused to mean equal to rather than less than. The notion of "equal to" is expressed by $\Theta(n)$.

The importance of this measure can be seen in trying to decide whether an algorithm is adequate, but may just need a better implementation, or the algorithm will always be too slow on a big enough input. For instance, *quicksort*, which is O(n log n) on average, running on a small desktop computer can beat *bubble sort*, which is $O(n^2)$, running on a supercomputer if there are a lot of numbers to sort. To sort 1,000,000 numbers, the quicksort takes 20,000,000 steps on average, while the bubble sort takes 1,000,000,000,000 steps.

1.7 TIME SPACE TRADE-OFF BETWEEN ALGORITHMS

A trade-off usually refers to losing one quality or aspect of something in return for gaining another quality or aspect. It implies a decision to be made with full comprehension of both the upside and downside of a particular choice.

Clearly, the parameter passing method used constrains the functionality of the called function: When pass-by-value is used, the called function cannot modify the actual parameters; when pass-by-reference is used, the called function is able to modify the actual parameters. In addition, the two methods have different time and space requirements that need to be understood in order to make the proper selection.

Pass-by-value creates a local variable and initializes that local variable by copying the value of the actual parameter. This means that space is used (on the stack) for the local variable and that time is taken to initialize that local variable. For small variables these penalties are insignificant. However, if the variable is large, the time and space penalties may become prohibitive.

On the other hand, pass-by-reference does not create a local variable nor does it require the copying of the actual parameter. However, because of the way that it must be implemented, every time a reference formal parameter is used to access the corresponding actual parameter, a small amount of extra time is taken to dereference the reference. As a result, it is typically more efficient to pass small variables by value and large variables by reference

A space-time or time-memory trade-off is a situation where the programmer can reduce memory use at the cost of slower program execution, or can reduce computation time at the cost of increased memory use.

The most common situation is an algorithm involving a lookup table: an implementation can include the entire table, which reduces computing time, but increases the amount of memory needed, or it can compute table entries as needed, increasing computing time, but reducing memory requirements.

A space-time tradeoff can be applied to the simple problem of data storage. If data is stored uncompressed, it takes more space but less time than if the data were stored compressed (since compressing the data reduces the amount of space it takes, but it takes time to run the compression algorithm). Depending on the particular instance of the problem, either way is practical.

For another example, bubble sort is a sort algorithm that uses O(1) (constant) memory space and O(n^2) (quadratic) time. In other words, its memory requirement is unrelated to the length of the list to be sorted, but its time requirement grows proportionally to the square of the length of the list. In the case of the sorting problem, a space-time tradeoff can be made by using a different algorithm such as binary tree sort. Its memory requirement is O(n) (linear), but its time requirement is O(n lg n) ("linearithmic") which is optimal for a general sort algorithm. Binary tree sort's time requirement grows more slowly than bubble sort's, but its memory requirement grows faster.

In t1he case of the sorting problem, all-around better algorithms exist, such as heapsort, which combines the good qualities of bubble sort and binary tree sort: its time requirement is O(n lg n), and its memory requirement is O(1).

1.8 STRING PROCESSING

In computer programming and some branches of mathematics, strings are sequences of various simple objects. These simple objects are selected from a predetermined set, each entry of which is usually allocated a code. Most commonly these simple objects will be printable characters and the control codes that are used with them. The data types in which these are stored are also called strings and it is fairly common to use these types to store arbitrary, variable-length sequences of binary data. Generally, a string can be placed directly in the code usually by surrounding it with some form of quote marks (usually ' or ", as these are typeable on most keyboards worldwide). Sometimes the term binary string is used to refer to an arbitrary sequence of bits.

A string datatype is a datatype modeled on the idea of a formal string. Strings are such an important and useful datatype that they are implemented in nearly every programming language. In some languages they are available as primitive types and in others as composite types. The syntax of most high-level programming languages allows for a string, usually quoted in some way, to represent an instance of a string datatype; such a meta-string is called a literal or string literal.

Although formal strings can have an arbitrary (but finite) length, the length of strings in real languages is often constrained to an artificial maximum. In general, there are two types of string datatypes: fixed length strings which have a fixed maximum length, and variable length strings whose length is not arbitrarily fixed. Most strings in modern programming languages are variable length strings. Despite the name, even variable length strings are limited in length; although, generally, the limit depends only on the amount of memory available.

Historically, string datatypes had one byte for each character, and although the exact character set varied by region, the character encodings were similar enough that programmers could generally get away with ignoring this — groups of character sets used by the same system in different regions either had a character in the same place, or did not have it at all. Mostly these character sets were based on ASCII, though IBMs mainframe systems went their own way and used EBCDIC.

Logographic languages such as Chinese, Japanese and Korean (known collectively as CJK) need far more than 256 characters — the limit of a one-byte-per-character encoding — for reasonable representation. The normal solutions involved keeping single-byte representations for ASCII and using two-byte representations for CJK ideographs. Use of these with existing code led to problems with matching and cutting of strings the severity of which depended on how the character encoding was designed. Some encodings such as the EUC family guarantee that a byte value in the ASCII range will only represent that ASCII character making the encoding safe for systems that use those characters as field separators or similar. Others such as ISO-2022 and shift-jis do not make such guarantees, making matching on byte codes unsafe. Another issue is that if the beginning of a string is cut off, important instructions for the decoder or information on position in a multibyte sequence may be lost. Another issue is that if strings are joined together (especially after having their ends truncated by code not aware of the encoding), the first string may not leave the encoder in a state suitable for dealing with the second string.

Unicode has complicated the picture somewhat. Most languages have a datatype for Unicode strings (usually UTF-16 as it was usually added before Unicode supplemental planes were introduced). Converting between Unicode and local encodings requires an understanding of the local encoding, which may be problematic for existing systems where strings of various encodings are being transmitted together with no real marking as to what encoding they are in.

Some languages like C++ implement strings as templates that can be used with any primitive type, but this is the exception not the rule.

Representations of strings depend heavily on the choice of character repertoire and the method of character encoding. Older string implementations were designed to work with repertoire and encoding defined by ASCII, or more recent extensions like the ISO 8859 series. Modern implementations often use the extensive repertoire defined by Unicode along with a variety of complex encodings such as UTF-8 and UTF-16.

Most string implementations are very similar to variable-length arrays with the entries storing the character codes of corresponding characters. The principal difference is that, with certain encodings, a single logical character may take up more than one entry in the array. This happens for example with UTF-8, where single characters can take anywhere from one to four bytes. In these cases, the logical length of the string differs from the logical length of the array.

The length of a string can be stored implicitly by using a special terminating character; often this is the null character having value zero, a convention used and perpetuated by the popular C programming language. Hence this representation is commonly referred to as C string. The length of a string can also be stored explicitly, for example by prefixing the string with integer value – a convention used in Pascal, consequently some people call it a P-string.

In terminated strings, the terminating code is not an allowable character in any string.

Here is an example of a null-terminated string stored in a 10-byte buffer, along with its ASCII representation:

F	R	A	N	K	NUL	k	e	f	w
46	52	41	4E	4B	00	6B	65	66	77

The length of a string in the above example is 5 characters, but it occupies 6 bytes. Characters after the terminator do not form part of the representation; they may be either part of another string or just garbage.

Here is the equivalent (old style) Pascal string:

length	F	R	A	N	K	k	f	f	w
05	46	52	41	4E	4B	6B	66	66	77

While these representations are common, others are possible. Using ropes makes certain string operations, such as insertions, deletions, and concatenations more efficient.

There are many algorithms for processing strings, each with various tradeoffs. Some categories of algorithms include

- String Searching – Algorithm for finding a given substring or pattern;
- Sorting Algorithms – Algorithm for sorting strings;
- Regular Expression Algorithms – Algorithms to generate regular expressions;
- Parsing a string – Algorithms to parsing a string.

GLOSSARY

1. Data structure - Collection of data organized in some fashion.
2. **Array -** A finite, ordered set of homogeneous elements stored in a contiguous memory location.
3. Linked list - A sequence of nodes, each containing arbitrary data fields and one or two references ("links") pointing to the next and/or previous nodes.
4. Stack - A collection of items in which only the most recently added item may be removed.
5. Tree - A tree is a finite set of a zero or more vertices such that there is one specially designated vertex called root and the remaining vertices are partitioned into a collection of sub-trees, each of which is also a tree.
6. **Binary Tree-** A tree that is either empty or consists of a root node & two disjoint trees called left & right sub-tree.
7. Graph - A collection of vertices (also called nodes) and edges (also called arcs) that connect these vertices.
8. Set - A collection of certain values without any particular order.

SUMMARY

1. Data structure = Organized data + Allowed operations
2. Types of data structure:
   a. Linear & Non-linear: which means the data stored in a sequence is called Linear, other is Non-linear (array is Linear & Tree is non-linear).
   b. Homogeneous & Non-homogeneous: Which means the data structure, which contains single type of data, is known as Homogeneous & other Non-Homogeneous.
   c. Static & Dynamic: This is means the allocation of memory, either static or Dynamic.
3. The allocation of memory is static if it is allocated in advance and dynamic if it is allocated at run time.
4. A Heap data structure is a binary tree with the following properties :

   Complete Binary tree - It is a **complete binary tree**; that is, each level of the tree is completely filled, except possibly the bottom level. At this level, it is filled from left to right.
5. Heap Order – It satisfies the heap-order property: The data item stored in each node is greater than or equal to the data items stored in its children.
6. $f(n) = O(g(n))$ means there are positive constants c and k, such that $0 \leq f(n) \leq cg(n)$ for all $n \geq k$. The values of c and k must be fixed for the function f and must not depend on n. **Also known as** O.

7. $f(n) = \Theta(g(n))$ means there are positive constants c_1, c_2, and k, such that $0 \leq c_1 g(n) \leq f(n) \leq c_2 g(n)$ for all $n \geq k$. The values of c_1, c_2, and k must be fixed for the function f and must not depend on n. **Also known as** theta.

REVIEW QUESTIONS

1. What is the purpose of studying data structure?
2. Differentiate between stack and queue.
3. Is tree a type of graph?
4. What are the applications of hash tables?
5. Explain in details:
   a. Array
   b. Linked list
   c. Stack
   d. Tree
   e. Binary Tree
   f. Graph.
   g. Set.

CHAPTER 2

UNIT 1

ANALYSIS OF ALGORITHMS

Dry Run → Review → Walk Through

2.1 INTRODUCTION

Objective of studying a topic concerned with algorithms and complexity analysis of algorithms is to learn how an efficient algorithm for any problem arising in computer science can be obtained.

Nowadays, computers have become a part of our lives, the underlying reason for that is the fastness of it. It is fast because it can do very long term work in very few minutes or seconds. The amount work done by a computer usually concerned with its configuration. However, almost the consisting algorithm in order to do work identifies the time required for work to be completed.

The term work involves a set of problems. We know that a problem is a ***question*** which we seek an answer. When we find one's answer, we consider the next and with that way, finally we complete the work. Problems are solved by step-by-step procedures, which are called ***algorithms***. The more efficient the algorithms become, the faster we obtain completion of the work.

What is an algorithm?

An algorithm may be defined as the step-by-step procedure or method that can be carried out by computer for solving programming problems.

These problems used algorithms and obtain result after the finite number of execution steps. In other words algorithms are precise specifications of a sequence of instruction that are executed in order to solve problems and obtain desired results. The step-by-step method or procedures has been in a use for a very long time in different object of life, and is not new in computer. An algorithm tells computer how to solve problem systematically to get desired output. For example, algorithm to read user name from keyboard and say hello to user can defined as follows:

Step # 1: START

Step # 2: Read user name from keyboard

Step # 3: Store INPUT to NAME

Step # 4: Say hello to user

Step # 5: STOP

Algorithm definition: An algorithm consists of a set of explicit and unambiguous (only one meaning) finite steps, which when carried out for a given set of initial conditions, produce the corresponding output, and terminate in a fixed amount of time.

2.2 Basic characteristics of algorithms

The basic characteristics of algorithms are as follows:

(i) Problems should be solved in finite number of step by step ALGORTHMS should be

(ii) Simple and easy to read

(iii) Problems should be solved in finite number of step-by-step direction.

(iv) It should be universal and leads to a unique solution of the problems.

(v) It should be capable of handing exception during the process of solving problems e.g.

(vi) Array index out of range or divide by zero.

(vii) It should be precise and unambiguous.

(viii) It should be provide result in finite amount of time.

(ix) It must be complete and correct.

(x) Desired result must be obtained after execution.

2.3.1 How to Write an Algorithm

There are different steps that should be in mind when you have to write algorithms for solving a particular type of problems.

Steps To Write Algorithms:

1. Take input from the user. This input is processed in subsequent instruction in the algorithms.
2. Process the input data entered by the user.
3. Produce one or more output after processing.
4. Show result.

2.3.2 Checking the Algorithms

To ensure the efficient execution of the program, it is necessary to check the algorithms before coding it. There are many different methods to check the algorithms. Some of them are.

1. **Dry Run:** This is the manual way to examination the algorithms. In this method we find the value of each variable after every step of algorithm.

2. **Review**: This method involves the studying the logic and computing it with a specification.

3. **Walk Through:** In this method algorithm is present to the team member for checking the efficiency of the algorithms.

2.3.3 Merit of the Algorithm

The merits of algorithm are as follows:

(i) Algorithm makes the program unambiguous mare understandable.

(ii) With algorithm program are portable and efficient.

(iii) It shows processing in easy step-by-step methods.

(iv) Modification deletion and updation as the existing program is quite easy.

(v) It promotes testing of program at developing stage.

(vi) Algorithm provides technique in program design on paper before it performs on computer.

(vii) They are also useful to determination output by just giving input.

(viii) They are quite useful to solve complex programming.

When analyzing the efficiency of an algorithm in terms of time - since we are talking about faster algorithms - we do not determine the actual number of CPU cycles, because this depends on the particular computer on which the algorithm is run. Instead, we are looking for faster algorithms in core, namely which are machine independent. Furthermore, we do not even want to count every executed instruction, because the numbers of instructions depend on the programming language used to implement the algorithm and the way the programmer writes the program. Rather, we want to measure which is independent of the computer, the programming language, the programmer, and all the complex details of the algorithms such as incrementing loop indices, setting of parameters, etc.

To sum up the things, dealing with the efficiency of algorithms involves steps such as: analyzing the problem, analyzing the inputs and creating alternative ways. Usually, a problem contains parameters that are not assigned specific values in the statement of the problem. These variables are called parameters to the problem.

Since a problem contains parameters, it represents a class of problems, one for each assignment of values to the parameters. Each specified assignment of values to the parameters is called an instance of the problem. A ***solution*** to an instance of a problem is the answer to the question asked by the problem in that instance.

Informally, an ***algorithm*** is any well-defined computational procedure that takes some value, or set of values, as ***input*** and produces some value, or set of values, as ***output***. An algorithm is thus a sequence of computational steps that transform the input into the output.

We can also view an algorithm as a tool for solving a well-specified ***computational problem***. The statement of the problem specifies in general terms the desired input/output relationship. The algorithm describes a specific computational procedure for achieving that input/output relationship.

We begin our study of algorithms with the problem of sorting a sequence of numbers into nondecreasing order. This problem arises frequently in practice and provides fertile ground for introducing many standard design techniques and analysis tools. Here is how we formally define the ***sorting problem***:

Input: A sequence of n numbers $(a_1, a_2, \ldots, a_n)$.

Output: A permutation (reordering) $\langle a'_1, a'_2, \ldots, a'_n \rangle$ of the input sequence such that $a'_1 \le a'_2 \le \cdots \le a'_n$.

Given an input sequence such as (31, 41, 59, 26, 41, 58), a sorting algorithm returns as output the sequence (26, 31, 41, 41, 58, 59). Such an input sequence is called an ***instance*** of the sorting problem. In general, an ***instance of a problem*** consists of all the inputs (satisfying whatever constraints are imposed in the problem statement) needed to compute a solution to the problem.

Sorting is a fundamental operation in computer science (many programs use it as an intermediate step), and as a result a large number of good sorting algorithms have been developed. Which algorithm is best for a given application depends on the number of items to be sorted, the extent to which the items are already somewhat sorted, and the kind of storage device to be used: main memory, disks, or tapes.

An algorithm is said to be ***correct*** if, for every input instance, it halts with the correct output. We say that a correct algorithm ***solves*** the given computational problem. An incorrect algorithm might not halt at all on some input instances, or it might halt with other than the desired answer. Contrary to what one might expect, incorrect algorithms can sometimes be useful, if their error rate can be controlled. We shall see an example of this in Chapter 33 when we study algorithms for finding large prime numbers. Ordinarily, however, we shall be concerned only with correct algorithms.

An algorithm can be specified in English, as a computer program, or even as a hardware design. The only requirement is that the specification must provide a precise description of the computational procedure to be followed.

2.4 COMPLEXITY OF AN ALGORITHM

In determining how efficiently an algorithm solves a problem, we need to analyze the algorithm. Informally, comparing elapsed time of algorithms, which do the similar jobs, can make efficiency analysis of algorithms. However, if we want to make analysis in a wide range we need more formal terminology and methods.

Time Complexity Analysis of Algorithms

Our measure of time for algorithms depends only the analysis, namely it is independent of questions like where the program is run and which language is used or who the programmer is.

In general the running time is roughly proportional to how many times some basic operation such as comparison of instructions is done. We therefore analyze the efficiency of algorithms by determining number of times some basic operation is done as a function of the size of the input.

2.5 EXPRESSING ALGORITHMS

Algorithms can be expressed in many kinds of notation, including natural languages, pseudo code, flowcharts, and programming languages. Natural language expressions of algorithms tend to be verbose and ambiguous, and are rarely used for complex or technical algorithms. Pseudo code and flowcharts are structured ways to express algorithms that avoid many of the ambiguities common in natural language statements, while remaining independent of a particular implementation language. Programming languages are primarily intended for expressing algorithms in a form that can be executed by a computer, but are often used as a way to define or document algorithms.

There is a wide variety of representations and one can express a given Turing machine program as a sequence of machine tables (finite state machine and state transition table), as flowcharts (state diagram), or as a form of rudimentary machine code or assembly code called "sets of quadruples" (at Turing machine).

Sometimes it is helpful in the description of an algorithm to supplement small "flow charts" (state diagrams) with natural-language and/or arithmetic expressions written inside "block diagrams" to summarize what the "flow charts" are accomplishing.

Representations of algorithms are generally classed into three accepted levels of Turing machine description:

1. **High-level description**: "...prose to describe an algorithm, ignoring the implementation details. At this level we do not need to mention how the machine manages its tape or head"

2. **Implementation description**: "...prose used to define the way the Turing machine uses its head and the way that it stores data on its tape. At this level we do not give details of states or transition function"

3. **Formal description**: Most detailed, "lowest level", gives the Turing machine's "state table".

For an example of the simple algorithm "Add m+n" described in all three levels .

2.6 IMPLEMENTATION

All algorithms are intended to be implemented as computer programs. However, algorithms are also implemented by other means, such as in a biological neural network (for example, the human brain implementing arithmetic or an insect looking for food), in an electrical circuit, or in a mechanical device.

Example:

One of the simplest algorithms is to find the largest number in an (unsorted) list of numbers. The solution necessarily requires looking at every number in the list, but only once at each. From this follows a simple algorithm, which can be stated in a high-level description English prose, as:

High-level description:

1. Assume the first item is largest.
2. Look at each of the remaining items in the list and if it is larger than the largest item so far, make a note of it.
3. The last noted item is the largest in the list when the process is complete.

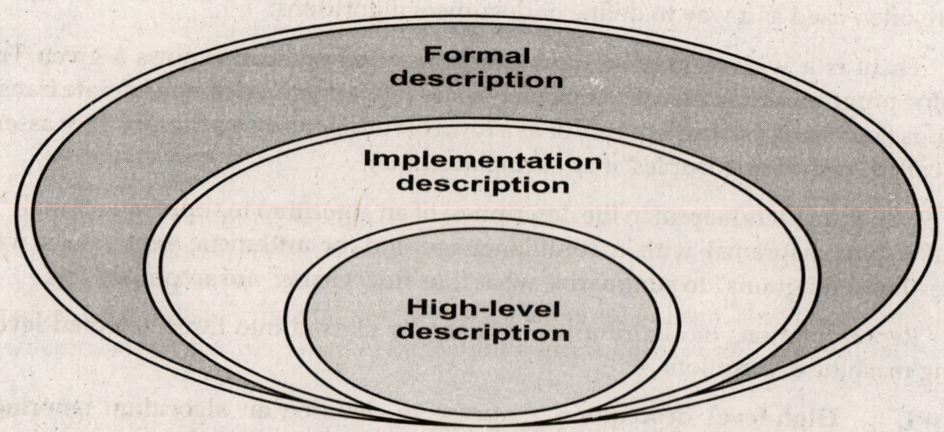

(Quasi-)formal description: Written in prose but much closer to the high-level language of a computer program, the following is the more formal coding of the algorithm in pseudo code or pidgin code:

Algorithm LargestNumber

Input: A non-empty list of numbers *L*.

Output: The *largest* number in the list *L*.

largest ← L_0

for each *item* **in** the list $L_{\geq 1}$, **do**

if the *item* > *largest*, **then**

largest ← the *item*

return *largest*

- "←" is a loose shorthand for "changes to". For instance, "*largest* ← *item*" means that the value of *largest* changes to the value of *item*.
- "**return**" terminates the algorithm and outputs the value that follows.

2.7 ALGORITHMIC ANALYSIS AND ITS CLASSIFICATION

It is frequently important to know how much of a particular resource (such as time or storage) is required for a given algorithm. Methods have been developed for the analysis of algorithms to obtain such quantitative answers; for example, the algorithm above has a time requirement of O(*n*), using the big O notation with *n* as the length of the list. At all times the algorithm only needs to remember two values: the largest number found so far, and its current position in the input list. Therefore it is said to have a space requirement of *O(1)*, if the space required to store the input numbers is not counted, or O(*n*) if it is counted.

Different algorithms may complete the same task with a different set of instructions in less or more time, space, or 'effort' than others. For example, a binary search algorithm will usually outperform a sequential search when used for table lookups on sorted lists.

Abstract Versus Empirical

The analysis and study of algorithms is a discipline of computer science, and is often practiced abstractly without the use of a specific programming language or implementation. In this sense, algorithm analysis resembles other mathematical disciplines in that it focuses on the underlying properties of the algorithm and not on the specifics of any particular implementation. Usually pseudo code is used for analysis as it is the simplest and most general representation. However, ultimately, most algorithms are usually implemented on particular hardware / software platforms and their algorithmic efficiency is eventually put to the test using real code.

Empirical testing is useful because it may uncover unexpected interactions that affect performance. For instance an algorithm that has no locality of reference may have much poorer performance than predicted because it thrashes the cache.

Classification

There are various ways to classify algorithms, each with its own merits.

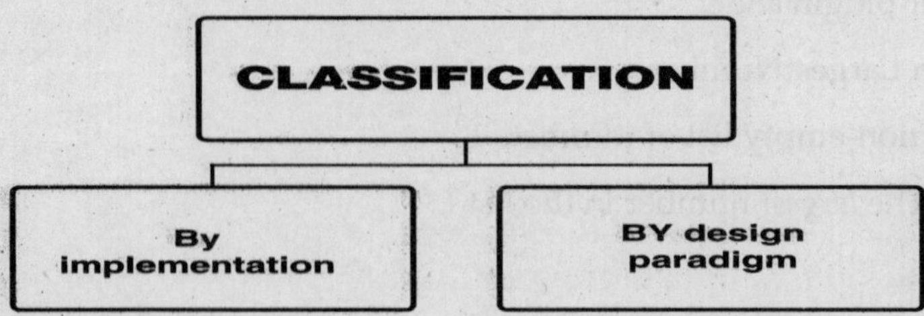

By implementation

One way to classify algorithms is by implementation means.

- **Recursion** or **iteration**: A recursive algorithm is one that invokes (makes reference to) itself repeatedly until a certain condition matches, which is a method common to functional programming. Iterative algorithms use repetitive constructs like loops and sometimes additional data structures like stacks to solve the given problems. Some problems are naturally suited for one implementation or the other. For example, towers of hanoi is well understood in recursive implementation. Every recursive version has an equivalent (but possibly more or less complex) iterative version, and vice versa.
- **Logical**: An algorithm may be viewed as controlled logical deduction. This notion may be expressed as: **Algorithm = logic + control** (Kowalski 1979). The logic component expresses the axioms that may be used in the computation and the control component determines the way in which deduction is applied to the axioms. This is the basis for the logic programming paradigm. In pure logic programming languages the control component is fixed and algorithms are specified by supplying only the logic component. The appeal of this approach is the elegant semantics: a change in the axioms has a well defined change in the algorithm.
- **Serial** or **parallel** or **distributed**: Algorithms are usually discussed with the assumption that computers execute one instruction of an algorithm at a time. Those computers are sometimes called serial computers. An algorithm designed for such an environment is called a serial algorithm, as opposed to parallel algorithms or distributed algorithms. Parallel algorithms take advantage of computer architectures where several processors can work on a problem at the same time, whereas distributed algorithms utilize multiple machines connected with a network. Parallel or distributed algorithms divide the problem into more symmetrical or asymmetrical subproblems and collect the results back together. The resource consumption in such algorithms is not only processor cycles on each processor but also the communication overhead between the processors. Sorting algorithms can be parallelized efficiently, but their communication overhead is expensive.

Iterative algorithms are generally parallelizable. Some problems have no parallel algorithms, and are called inherently serial problems.

- **Deterministic** or **non-deterministic**: Deterministic algorithms solve the problem with exact decision at every step of the algorithm whereas non-deterministic algorithm solve problems via guessing although typical guesses are made more accurate through the use of heuristics.
- **Exact** or **approximate**: While many algorithms reach an exact solution, approximation algorithms seek an approximation that is close to the true solution. Approximation may use either a deterministic or a random strategy. Such algorithms have practical value for many hard problems.

By design paradigm

Another way of classifying algorithms is by their design methodology or paradigm. There is a certain number of paradigms, each different from the other. Furthermore, each of these categories will include many different types of algorithms. Some commonly found paradigms include:

- **Divide and conquer**. A divide and conquer algorithm repeatedly reduces an instance of a problem to one or more smaller instances of the same problem (usually recursively) until the instances are small enough to solve easily. One such example of divide and conquer is merge sorting. Sorting can be done on each segment of data after dividing data into segments and sorting of entire data can be obtained in the conquer phase by merging the segments. A simpler variant of divide and conquer is called a **decrease and conquer algorithm**, that solves an identical subproblem and uses the solution of this subproblem to solve the bigger problem. Divide and conquer divides the problem into multiple subproblems and so conquer stage will be more complex than decrease and conquer algorithms. An example of decrease and conquer algorithm is the binary search algorithm.
- **Dynamic programming**. When a problem shows optimal substructure, meaning the optimal solution to a problem can be constructed from optimal solutions to subproblems, and overlapping sub problems, meaning the same subproblems are used to solve many different problem instances, a quicker approach called *dynamic programming* avoids recomputing solutions that have already been computed. For example, the shortest path to a goal from a vertex in a weighted graph can be found by using the shortest path to the goal from all adjacent vertices. The main difference between dynamic programming and divide and conquer is that subproblems are more or less independent in divide and conquer, whereas subproblems overlap in dynamic programming. The difference between dynamic programming and straightforward recursion is in caching or memoization of recursive calls. When subproblems are independent and there is no repetition, memoization does not help; hence dynamic programming is not a solution for all complex problems. By using memoization or maintaining a table of subproblems

already solved, dynamic programming reduces the exponential nature of many problems to polynomial complexity.

- **The greedy method**. A greedy algorithm is similar to a dynamic programming algorithm, but the difference is that solutions to the subproblems do not have to be known at each stage; instead a "greedy" choice can be made of what looks best for the moment. The greedy method extends the solution with the best possible decision (not all feasible decisions) at an algorithmic stage based on the current local optimum and the best decision (not all possible decisions) made in previous stage. It is not exhaustive, and does not give accurate answer to many problems. But when it works, it will be the fastest method. The most popular greedy algorithm is finding the minimal spanning tree as given by Kruskal.

- **Linear programming**. When solving a problem using linear programming, specific inequalities involving the inputs are found and then an attempt is made to maximize (or minimize) some linear function of the inputs. Many problems (such as the maximum flow for directed graphs) can be stated in a linear programming way, and then be solved by a 'generic' algorithm such as the simplex algorithm. A more complex variant of linear programming is called integer programming, where the solution space is restricted to the integers.

- **Reduction**. This technique involves solving a difficult problem by transforming it into a better known problem for which we have (hopefully) asymptotically optimal algorithms. The goal is to find a reducing algorithm whose complexity is not dominated by the resulting reduced algorithm's. For example, one selection algorithm for finding the median in an unsorted list involves first sorting the list (the expensive portion) and then pulling out the middle element in the sorted list (the cheap portion). This technique is also known as *transform and conquer*.

- **Search and enumeration**. Many problems (such as playing chess) can be modeled as problems on graphs. A graph exploration algorithm specifies rules for moving around a graph and is useful for such problems. This category also includes search algorithms, branch and bound enumeration and backtracking.

- **The probabilistic and heuristic paradigm**. Algorithms belonging to this class fit the definition of an algorithm more loosely.

1. Probabilistic algorithms are those that make some choices randomly (or pseudo-randomly); for some problems, it can in fact be proven that the fastest solutions must involve some randomness.

2. Genetic algorithms attempt to find solutions to problems by mimicking biological evolutionary processes, with a cycle of random mutations yielding successive generations of "solutions". Thus, they emulate reproduction and "survival of the fittest". In genetic programming, this approach is extended to algorithms, by regarding the algorithm itself as a "solution" to a problem.

3. Heuristic algorithms, whose general purpose is not to find an optimal solution, but an approximate solution where the time or resources are limited, they are not practical to find perfect solutions. An example of this would be local search, tabu search, or simulated annealing algorithms, a class of heuristic probabilistic algorithms that vary the solution of a problem by a random amount. The name "simulated annealing" alludes to the metallurgic term meaning the heating and cooling of metal to achieve freedom from defects. The purpose of the random variance is to find close to globally optimal solutions rather than simply locally optimal ones, the idea being that the random element will be decreased as the algorithm settles down to a solution.

Algorithm 1.1: (Sequential Search)

Problem: Is the key x in the array S of n keys?

Inputs: Positive integer n, array of keys S indexed from 1 to n, and a key x.

Output: location, the location of x in S (0 if x is not in S)

```
procedure seqsearch (n as integer; S as array[1...n] of keytype, x as keytype)
location =1;
while location and S[location]x do
location=location+1;
end while;
if location<n then
location = 0;
end if;
end procedure;
```

Algorithm 1.2: (Add Array Members)

Problem: Add all the numbers in the array S of n numbers.

Inputs: Positive integer n, array of keys S indexed from 1 to n.

Output: sum, the sum of the numbers in S.

```
function add (n as integer; S as array[1...n] of number) as number
i , sum = 0 as integer;
for i=1 to n-1 do
sum = sum + S[i];
end for;
end function;
```

Algorithm 1.3: (Exchange Sort)

Problem: Sort n keys in non-decreasing order.

Inputs: Positive integer n, array of keys S indexed from 1 to n.

Output: The array S containing the keys in non-decreasing order.

```
procedure exchange sort (n as integer; S as array[1...n] of keytype, x as keytype)
i, j as integer;
for i=1 to n-1 do
        for j=i+1 to n do
        if S[i]< S[j] then
        exchange S[i] and S[j];
        end if;
        end for;
end for;
end procedure;
```

Algorithm 1.4: (Binary Search)

Problem: Determine whether x is in the sorted array S of n keys.

Inputs: Positive integer n, sorted (non-decreasing order) array of keys S indexed from 1 to n, a key x.

Output: location, the location of x in S (0 if x is not in S).

```
procedure binsearch (n as integer; S as array[1...n] of keytype, x as keytype)
location as integer;
low, high, mid as integer;
low = 1; high=n; location = 0;
while low<=high and location = 0 do
mid = (low+high)/2;
if x =  S[mid] then
location=mid;
else if x < S[mid] then
high = mid-1;
else low=mid + 1;
end if;
end while;
end procedure;
```

Algorithm 1.5: (n^{th} Fibonacci Term Recursive)

Problem: Determine the nth term of the Fibonacci Sequence.

Inputs: Nonnegative integer n.

Output: fibo, the nth term of the Fibonacci Sequence.

```
function fibo (n as integer) as integer
if n <= 1 then fibo = n;
else fibo = fibo (n-1) + fibo (n-2)
end if;
end function
```

For many algorithms, it is easy to find a reasonable measure of the size of the input, which we call the input size. For the Algorithms 1.1 (Sequential Search), 1.3 (Add Array Members) and 1.4 (Binary Search), the measure of the size of the input, simply input size is the same as the input *n*, the number of elements in the array. In some algorithms, it is more appropriate to measure the size of the input using two numbers. For example, when the input to an algorithm is a graph we often measure the size of the input in terms of both the number of vertices and the number of edges. Therefore, we can say that the input size consists of both parameters.

So far, we call in the input size in our algorithms because is has been a reasonable measure of the amount of data in the input. For example, in the case of sorting algorithms, *n*, the number of keys to be sorted is a good measure of the amount of data in the input. So, we called in the input size.

However, we must not call *n* the input size in an algorithm. For example in Algorithm 1.5 (n^{th} Fibonacci Term Recursive), *n* is the input; it is not the size of the input it is the number of symbols used to encode *n*. More formally, we define the input size as in below:

INPUT SIZE

For a given algorithm, the input size is defined as the number of characters it takes to write the input.

If we use binary representation (more generally, it is used), the input size will be the number of bits it takes to encode *n*, which is

For example; if $n = 25 = 11001_2$

Thus the size of input $n = 25$ is $lg\ 25 + 1 = 5$

If compare two algorithms measure of the input size we can see the difference more apparently.

For the any sorting algorithm, if we calculate input size, we obtain the following results:

Suppose that we use binary encoding and we wish sort *n positive integers*. The integers to be sorted are inputs to the algorithm. Thus the input size is the count of the number of it takes to encode them. If the largest one is *L*, and we encode each integer in the number of bits needed to encode the largest, then it takes about $lg\ L$ bits to encode each of them. The input size for the *n* integers is therefore about $n\ lg\ L$.

Suppose that instead we choose to encode the integers in *base 10*. Then the characters used for the encoding are decimal digits, it takes about $log\ L$ characters to encode the largest, and the input size for the *n* integers is about $n\ log\ L$. The concept of basic operation is uniquely determined by some basic instructions for which the total work done by algorithm is proportional.

In general, a time complexity analysis of on algorithm is the determination of how many times the basic operation is done for each value of the input size.

In some cases the number of times the instructions are done depends not only on the input size, but also on the input values. For instance, in Algorithm 1.1 (Sequential Search), if x is the first item of the array, the basic operation is done once, whereas if x is not in the array, it is done *n-times*. Sometimes, whatever are the input sizes the basic operations are done some number of times depending on the input size. Therefore, here we need some terminology in order to encompass all the possibilities occurring when the inputs are changed.

2.7.1 Types of Complexities

The types of complexities are as follows:

Every-Case Time Complexity

If the basic operation is always done, the same number of times for every instance of size n. We call such time complexities of algorithms ***every-case time complexity*** and symbolize with $T(n)$.

Every-Time Complexity Analysis of Algorithm (Add Array Members):

Basic Operation: The addition of an item in the array to sum.

Input Size: n, the number of items in the array.

Analysis: Regardless of the instances of the array elements, there are n passes through the *for loop*. Therefore the basic operation is always done in times.

Therefore, there exists $T(n) = n$.

Every-Time Complexity Analysis of Algorithm (Exchange sort):

Basic Operation: The comparison of $S[j]$ with $S[i]$.

Input Size: n, the number of items to be sorted.

Analysis: We must determine how many passes through *for the " i" loop*. In the first pass through the *for "i" loop*, there are *n-1* passes through the *for " j" loop*, in the second pass there are *n-2* passes through the *for "j" loop*, in the third pass there are *n-3* passes through the *for "j" loop*, going on this way, in the last pass there is one pass through the *for "j" loop*.

Therefore, the total number of passes through the *for " j" loop* is:

$$T(n) = (n-1) + (n-2) + (n-3) + \ldots\ldots + 1 = (n-1).n$$

As we said before in some algorithms, the basic operation is not done the same number of times for instances of size n. So, these algorithms do not have an *every-case time complexity*.

In order to analyze such algorithms, we first con try the maximum number of times the basic operation is done.

Worst-Case Time Complexity

For a given algorithm, ***worst-case time complexity*** can be defined as the maximum number of times the algorithm will ever do its basic operation.

Clearly, for any algorithm if $T(n)$ exist then, $T(n) = W(n)$ holds.

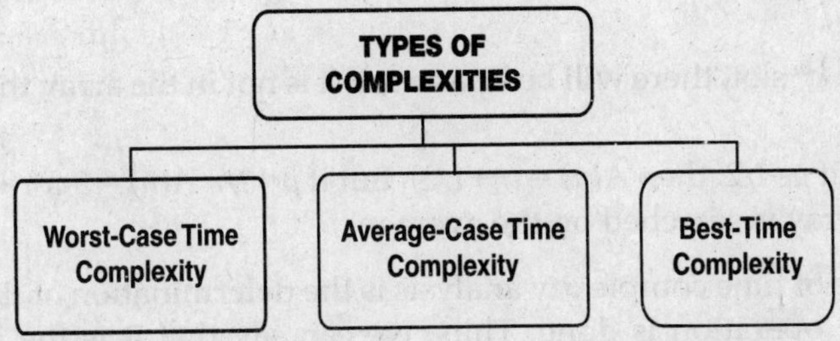

Worst-Case Time Complexity Analysis of Algorithm (Sequential Search)

Basic Operation: The comparison of an item in the array with x.

Input Size: n, the number of items in the array.

Analysis: The basic operation is done at most n times, which is the case if x is the last item in the array or if x is not in the array. Hence, $W(n) = n$.

Although the worst-case analysis informs us of the absolute maximum amount of time consumed, in some cases we may be more interested in knowing how the algorithm perform on the average.

Average-Case Time Complexity

For the input size of n, if we want to get an average overview on the behavior of algorithm, ***average-case time complexity*** is referred. So, $A(n)$ can be defined as the *average (expected value)* of the number of times the algorithm does the basic operation for an input size of n. The determination of $A(n)$ is called an ***average-case time complexity analysis***. Again if $T(n)$ exists, then $A(n) = T(n)$.

In order to compute $A(n)$, we need to assign probabilities to all possible inputs of size n. Determination of probabilities is based on all available information.

Average-case Time Complexity Analysis of Algorithm (Sequential Search):

Basic Operation: The comparison of an item in the array with x.

Input Size: n, the number of items in the array.

Analysis: We first analyze the case where it is known that x is in S. Namely, the available information must be analyzed first.

If we assume that the items in S are all distinct, then x is equally likely to be in any of the array slots. Based on this information, we assign equal probabilities to all array slots. Therefore, for, the probability that x is in the kth array slow is $1/n$.

If x is in the kth array slot, the number of times the basic operation is done to locate x (and, therefore, to exit the loop) is k. This means that the average time complexity is given by:

Let assign, the probability of the event that x is in the array top. Next, if x may not in the array, the probability then will be $1\text{-}p$. Again, if x in the kth slot the probability will be p/n.

If x is in the kth slot, there will be k passes, if it is not in the array there will be n passes so:

In general, if $p=1/2$, then $A(n) = (n+1/2)$. But if $p= 1/n$ $A(n) = 3n/n + 1$. This means that about $3/4$ of the array is searched on the average.

A final type of time complexity analysis is the determination of the smallest number of times the basic operation is done. Thus, we can say that it is the inverse analysis of worst-time complexity analysis.

Best-Time Complexity

For a given algorithm, B (n) is defined as the minimum number of times the algorithm will ever do its basic operation for an input size of n. And the determination of B (n) is called **a** ***best-case time complexity analysis.***

Again, if T (n) exists, then T $(n) = B$ (n).

Best-Case Time Complexity Analysis of Algorithm(Sequential Search):

Basic Operation: The comparison of on item the array with x.

Input Size: n, the number of items in the array.

Analysis: Because, there must be at least one pass through the loop. If $x = S$ $[1]$, then there will be one pass through the loop regardless of the size of n. Therefore, $B(n)=1$.

Among the type of analysis discussed above, worst-case and average-case analysis are referred more than every-case and best-case analysis because, indeed, we often not encounter algorithm which have every-case the complexities and best-case does not have any valuable meaning.

We have discussed analysis of the time complexity of an algorithm. All these same considerations also pertain to the analysis of memory complexity, which is an analysis of how efficient the algorithm in terms of memory.

Complexity Function

In general, a complexity function is a function from the nonnegative integers to the nonnegative real numbers, which gives the complexity of any algorithm with an input size n.

So the types of complexities discussed are special complexity functions.

Example: The functions

f(n)=n,

f(n)=n^2*,*

f(n)=lgn,

f(n)=3n2+4n.

are all examples of complexity functions because they all map the nonnegative integers to the nonnegative real numbers.

2.8 ANALYSIS DETAILS

When applying the theory of algorithm analysis, we must be aware general things that algorithms do and their time costs.

The general time consumers can be given as, consumed time for implementing basic operation, the overhead instructions, and the control instructions on the actual computer. Here, overhead instructions have the meaning of initialization instructions before a loop. The number of times these instructions executed is input size independent. Furthermore, *"control instructions"* have the meaning of incrementing an index to control a loop.

But the costing time of these instructions is input size dependent and increases with the input size.

The basic operation, overhead instructions, and control instructions are all properties of an algorithm, not of a problem. Thus, for one problem, we can have different algorithms with different properties.

When comparing two algorithms we have to consider these properties in order to get on exact result. For instance, if we have two different algorithms for the same problem, with every-time complexities n and n^2 respectively, without considering overhead and control instructions we can say that the first algorithm is much more efficient than the second one, for all instances of the input size. However, if we assume that the time it takes when executing control instructions is proportional to *1000* times of the input size, then,

Now, the efficiency-comparison of two algorithms has changed with the condition above. As a result, if the application never had an input size larger than *1000*, the second algorithm should be implemented.

But, in general, determining how control and overhead instructions have such dominant property precisely is not so easy. So, when comparing two algorithms some approximation techniques can be used.

2.8.1 Order of Algorithms Time Complexity Functions

Algorithms with time complexities such as n and $10n$ are called ***linear-time algorithms*** because their time complexities are *linear* in the input size n where as algorithms with time complexities such as n^2 and $0.001n^2$ are called ***quadratic-time algorithms*** because their time complexities are *quadratic* in the input size *n*. By neglecting overhead and control instructions it is possible to say that any linear-time algorithm is more efficient than the quadratic-time algorithms. In the case of making no neglecting linear-time algorithms become eventually more efficient than quadratic-time algorithms.

That eventual behavior of algorithms helps us in grouping them. With that way we can readily determine whether one algorithm's eventual behavior is better than another's.

Functions such as $3n^2$ and n^2+1000 are called ***pure quadratic*** functions since they contain no linear term, whereas a function such as $3n^2 +1000$ is called a complete quadratic function because of the involved linear term.

In both pure and complete quadratic functions the quadratic term dominates and the values of the other terms eventually become insignificant compared with the value of the quadratic term.

Thus, referring eventual behaviors we can group both pure and complete quadratic functions in one set. By the same way, we can use that classification method to cubic and higher order functions.

Therefore, intuitively, it is possible to throw away low-order terms and take the most high order as a criteria in classification.

The set of all complexity functions that can be classified with pure quadratic functions is called, where is the Greek capital letter 'theta'. If a function is a member of the set we say that the function is order of n^2. As an example,

Which means that $g(n)$ is order of n^2.

When an algorithm's time complexity is in, the algorithm is called a quadratic-time algorithm or a algorithm. We also say that the algorithm or a. *Exchange Sort* is a quadratic-time algorithm.

Now we call these sets ***complexity categories of algorithms.***

The following are some of the most common complexity categories:

$$N\ ,\ nlgn\ ,\ n^2, n^3, 2^n, lg\ n$$

N	f(n)=lg n	f(n)=n	f(n)=nlgn	f(n)=n²	f(n)=n³	f(n)=2ⁿ
10	0.003 μs	0.01 μs	0.033 μs	0.1 μs	1 μs	1 μs
20	0.004 μs	0.02 μs	0.086 μs	0.4 μs	8 μs	1 ms
30	0.005 μs	0.03 μs	0.147 μs	0.9 μs	27 μs	1 s
40	0.005 μs	0.04 μs	0.213 μs	1.6 μs	64 μs	18.3 min
50	0.006 μs	0.05 μs	0.282 μs	2.5 μs	125 μs	13 days
10^2	0.007 μs	0.10 μs	0.664 μs	10 μs	1 ms	$4*10^{13}$years
10^3	0.010 μs	1 μs	9.966 μs	1 ms	1 s	
10^4	0.013 μs	10 μs	130 μs	100 ms	16.7 min	
10^5	0.017 μs	0.10 ms	1.67 ms	10 s	11.6 days	
10^6	0.020 μs	1 ms	19.93 ms	16.7 min	31709years	
10^7	0.023 μs	0.01 s	0.23 s	1.16 days	$3.17*10^7$years	
10^8	0.027 μs	0.10 s	2.66 s	115.7days		
10^9	0.030 μs	1 s	29.90 s	31.7 years		

1 μs=10^{-6} second & 1 ms=10^{-3} second

Table 2.1: Execution times for algorithms with the given time complexities.

In the Table 2.1 above, the simplifying assumption is that it takes *1 nanosecond* (10^{-9} *second*) to process the basic operation for each algorithm.

The result is very surprising, even if the algorithms are not exponential-time, even in the quadratic- time algorithm it takes *31.7 years* to process an instance with an input size of *1 billion*. On the other hand the algorithm takes only *29.9 seconds* to process such an instance.

In general, an algorithm has to be or better for us to assume that it can process extremely large instances in tolerable amounts time. This does not mean that algorithms whose time complexities are in the higher-order categories are not useful. Algorithms with quadratic, cubic, and even higher-order time complexities can often handle the actual instances that arise in many applications.

Although, categorizing algorithms is very helpful for many instances, it is better to know the exact time complexity of any algorithm because if we know the exact value we will decide which one is more efficient without making generalization based its order.

2.9 TECHNIQUES IN ANALYZING ALGORITHMS

The common techniques in analyzing algorithms are as follows:

2.9.1 Divide and Conquer Method

Divide-and-conquer approach is first used by the French emperor Napoleon in the Battle of Austerliz on December 2, 1805. A combined army of Austrians and Russians army encompassed Napoleon's army by about 15000 soldiers. The Austria-Russian army launched a massive attack against the French right flank. Response to that attack, Napoleon drove against their center and split their forces in two. Because the two smaller armies were individually no match for Napoleon, they each give heavy losses and they compelled to retreat. By dividing the large army into two smaller armies and individually conquering these two smaller armies, Napoleon was able to conquer the large army.

By the same way, it is possible to use the same strategy on an instance of a problem. Thus, if we divide an instance of a problem into two or more smaller instances, where the smaller instances usually again instances of the original problem, and if we find solutions to the smaller instances, then combining these solutions will gave us the original solution. However, if it is not possible to find solutions to smaller instances we divide them again in two or more.

The divide-and-conquer approach is a *top-down* approach like it is in recursive technique. That is, the solution to a top-level instance of a problem is obtained by going down and obtaining solutions to smaller instances.

In general, the divide-and-conquer design strategy involves these following steps:

1. *Divide* an instance of a problem into one or more smaller instances.

2. *Conquer (solve)* each of the smaller instances. If a smaller instance is not sufficiently small, use recursion to do this.

3. If necessary, combine the solutions of the smaller instances to obtain the solution of the original instance.

Quick Sort (Partitioned Exchange Sort)

The Quick Sort Algorithm was developed by Hoare in 1962. In that algorithm, we divide the array to be sorted into two smaller partitions and then sort each partition recursively. The criteria on dividing the items in the array depend on some chosen pivot element. Thus, our partitions are defined as sub arrays which consist of the array elements smaller than the pivot item and the elements bigger or equal to the pivot item.

As an illustration the following example will give us how the quick sort works in general manner.

***Example*:**

Suppose we have the following array:

15 22 13 27 12 10 20 25

Let's chose 15 the first element of the array as the pivot item .According to the pivot item. Then,

1. We obtain,

   chosen pivot element

   ↓

   15 22 13 27 12 10 20 25

2. Sorting the sub arrays, we now obtain the desired result:

   10 12 13 15 20 22 25 27

Algorithm :Quick Sort

Problem: Sort n keys in non-decreasing order.

Inputs: positive integer n, array of keys S indexed from 1 to n.

Output: the array S containing the keys in non-decreasing order.

```
procedure quicksort (low, high as integer)
pivotpoint as integer;
if high > low then
partition ( low, high, pivotpoint );
quicksort ( low, high, pivotpoint-1 );
quicksort ( pivotpoint+1, high );
end if;
```

end procedure;

Algorithm: Partition into sub arrays

Problem: Partition the array S into sub arrays for quick sort.

Inputs: Two indices low and high and the sub array of S indexed from low to high.

Outputs: pivot point, the pivot point for the array S indexed from low to high.

```
procedure partition ( low, high, pivotpoint as integer )
        i, j as integer;
        pivotitem as integer;
        pivotitem= S[low];
        j=low;
        for i = low+1 to high do
                if S[i] < pivotitem then
        j = j+1;
                exchange S[i] and S[j]
        end for
        pivotpoint = j;
        exchange S[low] and S[pivotpoint]
        end procedure;
```

Every-Case Time Complexity Analysis of Algorithm (Partition into Sub arrays):

Basic Operation: The comparison of *S[i]* with pivot item.

Input Size: *high-low + 1*

Analysis: We compare every item except the first one. Then $T(n) = n-1$.

Here *n* is referred as the size of the sub arrays not the size of the full array S. But, for the time the procedure is called it is equal to the size of the full array *S*.

Worst-Case Time Complexity Analysis of Algorithm (Quick Sort)

Basic Operation: The comparison of *S[i]* with the pivot item in partition.

Input Size: n, the number of items in the array.

Analysis: As a strange situation, worst-case occurs when the array has already been sorted in non-decreasing order. The reason is a little bit tricky. If the array is already sorted in non decreasing order, no items are less than the first item in the array, which is the pivot item. Therefore, when partitions is called at the top level, no items are placed to the left of the pivot item, and the value of the pivot item assigned by partition is 1. Similarly, in each recursive call pivot point receives the value of low. Thus, the array is repeatedly partitioned into an empty sub array on the left and a sub array with one less item on the right. For the class of instances that are already sorted in non-decreasing order, we have

$$T(n) = T(0) + T(n-1) + n-1 \quad (1)$$

T (0): Time to sort left sub array

T (n-1): Time to sort right sub array

n- 1: Time to make partition

Here, we use the *T(n)* notation because, the notation we refer is the every-time complexity of the class of instances that are already sorted in non-decreasing order. Since *T(0) = 0,* we obtain the recurrence as:

$$T(n) = T(n-1)+ n-1 \text{ for } n>0$$

$$T(0) = 0 \quad (2)$$

Best, Worst, and Average-Case

The *worst case complexity* of the algorithm is the function defined by the maximum number of steps taken on any instance of size *n*.

The *best case complexity* of the algorithm is the function defined by the minimum number of steps taken on any instance of size *n*.

The *average-case complexity* of the algorithm is the function defined by an average number of steps taken on any instance of size *n*.

Each of these complexities defines a numerical function - time vs. size!

Insertion Sort

One way to sort an array of n elements is to start with empty list, then successively insert new elements in the proper position:

At each stage, the inserted element leaves a sorted list, and after *n* insertions contains exactly the right elements. Thus the algorithm must be correct.

But how *efficient* is it?

Note that the run time changes with the permutation instance! (even for a fixed size problem)

Insertion sort

We start with ***insertion sort,*** which is an efficient algorithm for sorting a small number of elements. Insertion sort works the way many people sort a bridge or gin rummy hand. We start with an empty left hand and the cards face down on the table. We then remove one card at a time from the table and insert it into the correct position in the left hand. To find the correct position for a card, we compare it with each of the cards already in the hand, from right to left, as illustrated in Figure below

Figure: Sorting a hand of cards using insertion sort.

Our pseudocode for insertion sort is presented as a procedure called `INSERTION-SORT`, which takes as a parameter an array $A[1 \, . \, . \, n]$ containing a sequence of length n that is to be sorted. (In the code, the number n of elements in A is denoted by $length[A]$.) The input numbers are ***sorted in place***: the numbers are rearranged within the array A, with at most a constant number of them stored outside the array at any time. The input array A contains the sorted output sequence when `INSERTION-SORT` is finished.

Insertion-Sort (*A*)

```
1.  for j ← 2 to length[A]
2.    do key ← A[j]
3.       Insert A[j] into the sorted sequence A[1 . . j – 1].
4.       i ← j – 1
5.       while i > 0 and A[i] > key
6.         do A[i + 1] ← A[i]
7.            i ← i – 1
8.       A[i + 1] ← key
```

Figure above shows how this algorithm works for $A = (5, 2, 4, 6, 1, 3)$. The index j indicates the "current card" being inserted into the hand. Array elements $A[1.. \, j - 1]$ constitute the currently sorted hand, and elements $A[j + 1 \, . \, . \, n]$ correspond to the pile of cards still on the table. The index j moves left to right through the array. At each iteration of the "outer" for loop, the element $A[j]$ is picked out of the array (line 2). Then, starting in position j - 1, elements are successively moved one position to the right until the proper position for $A[j]$ is found (lines 4-7), at which point it is inserted (line 8).

```
5  (2)  4   6   1   3
2   5  (4)  6   1   3
2   4   5  (6)  1   3
2   4   5   6  (1)  3
1   2   4   5   6  (3)
1   2   3   4   5   6   done
```

Figure: The operation of INSERTION-SORT on the array A = (5, 2, 4, 6, 1, 3). The position of index j is indicated by a circle.

Pseudo Code Conventions

We use the following conventions in our pseudocode.

1. Indentation indicates block structure. For example, the body of the **for** loop that begins on line 1 consists of lines 2-8, and the body of the **while** loop that begins on line 5 contains lines 6-7 but not line 8. Our indentation style applies to **if-then-else** statements as well. Using indentation instead of conventional indicators of block structure, such as **begin** and **end** statements, greatly reduces clutter while preserving, or even enhancing, clarity(In real programming languages, it is generally not advisable to use indentation alone to indicate block structure, since levels of indentation are hard to determine when code is split across pages).
2. The looping constructs **while, for,** and **repeat** and the conditional constructs **if, then**, and **else** have the same interpretation as in Pascal.
3. A multiple assignment of the form $i \leftarrow j \leftarrow e$ assigns to both variables i and j the value of expression e; it should be treated as equivalent to the assignment $j \leftarrow e$ followed by the assignment $i \leftarrow j$.
4. Variables (such as *i, j,* and *key*) are local to the given procedure. We shall not use global variables without explicit indication.
5. Array elements are accessed by specifying the array name followed by the index in square brackets. For example, $A[i]$ indicates the ith element of the array A. The notation ". ." is used to indicate a range of values within an array. Thus, $A[1 \,.\,.\, j]$ indicates the subarray of A consisting of elements $A[1], A[2], \ldots, A[j]$.
6. Compound data are typically organized into ***objects***, which are comprised of ***attributes*** or ***fields***. A particular field is accessed using the field name followed by the name of its object in square brackets. For example, we treat an array as an object with the attribute *length* indicating how many elements it contains. To specify the number of elements in an array A, we write $length[A]$. Although we use square brackets for both array indexing and object attributes, it will usually be clear from the context which interpretation is intended.
7. A variable representing an array or object is treated as a pointer to the data representing the array or object. For all fields f of an object x, setting $y \leftarrow x$ causes $f[y] = f[x]$. Moreover, if we now set $f[x] \leftarrow 3$, then afterward not only is $f[x] = 3$, but $f[y] = 3$ as well. In other words, x and y point to ("are") the same object after the assignment $y \leftarrow x$.

   Sometimes, a pointer will refer to no object at all. In this case, we give it the special value NIL.
8. Parameters are passed to a procedure ***by value***: the called procedure receives its own copy of the parameters, and if it assigns a value to a parameter, the change is *not* seen by the calling routine. When objects are passed, the pointer to the data representing the object is copied, but the object's fields are not. For example, if x is a parameter of a called procedure, the assignment $x \leftarrow y$ within the called procedure is not visible to the calling procedure. The assignment $f[x] \leftarrow 3$, however, is visible.

Exact Analysis of Insertion Sort

Count the number of times each line of pseudo code will be executed.

Line	InsertionSort(A)	#Inst.	#Exec.
1	for j:=2 to len. of A do	c1	n
2	key:=A[j]	c2	n-1
3	/* put A[j] into A[1..j-1] */	c3=0	/
4	i:=j-1	c4	n-1
5	while do	c5	tj
6	A[i+1]:= A[i]	c6	
7	i := i-1	c7	
8	A[i+1]:=key	c8	n-1

The for statement is executed (n-1)+1 times (why?)

Within the for statement, "key:=A[j]" is executed n-1 times.

Steps 5, 6, 7 are harder to count.

Worst Case

If the input is sorted in *descending* order, we will have to slide *all* of the already-sorted elements.

ANALYZING ALGORITHMS

Analyzing an algorithm has come to mean predicting the resources that the algorithm requires. Occasionally, resources such as memory, communication bandwidth, or logic gates are of primary concern, but most often it is computational time that we want to measure. Generally, by analyzing several candidate algorithms for a problem, a most efficient one can be easily identified. Such analysis may indicate more than one viable candidate, but several inferior algorithms are usually discarded in the process.

Before we can analyze an algorithm, we must have a model of the implementation technology that will be used, including a model for the resources of that technology and their costs. For most of this book, we shall assume a generic one-processor, ***random-access machine*** **(*RAM*)** model of computation as our implementation technology and understand that our algorithms will be implemented as computer programs. In the RAM model, instructions are executed one after another, with no concurrent operations. In later chapters, however, we shall have occasion to investigate models for parallel computers and digital hardware.

Analyzing even a simple algorithm can be a challenge. The mathematical tools required may include discrete combinatorics, elementary probability theory, algebraic dexterity, and the ability to identify the most significant terms in a formula. Because the behavior of an algorithm may be different for each possible input, we need a means for summarizing that behavior in simple, easily understood formulas.

Even though we typically select only one machine model to analyze a given algorithm, we still face many choices in deciding how to express our analysis. One immediate goal is to find a means of expression that is simple to write and manipulate, shows the important characteristics of an algorithm's resource requirements, and suppresses tedious details.

Analysis of Insertion Sort

The time taken by the INSERTION-SORT procedure depends on the input: sorting a thousand numbers takes longer than sorting three numbers. Moreover, INSERTION-SORT can take different amounts of time to sort two input sequences of the same size depending on how nearly sorted they already are. In general, the time taken by an algorithm grows with the size of the input, so it is traditional to describe the running time of a program as a function of the size of its input. To do so, we need to define the terms "running time" and "size of input" more carefully.

The best notion for ***input size*** depends on the problem being studied. For many problems, such as sorting or computing discrete Fourier transforms, the most natural measure is the *number of items in the input*--for example, the array size n for sorting. For many other problems, such as multiplying two integers, the best measure of input size is the *total number of bits* needed to represent the input in ordinary binary notation. Sometimes, it is more appropriate to describe the size of the input with two numbers rather than one. For instance, if the input to an algorithm is a graph, the input size can be described by the numbers of vertices and edges in the graph. We shall indicate which input size measure is being used with each problem we study.

The ***running time*** of an algorithm on a particular input is the number of primitive operations or "steps" executed. It is convenient to define the notion of step so that it is as machine-independent as possible. For the moment, let us adopt the following view. A constant amount of time is required to execute each line of our pseudocode. One line may take a different amount of time than another line, but we shall assume that each execution of the ith line takes time c_i, where c_i is a constant. This viewpoint is in keeping with the RAM model, and it also reflects how the pseudocode would be implemented on most actual computers.

Remember that Computational steps that we specify in English are often variants of a procedure that requires more than just a constant amount of time. For example, later in this book we might say "sort the points by x-coordinate," which, as we shall see, takes more than a constant amount of time. Also, note that a statement that calls a subroutine takes constant time, though the subroutine, once invoked, may take more. That is, we separate the process of ***calling*** the subroutine--passing parameters to it, etc.--from the process of ***executing*** the subroutine.

In the following discussion, our expression for the running time of INSERTION-SORT will evolve from a messy formula that uses all the statement costs c_i to a much simpler notation that is more concise and more easily manipulated. This simpler notation will also make it easy to determine whether one algorithm is more efficient than another. We start by presenting the INSERTION-SORT procedure with the time "cost" of each statement and the number of times each statement is executed. For each $j = 2, 3, \ldots, n$, where $n = length[A]$, we let t_j be the number of times the **while** loop test in line 5 is executed for that value of j. We assume that comments are not executable statements, and so they take no time.

INSERTION-SORT (A)	*Cost*	*Times*
1. for J ← 2 to *length[A)*	c_1	n
2. *do key ← A[j]*	c_2	n - 1
3. ▷ Insert *A[j]* into the sorted		
▷ Sequence *A*[1...*j* – 1].	O	n - 1
4. *i* ← *j* – 1	c_4	n - 1
5. while *i* > O and *A*[*i*] > *key*	c_5	$\sum_{j=2}^{n} i_j$
6. do *A*[*i* + 1] ← *A*[*i*] >	c_6	$\sum_{j=2}^{n} (i_j - 1)$
7. *i* ← *i* – 1	c_7	$\sum_{j=2}^{n} (i_j - 1)$
8. *A*[*i* + 1] ← *key*	c_8	n - 1

The running time of the algorithm is the sum of running times for each statement executed; a statement that takes c_i steps to execute and is executed n times will contribute $c_i n$ to the total running time. To compute $T(n)$, the running time of INSERTION-SORT, we sum the products of the *cost* and *times* columns, obtaining

$$T(n) = c_1 n + c_2 (n-1) + c_4 (n-1) + c_5 \sum_{j=2}^{n} t_j + \sum_{j=2}^{n} (t_j - 1) + c_7 \sum_{j=2}^{n} (t_j - 1) + c_8 (n-1)$$

This characteristic does not necessarily hold for a resource such as memory. A statement that references m words of memory and is executed n times does not necessarily consume mn words of memory in total.

Even for inputs of a given size, an algorithm's running time may depend on *which* input of that size is given. For example, in `INSERTION-SORT`, the best case occurs if the array is already sorted. For each $j = 2, 3, \ldots, n$, we then find that $A[i] \leq key$ in line 5 when i has its initial value of $j - 1$. Thus $tj = 1$ for $j = 2, 3, \ldots, n$, and the best-case running time is

$$T(n) = c_1 n + c_2 (n - 1) + c_4 (n - 1) + c_5 (n - 1) + c_8 (n - 1)$$

$$= (c_1 + c_2 + c_4 + c_8)n - (c_2 + c_4 + c_5 + c_8).$$

This running time can be expressed as $an + b$ for *constants a* and *b* that depend on the statement costs c_i; it is thus a ***linear function*** of n.

If the array is in reverse sorted order--that is, in decreasing order--the worst case results. We must compare each element $A[j]$ with each element in the entire sorted subarray $A[1..j-1]$, and so $t_j = j$ for $j = 2, 3, \ldots, n$. Noting that

$$\sum_{j=2}^{n} j = \frac{n(n+1)}{2} - 1$$

and

$$\sum_{j=2}^{n}(j-1)=\frac{n(n+1)}{2}$$

(we shall review these summations in Chapter 3), we find that in the worst case, the running time of INSERTION-SORT is

$$T(n)=c_1n+c_2(n-1)+c_4(n-1)+c_5\left(\frac{n(n+1)}{2}-1\right)+c_6\left(\frac{n(n+1)}{2}\right)+c_7\left(\frac{n(n+1)}{2}\right)+c_8(n-1)$$

$$=\left(\frac{c_5}{2}+\frac{c_6}{2}+\frac{c_7}{2}\right)n^2+\left(c_1+c_2+c_4+\frac{c_5}{2}-\frac{c_6}{2}-\frac{c_7}{2}+c_8\right)n-(c_2+c_4+c_5+c_8)$$

This worst-case running time can be expressed as $an^2 + bn + c$ for constants a, b, and c that again depend on the statement costs c_i; it is thus a ***quadratic function*** of n.

Typically, as in insertion sort, the running time of an algorithm is fixed for a given input, although in later chapters we shall see some interesting "randomized" algorithms whose behavior can vary even for a fixed input.

Worst-case and Aaverage-case Analysis

In our analysis of insertion sort, we looked at both the best case, in which the input array was already sorted, and the worst case, in which the input array was reverse sorted. For the remainder of this book, though, we shall usually concentrate on finding only the ***worst-case running time***, that is, the longest running time for *any* input of size n. We give three reasons for this orientation.

- The worst-case running time of an algorithm is an upper bound on the running time for any input. Knowing it gives us a guarantee that the algorithm will never take any longer. We need not make some educated guess about the running time and hope that it never gets much worse.
- For some algorithms, the worst case occurs fairly often. For example, in searching a database for a particular piece of information, the searching algorithm's worst case will often occur when the information is not present in the database. In some searching applications, searches for absent information may be frequent.
- The "average case" is often roughly as bad as the worst case. Suppose that we randomly choose n numbers and apply insertion sort. How long does it take to determine where in subarray $A[1..j-1]$ to insert element $A[j]$? On average, half the elements in $A[1..j-1]$ are less than $A[j]$, and half the elements are greater. On average, therefore, we check half of the subarray $A[1..j-1]$, so $t_j = j/2$. If we work out the resulting average-case running time, it turns out to be a quadratic function of the input size, just like the worst-case running time.

In some particular cases, we shall be interested in the ***average-case*** or ***expected*** running time of an algorithm. One problem with performing an average-case analysis, however, is that it may not be apparent what constitutes an "average" input for a particular problem.

Often, we shall assume that all inputs of a given size are equally likely. In practice, this assumption may be violated, but a randomized algorithm can sometimes force it to hold.

Order of Growth

We have used some simplifying abstractions to ease our analysis of the `INSERTION-SORT` procedure. First, we ignored the actual cost of each statement, using the constants c_i to represent these costs. Then, we observed that even these constants give us more detail than we really need: the worst-case running time is $an^2 + bn + c$ for some constants a, b, and c that depend on the statement costs c_i. We thus ignored not only the actual statement costs, but also the abstract costs c_i.

We shall now make one more simplifying abstraction. It is the ***rate of growth,*** or ***order of growth,*** of the running time that really interests us. We therefore consider only the leading term of a formula (e.g., an^2), since the lower-order terms are relatively insignificant for large n. We also ignore the leading term's constant coefficient, since constant factors are less significant than the rate of growth in determining computational efficiency for large inputs. Thus, we write that insertion sort, for example, has a worst-case running time of $\Theta(n^2)$ (pronounced "theta of n-squared").

We usually consider one algorithm to be more efficient than another if its worst-case running time has a lower order of growth. This evaluation may be in error for small inputs, but for large enough inputs a $\Theta(n^2)$ algorithm, for example, will run more quickly in the worst case than a $\Theta(n^3)$ algorithm.

2.9.2 Dynamic Programming

The divide-and-conquer method was a top-down approach where we solve an instance of a problem by dividing it into smaller instances and then blindly solve these smaller instances. Again, the smaller instances have no relation between them. For instance in Algorithm (Quick Sort) the each smaller instance consists of an array of keys that must be sorted independently. However in problems such as nth Fibonacci Term, the smaller instances are related, namely, in order to compute 4th Fibonacci term we refer 3rd, 2nd and the first Fibonacci Terms in an order. If we were using divide-and-conquer algorithm in finding Fibonacci Term, the algorithm would calculate each preceding term more than once. Therefore, it will be inefficient in calculating such term related algorithms.

Instead of using divide-and-conquer technique in such algorithms, we can use dynamic programming technique, which is similar in dividing the instances into smaller parts but, is an opposite approach. In dynamic programming, we again make partitions in order to obtain smaller instances, yet we solve smaller instances first, store results, and later, whenever we need any preceding result we refer the stored results other than recomputing it. Dynamic Programming is therefore a bottom-up approach. As we expressed before nth Fibonacci term constructing is a very good example for dynamic programming.

The steps in the development of dynamic programming algorithm are as follows:

1. Establish a recursive property that gives the solution to an instance of the problem.
2. Solve an instance of the problem in a bottom-up fashion by solving smaller instances first.

Dynamic Programming and Optimization

When dealing with optimization problems that we encounter in many areas, it is possible to get efficient algorithms with using dynamic programming concept. However, in that kind of problems there can be more than one candidate solution to an instance of the problem. Each candidate solution has a value associated with it, and a solution to that instance is any candidate that has an optimal value. Depending on the problem, the optimal value is either the minimum or the maximum. The steps of constructing such algorithms are as follows:

1. Establishing a recursive property that gives an optimal solution to an instance of the problem.
2. Computing the value of an optimal solution in a bottom-up fashion.
3. Constructing an optimal solution in a bottom-up fashion.

Definition: The **principle of optimality** is said to apply in a problem if an optimal solution to an instance of a problem always contains optimal solutions to all sub instances.

Shortest Path Problem

The Shortest Path Problem is an **optimization** problem, in which a candidate solution is a path from one vertex to another. However, our goal is to find the shortest one. An obvious algorithm for this problem would be to determine, for each vertex, the lengths of all the paths from that vertex to each other vertex, and compute the minimum of these paths, for which we obtain a time complexity worse than exponential-time.

The arising situation is most common one for all optimization problems. In order to reduce this time complexity we will use dynamic programming technique in which we store some possible results.

Algorithm : Floyd's Algorithm for Shortest Paths

Problem: Compute the shortest paths from each vertex in a weighted graph to each of the other vertices. The weights are nonnegative numbers.

Inputs: A weighted, directed graph and n, the number of vertices in the graph. The graph is represented by a matrix W, where *W[i , j]* is the weight on the edge from the ith vertex to the jth vertex.

Outputs: an array D containing the lengths of the shortest paths.

procedure floyd (n: integer; W: array [1…n,1…n] of number;var D:array[1…n,1….n] of number)

```
i, j, k as integer;
D =W;
    for k=1 to n do
    for i=1 to n do
```

```
                    for j=1 to n do
                         D[I,j] =minimum(D[I,j],D[I,k]+D[k,j])
                    end for;
               end for;
          end for;
     end procedure;
```

Every-Case Time Complexity Analysis of (Floyd's Algorithm for Shortest Paths)

Basic operation: The instructions in the for-j loop.

Input size: n, the number of vertices in the graph.

Analysis: We have a loop within a loop, with n passes through each loop. So

Algorithm : Floyd's Algorithm for Shortest paths

Problem: Same as in Above Algorithm , except shortest paths are also created.

Additional Outputs: an array *P*, where

Highest index of an intermediate vertex on the shortest path *P[i,j] = from* v_i *to* v_j if at least one intermediate vertex exists.

0 if no intermediate vertex exists.

```
Procedure floyd2 (n as integer, W as array[1....n,1....n] of number
D as array[1....n,1....n] of integer)

     i,j,k as integer;
     for i:=1 to n do
          for j:= 1 to n do
          P [i, j]=0
          end for;
     end for;
     D=W;
     for k:=1 to n do
     for i:= 1 to n do
          for j=1 to n do
          if D[i,k] + D[k,j]<D[i,j] then
          P[i,j] =k;
                    D [ i, j] = D[ i, k] + D[k, j];
               end if;
          end for;
          end for;
     end for;
     end procedure;
```

The Traveling Salesperson Problem

In general, the Traveling Salesperson Problem includes graph as an instance and then an analysis for that graph in order to find a minimum travel time. To minimize travel time it is needed to determine a shortest route that starts at some vertex (namely salesperson's home city) and passing each vertex once returning the started vertex again.

That problem differs from Floyd's Shortest Path algorithm because we generalize that problem to include the case where the weight (distance) going in one direction can be different than the weight going in another direction. Again the assumption made is that the weights are nonnegative numbers.

A tour (or Hamilton Circuit) in a directed graph is a path from vertex to itself that passes through each of the other vertices exactly once. Therefore, an optimal tour in a weighted, directed graph is such a path of minimum length.

In Traveling Salesperson Problem, it is possible to apply dynamic programming concept, because here the principle of optimality applies as it is in Floyd's Shortest Path's algorithm.

The traveling salesperson problem can be solved by using dynamic programming.

Example:

It is the last weekend of 1996 election campaign and candidate Walter Glenn is in New York City. Before Election Day, Walter must visit Miami, Dallas and Chicago then return to his New York City headquarters. Walter wants to minimize the total distance he must be travel. In what order should he visit cities? The distances in miles between the four cities are given in Table.

Cities	City 1 New York	City 2 Miami	City 3 Dallas	City 4 Chicago
New York	–	1334	1559	809
Miami	1334	–	1343	1397
Dallas	1559	1343	–	321
Chicago	809	1397	921	–

Figure 1.2: *All possible edges with length for each city to another.*

Solution:

We know that Walter must visit each city exactly once, the last city he must visit must be New York, and his tour originates in New York. When Walter has only one city left to visit, his problem is trivial: simply go from his current location to New York. Then it is possible to work backward to a problem in which he is in some city and has only two cities left to visit and finally it is possible to find the shortest tour that originates in New York and has four cities that Walter has already visited. At any stage, to determine which city should next be visited, it is needed to know two things: Walter's current location and the cities he has already visited. The state at any state consists of the last city visited and the set of cities that have already been visited. Defining $f_t\ (i\ ,\ s\ )$ to be the minimum distance that must be traveled to complete a tour if the t-1 cities in the set S have been visited and city i was the last city visited, and letting c_{ij} be the distance between cities i and j. It is possible to obtain the following stages.

Stage 4 Computations:

In backward analysis, assuming that all cities are visited except the last one, which is New York, we define three possibilities according to the Table. It is obvious that doing backward analysis helps us to solve the problem easily because dynamic programming is bottom-up approach. According to the backward analysis we obtain the following results:

f_4 (2,{2,3,4}) = c_{21} = 1334 (Go from city 2 to city1)
f_4 (3,{2,3,4}) = c_{31} = 1559 (Go from city 3 to city1)
f_4 (4,{2,3,4}) = c_{41} = 809 (Go from city 4 to city1)

Algorithm: The Dynamic Programming Algorithm for the Traveling Salesperson Problem

Problem: Determine an optimal tour in a weighted, directed graph. The weights are nonnegative numbers.

Inputs: A weighted, directed graph. And *n* is the number of vertices in the graph. The graph is represented by a matrix, where *W[i,j]* is the weight on the edge from v_i to v_j. *V* denotes the set of all vertices.

Outputs: A variable minlength, whose value is the length of an optimal tour, and an array P from which an optimal tour can be constructed. P[i,A] is the index of the first vertex after v_i on a shortest path from v_i to v_1 that passes through all the vertices in *A* exactly once.

```
Procedure travel (n as integer, W as array [1....n,1....n] of number,
    P as array [1....n, subset of V-{v1}] of index, minlength as integer);
    i, j, k as integer;
    D as array[1....n, subset of V-{vi}] of number;
            for i:= 2 to n do
    D [i, Ø] = W [ i , I];
    end for;
    for k:=1 to n-2 do
    for all subsets A V-{v1} containing k vertices do
            for i such that i 1 and vi is not in A do
            D[ i, A] =minimum[W[ i, j] + D[ vj, A-{vj}];
    P[i, A] = value of j that gave the minimum
    end for;
    end for;
    end for;
    D[1,V-{v1}] = minimum(W[1,j]+ D[vj,V-{v1}]);
    P[1,V-{vi}]:=value of j that gave the minimum
    minlength =D[1,V-{vi}]
    end procedure;
```

2.10 THEORY OF NP AND P TIME COMPLEXITY

So far, some problems arising in computer-science and their algorithms with time complexities have been discussed. Again for these algorithms better algorithms (algorithms which have less time complexity) have been developed.

Now, in that chapter we solely deal with just problems in general manner. We also will try to categorize the arising problems of computer-science in order to have a general overview about the problems. But, before starting a new terminology is needed in order to put the bricks in right order when constructing a wall.

Intractability

The dictionary defines ***intractable*** as "difficult to treat or work". This means that a problem in computer science is intractable if a computer has difficulty in solving it.

To make the definition more concrete we again define a new concept.

Definition: A polynomial-time algorithm is one whose worst-case time complexity is bounded above by a polynomial function of its input size. That is , if n is the input size, there exists a polynomial p(n) such that

Examples: *n, n^2, $nlgn$, $5n+10n$,* and n^{100} are some polynomial time algorithms, whereas 2^n, $2^{0.001n}$,, *and $n!$* are examples of non-polynomial time algorithms.

More definitely, in computer science, a problem is called ***intractable*** if it is impossible to solve it with a polynomial-time algorithm. The important point to be expressed here is:" Intractability is a property of a problem; it is not a property of any one algorithm for that problem". So, for a problem to be intractable means, that there must be no polynomial-time algorithm that solves it. However, obtaining a polynomial-time algorithm does not make it intractable.

In computer science arising problems are classified into three groups. These are:

(i) ***Problems which have polynomial-time algorithms:*** In that category, problems have at least one polynomial time algorithm (such as sorting having order, chained matrix multiplication having order where n is the measure of the input).

(ii) ***Problems that have been proven to be Intractable:***

Divided into two subcategories as:

(a) *Problems that require a (nonreasonable) nonpolynomial amounts of output.*

(b) *Problems that we don not require large (nonpolynomial) amounts of data but are proven not be solved by using polynomial-time algorithms.*

(iii) ***Problems that have not been proven to be Intractable but for which polynomial-time algorithms have not been found yet:***

That category includes the our famous Traveling Sales Person Problem, which has many application areas such as graph theory, network theory, and operations research. Moreover, 0-1 Knapsack Problem, the m-Coloring Problem for, and the Hamiltonian

Circuits Problem are in this category. Meanwhile, this category proves that computer science is not well developed yet. For bounded instances it is possible to get polynomial-time complexity but in general it is not possible yet.

THE SETS P AND NP

P Set: P is the set of all ***decision*** problems that can be solved by polynomial-time algorithms.

What is a decision problem? Decision problem is a problem, in which the output is simply "yes" or "no". Each optimization problem however has a corresponding decision problem, as it is in Traveling Salesperson Problem. The decision problem for Traveling Salesperson Problem is then as follows:

Let a weighted, directed graph be given. In that graph, the Traveling Salesperson Decision Problem is to determine for a given positive number d, whether there is a tour having total weight no greater than d. This problem has the same parameters as the Traveling Salesperson Optimization Problem plus the additional parameter d.

The decision problems for which polynomial-time algorithms have been found are all in P. For instance, the corresponding decision problem for the problem of determining whether a key is present in a sorted array is in P. It is known that the Traveling Salesperson problem lies in category 3 so, it is unknown whether it is P or not.

Now, it is time to define a new concept, NP. But before doing this it is needed to look at new algorithm that verifies if any candidate instance for the Traveling Salesperson Problem satisfies the decision problem.

Algorithm: (Verification)

Function verify (G **as weighted _digraph,** d **as given positive number,** S **as claimed_tour) as boolean**

if S is a tour **and** the total weight of the edges in S is **<= d then**

verify = true;

else verify = false;

end if;

end function;

This algorithm first checks whether S indeed a tour. If it is, the algorithm then adds the weights on the tour. If the sum of the weights is no greater than d, it returns *"true"*, otherwise *"false"*.

This verification algorithm is polynomial-time. Therefore, the problems like Travelling Salesperson Decision Problem are said to be polynomial-time non-deterministic algorithms.

Polynomial-time non-deterministic algorithm is a non-deterministic algorithm, which has polynomial-time verification stage. . What does that mean? That means, for any instance of the problem we guess a random solution and verify whether the solution is correct. Here, verification stage is in polynomial-time.

It is non-deterministic, since the candidate is found by guessing, namely as a non-deterministic process. But, the verification of such non-deterministic candidate is deterministic and also has polynomial-time algorithm.

NP Set: The set *NP* is defines the set of all problems, which can be solved by polynomial-time non-deterministic algorithms. It must be stressed that this does not mean that we necessarily have a polynomial-time algorithm that solves the problem.

Large numbers of problems are trivially in *NP*, because *every problem in P also in NP.*

The important question here is about which decision problems are not in NP? But, the answer is simple; *the problems that have been proven to be intractable are not in the set NP.*

NP-Completeness: The arising problems in the set *NP* can have the same approximately same difficulty level. So, if one of the problems in the set *NP* can be proved to be in the set *P* then thousands of problems are again in the set *P*. That behaviour or property of the set *NP* is called ***NP-Completeness***. In order to show this we need some definitions.

Suppose that we want to show decision problem *A* and we have an algorithm that solves problem *B*. Suppose further that we can write an algorithm creates an instance *y* of problem *B* from every instance *x* of problem *A* such that an algorithm for problem answers "yes" for *y* if and only if the answer to problem *A* is "yes" for *x*. Such an algorithm is called a ***transformation algorithm*** and actually a function that maps every instance of problem *A* to an instance of problem *B*. I t can be denoted as:

The transformation algorithm combined with an algorithm for problem *B* yields an algorithm for problem *A*.

Definition: If there exist a polynomial-time transformation algorithm from decision problem *A* to decision problem *B*, ***problem A is polynomial-time many-one reducible to problem B*** (usually we just say that problem *A* reduces to problem *B*.) In symbols, we wr ite

Definition: A problem *B* is called *NP-complete* if

1. it is in *NP* and
2. for every other problem *A* in *NP*,

Theorem: A problem C is *NP-complete* if

1. it is NP and
2. for some other NP-complete problem B,

Proof: Because *B is NP-complete*, for any problem *A* in. It is not hard to see that reducibility is transitive. Therefore,. Because C is *NP*, we can conclude that C is *NP-complete.*

Example: We have already written a polynomial-time verification algorithm for the usual *Travelling Salesperson Decision Problem.* Therefore this problem is in *NP*, and we can show that it is *NP-complete* by showing that

Travelling Salesperson (Undirected) Decision Problem Travelling Salesperson Decision Problem.

Transform an instance *(V,E)* of the *Travelling Salesperson (Undirected) Decision Problem* to the instance *(V,E′)* of the *Travelling Salesperson Problem* that has the same set of vertices *V* and has the edges <*u,v*> and *v*,u both in *E′ whenever (u,v)* is in *E*. The directed weights of <*u,v*> and <v,u> are the same as the inderected weight of *(u,v)*. Clearly, *(V,E)* has an undirected tour with total weight no greater than *d* if and only if *(V,E′)* has a directed tour with total weight no greater than *d*.

NP-HARD, NP-EASY, NP-EQUIVALENT PROBLEMS

So far we have discussed only decision problems. Next we extend our results to problems in general. Recall that previous Theorem implies that if decision problem *A* is polynomial-time many-one reducible to problem *B*, then we could solve problem *A* in polynomial time using a polynomial-time algorithm for problem *B*. We generalize this notation to nondecision problems with the following definition.

Definition: If problem *A* can be solved in polynomial time using a hypothetical polynomial-time algorithm for problem B, then problem *A* is polynomial-time *Turing reducible to problem* (usually we just say *Turing reduces to B*.)

This definition does not require that a polynomial-time algorithm for problem *B* exist. It only says that if one did exist, problem *A* would also be solvable in polynomial time.

***Example*: The Travelling Salesperson Optimization Problem is NP-hard.**

Suppose we had a hypothetical polynomial-time algorithm for the Travelling Salesperson Decision Problem containing the graph *G* and positive integer *d* be given. Apply the hypothetical algorithm to the graph G to obtain the optimal solution mindist.Then our answer for the instance of the decision problem would be *'yes'* if mindist and *'no'* otherwise.Clearly, the hypothetical polynomial-time algorithm for the optimization problem, along with this extra step, gives the answer to the decision problem in polynomial time.

Designing Algorithms

There are many ways to design algorithms. Insertion sort uses an ***incremental*** approach: having sorted the subarray *A*[1 . . *j* - 1], we insert the single element *A*[*j*] into its proper place, yielding the sorted subarray *A*[1 . . *j*].

In this section, we examine an alternative design approach, known as "divide-and-conquer." We shall use divide-and-conquer to design a sorting algorithm whose worst-case running time is much less than that of insertion sort. One advantage of divide-and-conquer algorithms is that their running times are often easily determined .

1.3.1 The divide-and-conquer Approach

Many useful algorithms are ***recursive*** in structure: to solve a given problem, they call themselves recursively one or more times to deal with closely related subproblems. These algorithms typically follow a ***divide-and-conquer*** approach: they break the problem into several subproblems that are similar to the original problem but smaller in size, solve the subproblems recursively, and then combine these solutions to create a solution to the original problem.

The divide-and-conquer paradigm involves three steps at each level of the recursion:

Divide the problem into a number of subproblems.

Conquer the subproblems by solving them recursively. If the subproblem sizes are small enough, however, just solve the subproblems in a straightforward manner.

Combine the solutions to the subproblems into the solution for the original problem.

The ***merge sort*** algorithm closely follows the divide-and-conquer paradigm. Intuitively, it operates as follows.

Divide: Divide the n-element sequence to be sorted into two subsequences of $n/2$ elements each.

Conquer: Sort the two subsequences recursively using merge sort.

Combine: Merge the two sorted subsequences to produce the sorted answer.

We note that the recursion "bottoms out" when the sequence to be sorted has length 1, in which case there is no work to be done, since every sequence of length 1 is already in sorted order.

The key operation of the merge sort algorithm is the merging of two sorted sequences in the "combine" step. To perform the merging, we use an auxiliary procedure `MERGE`(A,p,q,r), where A is an array and p, q, and r are indices numbering elements of the array such that $p \leq q < r$. The procedure assumes that the subarrays $A[p..q]$ and $A[q + 1..r]$ are in sorted order. It ***merges*** them to form a single sorted subarray that replaces the current subarray $A[p..r]$.

Although we leave the pseudocode as an exercise (see Exercise 1.3-2), it is easy to imagine a `MERGE` procedure that takes time $\Theta(n)$, where $n = r - p + 1$ is the number of elements being merged. Returning to our card-playing motif, suppose we have two piles of cards face up on a table. Each pile is sorted, with the smallest cards on top. We wish to merge the two piles into a single sorted output pile, which is to be face down on the table. Our basic step consists of choosing the smaller of the two cards on top of the face-up piles, removing it from its pile (which exposes a new top card), and placing this card face down onto the output pile. We repeat this step until one input pile is empty, at which time we just take the remaining input pile and place it face down onto the output pile. Computationally, each basic step takes constant time, since we are checking just two top cards. Since we perform at most n basic steps, merging takes $\Theta(n)$ time.

We can now use the `MERGE` procedure as a subroutine in the merge sort algorithm. The procedure `MERGE-SORT`(A,p,r) sorts the elements in the subarray $A[p..r]$. If $p \geq r$, the subarray has at most one element and is therefore already sorted. Otherwise, the divide step simply computes an index q that partitions $A[p..r]$ into two subarrays: $A[p..q]$, containing $n/2]$ elements, and $A[q + 1..r]$, containing $[n/2]$ elements.

The expression $[x]$ *denotes the least integer greater than or equal to* x, *and* $[x]$ denotes the greatest integer less than or equal to x.

```
MERGE-SORT (A,p,r)
    if p < r
    then q ← [(p + r)/2]
    MERGE-SORT (A,p,q)
    MERGE-SORT (A, q + 1, r)
    MERGE (A,p,q,r)
```

To sort the entire sequence $A = \{A[1], A[2], \ldots, A[n]\}$, we call MERGE-SORT($A$, 1, *length*[$A$]), where once again *length*[A] = n. If we look at the operation of the procedure bottom-up when n is a power of two, the algorithm consists of merging pairs of 1-item sequences to form sorted sequences of length 2, merging pairs of sequences of length 2 to form sorted sequences of length 4, and so on, until two sequences of length $n/2$ are merged to form the final sorted sequence of length n. Figure 1.3 illustrates this process.

1.3.2 Analyzing Divide-and-conquer Algorithms

When an algorithm contains a recursive call to itself, its running time can often be described by a ***recurrence equation*** or ***recurrence***, which describes the overall running time on a problem of size n in terms of the running time on smaller inputs. We can then use mathematical tools to solve the recurrence and provide bounds on the performance of the algorithm.

A recurrence for the running time of a divide-and-conquer algorithm is based on the three steps of the basic paradigm. As before, we let $T(n)$ be the running time on a problem of size n. If the problem size is small enough, say $n \le c$ for some constant c, the straightforward solution takes constant time, which we write as $\Theta(1)$. Suppose we divide the problem into a subproblems, each of which is $1/b$ the size of the original. If we take $D(n)$ time to divide the problem into subproblems and $C(n)$ time to combine the solutions to the subproblems into the solution to the original problem, we get the recurrence

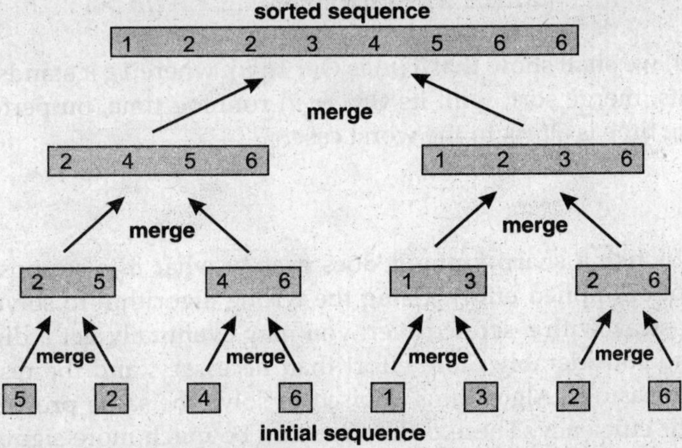

Figure 1.3 The operation of merge sort on the array A = ⟨5, 2, 4, 6, 1, 3, 2, 6⟩. The lengths of the sorted sequences being merged increase as the algorithm progresses from bottom to top.

$$G(n) = \begin{cases} \Theta(1) & \text{if } n \le c, \\ aT(n/b) + D(n) + C(n) & \text{otherwiese.} \end{cases}$$

In Chapter 4, we shall see how to solve common recurrences of this form.

Analysis of Merge Sort

Although the pseudocode for MERGE-SORT works correctly when the number of elements is not even, our recurrence-based analysis is simplified if we assume that the original problem size is a power of two. Each divide step then yields two subsequences of size exactly $n/2$. In Chapter 4, we shall see that this assumption does not affect the order of growth of the solution to the recurrence.

We reason as follows to set up the recurrence for $T(n)$, the worst-case running time of merge sort on n numbers. Merge sort on just one element takes constant time. When we have $n > 1$ elements, we break down the running time as follows.

Divide: The divide step just computes the middle of the subarray, which takes constant time. Thus, $D(n) = \Theta(1)$.

Conquer: We recursively solve two subproblems, each of size $n/2$, which contributes $2T(n/2)$ to the running time.

Combine: We have already noted that the MERGE procedure on an n-element subarray takes time $\Theta(n)$, so $C(n) = \Theta(n)$.

When we add the functions $D(n)$ and $C(n)$ for the merge sort analysis, we are adding a function that is $\Theta(n)$ and a function that is $\Theta(1)$. This sum is a linear function of n, that is, $\Theta(n)$. Adding it to the $2T(n/2)$ term from the "conquer" step gives the recurrence for the worst-case running time $T(n)$ of merge sort:

$$T(n) = \begin{cases} \Theta(1) & \text{if } n = 1, \\ 2T(n/2) + \Theta(n) & \text{if } n > 1. \end{cases}$$

In Chapter 4, we shall show that $T(n)$ is $\Theta(n \text{ 1g } n)$, where 1g n stands for $\log_2 n$. For large enough inputs, merge sort, with its $\Theta(n \lg n)$ running time, outperforms insertion sort, whose running time is $\Theta(n^2)$, in the worst case.

SUMMARY

A good algorithm is like a sharp knife--it does exactly what it is supposed to do with a minimum amount of applied effort. Using the wrong algorithm to solve a problem is like trying to cut a steak with a screwdriver: you may eventually get a digestible result, but you will expend considerably more effort than necessary, and the result is unlikely to be aesthetically pleasing. Algorithms devised to solve the same problem often differ dramatically in their efficiency. These differences can be much more significant than the difference between a personal computer and a supercomputer. As an example, let us pit a supercomputer running insertion sort against a small personal computer running merge sort. They each must sort an array of one million numbers. Suppose the supercomputer executes 100 million instructions per second, while the personal computer executes only one million instructions per second. To make the difference even more dramatic, suppose that the world's craftiest programmer codes insertion sort in machine language for the supercomputer, and the resulting code requires $2n^2$ supercomputer instructions to sort n numbers. Merge sort, on the other hand, is programmed for the personal computer by an average programmer using a high-level language with an inefficient compiler, with the resulting code taking $50n \lg n$ personal computer instructions. To sort a million numbers, the supercomputer takes

$$\frac{2\times(10^6)^2 \text{ instructions}}{10^8 \text{ instructions/second}} = 20{,}000 \text{ seconds} \approx 5.56 \text{ hours},$$

while the personal computer takes

$$\frac{50\times10^6 \lg 10^6 \text{ instructions}}{10^6 \text{ instructions/second}} \approx 1{,}000 \text{ seconds} \approx 16.67 \text{ minutes}.$$

By using an algorithm whose running time has a lower order of growth, even with a poor compiler, the personal computer runs 20 times faster than the supercomputer! This example shows that algorithms, like computer hardware, are a ***technology***. Total system performance depends on choosing efficient algorithms as much as on choosing fast hardware. Just as rapid advances are being made in other computer technologies, they are being made in algorithms as well.

REVIEW QUESTIONS

1. What is an algorithm? Elaborate the basic characteristics of algorithms.
2. What is the complexity of an algorithm? Explain how it can be calculated.
3. Explain algorithmic analysis and its classification
4. Explain algorithm classification with the help of examples.
5. Explain types of complexities of algorithms in details.
6. Elaborate all the techniques in analyzing algorithms.
7. Explain the theory of NP and P time complexity.

UNIT I

CHAPTER 3

GROWTH OF FUNCTIONS

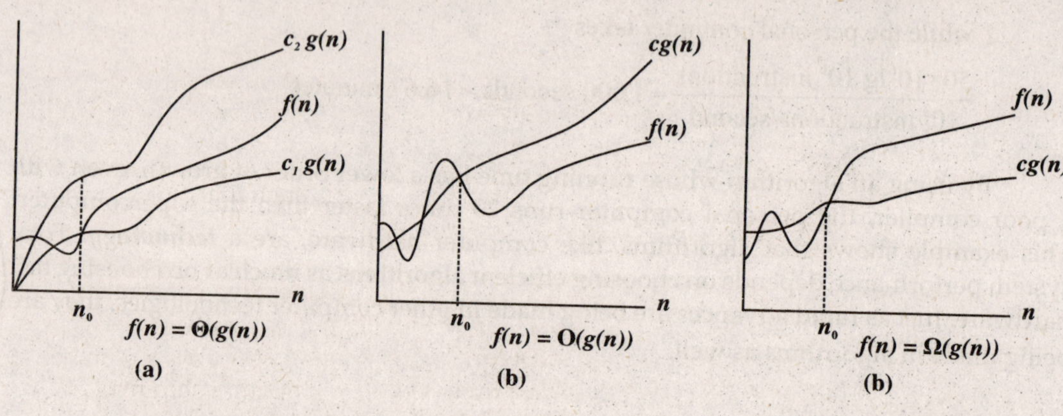

$f(n) = \Theta(g(n))$ (a) $f(n) = O(g(n))$ (b) $f(n) = \Omega(g(n))$ (b)

3.0 INTRODUCTION

The order of growth of the running time of an algorithm gives a simple characterization of the algorithm's efficiency and also allows us to compare the relative performance of alternative algorithms. Once the input size n becomes large enough, merge sort, with its $\Theta(n \lg n)$ worst-case running time, beats insertion sort, whose worst-case running time is $\Theta(n^2)$. Although we can sometimes determine the exact running time of an algorithm, as we did for insertion sort in earlier Chapters, the extra precision is not usually worth the effort of computing it. For large enough inputs, the multiplicative constants and lower-order terms of an exact running time are dominated by the effects of the input size itself.

When we look at input sizes large enough to make only the order of growth of the running time relevant, we are studying the ***asymptotic*** efficiency of algorithms. That is, we are concerned with how the running time of an algorithm increases with the size of the input *in the limit*, as the size of the input increases without bound. Usually, an algorithm that is asymptotically more efficient will be the best choice for all but very small inputs.

This chapter gives several standard methods for simplifying the asymptotic analysis of algorithms. The next section begins by defining several types of "asymptotic notation," of which we have already seen an example in Θ-notation. Several notational conventions used throughout this book are then presented, and finally we review the behavior of functions that commonly arise in the analysis of algorithms.

3.1 ASYMPTOTIC NOTATION

The notations we use to describe the asymptotic running time of an algorithm are defined in terms of functions whose domains are the set of natural numbers N = {0, 1, 2, . . .}. Such notations are convenient for describing the worst-case running-time function $T(n)$, which is usually defined only on integer input sizes. It is sometimes convenient, however, to *abuse* asymptotic notation in a variety of ways. For example, the notation is easily extended to the domain of real numbers or, alternatively, restricted to a subset of the natural numbers. It is important, however, to understand the precise meaning of the notation so that when it is abused, it is not *misused*. This section defines the basic asymptotic notations and also introduces some common abuses.

Θ-notation

In Chapter 1, we found that the worst-case running time of insertion sort is $T(n) = \Theta(n^2)$. Let us define what this notation means. For a given function $g(n)$, we denote by $\Theta(g(n))$ the *set of functions*

$\Theta(g(n))$ = {$\hat{a}(n)$: there exist positive constants c_1, c_2, and n_0 such that

$0 \le c_1 g(n) \le \hat{a}(n) \le c_2 g(n)$ for all $n \ge n_0$}.

A function $\hat{a}(n)$ belongs to the set $\Theta(g(n))$ if there exist positive constants c_1 and c_2 such that it can be "sandwiched" between $c_1 g(n)$ and $+c_2 g(n)$, for sufficiently large n. Although $\Theta(g(n))$ is a set, we write "$\hat{a}(n) = \Theta(g(n))$" to indicate that $\hat{a}(n)$ is a member of $\Theta(g(n))$, or "$\hat{a}(n) \in \Theta(g(n))$." This abuse of equality to denote set membership may at first appear confusing, but we shall see later in this section that it has advantages.

Figure 3.1 (a) gives an intuitive picture of functions $\hat{a}(n)$ and $g(n)$, where $\hat{a}(n) = \Theta(g(n))$. For all values of n to the right of n_0, the value of $\hat{a}(n)$ lies at or above $c_1 g(n)$ and at or below $c_2 g(n)$. In other words, for all $n \ge n_0$, the function $\hat{a}(n)$ is equal to $g(n)$ to within a constant factor. We say that $g(n)$ is an ***asymptotically tight bound*** for $\hat{a}(n)$.

The definition of $\Theta(g(n))$ requires that every member of $\Theta(g(n))$ be ***asymptotically nonnegative,*** that is, that $\hat{a}(n)$ be nonnegative whenever n is sufficiently large. Consequently, the function $g(n)$ itself must be asymptotically nonnegative, or else the set $\Theta(g(n))$ is empty. We shall therefore assume that every function used within Θ-notation is asymptotically non-negative. This assumption holds for the other asymptotic notations defined in this chapter as well.

In Chapter 1, we introduced an informal notion of Θ-notation that amounted to throwing away lower-order terms and ignoring the leading coefficient of the highest-order term. Let us briefly justify this intuition by using the formal definition to show that $1/2n^2 - 3n = \Theta(n^2)$. To do so, we must determine positive constants c_1, c_2, and n_0 such that

$$c_1 n^2 \le \frac{1}{2}n^2 - 3n \le c_2 n^2$$

for all $n \ge n_0$. Dividing by n^2 yields

$$c_1 \le \frac{1}{2} - \frac{2}{n} \le c_2$$

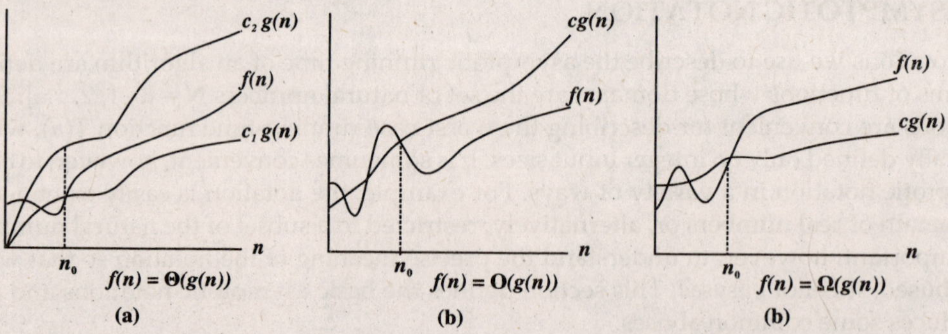

Figure 3.1 Graphic examples of the Θ, O, and Ω-notations. In each part, the value of n_0 shown is the minimum possible value; any greater value would also work. (a) Θ-notation bounds a function to within constant factors. We write $f(n) = \Theta(g(n))$ if there exist positive constants n_0, c_1, and c_2 such that to the right of n_0, the value of â(n) always lies between $c_1g(n)$ and $c_2g(n)$ inclusive. (b) O-notation gives an upper bound for a function to within a constant factor. We write â(n) = $O(g(n))$ if there are positive constants n_0 and c such that to the right of n_0, the value of â(n) always lies on or below $cg(n)$. (c) Ω-notation gives a lower bound for a function to within a constant factor. We write â(n) = $\Omega(g(n))$ if there are positive constants n_0 and c such that to the right of n_0, the value of â(n) always lies on or above $cg(n)$.

The right-hand inequality can be made to hold for any value of $n \geq 1$ by choosing $c_2 \geq 1/2$. Likewise, the left-hand inequality can be made to hold for any value of $n \geq 7$ by choosing $c_1 \leq 1/14$. Thus, by choosing $c_1 = 1/14$, $c_2 = 1/2$, and $n_0 = 7$, we can verify that $\frac{1}{2}n^2 - 3n = \Theta(n^2)$. Certainly, other choices for the constants exist, but the important thing is that some choice exists. Note that these constants depend on the function $\frac{1}{2}n^2 - 3n$; a different function belonging to $\Theta(n^2)$ would usually require different constants.

We can also use the formal definition to verify that $6n^3 \neq \Theta(n^2)$. Suppose for the purpose of contradiction that c_2 and n_0 exist such that $6n^3 \leq c_2n^2$ for all $n \geq n_0$. But then $n \leq c_2/6$, which cannot possibly hold for arbitrarily large n, since c_2 is constant.

Intuitively, the lower-order terms of an asymptotically positive function can be ignored in determining asymptotically tight bounds because they are insignificant for large n. A tiny fraction of the highest-order term is enough to dominate the lower-order terms. Thus, setting c_1 to a value that is slightly smaller than the coefficient of the highest-order term and setting c_2 to a value that is slightly larger permits the inequalities in the definition of Θ-notation to be satisfied. The coefficient of the highest-order term can likewise be ignored, since it only changes c_1 and c_2 by a constant factor equal to the coefficient.

As an example, consider any quadratic function â(n) = $an^2 + bn + c$, where a, b, and c are constants and $a > 0$. Throwing away the lower-order terms and ignoring the constant yields â(n) = $\Theta(n^2)$. Formally, to show the same thing, we take the constants $c_1 = a/4$, $c_2 = 7a/4$, and $n_0 = 2 \cdot \max\left((|b|/a), \sqrt{(|c|/a)}\right)$. The reader may verify that $0 \leq c_1n^2 \leq an^2 + bn + c \leq c_2n^2$ for all $n \geq n_0$. In general, for any polynomial $p(n) = \sum_{i=0}^{d} a_j n^i$ where the a_i are constants and $a_d > 0$, we have $p(n) = \Theta(n^d)$ (see Problem 2-1).

Since any constant is a degree-0 polynomial, we can express any constant function as $\Theta(n^0)$, or $\Theta(1)$. This latter notation is a minor abuse, however, because it is not clear what variable is tending to infinity. We shall often use the notation $\Theta(1)$ to mean either a constant or a constant function with respect to some variable.

O-notation

The Θ-notation asymptotically bounds a function from above and below. When we have only an ***asymptotic upper bound***, we use O-notation. For a given function $g(n)$, we denote by $O(g(n))$ the set of functions

$O(g(n)) = \{â(n)$: there exist positive constants c and n_0 such that

$0 \leq â(n) \leq cg(n)$ for all $n \geq n_0\}$.

We use O-notation to give an upper bound on a function, to within a constant factor. Figure 2.1 (b) shows the intuition behind O-notation. For all values n to the right of n_0, the value of the function $â(n)$ is on or below $g(n)$.

To indicate that a function $â(n)$ is a member of $O(g(n))$, we write $â(n) = O(g(n))$. Note that $â(n) = \Theta(g(n))$ implies $â(n) = O(g(n))$, since Θ-notation is a stronger notion than O-notation. Written set-theoretically, we have $\Theta(g(n)) \subseteq O(g(n))$. Thus, our proof that any quadratic function $an^2 + bn + c$, where $a > 0$, is in $\Theta(n^2)$ also shows that any quadratic function is in $O(n^2)$. What may be more surprising is that any *linear* function $an + b$ is in $O(n^2)$, which is easily verified by taking $c = a + |b|$ *and* $n_0 = 1$.

Some readers who have seen O-notation before may find it strange that we should write, for example, $n = O(n^2)$. In the literature, O-notation is sometimes used informally to describe asymptotically tight bounds, that is, what we have defined using Θ-notation. In this book, however, when we write $â(n) = O(g(n))$, we are merely claiming that some constant multiple of $g(n)$ is an asymptotic upper bound on $â(n)$, with no claim about how tight an upper bound it is. Distinguishing asymptotic upper bounds from asymptotically tight bounds has now become standard in the algorithms literature.

Using O-notation, we can often describe the running time of an algorithm merely by inspecting the algorithm's overall structure. For example, the doubly nested loop structure of the insertion sort algorithm from Chapter 1 immediately yields an $O(n^2)$ upper bound on the worst-case running time: the cost of the inner loop is bounded from above by $O(1)$ (constant), the indices i and j are both at most n, and the inner loop is executed at most once for each of the n^2 pairs of values for i and j.

Since O-notation describes an upper bound, when we use it to bound the worst-case running time of an algorithm, by implication we also bound the running time of the algorithm on arbitrary inputs as well. Thus, the $O(n^2)$ bound on worst-case running time of insertion sort also applies to its running time on every input. The $\Theta(n^2)$ *bound on the worst-case running time of insertion sort, however, does not imply a* $\Theta(n^2)$ bound on the running time of insertion sort on *every* input. For example, we saw in Chapter 1 that when the input is already sorted, insertion sort runs in $\Theta(n)$ time.

Technically, it is an abuse to say that the running time of insertion sort is $O(n^2)$, since for a given n, the actual running time depends on the particular input of size n. That is, the running time is not really a function of n. What we mean when we say "the running time is $O(n^2)$" is that the worst-case running time (which is a function of n) is $O(n^2)$, or equivalently, no matter what particular input of size n is chosen for each value of n, the running time on that set of inputs is $O(n^2)$.

Ω-notation

Just as O-notation provides an asymptotic *upper* bound on a function, Ω-notation provides an ***asymptotic lower bound.*** For a given function $g(n)$, we denote by $\Omega(g(n))$ the set of functions

$$\Omega(g(n)) = \{f(n): \text{there exist positive constants } c \text{ and } n_0 \text{ such that } 0 \le cg(n) \le f(n) \text{ for all } n \ge n_0\}.$$

The intuition behind Ω-notation is shown in Figure 2.1(c). For all values n to the right of n_0, the value of $f(n)$ is on or above $g(n)$.

From the definitions of the asymptotic notations we have seen thus far, it is easy to prove the following important theorem.

Theorem 3.1

For any two functions $f(n)$ and $g(n)$, $f(n) = \Theta(g(n))$ *if and only if* $f(n) = O(g(n))$ *and* $f(n) = \Omega(g(n))$.

As an example of the application of this theorem, our proof that $an^2 + bn + c = \Theta(n^2)$ for any constants a, b, and c, where $a > 0$, immediately implies that $an^2 + bn + c = \Omega(n^2)$ and $an^2 + bn + c = O(n^2)$. In practice, rather than using Theorem 3.1 to obtain asymptotic upper and lower bounds from asymptotically tight bounds, as we did for this example, we usually use it to prove asymptotically tight bounds from asymptotic upper and lower bounds.

Since Ω-notation describes a lower bound, when we use it to bound the best-case running time of an algorithm, by implication we also bound the running time of the algorithm on arbitrary inputs as well. For example, the best-case running time of insertion sort is $\Omega(n)$, which implies that the running time of insertion sort is $\Omega(n)$.

The running time of insertion sort therefore falls between $\Omega(n)$ and $O(n^2)$, since it falls anywhere between a linear function of n and a quadratic function of n. Moreover, these bounds are asymptotically as tight as possible: for instance, the running time of insertion sort is not $\Omega(n^2)$, since insertion sort runs in $\Omega(n)$ time when the input is already sorted. It is not contradictory, however, to say that the *worst-case* running time of insertion sort is $\Omega(n^2)$, since there exists an input that causes the algorithm to take $\Omega(n^2)$ time. When we say that the *running time* (no modifier) of an algorithm is $\Omega(g(n))$, we mean that *no matter what particular input of size n is chosen for each value of n*, the running time on that set of inputs is at least a constant times $g(n)$, for sufficiently large n.

USE OF ASYMPTOTIC NOTATION IN EQUATIONS

We have already seen how asymptotic notation can be used within mathematical formulas. For example, in introducing *O*-notation, we wrote "$n = O(n^2)$." We might also write $2n^2 + 3n + 1 = 2n^2 + \Theta(n)$. How you will interpret such formulas?

When the asymptotic notation stands alone on the right-hand side of an equation, as in $n = O(n^2)$, we have already defined the equal sign to mean set membership: $n \in O(n^2)$. In general, however, when asymptotic notation appears in a formula, we interpret it as standing for some anonymous function that we do not care to name. For example, the formula $2n^2 + 3n + 1 = 2n^2 + \Theta(n)$ means that $2n^2 + 3n + 1 = 2n^2 + f(n)$, where *$f(n)$ is some function in the set* $\Theta(n)$. In this case, *$f(n) = 3n + 1$, which indeed is in* $\Theta(n)$.

Using asymptotic notation in this manner can help eliminate inessential detail and clutter in an equation. For example, in Chapter I we expressed the worst-case running time of merge sort as the recurrence

$$T(n) = 2T(n/2) + \Theta(n).$$

If we are interested only in the asymptotic behavior of $T(n)$, there is no point in specifying all the lower-order terms exactly; they are all understood to be included in the anonymous function denoted by the term $\Theta(n)$.

The number of anonymous functions in an expression is understood to be equal to the number of times the asymptotic notation appears. For example, in the expression

$$\sum_{i=1}^{n} O(i)$$

there is only a single anonymous function (a function of i). This expression is thus *not* the same as $O(1) + O(2) + ... + O(n)$, which doesn't really have a clean interpretation.

In some cases, asymptotic notation appears on the left-hand side of an equation, as in

$$2n^2 + \Theta(n) = \Theta(n^2).$$

We interpret such equations using the following rule: *No matter how the anonymous functions are chosen on the left of the equal sign, there is a way to choose the anonymous functions on the right of the equal sign to make the equation valid.* Thus, the meaning of our example is that for any function $f(n) \in \Theta(n)$, there is some function $g(n) \in \Theta(n^2)$ such that $2n^2 + f(n) = g(n)$ for all n. In other words, the right-hand side of an equation provides coarser level of detail than the left-hand side.

A number of such relationships can be chained together, as in

$$2n^2 + 3n + 1 = 2n^2 + \Theta(n)$$
$$= \Theta(n^2).$$

We can interpret each equation separately by the rule above. The first equation says that there is *some* function $f(n) \in \Theta(n)$ such that $2n^2 + 3n + 1 = 2n^2 + f(n)$ *for all n. The second equation says that for* any *function $g(n) \in \Theta(n)$ (such as the* $f(n)$ just mentioned), there is *some* function $h(n) \in \Theta(n^2)$ such that $2n^2 + g(n) = h(n)$ for all n. Note that this interpretation implies that $2n^2 + 3n + 1 = \Theta(n^2)$, which is what the chaining of equations intuitively gives us.

O-notation

The asymptotic upper bound provided by O-notation may or may not be asymptotically tight. The bound $2n^2 = O(n^2)$ is asymptotically tight, but the bound $2n = O(n^2)$ is not. We use o-notation to denote an upper bound that is not asymptotically tight. We formally define $o(g(n))$ ("little-oh of g of n") as the set

$o(g(n)) = \{f(n)$: for any positive constant $c > 0$, there exists a constant $n_0 > 0$ such that $0 \le f(n) < cg(n)$ for all $n \ge n_0\}$.

For example, $2n = o(n^2)$, but $2n^2 \ne o(n^2)$.

The definitions of O-notation and o-notation are similar. The main difference is that in $f(n) = O(g(n))$, *the bound* $0 \le f(n) \le cg(n)$ holds for *some* constant $c > 0$, but in $f(n) = o(g(n))$, *the bound* $0 \le f(n) < cg(n)$ holds for all constants $c > 0$. Intuitively, in the o-notation, the function $f(n)$ becomes insignificant relative to $g(n)$ as n approaches infinity; that is,

$$\lim_{n\to\infty} \frac{f(n)}{g(n)} = 0 \qquad (3.1)$$

Some authors use this limit as a definition of the o-notation; the definition in this book also restricts the anonymous functions to be asymptotically nonnegative.

Ω-notation

By analogy, Ω-notation is to Ω-notation as o-notation is to O-notation. We use Ω-notation to denote a lower bound that is not asymptotically tight. One way to define it is by

$f(n) \in \Omega(g(n))$ if and only if $g(n) \in o(f(n))$.

Formally, however, we define $\Omega(g(n))$ ("little-omega of g of n") as the set

$\Omega(g(n)) = \{f(n)$: for any positive constant $c > 0$, there exists a constant $n_0 > 0$ such that $0 \le cg(n) < f(n)$ for all $n \ge n_0\}$.

For example, $n^2/2 = \Omega(n)$, *but* $n^2/2 \ne \Omega(n^2)$. *The relation* $f(n) = \Omega(g(n))$ *implies that*

$$\lim_{n\to\infty} \frac{f(n)}{g(n)} = \infty$$

if the limit exists. That is, $f(n)$ becomes arbitrarily large relative to $g(n)$ as n approaches infinity.

Comparison of Functions

Many of the relational properties of real numbers apply to asymptotic comparisons as well. For the following, assume that $f(n)$ and $g(n)$ are asymptotically positive.

Transitivity:

$\hat{a}(n) = \Theta(g(n))$ and $g(n) = \Theta(h(n))$ imply $\hat{a}(n) = \Theta(h(n))$,

$\hat{a}(n) = O(g(n))$ and $g(n) = O(h(n))$ imply $\hat{a}(n) = O(h(n))$,

$\hat{a}(n) = \Omega(g(n))$ and $g(n) = \Omega(h(n))$ imply $\hat{a}(n) = \Omega(h(n))$,

$\hat{a}(n) = o(g(n))$ and $g(n) = o(h(n))$ imply $\hat{a}(n) = o(h(n))$,

$\hat{a}(n) = \Omega(g(n))$ and $g(n) = \Omega(h(n))$ imply $\hat{a}(n) = \Omega(h(n))$.

Reflexivity:

$\hat{a}(n) = \Theta(\hat{a}(n))$,

$\hat{a}(n) = O(\hat{a}(n))$,

$\hat{a}(n) = \Omega(\hat{a}(n))$,

Symmetry:

$\hat{a}(n) = \Theta(g(n))$ if and only if $g(n) = \Theta(\hat{a}(n))$.

Transpose symmetry:

$f(n) = O(g(n))$ if and only if $g(n) = \Omega(f(n))$,

$f(n) = o(g(n))$ if and only if $g(n) = \Omega(f(n))$.

Because these properties hold for asymptotic notations, one can draw an analogy between the asymptotic comparison of two functions f and g and the comparison of two real numbers a and b:

$f(n) = O(g(n)) \approx a \leq b$,

$f(n) = \Omega(g(n)) \approx a \geq b$,

$f(n) = \Theta(g(n)) \approx a = b$,

$f(n) = o(g(n)) \approx a < b$,

$f(n) = \Omega(g(n)) \approx a > b$.

One property of real numbers, however, does not carry over to asymptotic notation:

Trichotomy: For any two real numbers a and b, exactly one of the following must hold: $a < b$, $a = b$, or $a > b$.

Although any two real numbers can be compared, not all functions are asymptotically comparable. That is, for two functions $f(n)$ and $g(n)$, it may be the case that neither $f(n) = O(g(n))$ nor $f(n) = \Omega(g(n))$ holds. For example, the functions n and $n^{1+\sin n}$ cannot be compared using asymptotic notation, since the value of the exponent in $n^{1+\sin n}$ oscillates between 0 and 2, taking on all values in between.

3.2 STANDARD NOTATIONS AND COMMON FUNCTIONS

This section reviews some standard mathematical functions and notations and explores the relationships among them. It also illustrates the use of the asymptotic notations

Monotonicity

A function $f(n)$ is ***monotonically increasing*** if $m \leq n$ implies $f(m) \leq f(n)$. Similarly, it is ***monotonically decreasing*** if $m \leq n$ implies $f(m) \geq f(n)$. A function $f(n)$ is **strictly increasing** if $m < n$ implies $f(m) < f(n)$ and ***strictly decreasing*** if $m < n$ implies $f(m) > f(n)$.

Floors and Ceilings

For any real number x, we denote the greatest integer less than or equal to x by $[x]$ (read "the floor of x") and the least integer greater than or equal to x by $[x[$ (read "the ceiling of x"). For all real x,

$$x - 1 < [x] \leq x \leq [x] < x + 1.$$

For any integer n,

$$[n/2] + [n/2] = n,$$

and for any integer n and integers $a \neq 0$ and $b \neq 0$,

$$[[n/a]/b] = [n/ab] \tag{2.3}$$

and

$$[[n/a]/b] = [n/ab] \tag{2.4}$$

The floor and ceiling functions are monotonically increasing.

Polynomials

Given a positive integer d, a ***polynomial in n of degree*** d is a function $p(n)$ of the form

$$p(n) = \sum_{i=0}^{d} a_i n^i,$$

where the constants $a_0, a_1, \ldots, a_d$ are the ***coefficients*** of the polynomial and $a_d \neq 0$. A polynomial is ***asymptotically positive*** if and only if $a_d > 0$. For an asymptotically positive polynomial $p(n)$ of degree d, we have $p(n) = \Theta(n^d)$. For any real constant $a \geq 0$, the function n^a is monotonically increasing, and for any real constant $a \leq 0$, the function n^a is monotonically decreasing. We say that a function $f(n)$ is ***polynomially bounded*** if $f(n) = n^{0(1)}$, which is equivalent to saying that $f(n) = O(n^k)$ for some constant k.

Exponentials

For all real $a \neq 0$, m, and n, we have the following identities:

$$a^0 = 1,$$
$$a^1 = a,$$
$$a^{-1} = 1/a,$$
$$(a^m)^n = a^{mn},$$
$$(a^m)^n = (a^n)^m,$$
$$a^m a^n = a^{m+n}.$$

For all n and $a \geq 1$, the function a^n is monotonically increasing in n. When convenient, we shall assume $0^0 = 1$.

The rates of growth of polynomials and exponentials can be related by the following fact. For all real constants a and b such that $a > 1$,

$$\lim_{n \to \infty} \frac{n^b}{a^n} = 0, \tag{2.5}$$

from which we can conclude that

$$n^b = 0(a^n)$$

Thus, any positive exponential function grows faster than any polynomial.

Using e to denote 2.71828 . . ., the base of the natural logarithm function, we have for all real x,

$$e^x = 1 + x + \frac{x^2}{2!} + \frac{x^3}{3!} + \ldots = \sum_{i=0}^{\infty} \frac{x^i}{i!}, \tag{2.6}$$

where "!" denotes the factorial function defined later in this section. For all real x, we have the inequality

$$e^x \geq 1 + x, \tag{2.7}$$

where equality holds only when x = 0. When $|x| \leq 1$, we have the approximation

$$1 + x \leq e^x \leq 1 + x + x^2. \tag{2.8}$$

When $x \to 0$, the approximation of e^x by $1 + x$ is quite good:

$$e^x = 1 + x + \Theta(x^2).$$

(In this equation, the asymptotic notation is used to describe the limiting behavior as $x \to 0$ rather than as $x \to \infty$.) We have for all x,

$$\lim_{n \to \infty} \left(1 + \frac{x}{n}\right)^n = e^x$$

Logarithms

We shall use the following notations:

$\lg n = \log_2 n$ (binary logarithm),
$\ln n = \log_e n$ (natural logarithm),
$\lg^k n = (\lg n)^k$ (exponentiation),
$\lg \lg n = \lg(\lg n)$ (composition).

An important notational convention we shall adopt is that *logarithm functions will apply only to the next term in the formula,* so that $\lg n + k$ will mean $(\lg n) + k$ and not $\lg(n + k)$. For $n > 0$ and $b > 1$, the function $\log_b n$ is strictly increasing.

For all real $a > 0$, $b > 0$, $c > 0$, and n,

(2.9)

$$a = b^{\log_b}$$

$$\log_c(ab) = \log_c a + \log_c b,$$

$$\log_b a^n = n \log_b a,$$

$$\log_b(1/a) = -\log_b a,$$

$$\log_b a = \frac{1}{\log_a b},$$

$$a^{\log_b n} = n^{\log_b a} \tag{2.9}$$

Since changing the base of a logarithm from one constant to another only changes the value of the logarithm by a constant factor, we shall often use the notation "lg n" when we don't care about constant factors, such as in O-notation. Computer scientists find 2 to be the most natural base for logarithms because so many algorithms and data structures involve splitting a problem into two parts.

There is a simple series expansion for $\ln(1 + x)$ when $|x| < 1$:

$$\ln(1+x) = x - \frac{x^2}{2} + \frac{x^3}{3} + \frac{x^4}{4} + \frac{x^5}{5} - \cdots$$

We also have the following inequalities for $x > -1$:

$$\frac{x}{1+x} \le \ln(1+x) \le x \tag{2.10}$$

where equality holds only for $x = 0$.

We say that a function $f(n)$ is ***polylogarithmically bounded*** if $f(n) = \lg^{O(1)} n$. We can relate the growth of polynomials and polylogarithms by substituting lg n for n and 2^a for a in equation (2.5), yielding

$$\lim_{n\to\infty} \frac{\lg^b n}{2^{a \lg n}} = \lim_{n\to\infty} \frac{\lg^b n}{n^a} = 0$$

From this limit, we can conclude that

$$\lg^b n = o(n^a)$$

for any constant $a > 0$. Thus, any positive polynomial function grows faster than any polylogarithmic function.

Factorials

The notation $n!$ (read "n factorial") is defined for integers $n \ge 0$ as

$$n! = \begin{cases} 1 & \text{if } n = 0, \\ n \cdot (n-1)! & \text{if } n > 0 \end{cases}$$

Thus, $n! = 1.2.3...n$.

A weak upper bound on the factorial function is $n! \le n^n$, since each of the n terms in the factorial product is at most n. ***Stirling's approximation,***

$$n! = \sqrt{2\pi n}\left(\frac{n}{e}\right)^n\left(1+\Theta\left(\frac{1}{n}\right)\right) \qquad (2.11)$$

where e is the base of the natural logarithm, gives us a tighter upper bound, and a lower bound as well. Using Stirling's approximation, one can prove

$n! = o(n^n)$,

$n! = \Omega(2^n)$,

$\lg(n!) = \Theta(n \lg n)$.

The following bounds also hold for all n:

$$\sqrt{2\pi n}\left(\frac{n}{e}\right)^n \le n! \le \sqrt{2\pi n}\left(\frac{n}{e}\right)^{n+(1/12n)}$$

The Iterated Logarithm Function

We use the notation $\lg^* n$ (read "log star of n") to denote the iterated logarithm, which is defined as follows. Let the function $\lg^{(i)} n$ be defined recursively for nonnegative integers i as

$$\lg^{(i)} n = \begin{cases} n & \text{if } i = 0 \\ \lg(\lg^{(i-1)} n & \text{if } i > 0 \text{ and } \lg^{(i-1)} n > 0, \\ \text{undefined} & \text{if } i > 0 \text{ and } \lg^{(i-1)} n \le 0 \text{ or } \lg^{(i-1)} \text{n is undefined} \end{cases}$$

Be sure to distinguish $\lg^{(i)} n$ (the logarithm function applied i times in succession, starting with argument n) from $\lg^i n$ (the logarithm of n raised to the ith power). The iterated logarithm function is defined as

$$\lg^* n = \min \{i \ge 0; \lg^{(i)} n \le 1\}$$

The iterated logarithm is a *very* slowly growing function:

$\lg^* 2 = 1$,

$\lg^* 4 = 2$,

$\lg^* 16 = 3$,

$\lg^* 65536 = 4$,

$\lg^*(2^{65536}) = 5$.

Since the number of atoms in the observable universe is estimated to be about 10^{80}, which is much less than 2^{65536}, we rarely encounter a value of n such that $\lg^* n > 5$.

Fibonacci Numbers

The ***Fibonacci numbers*** are defined by the following recurrence:

$$F_0 = 0,$$
$$F_1 = 1,$$
$$F_i = F_{i-1} + F_{i-2} \text{ for } i \geq 2. \tag{2.13}$$

Thus, each Fibonacci number is the sum of the two previous ones, yielding the sequence

$$0, 1, 1, 2, 3, 5, 8, 13, 21, 34, 55, \ldots .$$

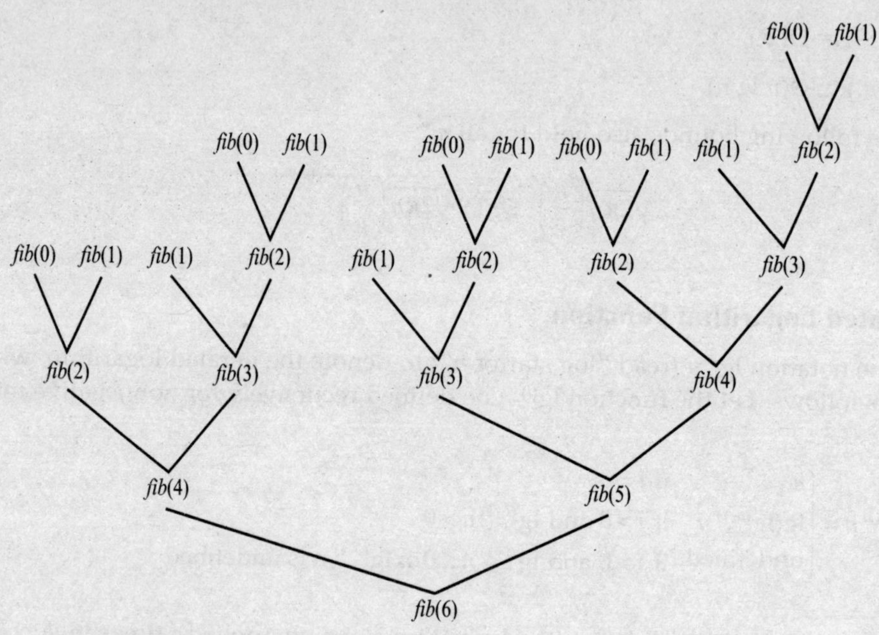

Fibonacci numbers are related to the ***golden ratio*** Φ and to its conjugate $\hat{\phi}$, which are given by the following formulas:

$$\phi = \frac{1+\sqrt{5}}{2}$$
$$\phi = 1.61803\ldots,$$
$$\hat{\phi} = \frac{1-\sqrt{5}}{2}$$
$$= -.61803\ldots \tag{2.14}$$

Specifically, we have

$$F_1 = \frac{\phi^i - \hat{\phi}^i}{\sqrt{5}} \tag{2.15}$$

which can be proved by induction (Exercise 2.2-7). Since $|\hat{\phi}| < 1$, we have $|\hat{\phi}^i| / \sqrt{5} < 1/\sqrt{5}1/2$, so that the ith Fibonacci number F_i is equal to $\phi^i / \sqrt{5}$ rounded to the nearest integer. Thus, Fibonacci numbers grow exponentially.

REVIEW QUESTIONS

1. If f(n) and g(n) be asymptotically nonnegative functions. Using the basic definition of Θ-notation, prove that $\max(f(n), g(n)) = \Theta(f(n) + g(n))$.

2. Justify the statement, "The running time of algorithm *A* is at least $O(n^2)$," is content-free.

3. Show that the running time of an algorithm is $\Theta(g(n))$ if and only if its worst-case running time is $O(g(n))$ and its best-case running time is $\Omega(g(n))$.

4. Give proper definitions for $\Omega(g(n, m))$ and $\Theta(g(n, m))$.

5. Why and Which is asymptotically larger: $\lg(\lg^* n)$ or $\lg^*(\lg n)$?

6. Prove that for $i \geq 0$, the $(i + 2)$nd Fibonacci number satisfies F_{i+2} $\Theta\Phi^i$.

7. Relative asymptotic growths

   Indicate, for each pair of expressions (*A*, *B*) in the table below, whether *A* is *O*, *o*, Ω, Ω, or Θ of *B*. Assume that $k \geq 1$, $\in > 0$, and $c > 1$ are constants. Your answer should be in the form of the table with "yes" or "no" written in each box.

	A	B	O	o	Ω	ω	Θ
a.	$\lg^k n$	n^e					
b.	n^k	c^n					
c.	$\sqrt{5}$	$n^{\sin n}$					
d.	2^n	$2^{n/2}$					
e	$n^{\lg m}$	$m^{\lg n}$					
f.	$\lg(n!)$	$\lg(n^n)$					

Q8. Let $f(n)$ and $g(n)$ be asymptotically positive functions. Prove or disprove each of the following conjectures.

a. $f(n) = O(g(n))$ implies $g(n) = O(f(n))$.

b. $f(n) + g(n) = \Theta(\min(\hat{a}(n), g(n)))$.

c. $f(n) = O(g(n))$ implies $\lg(f(n)) = O(\lg(g(n)))$, where $\lg(g(n)) > 0$ and $f(n) \geq 1$ for all sufficiently large *n*.

d. $f(n) = O(g(n))$ implies $2^{f(n)} = O(2^{g(n)})$.

e. $f(n) = O((f(n))^2)$.

f. $f(n) = O(g(n))$ implies $g(n) = \Omega(f(n))$.

g. $f(n) = \Theta(f(n/2))$.

h. $f(n) + o(f(n)) = \Theta(f(n))$.

UNIT 1

CHAPTER 4

SORTING ALGORITHMS

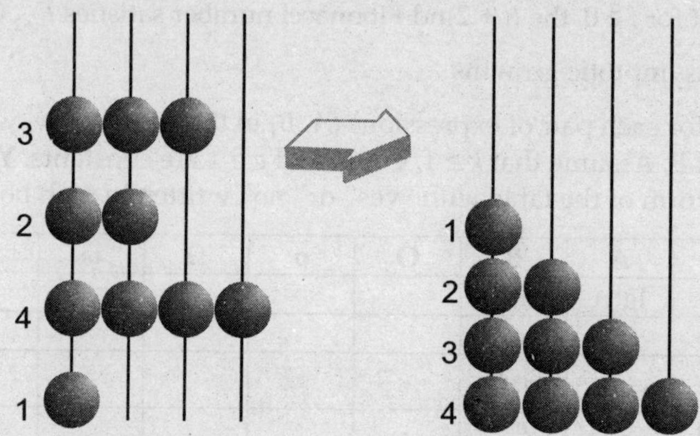

4.0 INTRODUCTION

Almost every long computer program has segments that sort and search data. On what basis is the computational complexity of sorting algorithms judged? There are two possibilities. The first possibility uses the number of object swaps while the second possibility is the total number of object comparisons. The number of object swaps is not a viable basis for determining complexity. When sorting internally, an array with objects already in order will never require a single swap. On the other hand there are worse case scenarios for many sorting algorithms where a swap occurs after every comparison.

External sorts do not 'swap' objects in the classic sense. These devices access their objects in a sequential manner. They operate as single linked queues that function in one of two modes, read only and write only. In the read only mode, objects can only be read from the front of the data stream. As an object is read, the pointer to the next object to be read is updated to the next object in the data stream. In the write only mode, an object is added to the rear of a second data stream. The added object becomes the new rear object. These objects cannot be individually addressed. For these reasons, externally based sorting algorithms decompose the file to be sorted into several scratch files and then merge these scratch files back into one longer file. These 'merged' files are 'more' sorted than the original scratch files. After several passes the original file is fully ordered or sorted. There is no swapping in the classical sense when sorting externally. It follows that the complexity of sorting algorithms must be based on the number of object comparisons.

Internally based sorts are characterized by the ability to compare and possibly swap any two objects in memory. There is no relationship between the number of object comparisons and the number of object swaps. An already sorted array need not swap at all. However, any key based sorting algorithm that sorts n objects must perform at least (n-1) compares. This follows because it takes at least (n-1) comparisons to determine whether or not an array containing n elements is in sorted order.

Here we start by reviewing two "brute force" sorting methods, Exchange Sort and Select Sort. Both of these algorithms have complexity O(n2). Both can be characterized by the fact that they compare adjacent array entries. Shell Sort, which starts out comparing non-adjacent elements is examined then and found to have complexity that is approximately O(n1.5). next section examines Quick Sort, Merge Sort, and Heap Sort, all of which are divide and conquer based algorithms. All three have complexity O(n*lg(n)). Next section examines Quick Sort in depth. Section four develops some theory and shows that no algorithm that sorts by comparing two objects can have computational complexity less than O(n*lg(n)). This chapter closes by illustrating a sorting algorithm that does not sort by key comparison. Finally a short discussion of external sorting closes the chapter. All of the methods studied apply to classes of objects where it is possible to assign objects and to determine whether or not one object precedes another object. Integers are easy to compare and determine which integer precedes another. If the objects to be sorted are address labels, then the label objects could be sorted by name or city or zip code because it is possible to define a method to determine which label precedes another based on those three criteria.

Sorting as a subject of study is also interesting in another respect. While there are many interesting sorting techniques presented, there are also several interesting theoretical results that limit the computational complexity of various general sorting techniques.

4. 1. O(N^2) SORTS: SELECTION SORT, EXCHANGE SORT

Selection Sort is the simplest sorting algorithm to describe. An array of length n is searched for its maximum object. After finding the location of the maximum object within the first n elements, Selection Sort swaps the object stored in the last location of the array with the array's maximum object. Selection sort then repeats the process on the first n-1 elements until the array is sorted. See Figure 1.

```
Void Select_Sort (Vertex<Class> T[1..n])
{
Integer max_index = 1;
For (integer I = n; I > 1; i--)
{
Max_index = 1;
For (integer j= 1; j?i; j++) (if (if (T[max_index] < T[j])( max_index = j;
}
}
If(max_index does not equal i){Swap {Swap (T[max_index],T[i]);
}
}
}
```

Figure 1 Selection Sort.

This basic sorting algorithm has computational complexity O(n2) as measured by the number of key comparisons. The number of swaps is O(n). It is assumed that the operator < is defined on the class encapsulated within the Vector class.

An examination of Figure 1 shows that the outer loop is executed n-1 times. (If n-1 objects are in their proper place in a sorted array, then the nth object must also be in its proper place.) The first time the outer loop executes, the inner loop does n-1 compares. The second time the outer loop executes there are n-2 compares, and so on. Thus using the arithmetic series formula we get that

$$\text{Number of compares} = (n-1)+(n-2)+(n-3)+\ldots 3+2+1 = n^*(n-1)/2$$

which implies that the number of compares in Selection Sort is $\Theta(n^2)$. Selection Sort swaps at most (n-1) times. Using swap criteria Selection Sort is efficient. No conceivable sorting algorithm can sort with fewer swaps. But Selection Sort is one of the most inefficient sorting algorithms when the criterion for computational efficiency is the number of object comparisons. For any input array of length n, Selection Sort always uses the same constant number of object comparisons.

SELECTION SORT

initial arrangement	8	6	1	4	9	2	5	3	0	7
after pass with r = 9	8	6	1	4	7	2	5	3	0	9
after pas with r = 8	0	6	1	4	7	2	5	3	8	9
after pass with r = 7	0	6	1	4	3	2	5	7	8	9
after pass with r = 6	0	5	1	4	3	2	6	7	8	9
after pass with r = 5	0	2	1	4	3	5	6	7	8	9
after pass with r = 4	0	2	1	3	4	5	6	7	8	9
after pass with r = 3	0	2	1	3	4	5	6	7	8	9
after pass with r = 2	0	2	2	3	4	5	6	7	8	9
after pass with r = 1	0	1	2	3	4	5	6	7	8	9

Selection Sort can not recognize when an array is already sorted. If it could, it could use this ability to terminate early. Exchange Sort can be modified to stop as soon as it recognizes that an array is sorted. The basic exchange sort algorithm looks somewhat like Selection Sort. See Figure 2. In Selection Sort the inner loop searches for the location of the maximum object.

In Exchange Sort the inner loop compares two adjacent array objects. If the two adjacent objects are out of order, then the two adjacent objects are immediately exchanged. The sort process then increments the array index, and repeats itself until the end of the loop is reached. Just like Selection Sort, at the end of the inner loop, the maximum object has been pushed to the last index of the array.

```
Void Exchange_Sort (Vector<class> T[m.n])
{integer length=n-m+1;
For (integer I = 0; I ? length-1; i++)
{
For (integer j=m+1;j?n-ij++)
{
If (T[j] < T[j-1]){ swap (T[j-1], T[j]);
}
}
}
}
```

Figure 2 Exchange Sort.

This sorting algorithm also has computational complexity Θ (n^2) as measured by the number of key comparisons. However, the number of swaps is O(n2). The analysis for determining the number of compares for Exchange Sort is the same as the analysis for determining the number of compares in Select Sort. Regular Exchange Sort has several disadvantages over selection sort. Both algorithms sort with the same Θ (n^2) complexity and both algorithms use the same number of compares for any array of length n. Selection Sort swaps at most n-1 array elements while Exchange Sort potentially swaps whenever a compare is made. If the array objects are stored in reverse order, Exchange Sort will swap n*(n-1)/2 times. This can be time consuming when the objects to be swapped occupy large amounts of memory.

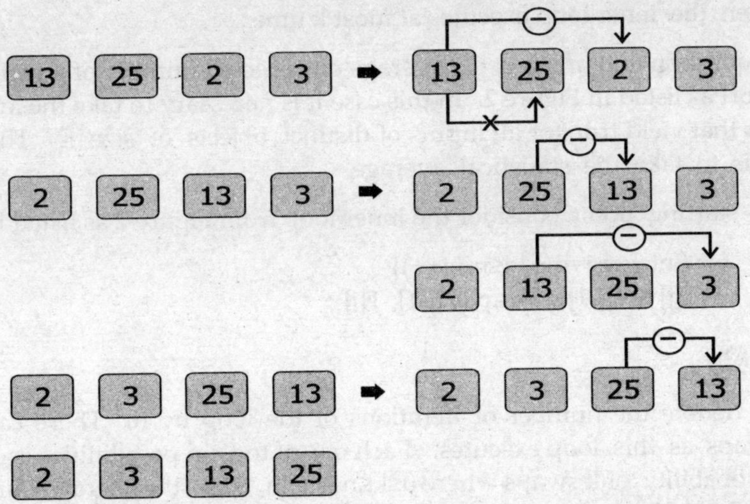

Exchange Sort can be improved by adding a simple boolean flag to signal when the array is finally sorted. An array is sorted when the inner loop iterates from start to finish without swapping any two adjacent objects. This boolean flag indicates whether or not the inner loop executed a swap. If the loop executes without a swap, then the algorithm terminates. Figure 3 lists the code for this improved Exchange Sort algorithm.

```
Void imnprovedExchangeSort (Vector<class> T[1..n])
{
Integer In_place = 0; Boolean Seap_occurred; repeat
{
Swap_occured = false;
for (integer j = 2; j ? n-Ln_place; j++)
{
If(array[j] < array[j-1]) { Swap (T[j-1], t[j]); Swap_occured = true;
}
}
Ln_place = In_place + 1;
} while (Swap_occurred equals true);
}
```

Figure 3 Improved Exchange Sort.

This sorting algorithm has computational complexity O(n2) as measured by the number of key comparisons. This version has a flag in the inner loop that signals when no swaps occurred and the array is sorted. However, the number of swaps is still O(n2).

Improved Exhange Sort has the same worst case as the version of Exchange Sort listed in figure 2. For this reason Improved Exchange Sort is O(n2). Are there cases where Improved Exchange Sort outperforms Selection Sort? Clearly nothing can outperform Improved Exchange Sort when the array of objects is sorted. improved Exchange Sort is almost linear, that is it also has complexity $\Omega(n)$, when all objects are initially 'close' to their final location. It can be shown that if every object is within k positions of their final location, then the inner loop executes at most k times.

One question that arises is the average or expected number of swap operations for Exchange Sort as listed in Figure 2. In this case it is necessary to take the average number of compares that yield true for all inputs of distinct objects of size n. The easiest way to do this is to take the statistical average.

As a starting point, consider the inner loop from Figure 2 as listed below.

```
for (integer j=m+1;j≤n-i;j++){
if (T[j] < T[j-1]){ Swap (T[j-1], T[j]);
}
}
```

First, denote the number of iterations of the loop by n. There can be between 0 and n swaps as this loop executes. Each one of these n possibilities is equally likely, that is the probability of k swaps where $0 \le k \le n$ is $1/n$. Thus the average number of swaps for this loop would be

$$\sum_{k=0}^{n} \text{(number of swaps)(probability of that number of swaps)}$$

$$= \sum_{k=0}^{n} (k)(1/n)$$

$$= (1/n)\sum_{k=1}^{n} k \;= (1/n)(n^*(n+1)/2$$

$$= (n+1)/2$$

Note that summation index changed from k=0 to k=1 because the term for k=0 has value zero. This analysis says that the average number of swaps generated by the inner loop is (n+1)/2 where n is the length of the inner loop. The outer look executes once for each value of n between 1 and the length of the outer loop.

$$\sum_{i=0}^{n-1}(i+1)/2=(1/2)\sum_{i=1}^{n}i=(1/2)(n*(n-1)/2)=n*(n-1)/4$$

which says that the average number of swaps is n*(n-1)/4 which is half the value of number of compares performed by Exchange Sort as listed in Figure 2.

In the exercises a sort method called Insert Sort will be analyzed. Given a vector T[1..n] to be sorted, Inert Sort assumes that the vector slice T[1..k] for k<n is sorted. At the (k+1)st stage the object T[k+1] is inserted by comparing and shifting from high to low until its final place is found. It is easy to show, using analysis similar to that used to analyze Exchange Sort, that worst case complexity of Insert Sort for both compares and assignments is n*(n+1)/2 but the average number of compares and sorts is half that value.

Is there something that theory can tell us about the design of efficient key-compare based sorting algorithms? The answer is yes. In the exchange sort algorithms above, two adjacent keys were compared. If the keys were out of order a swap occurred. This swap only corrected one out-of-order occurrence. The discussion that follows use the sequence [1,2,3, …,n] of integers. These n distinct integers can model any sequence of n distinct objects.

A permutation of [1,2,3, …,n] is a re-ordering of the first n integers. For example, [2,3,1,4] is one of twenty-four distinct permutations of [1,2,3,4]. Clearly the sequence of the first n distinct integers has n! distinct permutations. A general permutation is denoted by

[k1,k2,k3, …,kn] where ki denotes the integer in the ith place in the permutation.

An inversion in a permutation is a pair (ki,kj) where i<j but ki>kj. The permutation of [3,2,5,4,1] contains 6 inversions. These inversions are (3,2), (3,1), (2,1), (5,4), (5,1), and (4,1). Clearly a permutation is sorted if and only if it contains no inversions. Note that the maximum number of inversions occurs when the first number in the permutation is greater than all numbers that follow it, the second number is greater than all numbers that follow it and so on.

This implies that the permutation [n,n-1,n-2, …, 3, 2, 1] has the maximum number of inversions of any permutation of the first n integers. Since the first number n has n-1 inversions, the second number n-1 has n-2 inversions, and so on, then the total of the maximum number of inversions possible is (n-1) + (n-2) + … + 3 + 2 + 1 = n(n-1)/2

This implies that any sort algorithm based on comparison of keys must do, in the worst case, n(n-1)/2 comparisons if a comparison removes at most one inversion.

In fact the average number of inversions over all permutations is n(n-1)/4. To see this consider transpose of a permutation. If [k1,k2,k3, ...,kn] is any permutation of the first n integers, then its transpose is the same permutation in reverse order, that is [kn,kn-1,kn-2, ...,k1]

The transpose of the permutation of [2,4,1,5,3] is [3,5,1,4,2]. Observe that the arbitrary inversion (ki,kj) is only in the permutation or its transpose, but not both. This means that the total number of inversions in a permutation and its transpose is always a constant n(n-1)/2 inversions and the average number of inversions in any permutation and its transpose is a constant n(n-1)/4. Averaging all permutations and their transpose means that the average number of inversions in any permutation is again n(n-1)/4. In other words the complexity of any compare based sorting algorithm that removes at most one inversion per compare is $O(n^2)$. The implication of this fact is that any more efficient sorting strategy based on comparison of keys must be able to potentially remove more than one inversion per compare if its worst case is ever to be better than $O(n^2)$. The more efficient key based sorting algorithms examined in the remainder of the chapter are designed to remove more than one inversion, sometimes significantly more inversions, per compare.

4.2. SHELL SORT: AN 'IMPROVED' IMPROVED EXCHANGE SORT

Shell Sort gets its improved performance by noting that there is no requirement to always compare, and possibly swap, adjacent array objects. This makes Shell Sort a 'heuristic' Exchange Sort. Shell Sort first performs a bubble sort of objects that are a fixed distance apart. This effectively divides a list containing n objects into k sub lists each containing n/k objects. The first sub list is composed of the objects at locations 1,

1+k, 1+2*k, 1+3k ... while the second sub list is composed of the objects at locations 2, 2+k, 2+2*k, 2+3*k, ... and so on. After the k sub lists have been sorted, the whole procedure is repeated with k/2 lists composed of objects k/2 positions apart. This continues until there is just one list. In figure 3 a list containing 16 integers is first divided into 4 sub lists each containing 4 objects which are sorted at stage 1.

At stage 1 each object in each list is a distance k=4 from other objects in the same sub list. At stage 2 the 4 lists at the end of stage 1 are processed as two sub lists 2 indices apart. There are 8 objects in each of the two sub lists. At stage 2 adjacent objects in the same sub list at a distance k=2 apart. At the end of stage 2 these two lists are sorted and provide the input to stage 3. Stage 3 merges these last two lists. At this stage, the there is just one list.

Position

1	2	3	4	5	6	7	8	9	10	11	12	13	14	15	16
3	8	12	4	16	11	15	1	10	13	5	14	2	9	6	7

Beginning of first Stage 1 there are 4 sub lists

3	16	10	2
8	11	13	9
12	15	5	6
4	1	14	7

At the end of first Stage, the array to be sorted looks like

2 8 5 1 3 9 6 4 10 11 12 7 16 13 15 14

Beginning of second stage with 2 sub lists

2	5	3	6	10	12	16	15
8	1	9	4	11	7	13	14

At the end of second stage, the array to be sorted looks like

2 1 3 4 5 7 6 8 10 9 12 11 15 13 16 14

Last stage with 1 list

1 2 3 4 5 6 7 8 9 10 11 12 13 14 15 16

Figure: The mechanics of Shell Sort.

In Stage 1 the list of 16 is divided into 4 sub lists each containing 4 objects which are sorted. In stage 2 the list is divided into 2 sub lists which are then sorted. In the last stage the entire list is sorted. Note how the total list gets 'almost locally' sorted at the end of stage 2.

There is one interesting observation, not quite justified, that provides insight into the mechanics of Shell Sort. Shell Sort is an attempt to combine Improved Exchange Sort with a Merge Sort type algorithm. Each successive stage merges the results of two sorted lists from the previous stage into a combined sorted list. As noted above, if the objects in a sorted list are within a certain distance of there final location, then Improved Exchange Sort is almost linear. An examination of the locations of the objects at the end of each stage shows that objects tend to be 'closer' to their final location.

Figure 4 lists the pseudo code for Shell Sort. The outer loop divides the array into k sub lists, where two adjacent elements in each of the sub lists are a pre-set value gap apart. The two inner loops are essentially Improved Exchange Sort.

Shell Sort actually sorts a list because the last time the outer loop executes with the gap equals to one. At the terminal stage, this is exactly Improved Exchange Sort. Shell Sort uses the heuristic that it is less work to sort two short lists and then merge them together than to sort one long list.

```
void Shell_Sort(Vector<class? T[1..n])
{
integer gap = (T.highIndex() – T.lowIndex9) + 10)/2
boolean exchange_occured;
repeat
{
repeat
 {
exchange_occurred = false;
for (integer i=t.lowIndex();i?T.highIndex()-gap;i++){
if (T[I + gap} < T[i]){ Swap (T[i], t[I + gap]);
exchange_occured = true;
}
}
} while ( exchange_occurred equals true);
Gap = gap/2;
} while (gap>0);
}
```

Figure 4 Shell Sort.

This sorting algorithm has computational complexity of about O(n1.5) as measured by the number of key comparisons. This version can be tuned. Note that each sub list is checked until all sub lists are sorted. This will be done in the exercises. Another example is as:

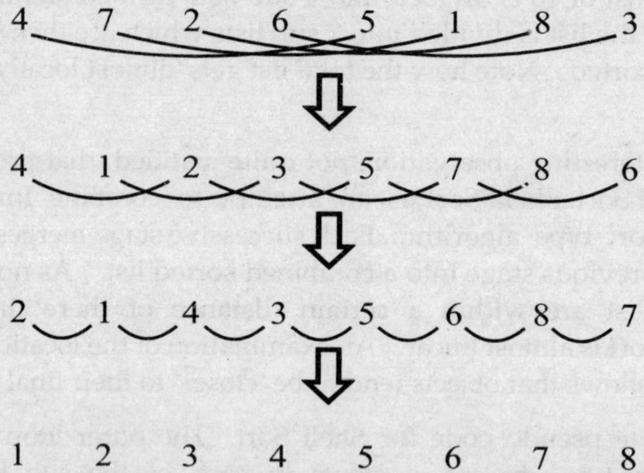

While it is not obvious, Shell Sort's computational complexity using the number of comparisons is $O(n^{1.5})$. This is a significant improvement over Select Sort and Improved Exchange Sort which both have complexity O(n2). Various strategies for choosing the values of gap have been studied. The strategy for dividing the lists into some power of two used in figure 4 is not optimal. Various strategies have been studied and these results are outlined in Knuth [xx]. The reader is referred to Knuth[xx] if they wish to review the derivation of the complexity bound. Other strategies for setting the gap are explored in the exercises. In summary, Shell Sort's object comparison strategy results in shorter inner loops and fewer comparisons in each inner loop.

4.3 QUICK SORT IN DEPTH

Quick is an example of a divide-and-conquer sorting algorithm. Under the assumption of the existence of a procedure 'partition' that reforms, in place, the array to be sorted into three parts. Not only does every object in the first part precedes the single object in the second part, and not only is the lone object in the second part less than or equal to every object in the third part, the partition procedure returns the array index location of the lone middle pivot object. Figure 5 lists a recursive version of Quick Sort under the assumption of the existence of the partition procedure.

```
void Quick_Sort (Vector<class> T[m..n])
 {
if ((m-n) > 0)
 {
integer part = Partition(t[m..n]);
if ((part-m)>0)
{
Quick_Sort (T[m..part-1]);
}
if ((n-part)>0){
Quick_Sort (T[part+1..n});
}
}
}
```

Figure 5: A recursive implementation of Quick Sort

It uses a simple partitioning strategy. Under most conditions this divide and conquer algorithm has computational complexity Θ(n*lg(n)).

Any divide-and-conquer algorithm, including Quick Sort, fails when it doesn't 'divide and conquer.' This occurs when the pivot object has position as either the first or last array object. This partition scheme fails to divide-and-conquer when the objects in the array start out in either an ascending or a descending order. To get the full benefit of Quick Sort's divide and conquer strategy, Quick Sort must place its pivot somewhere near the middle of the array being sorted. This does not occur when the array is either nearly sorted or in nearly reverse order.

```
25 11 43  67 91 55 15 82
          43
25 11 15  ▌  97 91 55 82
   15            67
11 ▌ 25      55 ▌ 91 82
11   25      55    91
                82 ▌
25 15 25 43  55 67 82 91
```

The odds of making a good or bad pivot object choice remain the same no matter what object is picked. The middle object is the best pivot object choice if the array is either ascending or descending, and in the random case it is as good a choice as any other, so this choice of the pivot object ought to be a better one.

```
integer partition (Vector<class> T[m..n})
{
Swap(T[m],T[m+n)/2])
integer j=m;
class pivolItem = t[j]
for (integer i=m+1; i?n; i++)
{
if(T[i]<pivotitem){j=j+1; Swap(T[i],T[j]);
}
Swap(T[m],T[j]; return j;
}
```

Figure 6

This partition procedure uses the middle element as the pivot element. For an array in random order this change does not affect the complexity of QuickSort but for an ordered, or sorted, array, this change guarantees a perfect split of the segment into two halves of equal length.

Another option for picking a good pivot object would be to pick three objects from the array and use the 'middle' object. While it takes a little overhead to pick the middle object, the choice of the middle object will always yield a split for an array in either ascending or descending order. This strategy is called the median-of-three strategy. The heuristic here is that the best of three guess ought to be the best. In practice the first, middle, and last objects are picked. In a sorted array this strategy always yields an optimum divide, but with slightly larger overhead than the partition version listed in figure 6. Figure 7 lists the pseudocode for the median-of-three strategy.

```
integer partition (Vector<class> T[m..n])
{
integer j=m, middle=(m+n)/2;
if (T[m]?T[middle]:
{
if (T[middle]?T[n]){ Swap(T[m],T{middle]);
{
else if (T[m]?T[n]){ if(T[m]>T[n]){ Swap(T[m],T[n]);
}
else{ Swap(T[m],T[middle]);
}
class pivolItem = T[m];
for (integer i=m+1; i?n; i++)
{
if(T[i]<pivotitem){j=j+1; Swap(T[i],T[j]);
} Swap(T[m],T[j]); return j;
}
```

Figure 7

This version of partition looks at the first, middle, and last components in the array. It determines which of the three is in the middle and uses that value as the pivot value.

It may require one additional swap and between two and three additional compares. The heuristic here is that the best guess of three guesses ought to result in a more even split most of the time.

A third version of using a random object as a pivot object was discussed earlier. The heuristic there is that a randomly chosen object has a random choice of being a good choice, but a randomly chosen object from a sorted array would always be a better choice that using the first or last object in the array.

There are several ways to enhance the performance of the QuickSort algorithm. First note that QuickSort eventually processes many short arrays. One way of avoiding the combined overhead due to recursion and the processing of small arrays is to stop the recursion when the number of objects in the sub-array is less than some threshold value. For small values of n, the $\Theta(n^2)$ performance of Select Sort is better than the expect Θ (n*lg(n)) performance of the recursively implemented Quick Sort.

QuickSort's computational complexity is technically O(n2). The reason is that some input arrays yield very poor performance. If QuickSort's partition procedure does a good job of dividing, then it appears to sort with complexity n*lg(n) when using the number of compares as the measure of complexity. It would be gratifying if the complexity Q(n) of Quick Sort, as measured by the number of compares, satisfied the difference equation Q(n) = 2*Q(n/2) + (n-1)

There is no guarantee that QuickSort splits the array to be sorted exactly down the middle at every step. What must be computed is the average of all the possible splits. This corresponds to finding the average or expected complexity over all possible n! inputs of length n. For a randomly ordered array, the final pivot element location is random. Thus if k denotes the pivot index, the difference equation is actually

$$Q(n) = Q(k-1) + Q(n-k) + (n-1)$$

for the correct split value k. This value of k is in a sense random over all possible n! input arrays. This implies that Q(n) must be computed statistically as the average over all possible pivot positions. By assumption the objects in the array are randomly placed. It follows that the probability the pivot will end up at any particular index value k where $1 \le k \le n$ is 1/n where n is the length of the array. The average must be computed over all values of k between 1 and n. Thus Q(n) must satisfy the recursive relation

$$Q(n) = 2 + (n-1) + (1/n)\sum_{k=1}^{n}(Q(k-1) + Q(n-k)) \quad n \le 2$$

$$Q(0) = Q(1) + 0$$

where the term 2 represents the two extra comparisons that occur when the pointers Left and Right cross and the term (n-1) is the number of compares used to partition the array which determines the location of the pivot element. Each individual term in the summation represents one possible location of the pivot element.

Note that terms of the form Q(k-1) go from Q(0), Q(1), Q(2) to Q(n-1) as k increments from one to n, while terms of the form Q(n-k) go from Q(n-1), Q(n-2), to Q(0) as k increments from 1 to n. It follows that the sum of the terms of the form Q(k-1) with increasing index equals the sum of the terms of form Q(n-k) with decreasing index. This allows the terms to be combined yielding

$$Q(n) = (n+1) + (2/n)\sum_{k=1}^{n} Q(k-1)$$

Multiplying every term by n removes the denominator and produces

$$n*Q(n) = n*(n+1) + 2\sum_{k=1}^{n} Q(k-1) \qquad (5)$$

But formula 5 is true for all values of n, so this recurrence relation is also true when (n-1) is substituted for

n, that is

$$(n-1)*Q(n-1) = (n-1)*n + 2*\sum_{k=1}^{n-1} Q(k-1) \qquad (6)$$

Subtracting formula.6 from formula 5 yields the difference equation in formula .7

$$n*Q(n) = (n+1)*Q(n-1) + 2*n \qquad (7)$$

Dividing both sides by n*(n+1) produces formula 8.

$$Q(n)/(n+1) = Q(n-1)/n + 2/(n+1) \qquad (8)$$

Again, this relation is good for all values of n, so substituting the values for Q(n-1), Q(n-2) etc. yields

$$\begin{aligned} Q(n)/(n+1) &= Q(n-2)/(n-1) + 2/n + 2/(n+1) \\ &= Q(n-3)/(n-2) + 2/(n-1) + 2/n + 2/(n+1) \\ &= Q(2)/3 + 2*\sum_{k=3}^{n}(1/k) \\ &\le 2*\sum_{k=1}^{n}(1/k) \end{aligned}$$

The term Q(2)/3 is one third the number of compares needed to sort an array of two elements, but this value is less than the terms added to the summation. The standard 'trick' from the calculus for estimating sums of positive terms with decreasing slope is to substitute the value of the related integral, thus it follows that

$$2*\sum_{k=1}^{n}(1/k) \approx 2*\sum_{1}^{n}(1/x)\,dx = 2*\ln(n)$$

But 2*ln(n) ≈ 1.38*lg(n) so

or

$$Q(n)/(n+1) \le 1.38*lg(n)$$

$$Q(n) \le 1.38*n*lg(n) \quad (9)$$

which implies that the average or expected computational complexity of Quick Sort, as measured by statistical techniques, is$\Theta(n*lg(n))$. Another interpretation of this last relation is that Q(n) is 38% slower than a similar sorting technique would be if the pivot element was always in the middle of the array. This 38% term says that if one averages all the 'good' inputs and 'bad' inputs with the 'just ok' inputs yields a process that is 38% less than an optimum process.

Suppose it is necessary to find the median value in an array of unsorted elements. This is a special case of a more general problem called the Selection Problem. The Selection problem says that given a set of n data points that can be unambiguously ordered, then one must pick the kth largest for any value of k between 1 and n. The partition technique used in QuickSort can be applied to the Selection Problem.

4.4 OTHER O(N*LG(N)) SORTS: MERGE SORT AND HEAP SORT

Divide and conquer strategies assume that it is less work to sort two short lists than to sort one long list. This section examines two such algorithms. The first, Merge Sort, starts with a heuristic that it is easier to merge two already sorted smaller lists than it is to sort one large list.

Merging two sorted lists of length n/2 items could take as few as n/2 compares (every object in one array precedes every object in the second array) to (n-1) compares (at the end of the merging process there is one object left in each array). If an array of n objects is divided in half, and each half is sorted using Select Sort, then the number of compares, before merging, would be

(2 sub arrays to sort)*((n/2)*((n/2)-1)/2 = n*(n-2)/4

and then assuming the worse case for merging takes (n-1) compares, then

total compares ≤ n*(n-2)/4 + (n-1) = (n2 +2*n +2)/4

If the original list had been sorted directly with Select Sort, it would have required n*(n-1)/2 compares so the savings would be at least

(Compares Select Sort)-(Compares Simple Merge)

≥ n*(n-1)/2 – (n2 + 2n +2)/4

= (n2 –4*n - 2)/4

which is a savings of almost half the compares over the basic Select Sort. The Merge Sort procedure recursively applies the same heuristic to all the sub arrays of objects. The second $\Theta(n*lg(n))$ sorting method, Heap Sort, is based on a clever data representation call a heap.

Merge Sort can be motivated with a simple example. Suppose that a large stack of name cards must be sorted. Instead of trying to sort all the cards at once, the large stack is divided into several smaller stacks. Each of these smaller stacks is sorted.

Then pairs of these smaller sorted stacks are merged into a combined sorted big stack. These combined sorted stacks are further combined into a still larger sorted stack of cards. See Figure 8. This process continues until all the stacks are combined into one stack. This is the strategy of Merge Sort.

Merge Sort is best implemented as a recursive algorithm. Arrays are split in half until the base case of a sub array consisting of a single object is reached. An array containing exactly one object is trivially sorted. After the base case is reached, two adjacent sub arrays are merged into one combined sub array so that the resulting sub array is sorted. This process continues until the last two sub arrays are merged into the combined array. Figure 9 contains the code for Merge Sort.

Position

1 2 3 4 5 6 7 8 9 10 11 12 13 14 15 16

Starting with 16 lists of length 1

3 8 12 4 16 11 15 1 10 13 5 14 2 9 6 7

Which are merged into 8 sorted lists of length 2

[3 8] [4 12] [11 16] [1 15] [10 13] [5 14] [2 9] [6 7]

Which are further merged into 4 sorted lists of length 4

[3 4 8 12] [1 11 15 16] [5 10 13 14] [2 6 7 9]

Which are further merged into 2 sorted lists of length 8

[1 3 4 8 11 12 15 16] [2 5 6 7 9 10 13 14]

Which are finally merged into 1 sorted list of length 16

[1 2 3 4 5 6 7 8 9 10 11 12 13 14 15 16]

Figure 8. Outline of the mechanics of Merge Sort.

Merge Sort starts out with trivially sorted lists of length 1. Two adjacent lists are merged into a larger list at each stage. The merged sub lists are denoted by brackets [...] in the figure above.

```
void Merge_Sorted_Arrays (Vector<class> T[m..n], integer mid, Vector <class>
        temp[m..n]) {
integer i = m, index1, index2;
integer Length=n - m + 1;
for (index1=m,index2=mid;
(index1<mid) and (index2 ≤ Length); i++){
if (T[index1] < T[index2]){ temp[i] = T[index1]; index1 = index1 + 1; } else{
temp[i] = T[index2];
index2 = index2 + 1; }
}
while (index1 < mid){
temp[i] = T[index1]
```

```
i = i + 1;
index1 = index1 + 1;
}
while (index2 ≤ Length){
temp[i] = T[index2];
i = i + 1;
index2 = index2 + 1;
}
// Copy merged array back to the source array. for (i = m; i ≤ n; i++){
T[i] = temp[i];
}
}

void Merge_Helper (Vector<class> T[m..n], Vector<class> temp[m..n]){
integer Length = n - m + 1;
if (Length < 2){
return; }
integer middle = m + Length/2;
Merge_Helper(T[m..midddle-1],temp[m..midddle-1]);Merge_Helper(T[middle..n],
    temp[middle..n]); Merge_Sorted_Arrays (T[m..n], middle, temp[m..n]);
}

void Merge_Sort ( Vector<class> T[m..n]){ Vector<class> temp[m..n]; // Get scratch
    array
Merge_Helper(T[m..n],temp[m..n]);
}
```

*Figure 9. The routine Merge_Sort has computational complexity □(n*lg(n)) but it uses twice as much memory to achieve this improved performance.*

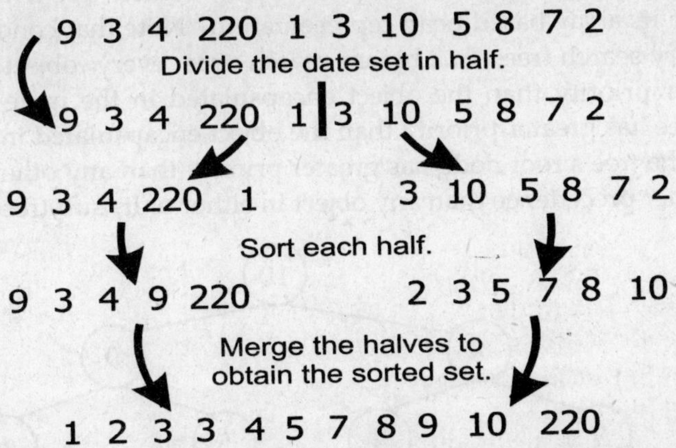

Merge Sort uses the fewest compares when the array to be sorted is already in ascending order. Under this scenario, the number of compares M(n) for an array of length n satisfies the recurrence relation

$$M(n) = 2*M(n/2) + n/2$$

Merge Sort's worst case occurs when the merge phase does (n-1) compares for each merge phase. In this case, the number of compares M(n) for an array of length n must satisfy the recurrence relation

$$M(n) = 2*M(n/2) + (n-1)$$

Both of these relations are derived by noting that the number of comparisons equals the work done in sorting two lists of half the length, which is represented by the terms 2*M(n/2), and then merging these two lists into one combined list.

The solution of both recurrence relations is O(n*lg(n)), hence the complexity of Merge Sort for any array as measured by the number of comparisons is O(n*lg(n)). Merge Sort does not, like Exchange Sort, Shell Sort, or Select Sort, sort in place. Merge Sort always achieves O(n*lg(n)) performance regardless of the initial order of objects in the array to be sorted. Merge Sort's performance can be slightly improved in two ways. One strategy is to sort short arrays in order to take advantage of the fact that for small values of n, O(n2) methods often outperform O(n*lg(n)) methods. This strategy also reduces the processing overhead due to recursion. Eliminating recursion by use of a stack also improves performance. These ideas will be explored further in the exercises.

The next sort to be analyzed, Heap Sort, uses a special data representation to improve sorting performance. Heaps are often used to implement priority queues. A priority queue removes the object with highest priority next. A heap is an array based representation of a complete binary tree where

1. the root of the tree is at array index 1,
2. the left child of an element at index i, if it exists, is located at index 2*i and the right child is located at index 2*i+1
3. the parent node has a higher priority than any of its children.

Figure 3a shows a heap as a complete binary search tree while figure 3b shows the same tree with its array based heap representation. Note that condition 3 says that a heap is not a binary search tree. In a binary search tree every object in a node's left sub-tree has lower priority than the object encapsulated in the node while every object in the right sub-tree has greater priority than the object encapsulated in the sub-trees root node. In a heap, the tree's root node has greater priority than any other object in the tree because it has higher precedence than any object in either of its sub-trees.

a.

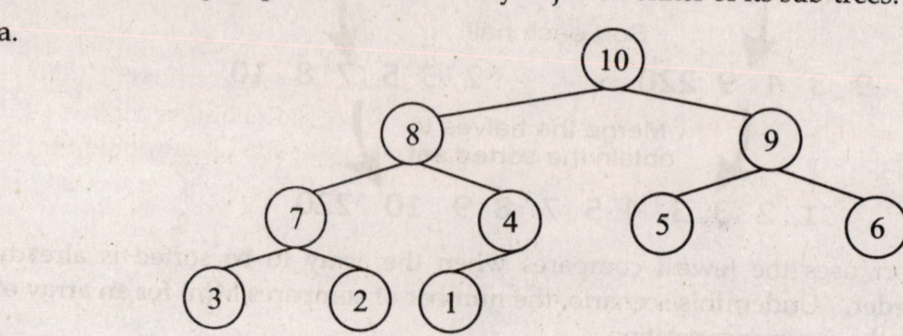

b. Heap array Index = 1 2 3 4 5 6 7 8 9 10

Value = 10 8 9 7 4 5 6 3 1 2

Figure .3(a) The heap represented as a binary tree. Note that the maximum object is located in the root and the value of the object in any node is greater or equal to the value of any child. (b) The heap in part (a) represented as an array. Note the root of the heap is always located at index=1, and the left child of a node with index I is located at the node whose index is 2*I while the right child of the node with index I is located at the node whose index is 2*I+1.

There are two 'heap' facts that make the heap structure a good candidate for a sort routine. First, the maximum object in a heap is always located at the heap's root, that is at array index=1. In Heap Sort, the maximum array element is found, and then swapped with the end element. At that point the array to be sorted length is reduced by one, the heap rebuilt, and the whole process is applied on the shortened array. Second, since a Heap is a complete binary tree, the heap of size n has lg(n) levels. This implies that the basic heap based operations should have computational complexity $\Theta(\lg(n))$. After the root is removed from the heap, the heap operation RebuildHeap should be $\Theta(\lg(n))$. The strategy for HeapSort is now clear. First build the heap. Then once the heap is built, swap the maximum element located at the heap's root with the last element in the heap, reduce the heap's size by 1, and rebuild the heap. Continue the process of swapping, reducing, and rebuilding until the size of the heap has been reduced to a single object. The pseudocode outline for heap sort is

```
BuildHeap(V);
Set n = length of V;
while (n doe s not equal 1) {
Swap object at index 1 with object at index n;
set n=n-1;
RebuildHeap on first n elements of V;
}
```

The pseudocode above assumes the first index of the array to be sorted is 1.

The idea behind building the original heap is relatively simple. For any arbitrary array of objects indexed from 1 to n, the objects located at positions (n/2)+1 to n starts in a heap. One starts with a half empty heap and then uses the heap insert operation to build up the heap from position (n/2) to position one object at a time. Insert consists of adding the new object at the next position and checking to see if it is larger than any of its children. If it is larger, then start to add the next object to the heap. If it is not larger, then swap that object with the larger of its children and continue the process until either the end of the heap is reached the object is larger than both its children. The procedure BuildHeap in figure.4 builds a heap using this strategy. Again note that the array stores objects in locations with indices between one and n.

```
void Add_to_Heap(Vector<class> T[1..n], integer index){
integer Largest = index; integer L = 2*index; integer R = L + 1;
if ((L≤n)and (T[L]>T[index])){ Largest = L;
```

```
}
if ((R≤n) and (T[R]>T[Largest])){ Largest = R;
}
if (Largest does not equal index){ Swap (T[index], T[Largest]);
Add_to_Heap (array, Largest, num_elements);
}
}

void BuildHeap (Vector<class> T[1..n])
{
for (integer i = n/2; i≥1; i--){ Add_to_Heap (T[1..n], i);
}
}
```

Figure.4. BuildHeap builds a heap in place. BuildHeap only needs to be called for the first

half of the array. The auxiliary procedure Add_to_Heap first finds the largest value of the elements at the index i, its left child at index and its right child. The largest value is moved into index i. The process continues recursively until no swapping is necessary.

BuildHeap has worst case complexity, as measured by the number of compares, of O(n*lg(n)). Since the kth object can be inserted with fewer than lg(k) compares, it follows that the number of compares BH(n) to build a heap of n elements cannot exceed

$$BH(n) \leq lg(1) + lg(2) + lg(3) + \ldots lg(n-1) + lg(n)$$

but the logarithm is an increasing function, so for k≤n it follows that lg(k)≤lg(n). Replacing each of the n terms of the form lg(k) in the expression on the right hand side by lg(n), it follows that BH(n)≤n*lg(n). This implies BuildHeap has complexity O(n*lg(n)).

Now that the heap has been built, the sorting can begin. The largest object on the heap, located at the root index = 1, is swapped with the last object in the heap and the heap's size is reduced by 1. Since the last object in the heap has lower priority than its parent, the new object at the root no longer has the maximum precedence of all objects on the heap. The heap must be rebuilt before the sort process can continue. Starting at index i=1, the rebuild operation recursively replaces the object at index i with the larger of its two children at indices 2*i and 2*i+1 provided the larger of the two children has higher priority than its parent. This process continues until the object at index i is larger than either of its two children or until 2*i or 2*i+1 is greater than the last index of the heap. This code for the HeapSort algorithm is listed in figure.5. Note how the case of an index i that only has one child at location 2*i is handled. This is the case when the number of objects on the heap is even.

```
void HeapSort (Vector<class> T[1..n]) {
integer Size = n; BuildHeap (T[1..n]);
for (integer i = n; i≥1; i--){ Swap (T[1],T[i]);
Size = Size - 1; Add_to_Heap(T[1..Size], 1);
```

```
    }
}
```

Figure 5 The code for Heap Sort first turns the array to be sorted into a heap. The heap is then turned into a sorted array by swapping the highest priority object stored at heap index=1 into the last element of the heap, decreasing the size of the heap and rebuilding the heap.

The rebuild operation does at most two comparisons per iteration. It takes at most lg(k) iterations to rebuild a heap of size k. Thus the total number of compares to rebuild the heap is less than

$$2^*(\lg(n) + \lg(n-1) + \lg(n-2) + \ldots \lg(2) + \lg(1)) \leq 2^*n^*\lg(n)$$

so the computational complexity of the sorting portion of Heap Sort as measured by the number of compares is at most 2*n*lg(n). This implies that the combined HeapSort algorithm, which combines the code for BuildHeap in figure 4 and the code for Heap Sort figure 5, has complexity less than 3*n*lg(n). This bound can be sharpened to 2*n*lg(n). Unlike Quick Sort, the bound on HeapSort is an absolute bound. Heap Sort, regardless of objects initial order, is always □(n*lg(n)).

Heap Sort, like Quick Sort but unlike Merge Sort, sorts in place.

Merge Sort always achieves its □(n*lg(n)) complexity with the added cost of the extra space needed to merge the short arrays, while Quick Sort sorts in place and, on the average, achieves its □(n*lg(n)) bound.

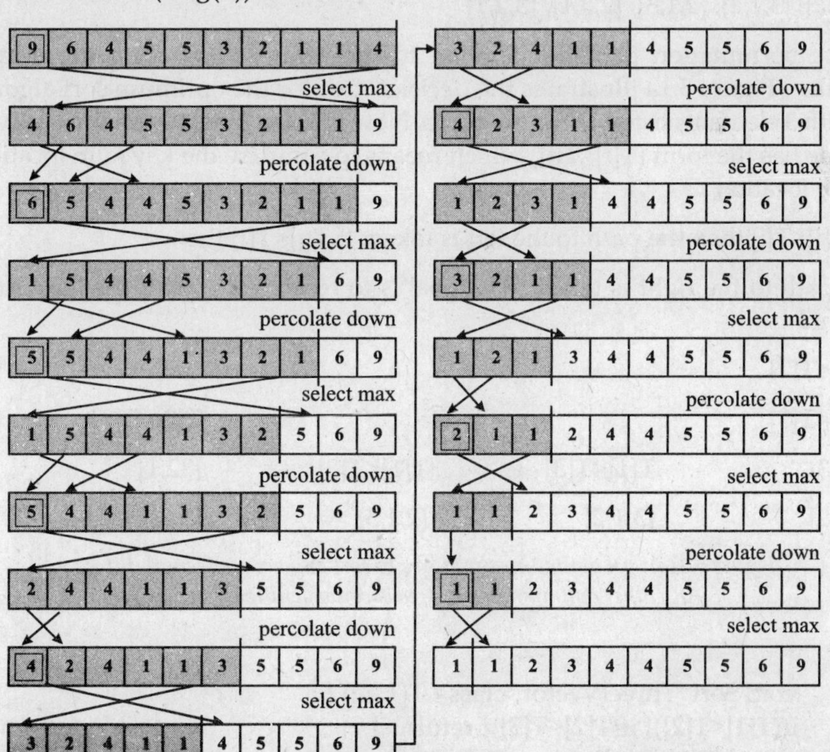

4.5 LOWER BOUNDS FOR SORTING BY KEYS

Three distinct approaches to sorting by keys have achieved Θ(n*lg(n)) but none has been found to do better. Is there an approach to sorting by keys that has lower computational complexity than Θ (n*lg(n))? If so, the search needs to continue. If not, there is no reason to search further. The question becomes, "Is there a lowest theoretical complexity bound for sorting algorithms that sort by comparing keys?" This section proves that the answer to this question is a resounding no. There is no reason to look for more efficient classes of key based sorting algorithms. In particular there is no linear sorting algorithm, i.e. one whose computational complexity is Θ (n), based on the comparison of keys. To do this a decision tree will be developed that can model anyalgorithm that sorts by comparing keys. The structure of this tree will show that for any sorting algorithm based on keys, there has at least one input that takes at least n*lg(n) comparison of keys.

Let [x1, x2, ... , xn] be an integer array that contains n distinct integers. There are n! different ways these n distinct integers can be arranged in the array. Any valid sorting algorithm must be able to sort any one of these

n! object orderings, or permutations. Obviously, any optimum sorting algorithm will not do any extra work. Any sorting algorithm selects the correct permutation and applies it against the original array. Suppose [a,b,c] are three distinct integers.

There are 3! = 6 permutations of the integers {1,2,3}. These six permutations are [1,2,3], [1,3,2], [3,1,2], [2,1,3], [2,3,1], [3,2,1]

If the permutation [2,3,1] is applied to the array [a,b,c], then the array [b,c,a] is the result. Figure 5.1a illustrates the decision tree for the optimum sort algorithm for an array with 3 elements listed in figure 9.5.1b. Note that the tree has exactly 6 leaves. Each interior node has the form (T[i]<T[j]) which means to compare the key ki in location i with the key kj in location j.

If T[i]<T[j] then the path to the left is taken. If T[j]<T[i] then

the path to the right is taken. The goal is to reach a leaf with the least number of comparisons.

T[1]<T[2]

T[2]<T[3] T[2]<T[3]

[1,2,3] T[1]<T[3] T[1]<T[3] [32,1]

[1,3,2] [3,1,2] [2,1,3] [2,31]

Figure 5.1(a) An optimum search tree to sort any array of length three. Any other optimum search tree is equivalent to this tree.

```
void Sort_Three(Vector<class> T[1..3]) {
if(T[1]<T[2]){ if(T[2]<T[3]){ return; }
else if (T[1]<T[3]){ Swap(T[2],T[3]); return; }
```

```
else { Swap(T[1],T[3]); Swap(T[2],T[3]); return; }
}
else {
if(T[3]<T[2]){ Swap(T[1],T[3]); return; }
else if (T[1]<T[3]){ Swap(T[2],T[1]); return; }
else { Swap(T[1],T[2]); Swap(T[2],T[3]); return; }
}
}
}
```

Figure 5.1(b): One possible implementation in pseudocode that sorts an array T[1..3] of integers. Whatever ordering of three distinct integers is returned sorted with at most three compares. Note that any algorithm that sorts an array of three keys has four possible inputs that require three compares. Note also that every input requires at least two compares in order to verify whether or not the input array is already sorted.

Suppose it is known that T[1]<T[2] is true. The algorithm diagramed in figure.5.1(a) says to take the left path and check to see if T[2]<T[3]. If that comparison is true, then it is now known that T[1]<T[2]<T[3] or the permutation [1,2,3] applied against the array T[1..3] yields the sorted array. If the comparison T[2]<T[3] is false, then it is known that T[1]<T[2] (a<b) and T[3]<T[2] (c<b). Clearly T[2] is the maximum object in the array but it is not known whether T[1]<T[3] (a<c) or T[3]<T[1] (c<a). Figure 5.1(a) now checks (T[1]<T[3]) to answer this question. Suppose T[1]<T[3] (a<c) is false, then T[3]<T[1]<T[2] from which it follows that the permutation [3,1,2] when applied to the array T[1..3] yields a sorted array.

Each leaf of the comparison tree is identified with a possible permutation. There are no duplicate leaves because the sort algorithm must be deterministic. The decision tree for any optimal key based sorting algorithm will have exactly n! leaves because this n! equals the number of possible permutations of n elements. An optimum algorithm, as diagramed in its decision tree, will not make any redundant comparisons. There is no need to check if ka<kc if it is already known that both ka<kb and kb<kc are true. These observations reduce the problem of determining the minimum number of comparisons needed by any optimum sorting algorithm to the problem of finding the minimum number of interior nodes (where each interior node represents a single comparison between two particular keys) of a tree with n! leaves (remember, each leaf represents a permutation that converts some input into a properly sorted output).

The optimum tree, in addition to having exactly n! leaves, will have a minimum number of levels. Each level represents one comparison. Minimizing comparisons minimizes interior nodes. Let k be the height of this minimum tree. Since each level represents a comparison needed to find the minimum path down to the correct leaf (permutation) of the optimum sort algorithm, the problem reduces to finding the minimum height of the decision tree with n! leaves. Thus the height of the tree equals the number of comparisons needed in the worst case.

Recall that a tree's root node has level 0. The maximum number of nodes on level k is 2k, which implies that

Minimum number of permutations = $n! \leq 2k$

for some integer k because an input array with n objects has n! possible permutations. Taking the logarithm to the base 2 of both sides and noting that k is an integer yields

$k \geq \Theta\ lg(n!)!$

Using Stirling's Formula $(n! \approx sqrt(2^* \Theta *n)(n/e)n)$ to approximate the value of n! produces $lg(n!) \approx lg(n)/2 + lg(2^* \Theta)/2 + n^*lg(n) - n^*lg(e)$

$= n^*lg(n) + lg(n)/2 - n^*ln(e) + O(1)$

Taking the ceiling of both sides yields

$k \approx \Theta\ n^*lg(n)!$

The conclusion of this argument implies that there is no faster class of sorting algorithms based on the comparison of keys than those that sort in Θ (n*lg(n)). If a faster sorting method exists, it must be based on some method other than the comparison of keys. Radix Sort, which is an O(n) sorting algorithm, is studied in the next section. Radix Sort does not sort by comparing keys. It assumes a fixed length key and sorts based on the components of the key.

4.6 A SORT NOT BASED ON KEY COMPARISON: RADIX SORT

This section on external sorting concludes with a study of radix sort, which has computational complexity Θ (n). Radix sort does not compare keys, so it does not violate the fact that a sorting algorithm which is based on the comparison of keys can not have complexity less than Θ (n*lg(n)). Radix sort is based on the key structure. The key must be composed fixed number of components, and each component must have a finite range. The standard 10 digit area code plus phone number is an example of such a key. The key has exactly ten components and each component is one of ten digits.

Radix sorting had its beginnings in the era of mechanical card sorters where decks of cards had to be sorted. Punch cards typically had eighty columns and each column had about ten locations for punch holes. Suppose that the key was in columns 1-4 of the cards, and each column contained only contained a digit between 0 and 9. The sorting process takes four passes (one pass for each component of the key). The key is scanned from right to left. On the first pass the components in column four are scanned. The sorter places all cards with 0 digit in the first bin, all cards with a 1 are placed in the second bin, and so on. The operator then removes the cards from the last or the 9-th digit bin first. The cards from the next to last bin, or the 8-th digit bin, are removed next and placed on top of the deck. Then the third from the last bin or the 7-th digit bin cards are removed and placed on top of the deck and so on. The process is repeated using digits in column 3 and the deck is combined, then the process is repeated for digits in column 2 and the decks are combined, and finally the process is repeated for column 1. At this point, the deck of cards is in sorted order.

This process is illustrated in figure.6.1. Suppose the objects all have three digit keys and each digit is either the digit 1, the digit 2 or the digit 3. In figure 6.1(a) the original numbers in TAPE0 have been placed in three files TAPE1, TAPE2 and TAPE3 depending on whether the right digit ends in 1, 2, or 3 respectively. TAPE0 in figure 6.1(b) is the result of copying TAPE1 from figure .6.1(a) to TAPE0, then copying TAPE2, and then TAPE3 respectively. TAPE1, TAPE2, and TAPE3 in figure.6.1(b) are the result of placing the objects on the file on the basis of the middle key. Figure.6.1(c) follows as before. TAPE0 in figure.6.1(d) is the final result. TAPE0 TAPE1

TAPE2		TAPE3	
132	131	132	213
112	331	112	323
131	232	223	
213			
323			
331			
232			
223			

Figure 6.1(a) Original file is shown under TAPE0 and first distribution of Radix Sort based on third digit of the key. Note that the data on TAPE0 is random.

TAPE0	TAPE1	TAPE2	TAPE3
131	112	323	131
331	213	223	331
132	132		
112	232		
232			
213			
323			
223			

Figure.6.1(b) Merged file and second distribution of Radix Sort based on second digit of the key. Note that the Merged file TAPE0 after gather data from first distribution in figure

6.1(a) is in ascending order based on the last digit only. The distribution in this second phase is based on the key component second from the right.

TAPE0	TAPE1	TAPE2	TAPE3
112	112	213	323
213	131	223	331
323	132	232	
223			
131			
331			
132			
232			

Figure .6.1(c) Merged file from phase 2 distribution listed in figure 6.1(b) and the third distribution of Radix Sort based on third digit counting from theleft. Note that the Merged file TAPE0 is in order if last two digits are considered to be the key.

TAPE0	TAPE1	TAPE2	TAPE3
112			
131			
132			
213			
223			
232			
323			
331			

Figure .6.1(d): Merged file after TAPE1, TAPE2 and TAPE3 are copied from the third distribution in figure 6.1(c), in that order, to TAPE0. Note that TAPE0 is now in ascending order. The total number of distributions equaled the number of key components and the number of scratch files equaled the number of different possible key values.

Radix sort is clearly Θ (n). In radix sort, the tape read and tape write are the time consuming operations. One read and one write per key component is required to move the object from the file to the component based scratch file, and another read and write are required to move objects back from the scratch file back to the original file. This yields a total of 2 reads and 2 writes per pass. The number of passes equals the number of components in the key. Suppose the time to read one object equals the time to write one object. Let T denote the time per read or write, let L denote the key length, and let n denote the number of objects to be sorted. Thus an estimate of the execution time to sort a file based on the radix sort strategy is 4*L*T*n. This implies that radix sort is linear, or it has computational complexity Θ (n). It is important to note that not one comparison between two keys was done in sorting these keys using Radix Sort.

4.7 EXTERNAL SORTS: SEQUENTIAL VARIATIONS OF MERGE SORT

External Sorts do some work internally but store their beginning, intermediate, and final results externally. The external storage device is either a disk drive or a tape drive.

Files are assumed to be sequential. Sequential files operate in one of two modes. In the Read mode, only the next object on the file can be read. The file cannot be backed up to access a previous object. If it is necessary to read a previous object, the file must be rewound and reading starts again at the very first object in the file. There is a boolean operation to detect whether the end-of-file has been reached. When the file is in write mode, it starts out with an empty file and writes the object at the end of the file.

An object can only be written at the end of the file. It is impossible to write anywhere but at the end of the file. If a file's mode is changed from read to write, all the data on the file is lost. Other file operations in the sequential file class open and close the file. This section deals only with the sorting of data on sequential files. There are other file classes called indexed files and indexed sequential files. The indexed file structure allows elements to be accessed like large arrays while the indexed sequential file structure is a composite of the indexed file structure with the sequential file structure. Neither of these file structures is discussed further.

Minimizing file access is the single most important consideration when sorting sequential files. The time spent accessing an internal memory address is measured in nanoseconds. The time spent reading or writing to an external file is measured in milliseconds. This is a difference in access time of four to six orders of magnitude.

It takes literally minutes to rewind a sequential file stored on a magnetic tape. Hardware designers and operating systems programmers have spent considerable effort to reduce the access time of external devices. Reading and writing is done to internal buffers. Once the buffer is empty, in the case of the mode being read, then and only then is the external device accessed and enough data is read to fill the buffer. To decrease the execution time external devices read and write groups of objects, not single objects. The use of buffers is usually transparent to the programmer.

There are tricks to further speed this process up such as double buffering. In double buffering data is being read into one buffer while data in the other buffer is being processed. While these standard programming techniques decrease execution time, they do not alter the fact that accessing external devices is much slower than accessing internal memory.

In this section, external files are assumed to be very large. If the complete file can fit into internal memory, then the best sort strategy would be to read the entire file into memory, sort the file internally with an in-place sort like Quick Sort, and then write the entire array back to the external device. The choice of methods to sort external files is often limited by the hardware devices that are available on the particular system. Any algorithm that requires four tape drives will not work at an installation that has only three tape drives. Since multiple files can be open or stored on the same disk drive, this consideration is of less importance than it used to be. The tape medium is now used more for permanently archiving data than for manipulating data.

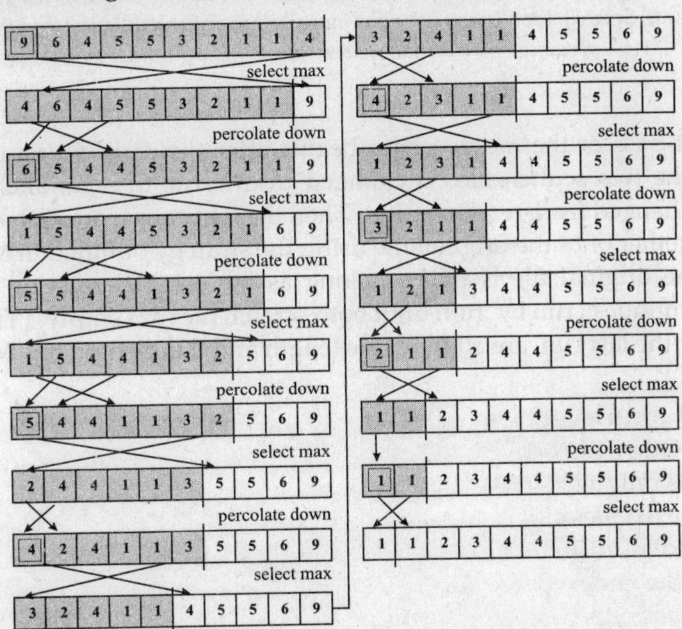

Since only large files are under consideration, efficient strategies must be chosen. Strategies that have complexity ! (n2) are unacceptable. Strategies that are ! (n*lg(n)) are barely acceptable. If the key has a certain form, then ! (n) strategies such as Radix Sort are possible and perhaps desirable.

Most external sorting is based on merging. A run is defined to be a sequence of objects in ascending order and known length. The simplest merge strategy starts out in an initializing phase that distributes the data to two scratch files. See Figure 7.1(a). An internal scratch array is filled with data and sorted. The objects in this array are then written as a run to the first scratch file. The next batch of data is read into the scratch array, sorted, and written as a run to the second scratch file. The process continues.

Sorted runs are written to alternate files. All runs, except possibly the last run, have the same length. The process terminates when all the data has been read, sorted, and written to the two initial scratch files. At the end of this initial distribution phase, the two scratch files are composed of sorted runs.

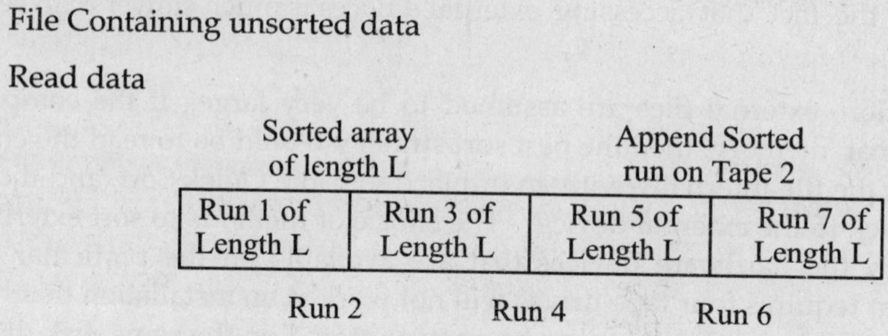

File Containing unsorted data

Read data

Sorted array of length L

Append Sorted run on Tape 2

Run 1 of Length L	Run 3 of Length L	Run 5 of Length L	Run 7 of Length L

Run 2 Run 4 Run 6

Figure 7.1(a) : External sort initial distribution phase, Unsorted data is first read into an array of fixed length and sorted using a $\Theta(n*lg(n))$ Sort. These sorted 'runs' are appended onto the end of two scratch tapes. This phase ends when the external file containing the unsorted data is completely processed. Scratch Tape 1 may have one more run than Scratch tape 2 and the last run processed may contain fewer objects than the other runs.

The first pass of the merge phase begins after the distribution phase terminates. The mode of the two scratch files is changed from write to read, and the mode of the original file is changed from read to write. Then the first runs from each of the scratch files are merged together onto the original file using the strategy outlined in Merge Sort. This new run on the original file is twice as long as the original runs on the scratch files. This process continues, run by run, until both scratch files are empty. The resulting runs, except possibly the last run, are all the same length and their length has been doubled. See figure 9.7.1.(b)

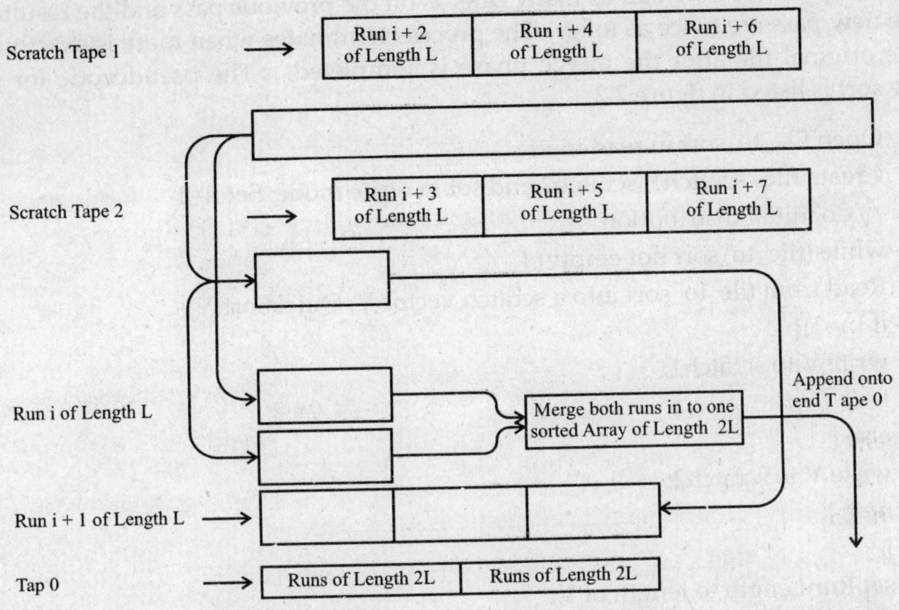

Figure.7.1.b. External sort merge phase. Two runs are read, one from Tape 1 and one from Tape 2, merged and the result appended onto the end of Tape 0. Tape 0 has runs twice as long as the original runs. The next phase is a modified distribution phase where runs are split between two scratch tapes and then these runs are combined. The process is complete when tape 0 has only one run.

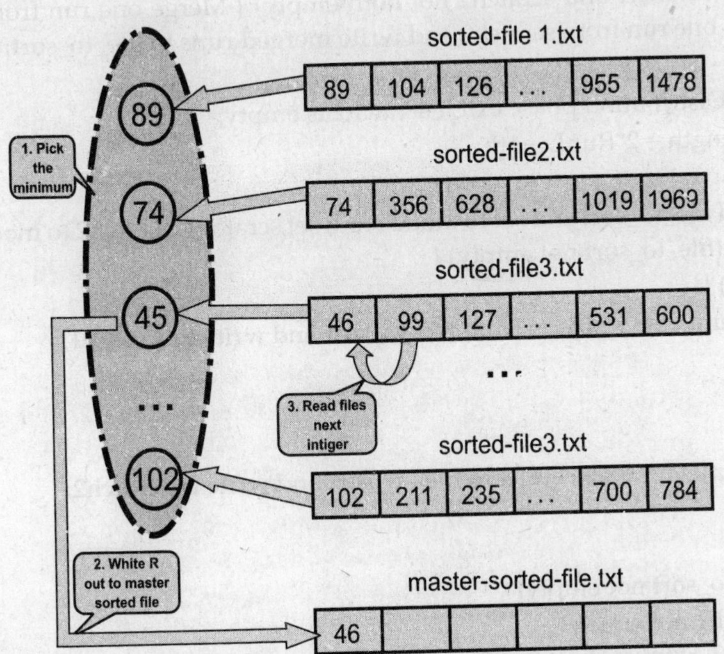

A modified distribution phase now follows. This time the already sorted runs are distributed to the two scratch files, and then merged back again onto the original file.

After each pass there are half as many runs as on the previous pass and the resulting runs on the new pass are twice as long. The process terminates when there is exactly one run on the original file after the merge phase is completed. The pseudocode for external merge sort is listed in figure 7.2.

```
Open file_to_sort in read mode;
Create files scratch1, scratch2 and set in write mode; Set n=1
//do initial distribution
while (file_to_sort not empty) {
Read from file_to_sort into a scratch vector V; QuickSort(V)
if (n=1){
write V to scratch1;
n=2; }
else {
write V to scratch2;
n=1; }
}
set RunLength to length of V;
while (scratch2 not empty){
//Merge phase
rewind scratch1, scratch2 and set mode to read;
set file_to_sort to mode write;
while (scratch1 and scratch2 not both empty) { Merge one run from scratch1 and
        one run from scratch2 and write merged runs to file_to_sort;
}
//Re-Distribution phase exit if scratch2 is empty;
RunLength = 2*RunLength;
n=1;
rewind file_to_sort and set to mode read; set scratch1, scratch2 to mode write; while
        (file_to_sort not empty) {
if (n=1) {
read RunLength objects from file_to_sort and write to scratch1;
n=2;
}
else {
read RunLength objects from file_to_sort and write to scratch2;
n=1;
}
} {file_to_sort not empty}
} {scratch1 not empty}
```

Figure 7.2. External Merge Sort Pseudocode. Scratch1 and scratch2 are two temporary files where intermittent data is stored. The pseudocode assumes each run except possibly the last has the same length. The algorithm terminates when the merge phase fails to put a run on scratch2.

This algorithm clearly terminates. If R(k) denotes the length of the run after k merges, then

$$R(k) = 2(k-1)*n$$

where n is the length of the original run. If there were N objects on the file, then it takes k passes to sort the original file where K is the first integer such that $2(k-1)*n \geq N$. If n=1, then k=lg(N). This intuitively implies that external based merge sort has complexity $\Theta(N*lg(N))$. The computational complexity of external sort algorithms is based on the number of times an object is read or written, not the number of times two objects are compared. Comparisons are done internally while reads and writes are done externally. The tape or disk read and write operations are the time consuming operations. Each object is read and written once in the distribution phase and read and written once in each merge phase. The total number of read-write operations per cycle is 4*N while the number of cycles is lg(N/n) where n is the length of the first run. The computational complexity for this merge based sort is O(N*lg(N)).

Heapsort in Detail

We introduce another sorting algorithm. Like merge sort, but unlike insertion sort, heapsort's running time is O(n lg n).Like insertion sort, but unlike merge sort, heapsort sort in place: only a constant number of array element are stored out side the input array at any time. Thus, heapsort combines the better attributes of the two sorting algorithms we have already discussed.

Heapsort also introduces another algorithm design technique: the use of data structure, in this case one we call a "heap," to manage information during the execution of the algorithm. Not only is the heap data structure will reappear in algorithms in the later chapters.

We note that the term "heap" was originally coined in the context of heapsort, but it has since come to refer to "garbage-collected storage," such as the programming lanuages Lisp and java provide. Our heap data structure is not garbage-collected storage, and whenever we refer to heaps in our discussion , we shall mean the structure defined in this topic.

Heaps

The heap data structure is an array object that can viewed as a nearly complete binary tree. Each node of the tree corresponds to an element of the array that stores the value in the node. The tree is completely filled on all levels except possibly the lowest, which is filled from the left up to a point. An array A that represents a heap is an object with two attributes: length[A], which is the number of elements in the array, and heap-size[A], the number of elements in the heap stored within array A. that is ,although A[1.. length[A]] may contain valid numbers of the heap.

The root of the tree is A[1], and given the index I of a node, the indices of its parent PARENT (i), left child LEFT(i), and right child RIGHT(I) can be computed simply:

```
PARENT(i)
  return [i/2]
LEFT(i)
  retrun 2i
RIGHT(i)
  return 2i + 1
```

on most computers, the LEFT procedure can computer 2i in one instruction by simply shifting the binary representation of I left one bit position. Similarly, the RIGHT procedure can quickly compute 2i + 1 by shifting the binary representation of I left one bit position and adding in a 1 as the low-order bit position. In a good implementation of heap sort, these three procedures are often implemented as "macros" or "in-line" procedures.

The study of heap structure is further divided in two types namely max heaps and min heaps. In both kinds, the values in the nodes satisfy a heap property, the specifics of which depend on the kind of heap. In a max-heap,the max-heap property is that for every node I other then the root, A[PARENT (i)] $\geq$ A[I] .

That is ,the value of a node is at most the value of its parent. Thus, the largest element in a max-heap is stored at the root, and the sub tree rooted at a node contains values no larger then that contained at the node itself. A min-heap is organized in the opposite way; the min-heap property is that for every node I other then the root,

A[PARENT(i)] $\leq$ A[i]

The smallest element in a min-heap is the root.

For the heapsort algorithm, we use max-heaps. Min-heaps are commonly used in priority queues. We shall be precise in specifying whether we need a max-heap or a min-heap for any particular application, and when properties apply to either max-heaps, we just use the term"heap."

Viewing a heap as a tree, we define the height of anode in a heap to be the number of edges on the longest simple downward path from the node to a leaf, and we define the height the height of the heap to be the height of its root. Since a heap of n elements is based on a complete binary tree, its height is O(lg n).we shall see that the basic operations on heaps run in time at most proportional to the height of the tree and thus take O(lg n) time. The remainder of this chapter presents five basic procedures and shows how they sre used in a sorting algorithm and a priority-queue data structure.

The MAX-HEAPIFY procedure, which runs in O(lg n) time, is the key to maintaining the max-heap property.

The BUILD-MAX-HEAP procedure, which runs in linear time,produces a max-heap from an unordered input array.

The HEAPSORT procedure, which runs in O(n lg n) time, sorts an array in place.

The MAX-HEAP-INSERT, HEAP-EXTRACT-MAX, HEAP-INCREASE-KEY, and HEAP-MAXIMUM procedures, which run in O(lg n) time .allow the heap data structure to be used as a priority queue.

Maintaining the Heap Property

MAX-HEAPIFY is an important subroutine for manipulating max-heap. Its inputs are an array A and an index I into the array. When max-heapify is called, it is assumed that the binary tree rooted at LEFT(i) and RIGHT(i) are max-heaps, but that A[I] may be smaller then its children, thus violating the max-heap property.

The function of MAX-HEAPIFY is to let the value at A[I]"float down" in the max heap so that the subtree rooted at index I becomes a max-heap.

MAX-HEAP IF Y(A.i)

```
1.   l ← LEFT(i)
2.   r ← RIGHT(i)
3.   if l ≤ heap-size[A] and A[l] > A[i]
     then largest ← l
     else largest ← i
      if r ≤  heap-size[A] and A[r] > A[largest]
     then largest ← r
     if largest  ≠  i
     then exchange A ↔ A[largest]
```

MAX-HEAP IF Y(A,lagest)

At each step, the largest of the elements A[i] , A[LEFT(i)] ,and A[RIGHT(i)] is determined, and its index is stored in largest ,then the subtree rooted at node I is a max-heap and the procedure terminates. Otherwise, one of the two children has the largest element, and A[i] is swaped with A [largest], which causes node I and its children to satisfy the max-heap property. The node index by largest, however, now has the original value A[i], and thus the subtree rooted at the largest may violate the max-heap property. Consequently, MAX-HEAPIFY must be called recursively on that subtree.

The running time of MAX-HEAPIFY on a a sub tree of size n rooted at given node i is the O(1) time to fix up the relationship among the elements A[i], A [LEFT(i)] ,and A[RIGHT(i)], plus the time to run MAX-HEAPIFY on a subtree of size n rooted at given node i. The children's subtrees each have size at most 2n / 3 – the worst case occurs when the last row of the tree is exactly half full—and the running time of MAX-HEAPIFY can therefore be described by the recurrence.

Building a Heap

We can use the procedure MAX-HEAPIFY in a bottom-up manner toconvert an array A[l .. n], where n =length[A], into a amax-heap. The elements in the subarray A[($\lfloor n/2 \rfloor$ +1)..n] are allleaves of the tree, and so each is a 1-element heap to begin with. The procedure BUILD-MAX-HEAP goes through the remaining nodes of the tree and runs MAX-HEAPIFY on each one.

```
BUILD-MAX-HEAP(A)
heap-size[A] ← length[A]
for i ←⌊length[A] / 2⌋ downto 1
    do MAX-HEAPIFY(A,i)
```

To show why BUILD-MAX-HEAP works correctly, we use the followingloop invariant:

At the start of each iteration of the loop of lines 2-3, each node i+1 I+2,…..,n is the root of a max-heap.

We need to show that this invariant is true prior to the loop iteration, that each iteration of the loop maintains the invariant, and that the invariant provies a useful property to show correctness when the loop terminates.

Initialization: prior to the first itaration of the loop, $i = \lfloor n/2 \rfloor$. Each node $\lfloor n/2 \rfloor+1, \lfloor n/2 \rfloor+2, \ldots, n$ is a aleaf and is the root of a trivial max- heap.

Maintenance

To see that each iteration maintains the loop invariant, observe that the children of node i are numbered higher then i. By the loop invariant , therefore, they are both root of max-heaps. This is precisely the condition required for the call MAX-HEAPIFY(A,i) to make node i a max-heap root. Moreover, the MAX-HEAPIFY call preserves the property that nodes i+1, i=2,….,n are all roots of max-heaps. Decrementing i in the for loop update reestablishes the loop invariant for the next iteration.

Termination

At termination, i=0. by the loop invariant, each node 1,2,….,n is the root of the max heap. In particular, node 1 is.

We can compute a simple upper bound on the running tıme of BUILD-MAX-HEAP as follows. Each call to MAX-HEAPIFY cost O(lg n) time, and there are O(n) such calls. Thus, the running time is O(lg n). this upper bound, though correct, is not asymptotically tight.

We can derive a tighter bound by observing that for MAX-HEAPIFY to run at a node varies with the height of the node in the tree, and the heights of heap has height$\lfloor \lg n \rfloor$ and at most$\lceil n/2h+1 \rceil$nodes of any height h .

This time required by MAX-HEAPIFY when called on a node of height h is O(h), so we can express the total cast of BUILD-MAX-HEAP as

$$\sum_{h=0}^{\lg n} [n/2^{h+1}]O(h) = O(n\sum_{h=0}^{\lg n} h/2h$$

The last summation can be evaluated by substituting x=1/2 in the formula (A.8), which yields

$$\sum_{h=0}^{\infty} h/2^h = 1/2/(1-1/2)^2$$

$= 2$

Thus, the running time of BUILD-MAX-HEAP can be bounded as

$$\sum_{h=0}^{\lg n} h/2^h = O(n\sum_{h=0}^{\infty} h/2^h$$

$= O(n)$

Hence, we can build a max-heap from an unordered array in linear time.

We can build a mix-heap by the procedure BUILD-MIN-HEAP, which is the same as BUILD-MAX-HEAP but with the call to MAX-HEAPIFY in line 3 replaced by a call to MIN-HEAPIFY. BUILD-MIN-HEAP PRODUCES A min-heap from an unordered linear array in linear time.

The Heapsort Algorithm

The heapsort algorithm starts by using BUILD-MAX-HEAP to build a max-heap on the input array A[1..n], where n= length[A]. since the maximum element of the array is stored at the root A[1], it can be put into its correct final positionby exchanging it with A[n]. if we now"discard" node n from the heap(by decrementing heap-size[A]), we observe that A[1..(n –1)] can easily be made into a max-heap. The children of the root remain max-heaps,but the new root element may violate the max-heap property. All that is needed to restore the max-heap property, however, is one call to MAX-HEAPIFY(A,1), which leavea a max-heap in A[1..(n –1)]. The heapsort algorithm then repeats this process for the max-heap of size n-1 down to a heap of size 2.

```
HEAPSORT(A)
BUILD-MAX-HEAP(A)
for i ← length[A] downto 2
do exchange A[1]↔ A[i]
heap-size[A] ← heap-size[A] –1
MAX-HEAPIFY(A,1)
```

The heapsort procedure takes time O(n lg n), since the call to BUILD-MAX-HEAP takes time O(n) and each of the n –1 call to MAX-HEAPIFY takes time O(lg n).

Priority queues

Heapsort is an excellent algorithm, but a good implementation of quicksort, usually beats it in practice. Nevertheless, the heap data structure ture itself has enormous utility. In this section, we present one of the most popular application of a heap: its use as efficient priority queue. As with heaps these are two kinds of priority queues: max-priority and min-priority queues. We will focus here on how to implement max-priority, which are in turn based on max heaps

A priority queue is a data structure for maintaining a set S of elements ,each with an associated value called a key. A max –priority queue supports the following operations.

INSERT(S,x) insert the element x into the set S.

This operation could be written as $S \leftarrow S \cup \{x\}$.

MAXIMUM(S)returns the elements of S with the largest key.

EXTRACT-MAX(S)removes and returns the elements of S with the largest key.

INCREASE-KEY(S,x,k)increase the value of element x's key to new value k, which is assumed to be at least as x's current key value.

One application of max-priority queues is to schedule jobs on a shared computer. The max-priority queue keeps track of th jobs to be performed and their relative priorities. When a jobs is finished or interrupted, the highest-priority job is selected from those pending using EXTRACT-MAX.A new job can be added to the queue at any time using INSERT.

Alternatively, a min –priority queue supports the operations INSERT, MINIMUM, EXTRACT-MIN, and DECREASE-KEY. A min-priority queue can be used in an event-driven simulator. The items in the queue are events to be simulated, each with an associated time of occurrence that serves as its key. The events must be simulated in the future. The simulation program uses EXTRACT-MIN at each step to choose the next event to simulate. As new events are produced, they are inserted into the min-priority queue using INSERT. We shall see other uses for min-priority queues, highlighting the DECREASE-KEY operation.

Not surprisingly, we can use a heap to implement a priority queue. In a given application, such as job scheduling or event-driven simulation, elements of a priority queue correspond to objects in the application. It is often necessary to determine which application object corresponds to a given priority-queue element, and vice-versa. When a heap is used to implement a priority queue, therefore, we often need to store a handle to the corresponding application object in each heap element. The exact makeup of the handle (i.e., a pointer, an integer, etc) depends upon the application. Similarly, we need to store a handle to the corresponding heap element in each application object. Here the handle would typically be an array index. Because heap elements change locations with in the array during heap operations, an actual implementation, upon relocating a heap element, would also have to update the array index in the corresponding application object. Because the details of accessing application object depend heavily on the application and its implementation, we shall not pursue them here, other noting that in practice, these handles do need to be correctly maintained.

Now we discuss how to implement the operations of a max-priority queue. The procedure HEAP-MAXIMUM implements the MAXIMUM operation in $\Theta(1)$ time.

HEAP-MAXIMUM(A)

return A[1]

The procedure HEAP-EXTRACT-MIX implements the EXTRACT-MAX operation. It is similar to the for loop body (lines 3-5) of the HEAPSORT procedure.

```
HEAP-EXTRACT-MAX(A)
if heap-size[A] <1
then error " heap underflow "
max←A[1]
A[1]← A[heap-size[A]]
heap-size[A]←heap-size[A] –1
MAX-HEAPIFY(a,1)
return max
```

The running time of HEAP-EXTRACT-MAX is O(lg n), since it performs only a conatant amount of work on top of O(lg n) time for MAX-HEAPIFY.

The procedure HEAP-INCREASE-KEY implements the INCREASE-KEY operation. The priority-queue element whose key is to be increased is identified by an index i into the array. The procedure first updates the key of element A[i] to its new value. Because then, in a manner reminiscent of the insertion loop of INSERTION-SORT, traverses a path from this node toward the root to find a proper place for the newly increased Key. During the traversal, it repeatedly compares an element to its parent, exchanging their keys and continuing if the element's key is larger, and terminating if the element's key is smaller, since the max-heap property now holds.

HEAP-INCREASE-KEY(A,i,key)

```
if key < A[i]
then error "new key is smaller then current key"
A[i] ← key
while i > 1 and A[PARENT(i)] <A[i]
do exchange A[i] ↔ A[PARENT(i)]
i ← PARENT(i)
```

Figure shows an example of an a HEAP-INCREAES –KEY operation. The running time of HEAP-INCREAES –KEY on an n-element heap is O(lg n), since the path traced from the node updated in line 3 to the root length O(lg n).

The procedure MAX-HEAP-INSERT implements the INSERT operation. It takes as an input the key to the new element to be inserted into max-heap A. the procedure first expends the max-heap by adding to the tree a new leaf whose key is –∞. Then it calls HEAP-INCREASE-KEY to set the key of this new node to its correct value and maintain the max-heap property.

MAX-HEAP-INSERT (A,key)

```
heap-size[A] ← heap-size{A] +1
A[heap-size[A]] ← –∞
HEAP-INCREASE-KEY (A,heap-size[A],key)
```

The running time of MAX-HEAP-INSERT on an n-element heap is O(lg n).

In summary, a heap can support any priority-queue operation on a set size n in O(lg n) time.

SUMMARY

Sort method	Stable	Space	Running times	
			Average	Worst
Bubblesort	Yes	1	n^2	n^2
Bucket sort	Yes	n	n	n
Comparison counting	Yes	n	n^2	n^2
Distribution counting	Yes	$n + m$	$n + m$	$n + m$
Heapsort	No	1	$n\lg n$	$n\lg n$
Mergesort	Yes	n	$n\lg n$	$n\lg n$
Quicksort	No	1	$n^{1.25}$	$n^{1.5}$
Shell's sort	No	1	$n^{1.25}$	$n^{1.5}$
Straight insertion	Yes	1	n^2	n^2
Straight selection	Yes	1	n^2	n^2
Radix sort	Yes	1	$d(n + m)$	$d(n + m)$

REVIEW QUESTIONS

1. What is the purpose of studying sorting algorithms?
2. What are the applications of a heap?
3. Explain the following sorting algorithms in details:
   (a) Quick
   (b) Insertion
   (c) Heap
   (d) Selection
   (e) Merge.

UNIT 2

ADVANCE DATA STRUCTURES

B-TREES: BALANCED TREES

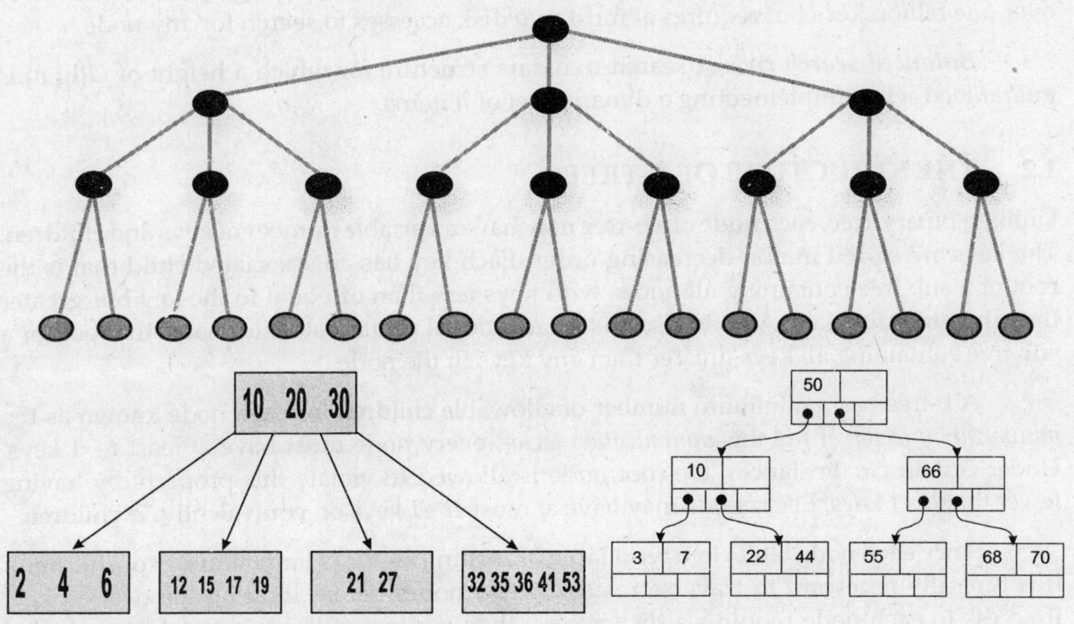

1.1 INTRODUCTION

Tree structures support various basic dynamic set operations including *Search*, *Predecessor*, *Successor*, *Minimum*, *Maximum*, *Insert*, and *Delete* in time proportional to the height of the tree. Ideally, a tree will be balanced and the height will be *log n* where *n* is the number of nodes in the tree. To ensure that the height of the tree is as small as possible and therefore provide the best running time, a balanced tree structure like a red-black tree, AVL tree, or b-tree must be used.

When working with large sets of data, it is often not possible or desirable to maintain the entire structure in primary storage (RAM). Instead, a relatively small portion of the data structure is maintained in primary storage, and additional data is read from secondary storage as needed. Unfortunately, a magnetic disk, the most common form of secondary storage, is significantly slower than random access memory (RAM). In fact, the system often spends more time retrieving data than actually processing data.

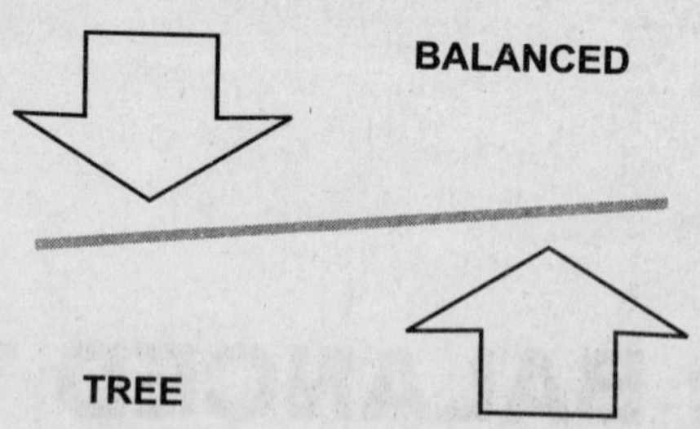

B-trees are balanced trees that are optimized for situations when part or the entire tree must be maintained in secondary storage such as a magnetic disk. Since disk accesses are expensive (time consuming) operations, a b-tree tries to minimize the number of disk accesses. For example, a b-tree with a height of 2 and a branching factor of 1001 can store over one billion keys but requires at most two disk accesses to search for any node .

Balanced search tree: A search-tree data structure for which a height of $O(\lg n)$ is guaranteed when implementing a dynamic set of n items.

1.2 THE STRUCTURE OF B-TREES

Unlike a binary-tree, each node of a b-tree may have a variable number of keys and children. The keys are stored in non-decreasing order. Each key has an associated child that is the root of a sub tree containing all nodes with keys less than or equal to the key but greater than the preceding key. A node also has an additional rightmost child that is the root for a sub tree containing all keys greater than any keys in the node.

A b-tree has a minimum number of allowable children for each node known as the *minimization factor*. If t is this *minimization factor*, every node must have at least $t - 1$ keys. Under certain circumstances, the root node is allowed to violate this property by having fewer than $t - 1$ keys. Every node may have at most $2t - 1$ keys or, equivalently, $2t$ children.

Since each node tends to have a large branching factor (a large number of children), it is typically necessary to traverse relatively few nodes before locating the desired key. If access to each node requires a disk access, then a b-tree will minimize the number of disk accesses required. The minimization factor is usually chosen so that the total size of each node corresponds to a multiple of the block size of the underlying storage device. This choice simplifies and optimizes disk access. Consequently, a b-tree is an ideal data structure for situations where all data cannot reside in primary storage and accesses to secondary storage are comparatively expensive (or time consuming).

Height of B-Trees

For n greater than or equal to one, the height of an n-key b-tree T of height h with a minimum degree t greater than or equal to 2,

$$h \leq \log_t \frac{n=1}{2}$$

The worst case height is $O(\log n)$. Since the "branchiness" of a b-tree can be large compared to many other balanced tree structures, the base of the logarithm tends to be large; therefore, the number of nodes visited during a search tends to be smaller than required by other tree structures. Although this does not affect the asymptotic worst case height, b-trees tend to have smaller heights than other trees with the same asymptotic height.

1.3 OPERATIONS ON B-TREES

The algorithms for the *search, create,* and *insert* operations are shown below. Note that these algorithms are single pass; in other words, they do not traverse back up the tree. Since b-trees strive to minimize disk accesses and the nodes are usually stored on disk, this single-pass approach will reduce the number of node visits and thus the number of disk accesses. Simpler double-pass approaches that move back up the tree to fix violations are possible.

Since all nodes are assumed to be stored in secondary storage (disk) rather than primary storage (memory), all references to a given node be be preceeded by a read operation denoted by *Disk-Read*. Similarly, once a node is modified and it is no longer needed, it must be written out to secondary storage with a write operation denoted by *Disk-Write*. The algorithms below assume that all nodes referenced in parameters have already had a corresponding *Disk-Read* operation. New nodes are created and assigned storage with the *Allocate-Node* call. The implementation details of the *Disk-Read, Disk-Write,* and *Allocate-Node* functions are operating system and implementation dependent.

B-Tree-Search(x, k)

```
i <- 1
while i <= n[x] and k > key_i[x]
        do i <- i + 1
if i <= n[x] and k = key_i[x]
        then return (x, i)
if leaf[x]
        then return NIL
            else Disk-Read(c_i[x])
                return B-Tree-Search(c_i[x], k)
```

The search operation on a b-tree is analogous to a search on a binary tree. Instead of choosing between a left and a right child as in a binary tree, a b-tree search must make an n-way choice. The correct child is chosen by performing a linear search of the values in the node. After finding the value greater than or equal to the desired value, the child pointer to the immediate left of that value is followed. If all values are less than the desired value, the rightmost child pointer is followed. Of course, the search can be terminated as soon as the desired node is found. Since the running time of the search operation depends upon the height of the tree, *B-Tree-Search* is $O(\log_t n)$.

```
B-Tree-Create(T)
x <- Allocate-Node()
leaf[x] <- TRUE
```

```
n[x] <- 0
Disk-Write(x)
root[T] <- x
```

The *B-Tree-Create* operation creates an empty b-tree by allocating a new root node that has no keys and is a leaf node. Only the root node is permitted to have these properties; all other nodes must meet the criteria outlined previously. The *B-Tree-Create* operation runs in time *O(1)*.

```
B-Tree-Split-Child(x, i, y)
z <- Allocate-Node()
leaf[z] <- leaf[y]
n[z] <- t - 1
for j <- 1 to t - 1
    do key_j[z] <- key_j+t[y]
if not leaf[y]
    then for j <- 1 to t
        do c_j[z] <- c_j+t[y]
n[y] <- t - 1
for j <- n[x] + 1 downto i + 1
    do c_j+1[x] <- c_j[x]
c_i+1 <- z
for j <- n[x] downto i
    do key_j+1[x] <- key_j[x]
key_i[x] <- key_t[y]
n[x] <- n[x] + 1
Disk-Write(y)
Disk-Write(z)
Disk-Write(x)
```

If is node becomes "too full," it is necessary to perform a split operation. The split operation moves the median key of node x into its parent y where x is the ith child of y. A new node, z, is allocated, and all keys in x right of the median key are moved to z. The keys left of the median key remain in the original node x. The new node, z, becomes the child immediately to the right of the median key that was moved to the parent y, and the original node, x, becomes the child immediately to the left of the median key that was moved into the parent y.

The split operation transforms a full node with $2t - 1$ keys into two nodes with $t - 1$ keys each. Note that one key is moved into the parent node. The *B-Tree-Split-Child* algorithm will run in time $O(t)$ where t is constant.

```
B-Tree-Insert(T, k)
r <- root[T]
if n[r] = 2t - 1
```

```
    then s <- Allocate-Node()
        root[T] <- s
    leaf[s] <- FALSE
    n[s] <- 0
    c1 <- r
    B-Tree-Split-Child(s, 1, r)
    B-Tree-Insert-Nonfull(s, k)
    else B-Tree-Insert-Nonfull(r, k)
```

B-Tree-Insert-Nonfull(x, k)

```
i <- n[x]
if leaf[x]
    then while i >= 1 and k < keyi[x]
            do keyi+1[x] <- keyi[x]
        i <- i - 1
        keyi+1[x] <- k
    n[x] <- n[x] + 1
    Disk-Write(x)
        else while i >= and k < keyi[x]
            do i <- i - 1
    i <- i + 1
    Disk-Read(ci[x])
    if n[ci[x]] = 2t - 1
        then B-Tree-Split-Child(x, i, ci[x])
            if k > keyi[x]
                then i <- i + 1
```

B-Tree-Insert-Nonfull(c_i[x], k)

To perform an insertion on a b-tree, the appropriate node for the key must be located using an algorithm similiar to *B-Tree-Search.* Next, the key must be inserted into the node. If the node is not full prior to the insertion, no special action is required; however, if the node is full, the node must be split to make room for the new key. Since splitting the node results in moving one key to the parent node, the parent node must not be full or another split operation is required. This process may repeat all the way up to the root and may require splitting the root node. This approach requires two passes. The first pass locates the node where the key should be inserted; the second pass performs any required splits on the ancestor nodes.

Since each access to a node may correspond to a costly disk access, it is desirable to avoid the second pass by ensuring that the parent node is never full. To accomplish this, the presented algorithm splits any full nodes encountered while descending the tree. Although this approach may result in unecessary split operations, it guarantees that the parent never needs to be split and eliminates the need for a second pass up the tree. Since a split runs in linear time, it has little effect on the $O(t \log_t n)$ running time of *B-Tree-Insert*.

Splitting the root node is handled as a special case since a new root must be created to contain the median key of the old root. Observe that a b-tree will grow from the top.

B-Tree-Delete

Deletion of a key from a b-tree is possible; however, special care must be taken to ensure that the properties of a b-tree are maintained. Several cases must be considered. If the deletion reduces the number of keys in a node below the minimum degree of the tree, this violation must be corrected by combining several nodes and possibly reducing the height of the tree. If the key has children, the children must be rearranged.

Example of B-Tree

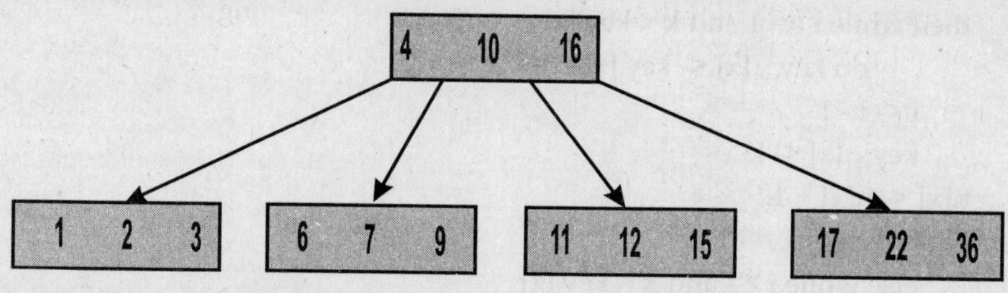

Searching a B-Tree for Key 21

B-Tree: Minimization Factor t=3, Minimum Degree=2, Maximum Degree = 5

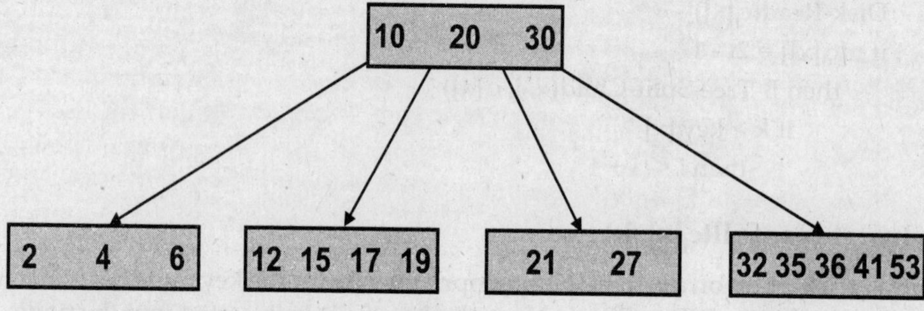

Inserting Key 33 into a B-Tree (w/ Split)

1.4 VARIOUS APPLICATIONS OF B-TREES

Databases

A database is a collection of data organized in a fashion that facilitates updating, retrieving, and managing the data. The data can consist of anything, including, but not limited to names, addresses, pictures, and numbers. Databases are commonplace and are used everyday. For example, an airline reservation system might maintain a database of available flights, customers, and tickets issued. A teacher might maintain a database of student names and grades.

Because computers excel at quickly and accurately manipulating, storing, and retrieving data, databases are often maintained electronically using a *database management system*. Database management systems are essential components of many everyday business operations. Database products like *Microsoft SQL Server*, *Sybase Adaptive Server*, *IBM DB2*, and *Oracle* serve as a foundation for accounting systems, inventory systems, medical recordkeeping sytems, airline reservation systems, and countless other important aspects of modern businesses.

It is not uncommon for a database to contain millions of records requiring many gigabytes of storage. For examples, TELSTRA, an Australian telecommunications company, maintains a customer billing database with 51 billion rows (yes, billion) and 4.2 terabytes of data. In order for a database to be useful and usable, it must support the desired operations, such as retrieval and storage, quickly. Because databases cannot typically be maintained entirely in memory, b-trees are often used to index the data and to provide fast access. For example, searching an unindexed and unsorted database containing n key values will have a worst case running time of $O(n)$; if the same data is indexed with a b-tree, the same search operation will run in $O(\log n)$. To perform a search for a single key on a set of one million keys (1,000,000), a linear search will require at most 1,000,000 comparisons. If the same data is indexed with a b-tree of minimum degree 10, 114 comparisons will be required in the worst case. Clearly, indexing large amounts of data can significantly improve search performance. Although other balanced tree structures can be used, a b-tree also optimizes costly disk accesses that are of concern when dealing with large data sets.

Concurrent Access to B-Trees

Databases typically run in multiuser environments where many users can concurrently perform operations on the database. Unfortunately, this common scenario introduces complications. For example, imagine a database storing bank account balances. Now assume that someone attempts to withdraw $40 from an account containing $60. First, the current balance is checked to ensure sufficent funds. After funds are disbursed, the balance of the account is reduced. This approach works flawlessly until concurrent transactions are considered. Suppose that another person simultaneously attempts to withdraw $30 from the same account. At the same time the account balance is checked by the first person, the account balance is also retrieved for the second person. Since neither person is requesting more funds than are currently available, both requests are satisfied for a total of $70. After the first person's transaction, $20 should remain ($60 - $40), so the new balance is recorded as $20. Next, the account balance after the second person's transaction, $30 ($60 - $30), is recorded overwriting the $20 balance. Unfortunately, $70 have been disbursed, but the account balance has only been decreased by $30. Clearly, this behavior is undesirable, and special precautions must be taken.

A b-tree suffers from similar problems in a multiuser environment. If two or more processes are manipulating the same tree, it is possible for the tree to become corrupt and result in data loss or errors.

The simplest solution is to serialize access to the data structure. In other words, if another process is using the tree, all other processes must wait. Although this is feasible in many cases, it can place an unecessary and costly limit on performance because many operations actually can be performed concurrently without risk. *Locking*, introduced by Gray and refined by many others, provides a mechanism for controlling concurrent operations on data structures in order to prevent undesirable side effects and to ensure consistency.

B-tree algorithms

A B-tree is a data structure that maintains an ordered set of data and allows efficient operations to find, delete, insert, and browse the data. In this discussion, each piece of data stored in a B-tree will be called a "key", because each key is unique and can occur in the B-tree in only one location.

A B-tree consists of "node" records containing the keys, and pointers that link the nodes of the B-tree together.

Every B-tree is of some "order n", meaning nodes contain from n to 2n keys, and nodes are thereby always at least half full of keys. Keys are kept in sorted order within each node. A corresponding list of pointers are effectively interspersed between keys to indicate where to search for a key if it isn't in the current node. A node containing k keys always also contains k+1 pointers.

For example, here is a portion of a B-tree with order 2 (nodes have at least 2 keys and 3 pointers). Nodes are delimited with [square brackets]. The keys are city names, and are kept sorted in each node. On either side of every key are pointers linking the key to subsequent nodes:

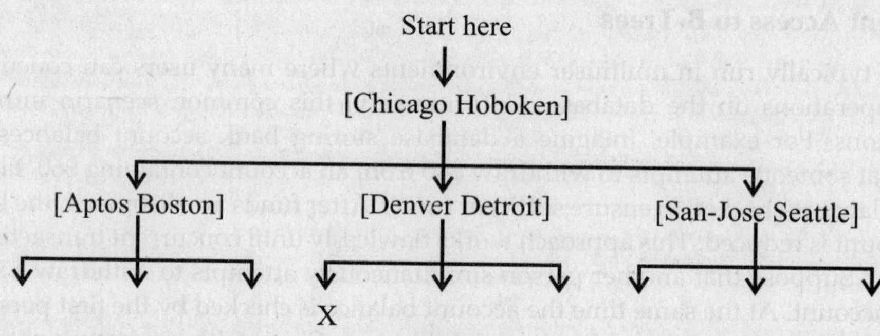

To find the key "Dallas", we begin searching at the top "root" node. "Dallas" is not in the node but sorts between "Chicago" and "Hoboken", so we follow the middle pointer to the next node. Again, "Dallas" is not in the node but sorts before "Denver", so we follow that node's first pointer down to the next node (marked with an "X"). Eventually, we will either locate the key, or encounter a "leaf" node at the bottom level of the B-tree with no pointers to any lower nodes and without the key we want, indicating the key is nowhere in the B-tree.

Below is another fragment of an order 1 B-tree (nodes have at least 1 key and 2 pointers). Searching for the key "Chicago" begins at "Marin", follows the first pointer to "Aptos" (since Chicago sorts before Marin), then follows that node's second pointer down to the next level (since Chicago sorts after Aptos), as marked with an "X".

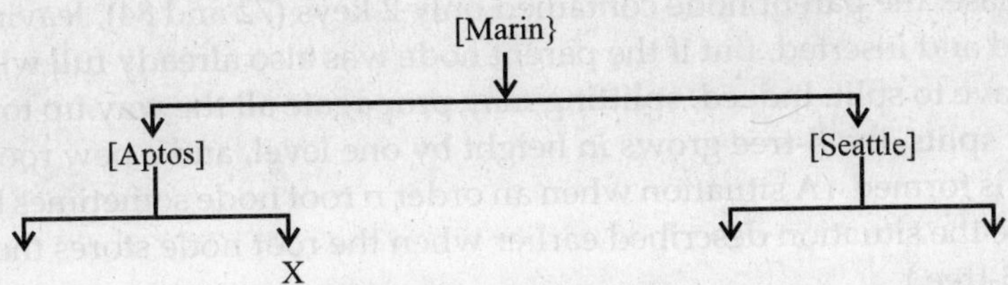

Searching a B-tree for a key always begins at the root node and follows pointers from node to node until either the key is located or the search fails because a leaf node is reached and there are no more pointers to follow.

B-trees grow when new keys are inserted. Since the root node initially begins with just one key, the root node is a special exception and the only node allowed to have less than n keys in an order n B-tree.

Here is an order 2 B-tree with integer keys. Except for the special root node, order 2 requires every node to have from 2 to 4 keys and 3 to 5 pointers. Empty slots are marked with " . ", showing where future keys have not yet been stored in the nodes:

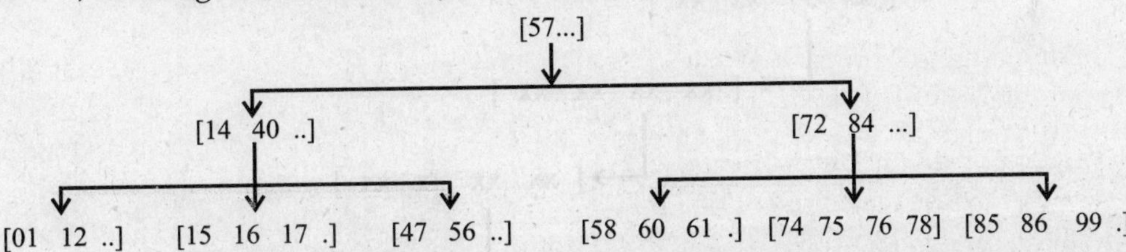

To insert the key "59", we first simply search for that key. If 59 is found, the key is already in the tree and the insertion is superfluous. Otherwise, we must end up at a leaf node at the bottom level of the tree where 59 would be stored. In the above case, the leaf node contains 58, 60, 61, and room for a fourth key, so 59 is simply inserted in the leaf node in sorted order:

[58 59 60 61]

Now we'll insert the key "77". The initial search leads us to the leaf node where 77 would be inserted, but the node is already full with 4 keys: 74, 75, 76, and 78. Adding another key would violate the rule that order 2 B-trees can't have more than 4 keys. Because of this "overflow" condition, the leaf node is split into two leaf nodes. The leftmost 2 keys are put in the left node, the rightmost 2 keys are put in the right node, and the middle key is "promoted" by inserting it into the parent node above the leaf. Here, inserting 77 causes the 74-75-76-78 node to be split into two nodes, and 76 is moved up to the parent node that contained 72 and 84:

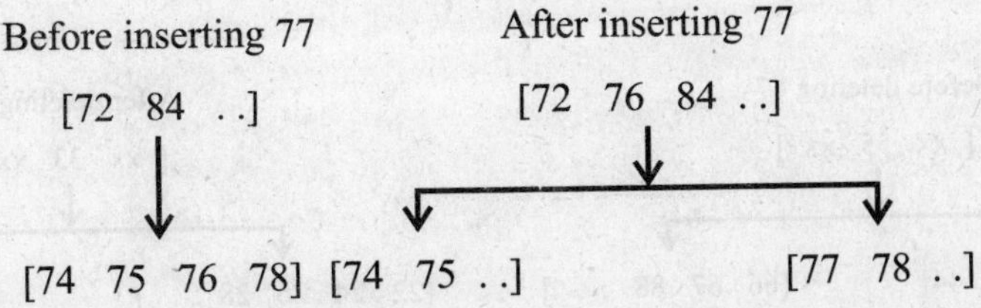

In this case, the parent node contained only 2 keys (72 and 84), leaving room for 76 to be promoted and inserted. But if the parent node was also already full with 4 keys, then it too would have to split. Indeed, splitting may propagate all the way up to the root node. When the root splits, the B-tree grows in height by one level, and a new root with a single promoted key is formed. (A situation when an order n root node sometimes has fewer than n keys, just like the situation described earlier when the root node stores the very first key placed in the B-tree.)

B-trees shrink when keys are deleted. To delete a key, first perform the usual search operation to locate the node containing the key. (If the key isn't found, it isn't in the tree and can't be deleted.)

If the found key is not in a leaf, move it to a leaf by swapping the key with the logical "next" key. In a B-tree, the "next" key is always the first key in the leftmost leaf of the right subtree.

For example, in this B-tree we want to delete "37", which is not in a leaf. "xx" indicates key values that don't matter:

```
[ xx 37 xx xx ]
      |
      └──> [ xx xx xx xx ]
                 |
                 └──> [ xx xx xx xx ]
                           |
                           └──> [ 41 43 . . ]
```

We follow the pointer immediately to the right of 37 to find 37's right subtree, then follow the leftmost pointers in each subnode until we reach a leaf. The first key in the leaf is "41", the logical "next" key after 37 in the list of all keys in the tree. By swapping 37 and 41, we can move 37 to a leaf node to set up a deletion without violating the key order or pointer order of the overall B-tree.

Once the key we want is in a leaf, we can delete it. If at least n keys remain in the node, we're done, otherwise it is an "underflow", since every node (except the root) must have at least n keys.

If a node underflows, we may be able to "redistribute" keys by borrowing some from a neighboring node. For example, in the order 3 B-tree below, the key 67 is being deleted, which causes a node to underflow since it only has keys 66 and 88 left. So keys from the neighbor on the left are "shifted through" the parent node and redistributed so both leaf nodes end up with 4 keys:

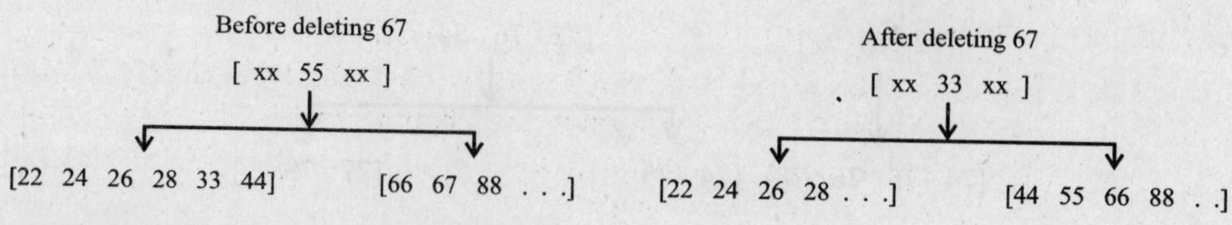

But if the underflow node and the neighbor node have less than 2n keys to redistribute, the two nodes will have to be combined. For example, here key 52 is being deleted from the B-tree below, causing an underflow, and the neighbor node can't afford to give up any keys for redistribution. So one node is discarded, and the parent key moves down with the other keys to fill up a single node:

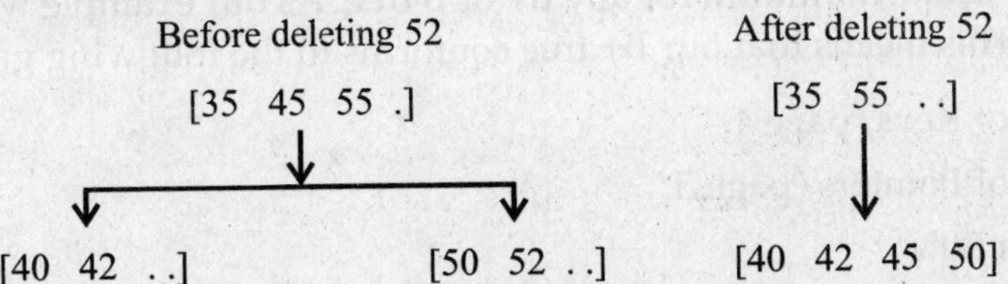

In the above case, moving the key 45 out of the parent node left two keys (35 and 55) remaining. But if the parent node only had n keys to begin with, then the parent node also would underflow when the parent key was moved down to combine with the leaf key. Indeed, underflow and the combining of nodes may propagate all the way up to the root node. When the root underflows, the B-tree shrinks in height by one level, and the nodes under the old root combine to form a new root.

The payoff of the B-tree insert and delete rules are that B-trees are always "balanced". Searching an unbalanced tree may require traversing an arbitrary and unpredictable number of nodes and pointers.

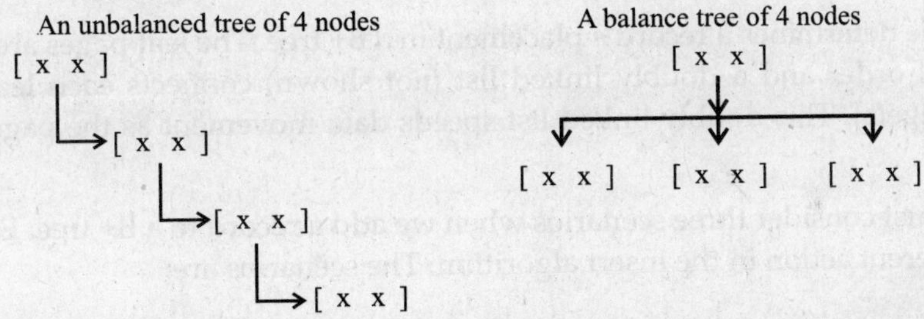

Searching a balanced tree means that all leaves are at the same depth. There is no runaway pointer overhead. Indeed, even very large B-trees can guarantee only a small number of nodes must be retrieved to find a given key. For example, a B-tree of 10,000,000 keys with 50 keys per node never needs to retrieve more than 4 nodes to find any key.

1.5 B+ TREES

B Trees. B Trees are multi-way trees. That is each node contains a set of keys and pointers. A B Tree with four keys and five pointers represents the minimum size of a B Tree node. A B Tree contains only data pages.

B Trees are dynamic. That is, the height of the tree grows and contracts as records are added and deleted.

B+ Trees A B+ Tree combines features of ISAM and B Trees. It contains index pages and data pages. The data pages always appear as leaf nodes in the tree. The root node and intermediate nodes are always index pages. These features are similar to ISAM. Unlike ISAM, overflow pages are not used in B+ trees.

The index pages in a B+ tree are constructed through the process of inserting and deleting records. Thus, B+ trees grow and contract like their B Tree counterparts. The contents and the number of index pages reflects this growth and shrinkage.

B+ Trees and B Trees use a "fill factor" to control the growth and the shrinkage. A 50% fill factor would be the minimum for any B+ or B tree. As our example we use the smallest page structure. This means that our B+ tree conforms to the following guidelines.

Number of Keys/page 4

Number of Pointers/page 5

Fill Factor 50%

Minimum Keys in each page 2

As this table indicates each page must have a minimum of two keys. The root page may violate this rule.

The following table shows a B+ tree. As the example illustrates this tree does not have a full index page. (We have room for one more key and pointer in the root page.) In addition, one of the data pages contains empty slots.

B+ Tree with four keys

Adding Records to a B+ Tree

The key value determines a record's placement in a B+ tree. The leaf pages are maintained in sequential order and a doubly linked list (not shown) connects each leaf page with its sibling page(s). This doubly linked list speeds data movement as the pages grow and contract.

We must consider three scenarios when we add a record to a B+ tree. Each scenario causes a different action in the insert algorithm. The scenarios are:

The insert algorithm for B+ Trees

Leaf Page
Full
Index Page
FULL Action

NO NO Place the record in sorted position in the appropriate leaf page

YES NO

1. Split the leaf page
2. Place Middle Key in the index page in sorted order.
3. Left leaf page contains records with keys below the middle key.

Right leaf page contains records with keys equal to or greater than the middle key.

YES YES

1. Split the leaf page.
2. Records with keys < middle key go to the left leaf page.
3. Records with keys >= middle key go to the right leaf page.
4. Split the index page.
5. Keys < middle key go to the left index page.
6. Keys > middle key go to the right index page.

   The middle key goes to the next (higher level) index.

   IF the next level index page is full, continue splitting the index pages.

Illustrations of the insert algorithm

The following examples illustrate each of the **insert** scenarios. We begin with the simplest scenario:

(a) inserting a record into a leaf page that is not full. Since only the leaf node containing 25 and 30 contains

(b) expansion room, we're going to insert a record with a key value of 28 into the B+ tree.

Add Record with Key 28

Adding a record when the leaf page is full but the index page is not

Next, we're going to insert a record with a key value of 70 into our B+ tree. This record should go in the leaf page containing 50, 55, 60, and 65. Unfortunately this page is full. This means that we must split the page as follows:

Left Leaf Page Right Leaf Page

50 55 60 65 70

The middle key of 60 is placed in the index page between 50 and 75.

The following table shows the B+ tree after the addition of 70.

Add Record with Key 70

Adding a record when both the leaf page and the index page are full

As our last example, we're going to add a record containing a key value of 95 to our B+ tree. This record belongs in the page containing 75, 80, 85, and 90. Since this page is full we split it into two pages:

Left Leaf Page Right Leaf Page

75 80 85 90 95

The middle key, 85, rises to the index page. Unfortunately, the index page is also full, so we split the index page:

Left Index Page Right Index Page New Index Page

25 50 75 85 60

The following table illustrates the addition of the record containing 95 to the B+ tree.

Add Record with Key 95

Rotation

B+ trees can incorporate rotation to reduce the number of page splits. A rotation occurs when a leaf page is full, but one of its sibling pages is not full. Rather than splitting the leaf page, we move a record to its sibling, adjusting the indices as necessary. Typically, the left sibling is checked first (if it exists) and then the right sibling.

As an example, consider the B+ tree before the addition of the record containing a key of 70. As previously stated this record belongs in the leaf node containing 50 55 60 65. Notice that this node is full, but its left sibling is not.

Add Record with Key 28

Using rotation we shift the record with the lowest key to its sibling. Since this key appeared in the index page we also modify the index page. The new B+ tree appears in the following table.

Illustration of Rotation

Deleting Keys from a B+ tree

We must consider three scenarios when we delete a record from a B+ tree. Each scenario causes a different action in the delete algorithm. The scenarios are:

The delete algorithm for B+ Trees

Leaf Page
Below Fill
Factor
Index Page
Below Fill
Factor
Action

NO NO

Delete the record from the leaf page. Arrange keys in ascending order to fill void. If the key of the deleted record appears in the index page, use the next key to replace it.

YES NO Combine the leaf page and its sibling. Change the index page to reflect the change.

YES YES

1. Combine the leaf page and its sibling.
2. Adjust the index page to reflect the change.

Combine the index page with its sibling.

Continue combining index pages until you reach a page with the correct fill factor or you reach the root page.

As our example, we consider the B+ tree after we added 95 as a key. As a refresher this tree is printed in the following table.

Add Record with Key 95

Delete 70 from the B+ Tree

We begin by deleting the record with key 70 from the B+ tree. This record is in a leaf page containing 60, 65 and 70. This page will contain 2 records after the deletion. Since our fill factor is 50% or (2 records) we simply delete 70 from the leaf node. The following table shows the B+ tree after the deletion.

Delete Record with Key 70

Delete 25 from the B+ tree

Next, we delete the record containing 25 from the B+ tree. This record is found in the leaf node containing 25, 28, and 30. The fill factor will be 50% after the deletion; however, 25 appears in the index page. Thus, when we delete 25 we must replace it with 28 in the index page.

The following table shows the B+ tree after this deletion.

Delete Record with Key 25

Delete 60 from the B+ tree

As our last example, we're going to delete 60 from the B+ tree. This deletion is interesting for several resasons:

The leaf page containing 60 (60 65) will be below the fill factor after the deletion. Thus, we must combine leaf pages.

1. With recombined pages, the index page will be reduced by one key. Hence, it will also fall below the fill factor. Thus, we must combine index pages.
2. Sixty appears as the only key in the root index page. Obviously, it will be removed with the deletion.

The following table shows the B+ tree after the deletion of 60. Notice that the tree contains a single index page.

Delete Record with Key 60

1.6 B-TREES: PERFECTLY HEIGHT-BALANCED M-WAY SEARCH TREES

A B-tree is an M-way search tree with two special properties:

1. It is perfectly balanced: every leaf node is at the same depth.
2. Every node, except perhaps the root, is at least half-full, i.e. contains M/2 or more values (of course, it cannot contain more than M-1 values). The root may have any number of values (1 to M-1).

The 3-way search tree above is clearly *not* a B-tree. Here is a 3-way B-tree containing the same values:

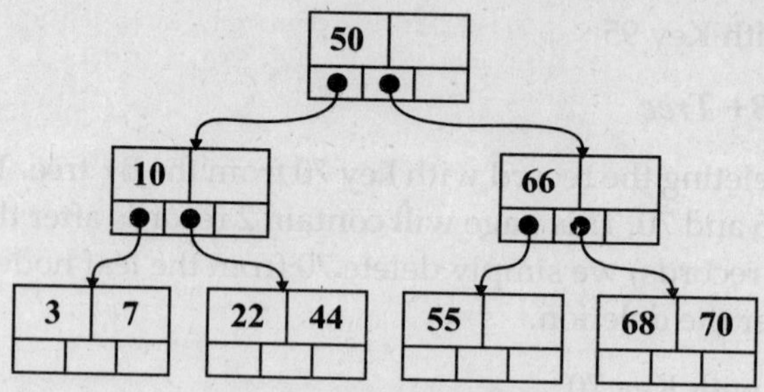

And here is a 5-way B-tree (each node other than the root must contain between 2 and 4 values):

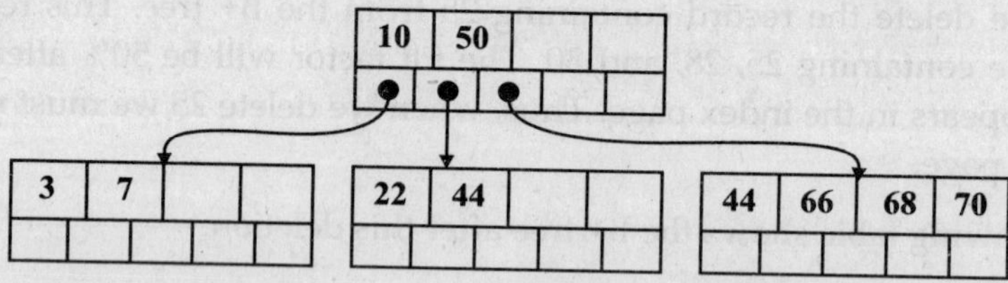

In the descriptions of our algorithms, we assume that M is odd; therefore each node (other than the root) must contains between (M-1)/2 and M-1 values.

- Insertion Into a B-Tree
- Deleting a Value From a B-Tree

1.6.1. Insertion Into a B-Tree

To insert value X into a B-tree, there are 3 steps:

1. Using the SEARCH procedure for M-way trees (described above) find the leaf node to which X should be added.
2. Add X to this node in the appropriate place among the values already there. Being a leaf node there are no subtrees to worry about.
3. If there are M-1 or fewer values in the node after adding X, then we are finished.

   If there are M nodes after adding X, we say the node has *overflowed*. To repair this, we split the node into three parts:

   Left:

the first (M-1)/2 values
Middle:
the middle value (position 1+((M-1)/2)
Right:
the last (M-1)/2 values

Notice that Left and Right have just enough values to be made into individual nodes. That's what we do... they become the left and right children of Middle, which we add in the appropriate place in this node's parent.

But what if there is no room in the parent? If it overflows we do the same thing again: split it into Left-Middle-Right, make Left and Right into new nodes and add Middle (with Left and Right as its children) to the node above. We continue doing this until no overflow occurs, or until the root itself overflows. If the root overflows, we split it, as usual, and create a new root node with Middle as its only value and Left and Right as its children (as usual).

For example, let's do a sequence of insertions into this B-tree (M=5, so each node other than the root must contain between 2 and 4 values):

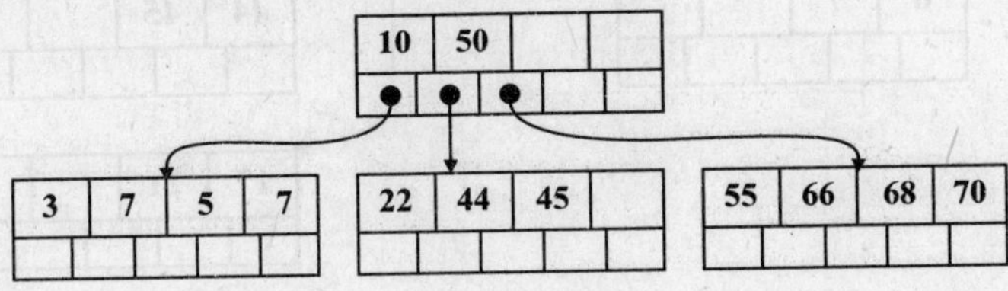

Insert 17: Add it to the middle leaf. No overflow, so we're done.

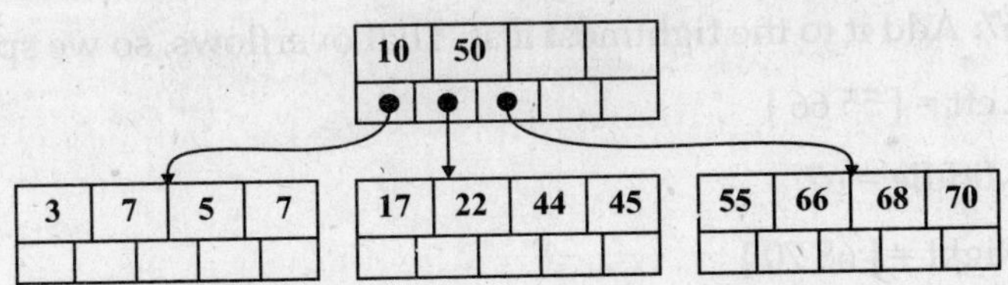

Insert 6: Add it to the leftmost leaf. That overflows, so we split it:

- Left = [2 3]
- Middle = 5
- Right = [6 7]

Left and Right become nodes; Middle is added to the node above with Left and Right as its children.

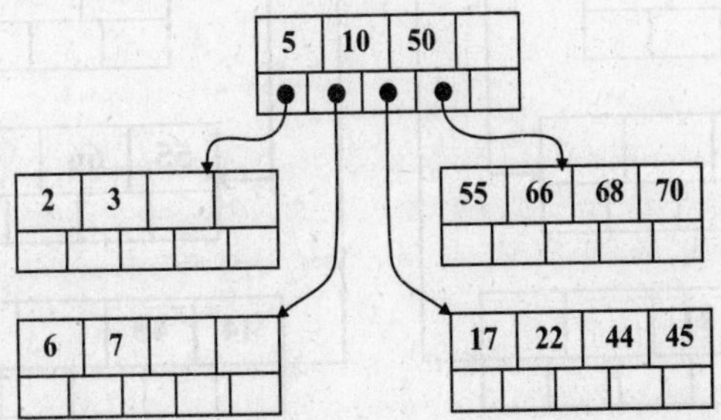

UNIT 2

The node above (the root in this small example) does not overflow, so we are done.

Insert 21: Add it to the middle leaf. That overflows, so we split it:

- left = [17 21]
- Middle = 22
- Right = [44 45]

Left and Right become nodes; Middle is added to the node above with Left and Right as its children.

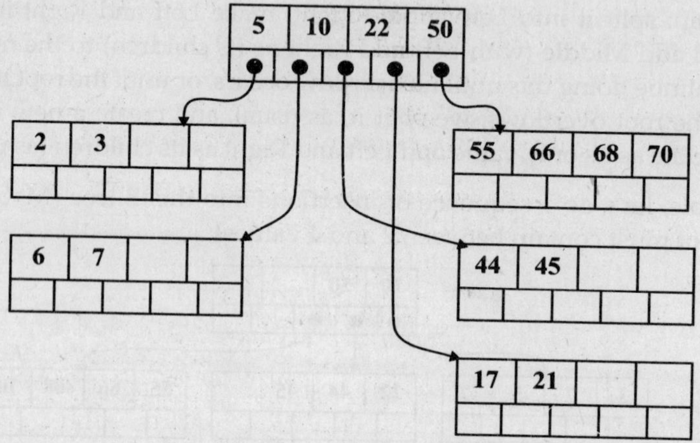

The node above (the root in this small example) does not overflow, so we are done.

Insert 67: Add it to the rightmost leaf. That overflows, so we split it:

- Left = [55 66]
- Middle = 67
- Right = [68 70]

Left and Right become nodes; Middle is added to the node above with Left and Right as its children.

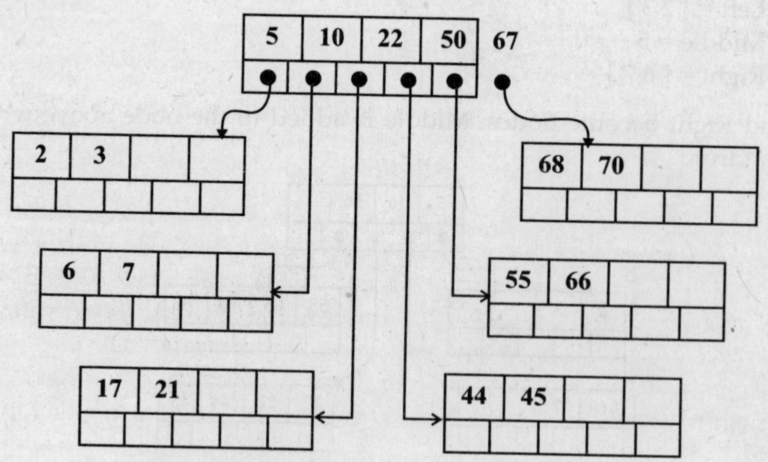

But now the node above does overflow. So it is split in exactly the same manner:

- Left = [5 10] (along with their children)
- Middle = 22
- Right = [50 67] (along with their children)

Left and Right become nodes, the children of Middle. If this were not the root, Middle would be added to the node above and the process repeated. If there is no node above, as in this example, a new root is created with Middle as its only value.

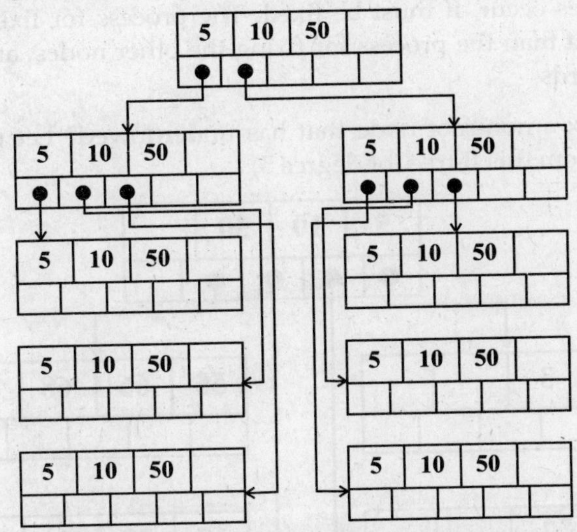

The tree-insertion algorithms we're previously seen add new nodes at the bottom of the tree, and then have to worry about whether doing so creates an imbalance. The B-tree insertion algorithm is just the opposite: it adds new nodes at the *top* of the tree (a new node is allocated only when the root splits). B-trees grow at the root, not at the leaves. Because of this, there is never any doubt that the tree is always perfectly height balanced: when a new node is added, all existing nodes become one level deeper in the tree.

1.6.2. Deleting a Value From a B-Tree

Recall our deletion algorithm for binary search trees: if the value to be deleted is in a node having two subtrees, we would replace the value with the largest value in its left subtree and then delete the node in the left subtree that had contained the largest value (we are guaranteed that *this* node will be easy to delete).

We will use a similar strategy to delete a value from a B-tree. If the value to be deleted does not occur in a leaf, we replace it with the largest value in its left subtree and then proceed to delete that value from the node that originally contained it. For example, if we wished to delete 67 from the above tree, we would find the largest value in 67's left subtree, 66, replace 67 with 66, and then delete the occurrence of 66 in the left subtree. In a B-tree, the largest value in any value's left subtree is guaranteed to be in leaf. Therefore wherever the value to be deleted initially resides, the following deletion algorithm always begins at a leaf.

1. To delete value X from a B-tree, starting at a leaf node, there are 2 steps:
2. Remove X from the current node. Being a leaf node there are no subtrees to worry about.

   Removing X might cause the node containing it to have *too few* values.

   Recall that we require the root to have at least 1 value in it and all other nodes to have at least (M-1)/2 values in them. If the node has too few values, we say it has *underflowed.*

   If underflow does not occur, then we are finished the deletion process. If it does occur, it must be fixed. The process for fixing a root is slightly different than the process for fixing the other nodes, and will be discussed afterwards.

How do we fix a non-root node that has underflowed? Let us take as a specific example, deleting 6 from this B-tree (of degree 5):

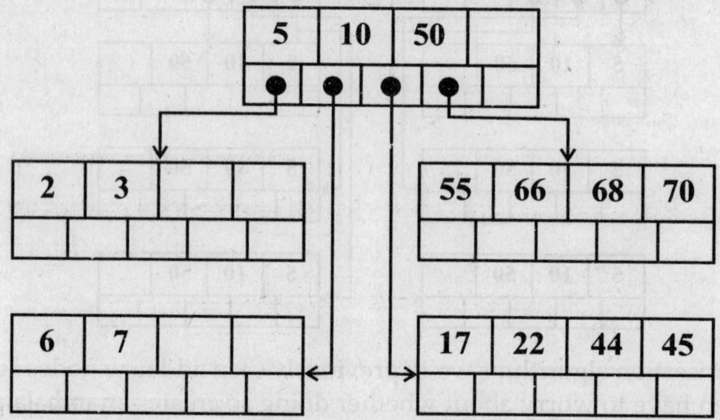

Removing 6 causes the node it is in to underflow, as it now contains just 1 value (7). Our strategy for fixing this is to try to `borrow' values from a neighbouring node. We join together the current node and its more populous neighbour to form a `combined node' - and we must also include in the combined node the value in the parent node that is in between these two nodes.

In this example, we join node [7] with its more populous neighbour [17 22 44 45] and put `10' in between them, to create

[7 10 17 22 44 45]

How many values might there be in this combined node?

- The parent node contributes 1 value.
- The node that underflowed contributes exactly (M-1)/2-1 values.
- The neighbouring node contributes somewhere between (M-1)/2 and (M-1) values.

The treatment of the combined node is different depending on whether the neighbouring contributes exactly (M-1)/2 values or more than this number.

Case 1

Suppose that the neighbouring node contains more than (M-1)/2 values. In this case, the total number of values in the combined node is strictly greater than 1 + ((M-1)/2 – 1) + ((M-1)/2), i.e. it is strictly greater than (M-1). So it must contain M values or more.

We split the combined node into three pieces: Left, Middle, and Right, where Middle is a single value in the very middle of the combined node. Because the combined node has M values or more, Left and Right are guaranteed to have (M-1)/2 values each, and therefore are legitimate nodes. We replace the value we borrowed from the parent with Middle and we use Left and Right as its two children. In this case the parent's size does not change, so we are completely finished.

This is what happens in our example of deleting 6 from the tree above. The combined node [7 10 17 22 44 45] contains more than 5 values, so we split it into:

- Left = [7 10]
- Middle = 17
- Right = [22 44 45]

Then put Middle into the parent node (in the position where the `10' had been) with Left and Right as its children (**there is an error in this figure, it should not contain 6**):

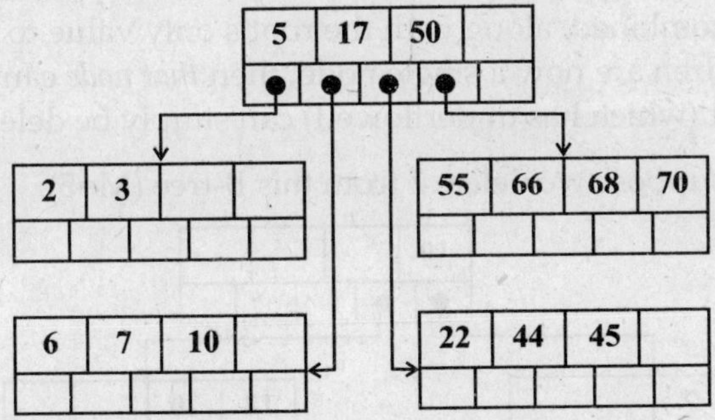

Case 2

Suppose, on the other hand, that the neighbouring node contains exactly (M-1)/2 values. Then the total number of values in the combined node is 1 + ((M-1)/2 - 1) + ((M-1)/2) = (M-1)

In this case the combined node contains the right number of values to be treated as a node. So we make it into a node and remove from the parent node the value that has been incorporated into the new, combined node. As a concrete example of this case, suppose that, in the above tree, we had deleted 3 instead of 6. The node [2 3] underflows when 3 is removed. It would be combined with its more populous neighbour [6 7] and the intervening value from the parent (5) to create the combined node [2 5 6 7]. This contains 4 values, so it can be used without further processing. The result would be:

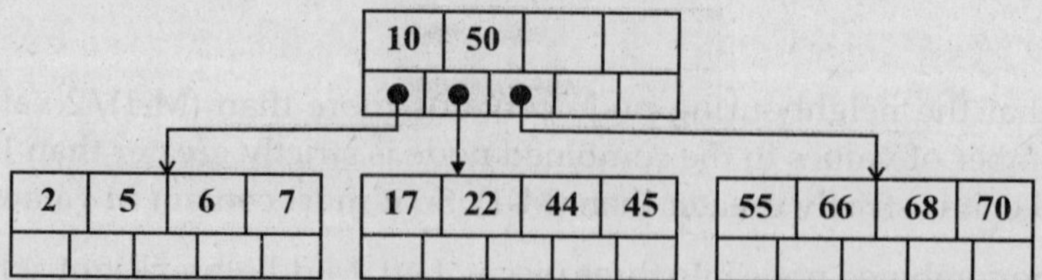

It is very important to note that the parent node now has one fewer value. This might cause *it* to underflow - imagine that 5 had been the *only* value in the parent node. If the parent node underflows, it would be treated in exactly the same way - combined with *its* more populous neighbour etc. The underflow processing repeats at successive levels until no underflow occurs or until the root underflows (the processing for root-underflow is described next).

Now let us consider the root. For the root to underflow, it must have originally contained just one value, which now has been removed. If the root was also a leaf, then there is no problem: in this case the tree has become completely empty.

If the root is not a leaf, it must originally have had two subtrees (because it originally contained one value). How could it possibly underflow?

The deletion process always starts at a leaf and therefore the only way the root could have its value removed is through the Case 2 processing just described: the root's two children have been combined, along with the root's only value to form a single node. But if the root's two children are now a single node, then *that node* can be used as the new root, and the current root (which has underflowed) can simply be deleted.

To illustrate this, suppose we delete 7 from this B-tree (M=5):

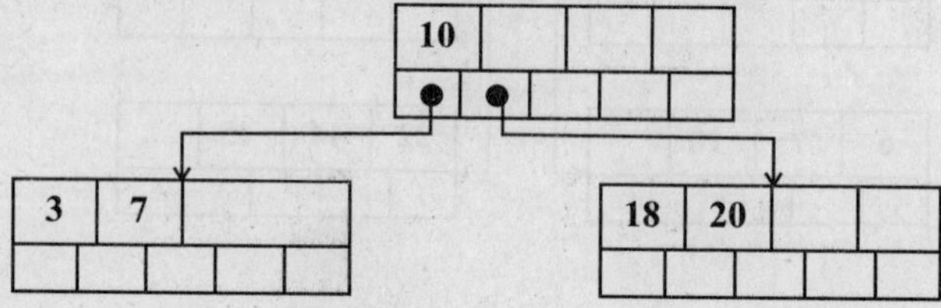

The node [3 7] would underflow, and the combined node [3 10 18 20] would be created. This has 4 values, which is acceptable when M=5. So it would be kept as a node, and `10' would be removed from the parent node - the root. This is the only circumstance in which underflow can occur in a root that is not a leaf. The situation is this:

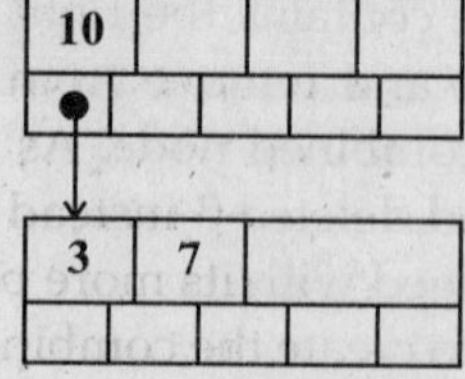

Clearly, the current root node, now empty, can be deleted and its child used as the new root.

REVIEW QUESTIONS

1. What are b-trees? Discuss the structure of b-trees.
2. Explain all the operation s that can be performed on b-trees.
3. Elaborate all the applications of b-trees.
4. Explain b-tree algorithms.
5. What are b+ trees? Explain the operations that can be performed on b+ trees in details.
6. Explain perfectly height-balanced m-way search trees and its algorithms in details.

UNIT 2

CHAPTER 1

BINARY SEARCH TREES

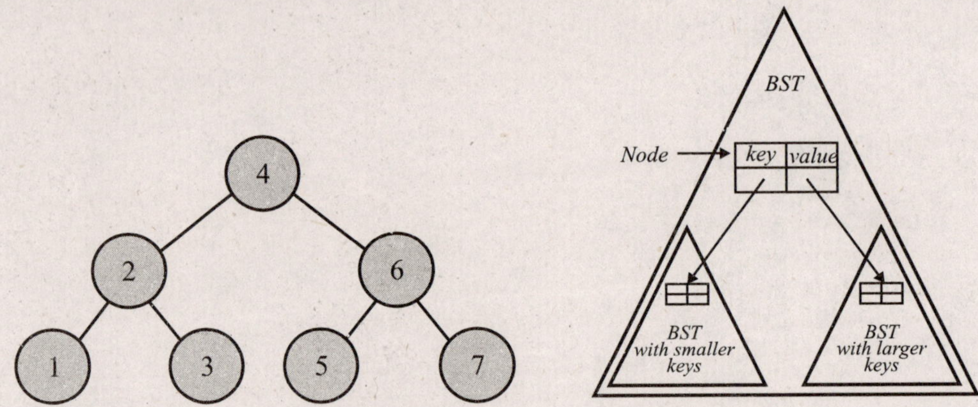

2.1 INTRODUCTION TO BINARY SEARCH

Before discussing the trees in details, we first need to understand the idea of binary search. Suppose we have a list L and in this list we are searching for a value X. If L has no special properties, if it might be any old list, then there is no better way to search it than to start at the beginning and go through the list one step at a time comparing each element to X in turn. This is called *linear* search - the time it takes (on average, and in the worst case) is *linear*, or O(N), in the length of the list.

But if L is a sorted list, there is a much faster way to search for X:

1. Compare X to the middle value (M) in L.
2. If X = M we are done.
3. If X < M we continue our search, but we can confine our search to the first half of L and entirely ignore the second half of L.
4. If X > M we continue, but confine ourselves to the second half of L.

Example: L = 1 3 4 6 8 9 11. X = 4.

- Compare X to 6. It's smaller. Repeat with L = 1 3 4.
- Compare X to 3. It's bigger. Repeat with L = 4.
- Compare X to 4. It's equal. We're done, we found X.

This is called *Binary Search:* each iteration of (1)-(4) the length of the list we are looking in gets cut in half. Therefore, the total number of iterations cannot be greater than logN.

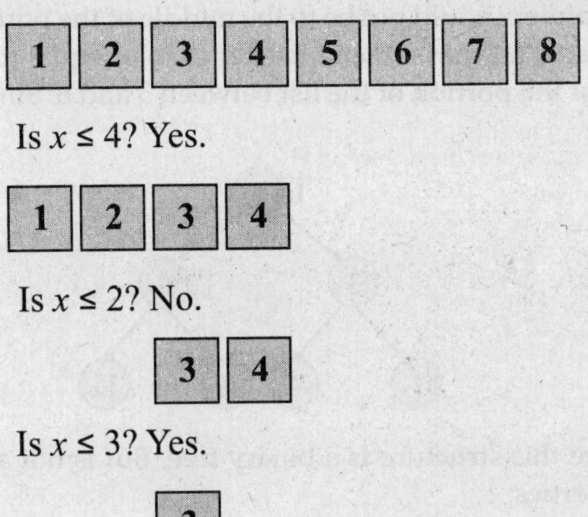

The difference between O(logN) and O(N) is extremely significant when N is large: for any practical problem it is crucial that we avoid O(N) searches. For example, suppose your list contained 2 billion (2 * 10**9) values. Linear search would involve about a billion comparisons; binary search would require only 32 comparisons!

Binary search works perfectly if lists are implemented with arrays. But, there is a problem with *linked* implementations of lists. Can anyone see what it is?

With a linked implementation we cannot find the middle of the list in constant time: it takes linear time (not just in our implementation, but in any linked implementation), and this takes away all the speedup we get from binary search.

What can we do about this? We need linked implementations for their memory efficiency and flexibility, but we cannot afford to do linear search.

Let's design a linked structure specifically for doing binary search very efficiently. It will contain exactly the pointers needed for binary search. What's the first thing we need? A pointer to the middle element.

Using our previous example (L -> 6), what should the node `6' point to? Well, when we compare X to 6 there are two possible outcomes that involve further search: X < 6 and X > 6. In the first case we need a pointer from `6' to the middle of the front half of L, i.e. from `6' to `3'. In the second case we need a pointer from `6' to the middle of the last half of L, i.e. to `9'.

So the pointers we've got so far:

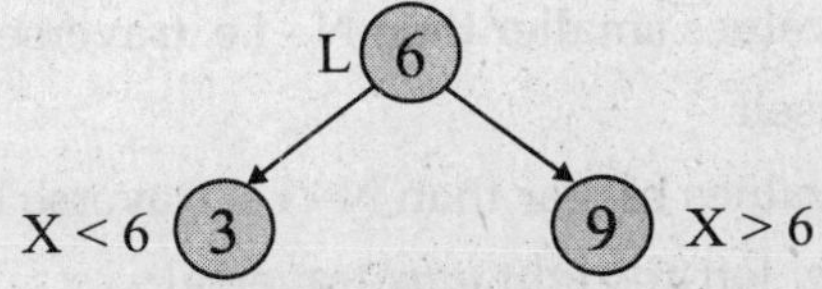

What pointers do we need emanating out of `3'? Again there are two, one for each possible outcome of comparing X to 3 that requires further search. If X < 3 we need a pointer to the middle of the portion of L less than 3. If X > 3 we need a pointer to ... be careful here ... this pointer should not be to the middle of the portion of L bigger than 3. We have already eliminated all the elements bigger than or equal to 6. So this pointer should point to the middle of the portion of the list between 3 and 6. Similarly for 9. So here is our final data structure:

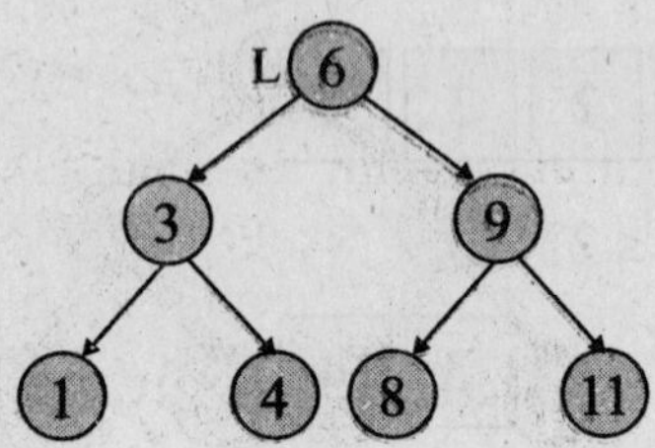

As you can see this structure is a binary tree. But is not an arbitrary binary tree; it has two special properties:

1. Everything in a node's left subtree is smaller than the node's value
2. Everything in a node's right subtree is bigger than the node's value

These hold for every node in the tree.

A binary tree with these properties is called a *Binary Search Tree*. In a binary search tree we can *search* for a value in O(logN) time, where N is the number of nodes in the tree. The algorithm is exactly the binary search algorithm, but translated in terms of `root' and `subtrees':

1. Compare X to the *root* (i.e. *middle value*) (M) in L.
2. If X = M we are done.
3. If X < M we recursively search for X in L's *left subtree.*
4. If X > M we recursively search for X in L's *right subtree.*

I have not mentioned what happens if the subtree is empty (does not exist). Obviously when this happens, we are finished and X is known NOT to be in the tree.

Example

Search for 5 in the above tree.

The properties defining a BST (my abbreviation for Binary Search Tree), mean that it is very easy to *traverse* the tree in increasing (or in decreasing order). To traverse a BST in increasing order here is what we must do:

From the node containing the value N:

1. process all values smaller than N - i.e. traverse N's *left* subtree.
2. process N itself.
3. process all values bigger than N - i.e. traverse N's *right* subtree.

This is just ordinary left-to-right *infix* traversal.

How would we traverse the BST in decreasing order?

Answer: *Right to Left infix traversal.*

2.2 OPERATIONS ON BINARY SEARCH TREES

BSTs are binary trees, so all the operations we've defined for binary trees can be applied to BSTs. However, one of our tree operations does not *preserve* the special properties of a BST. The problematic operation is JOIN. Recall that JOIN was a problem with sorted lists - we have the same problem, for the same reasons, when we JOIN two BSTs: the result may not be a BST.

Our solution for sorted lists was to recognize that there is always has a unique correct position in a sorted list for any new value. The same is true of a BST - if you give me a BST and an value, there is a *unique* position for that new value in the BST - assuming that we are not allowed/willing to re-arrange the existing values. If the existing values must stay where they are, we have no choice about where to put a new value. If it is smaller than the root value, it must go in the left subtree; if larger it must go in the right subtree. This reasoning applies recursively until we reach a node where the required subtree does not exist. And that is where we place the new value.

Example

Where to place `2' in our example tree:

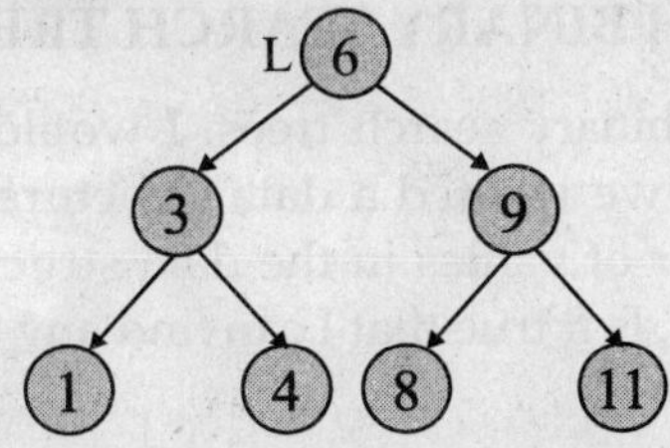

Answer: *It must go in 6's left subtree, 3's left subtree, 1's right subtree. 1 has no right subtree, so we make a singleton with `2' and it becomes 1's right subtree.*

Where to place `7'? `10'?

Here is the general pseudocode for BSTINSERT(V,T) (assume V is not in T):

```
BSTINSERT(V,T) {
if T is empty
    then T = create_singleton(V)
        else if V > rootvalue(T)
            then if T's right subtree exists
                then BSTINSERT(V,T's right subtree)
            else T's right subtree = create_singleton(V)
        else if T's left subtree exists
    then BSTINSERT(V,T's left subtree)
else T's left subtree = create_singleton(V) }
```

I hope you can see that this can very easily be written using our tree operations. I also hope you see that this is exactly the same as the SEARCH(V,T) operation described above, except for

1. the processing we do in the base case (empty tree or subtree)
2. the assumption that V is not in the tree for INSERT.

Special Precondition: Things can go wrong if we allow the user to INSERT a value directly into a subtree. If he tried to insert 99 into the subtree rooted at 3, it would end up in the wrong part of the whole tree (it ought to be in `6's right subtree, but the user started the process out in its left subtree). So we must add a precondition: argument T must not be a subtree. But then, strictly speaking, this procedure may not call itself recursively, because this violates the precondition. What we actually need is a procedure called INSERT_IN_SUBTREE which is not available to the user and which does not have this precondition.

There is one final operation on BSTs to discuss. And that is, how to DELETE a value from a BST. Although we have not included DELETE as a primitive operation on general binary trees, many people do! Furthermore DELETE is particularly important for BSTs because DELETE is a standard operation on Collections and the primary use of BSTs is as a very efficient way to implement Collections.

It is not perfectly obvious *how* we can delete a node from a BST and have the resulting tree still have the special properties of a BST.

2.3 A PROBLEM WITH BINARY SEARCH TREES

To finish off the subject of binary search trees, I would like to return to the issue that originally motivated them - we wanted a data structure that could be searched in logN time, where N is the number of values in the data structure. Do BSTs actually meet this requirement? In other words, Is it true that I can find any value X in any BST in logN time? What do you think? Yes, no?

Well, while you think about that, here is something that *is* certainly true. The time to search in a BST is definitely limited by the *height* (or depth) of the tree. Each step in the search goes down one level, so in the absolute worst case, we will have to go all the way from the root to the deepest leaf in order to find X, or to find out that X is not in the tree. So we can say with certainty that search is O(Height).

But we want to know, is search O(logN)? Well, since we know search is O(Height), this is really asking is Height O(logN) ... is it always the case that the height of a BST is proportional to the logarithm of the # of nodes?

Unfortunately, the answer to all the questions is *no*. There are BSTs in which Height and # of Nodes are *equal*! In these trees, searching is O(N), linear time, not log time. It's obvious once I draw one:

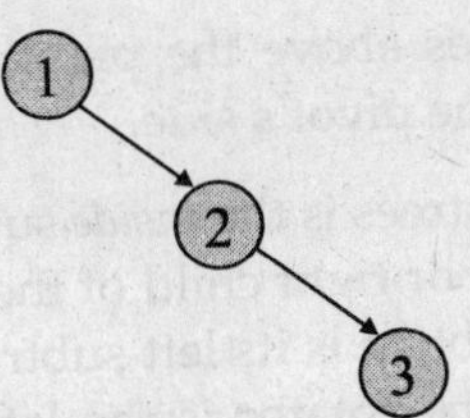

This is called a Degenerate tree, or linear tree. In it, no node has two subtrees, every node has 1 (except the lone leaf who has 0). Obviously this is nothing more than a sorted *linked list*, which was where all our problems began!

So, aren't we are back where we started? Not quite. Most Binary Search Trees are not degenerate: in most of them Height is proportional to LOG(# nodes), and we get efficient search.

For example, the book cites a theorem (page 267) that if you start with an empty BST and add to it N randomly generated values, the expected Height of the tree is 1.4(log(N+1)). This is good news. It basically says that you only get a degenerate BST if you insert values in a *systematic* way. So, whenever you build a BST make sure you do not insert the values in increasing or decreasing order. Or if you find yourself with a degenerate tree it is worthwhile to rebuild it by removing all its values and re-inserting them in random order.

There is another approach to keeping Height related to log(# nodes), based on the observation that in all degenerate BSTs, there is a node that has one subtree that is much deeper than the other ... in our example, the right subtree of `1' is much taller than the left subtree. What would happen if we absolutely required that the subtrees be the same height (within 1)?

Height would always be O(log(# nodes)), so search would always be O(logN).

Trees with this property are called *Balanced Trees*, and that's our next topic.

2.4. TREE ROTATION: THE GENERAL ALGORITHM

The *pivot* node is the deepest node at which there is an imbalance. The *rotator* node is the root of the *pivot*'s taller subtree.

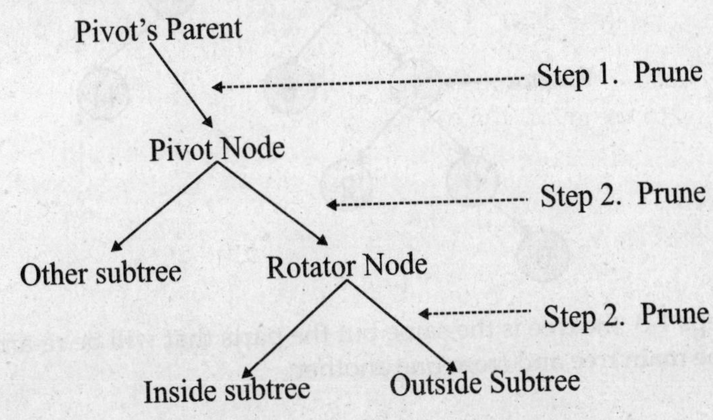

There may be more nodes above the pivot's parent. Step 3 prunes the rotator's `inside' subtree, i.e. the one on the pivot's side.

Which of the rotator's subtrees is the *inside* subtree, which is the *outside*? It depends on whether the rotator is the left or right child of the pivot. If the rotator is the right child (as in this picture), the inside subtree is its left subtree and the outside subtree is its right subtree. On the other hand, if the rotator is the left child the inside subtree is its right subtree and the outside subtree is its left subtree.

Step 4: Join the pruned *inside* subtree to the *pivot* (in the place where the rotator had been).

Step 5: Join the *pivot* to the rotator (in the place where *inside* had been).

Step 6: Join the rotator to the *pivot*'s (original) *parent* (in the place where the *pivot* had been).

Following these steps, the result of the rotation is this: the rotator has rotated up, the pivot has rotated down on the other side, and the inside subtree has jumped across to join the pivot:

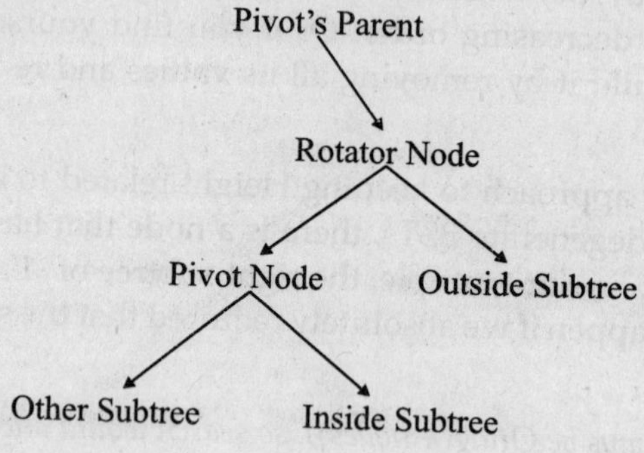

Example:

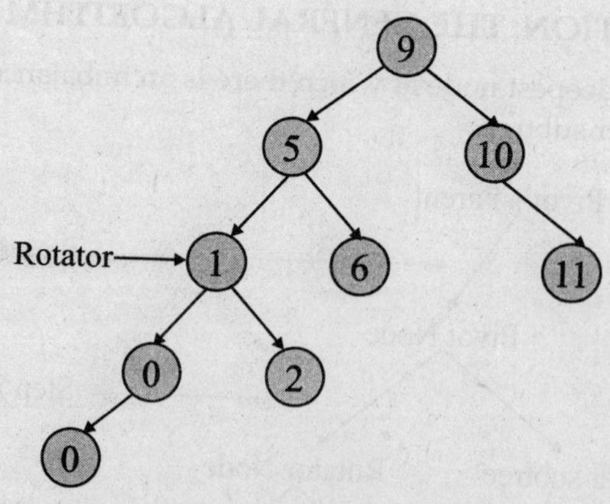

After steps 1-3, the tree is the same but the parts that will be re-arranged have been pruned from the main tree and from one another:

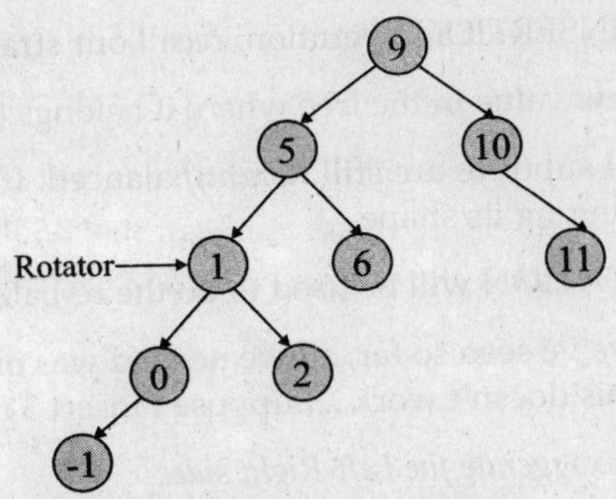

Step 4: Join the pruned *inside* subtree to the *pivot*:

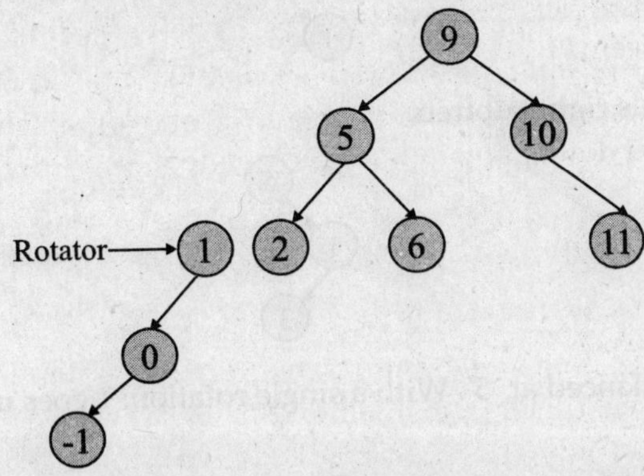

Step 5: Join the *pivot* to the rotator (in the place where *inside* had been):

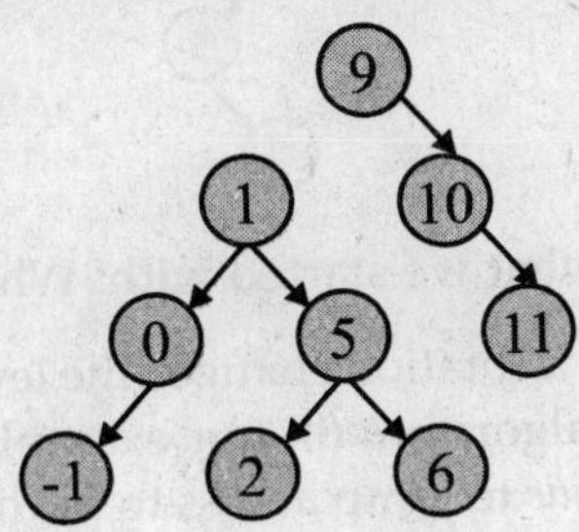

Step 6: Join the rotator to the *pivot*'s (original) *parent*:

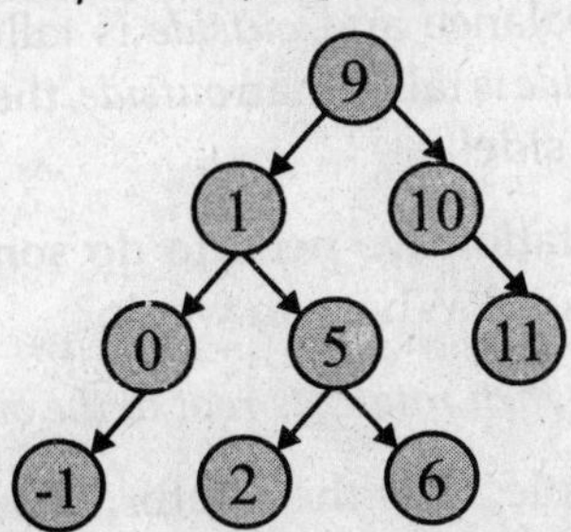

The result of the rotation in this example is: `1' rotates up, `5' rotates down on the other side, and `2' jumps across to join `5'.

Returning to the INSERTION operation, recall our strategy:

1. Add the new value in the tree where it belongs (normal BST insertion).
2. Check if all subtrees are still height-balanced. If they are not, re-balance the tree by changing its shape.

In particular, ROTATION will be used to do the re-balancing.

In the examples we've seen so far, all we needed was one rotation to re-balance the whole tree. Sometimes this doesn't work... Suppose I insert 3 into the following tree:

On the blackboard, exaggerate the Left-Right sides

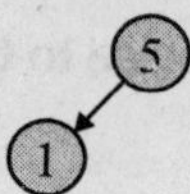

First add 3 as 1's right subtree:

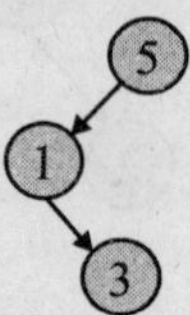

But this is unbalanced at `5'. With a single rotation: 1 goes up, 5 goes down, 3 jumps across, and we get:

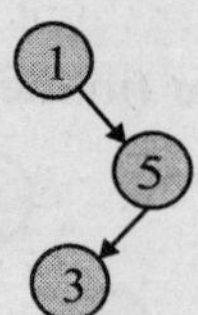

Which is just as bad as what we started with! What has gone wrong?

Let's look closely at how a rotation changes the level of two subtrees – the *inside* and *outside* subtrees in the general algorithm (in our example `3' is the inside subtree, outside is empty). A rotation causes *inside* to jump across to the other side – but it stays at the same level. *Outside* stays on the same side, but it goes up one level.

If there is a height-imbalance and *outside* is taller than *inside* then a rotation will correct the imbalance. But if *inside* is taller than *outside*, the rotation will not *fix* the imbalance, it will just move it to the other side!

So, before doing the rotation we need to do something to ensure that the *outside* subtree is taller than the *inside* one. What can we do?

Answer: *If inside is taller then rotate its root to the outside!*

Going back to our example, `1' is the rotator, `3' is the *inside* subtree. It is taller than the *outside* subtree (which is empty), so we rotate `3' up, and `1' down (to the *outside*) etc. giving:

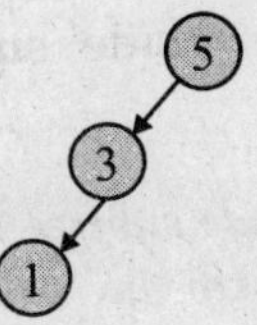

And now we do the main rotation (3 up, 5 down):

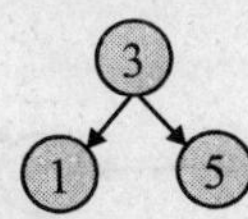

2.5 GENERAL INSERTION ALGORITHM

1. Do a normal BST insert
2. If the tree is balanced, you are finished. otherwise do 3-4.
3. Starting at the newly inserted node, work your way up the tree until you find the first node whose subtrees' heights differ by 2. This node is the *pivot*, the root of its taller subtree is the *rotator*.
4. It is necessarily the case that the new value was inserted in one of the *rotator*'s subtrees. If it was inserted in the *rotator*'s *outside* subtree, then this subtree will be taller than *inside*, and a single rotation (of the *rotator*) will correct the imbalance. Otherwise you must first rotate the root of the rotator's inside subtree up into the rotator's position (the rotator does down the other side), and then rotate the node that replaced the rotator up into the pivot's position.

Example: insert 2 into this tree:

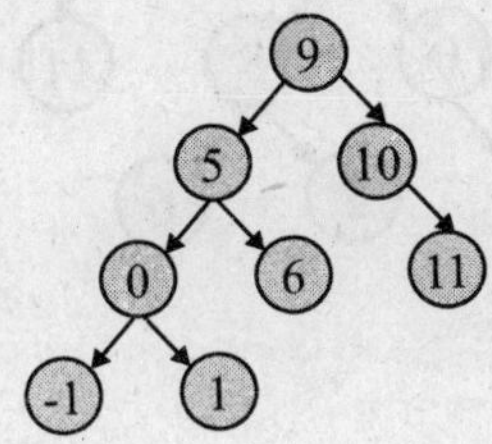

First, we obtain:

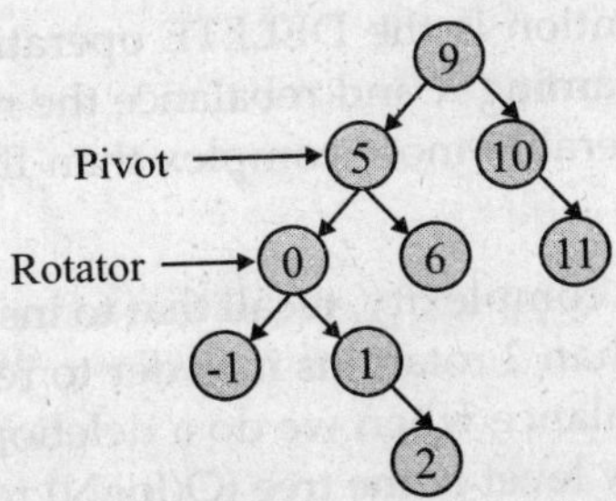

The pivot is the lowest node whose subtrees' heights differ by 2. The rotator is the root of the pivot's taller subtree (the one in which the new value was inserted).

UNIT 2

The new value is in the rotator's `inside' subtree. Therefore, we must rotate this subtree before correcting the imbalance.

> ***Remember:*** *If the rotator's inside subtree was already shorter than its outside subtree we would just skip the `setup' step that follows and go straight to the last step.*

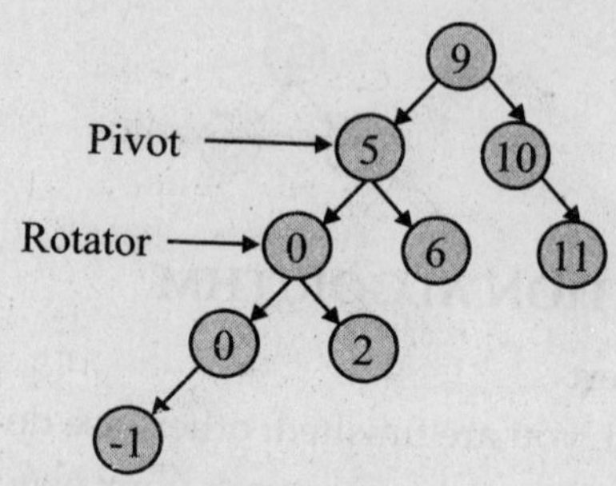

This rotation does not change the imbalance at all; all it does it make the rotator's outside subtree taller than its inside one. The pivot node does not change and the rotator is the same node as before (different value).

When the rotator's outside subtree is taller, a single rotation of the rotator will correct the height imbalance in the whole tree.

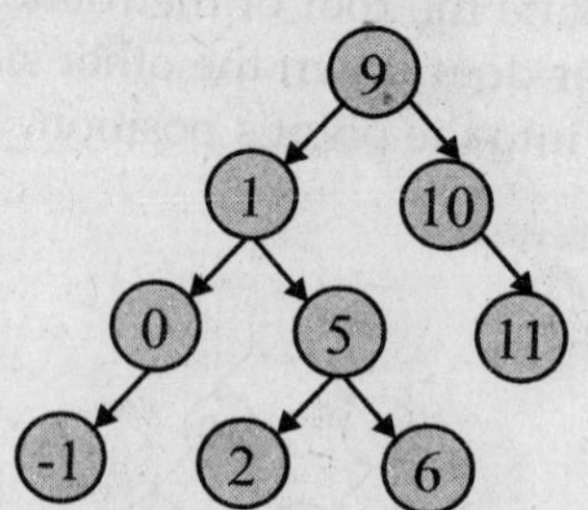

Exercise: add 4 or 7 to this tree.

2.6 DELETION OF A NODE FROM AN AVL TREE

The inverse of the INSERT operation is the DELETE operation: given a value X and an AVL tree T, delete the node containing X and rebalance the resulting tree, if necessary. It turns out that DELETE is considerably more complex than INSERT - we will not go into the details in this course.

To illustrate the additional complexity, recall that to insert a new value into an AVL tree, we never need to do more than 2 rotations in order to restore the tree's balance. We can use rotations to restore the balance when we do a deletion, too, but in some cases we may have to do a rotation at every level of the tree (O(logN) rotations in the worst case).

Here is a tree that causes this worse case # of rotations (we're deleting X). At every node the left subtree is one shorter than the right subtree (numbers shown are height of subtrees):

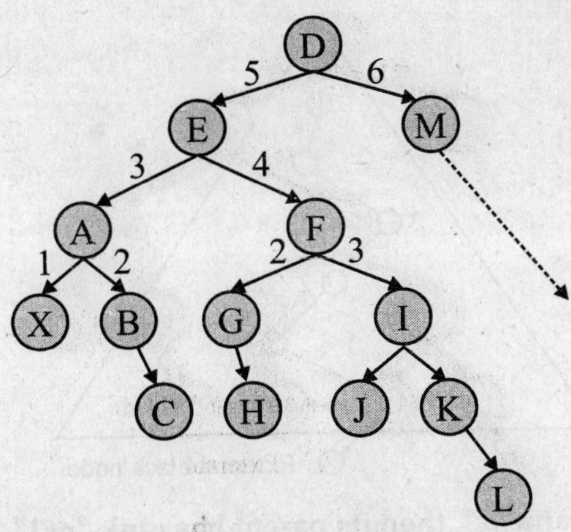

Deleting X upsets the balance at `A'. When we rotate (B up, A down) to fix this, the whole of this subtree - which is E's left subtree - gets shorter. This means the balance at `E' is upset. When we fix this with a rotation (F up, E down) This subtree (D's left subtree) gets shorter - the subtree heights at this stage are 4 on the left and 6 on the right. When we rotate to fix this (D down, M up), we will get a 5-5 balance at D - so now it is one shorter and its parent is out of balance. This can propagate right to the top of the tree.

2.7 RED-BLACK TREES

Red-black trees are binary search trees with worst-case height no more than 2 log_2 n. Standard dictionary operations (insert, delete, search, minimum, maximum) take O (log n) time. In contrast, standard binary search trees have Omega (n) height in the worst-case and O (log n) height on the average. They are, however, easier to implement.

Definition

Red-black trees have all the characteristics of binary search trees. In addition, red-black trees have the following characteristics.

- Each node of the tree contains the fields color, key, left, right, parent and an optional field rank.

  Every node is colored either "red" or "black".

Red Node

Black Node

Either red or black node

- The rank in a tree goes from zero up to the maximum rank which occurs at the root. The rank roughly corresponds to the height of a node. The rank of two consecutive nodes differs by at most one. **All the external nodes are black and have a rank zero.**

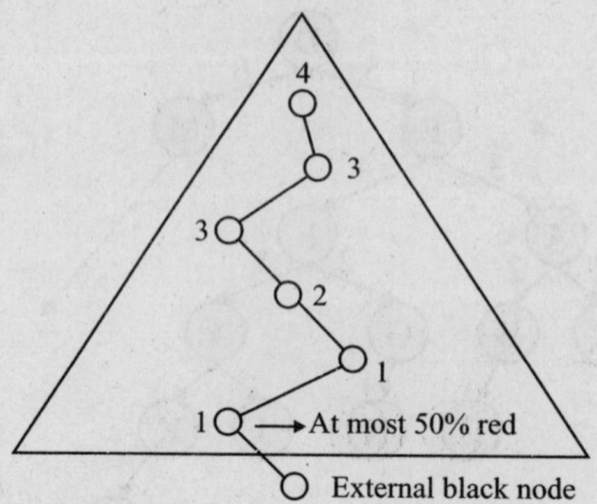

If a black node has rank "r", then its parent has rank "r+1".

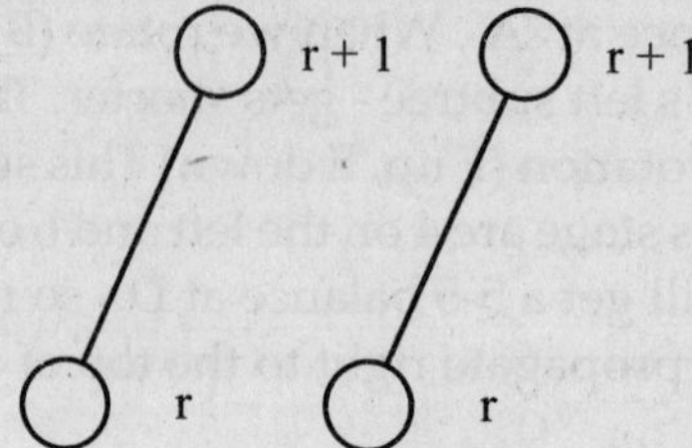

If a red node has rank "r", then its parent will have rank "r" as well.

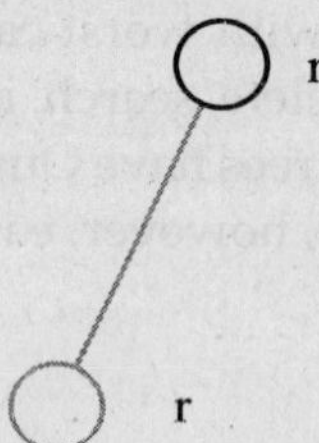

- **Consecutive red nodes are disallowed**. This means every red node is followed by a black node, on the other hand a black node may followed by a black or red node. This implies that at most 50% of the nodes on any path from external node to root are red.

- **Every path from the root to a leaf contains the same number of black nodes.** This number called black-height of the tree.

In this section, we give an example of red-black tree with five levels. We set the ranks starting at the bottom and show some sample ranks. Note that there is some freedom in assigning ranks to nodes.

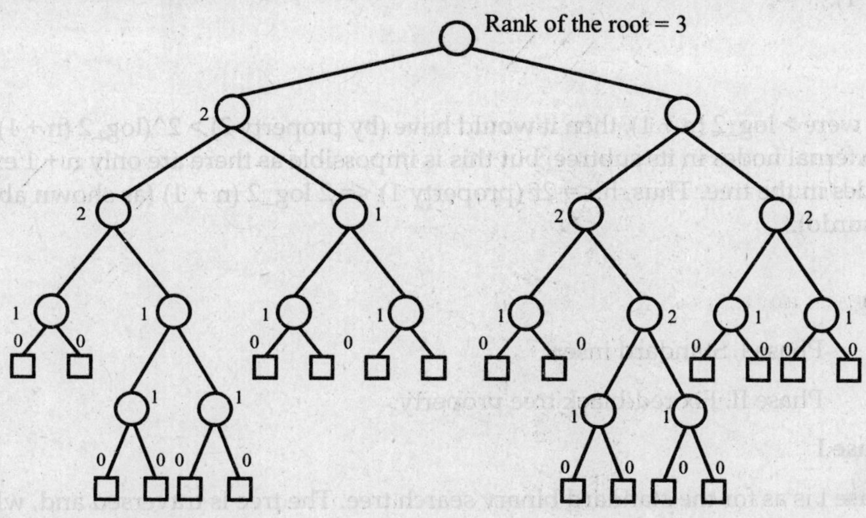

Properties of red-black trees

Let h is the height of a tree and r is the rank of the root.

Property 1: h/2 <= r <= h.

Proof:

The rank of the root "r" is greater than or equal to "h/2", since there are at least 50% black nodes on any path from external node to root. "r" is also less than or equal to the height of the tree "h".

Property 2: A node of rank r has >= 2^r external nodes in its subtree.

Proof (by induction):

(i) **Base case:** Let r = 1 then root 1 has 2^1 external nodes.

(ii) **Assumption:** Assume true up to but not including r.

(iii) **Verification:** Verify the claim for r.

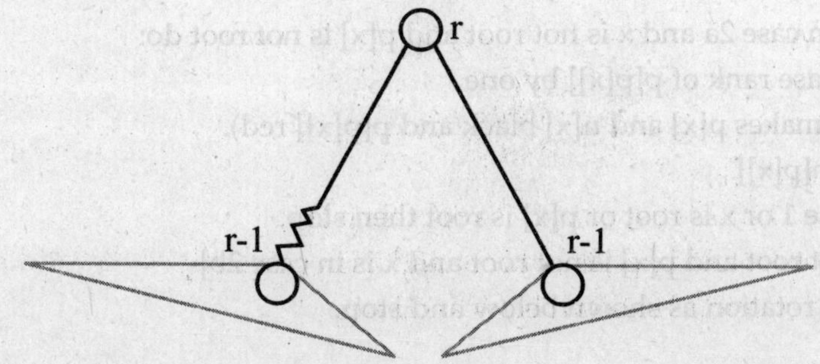

Since the number of external nodes in the subtrees >= 2^(r-1) + 2^(r-1) = 2^r, then 2^r <= n + 1 external nodes as required.

Main property: The height of a red-black tree with n internal nodes is at most 2 log_2 (n + 1).

Proof

If r were > log_2 (n + 1), then it would have (by property 2) > 2^(log_2 (n + 1)) = n + 1 external nodes in its subtree, but this is impossible as there are only n + 1 external nodes in the tree. Thus, h <= 2r (property 1) <= 2 log_2 (n + 1) (as shown above ex absurdo).

Insertion

- Phase I, Standard insert.
- Phase II, Fix red-black tree property.

Phase I

Phase I is as for the standard binary search tree. The tree is traversed and, when an external node is encountered, it is replaced with the new node. The new node must be colored red in order to preserve the characteristics of the red-black tree.

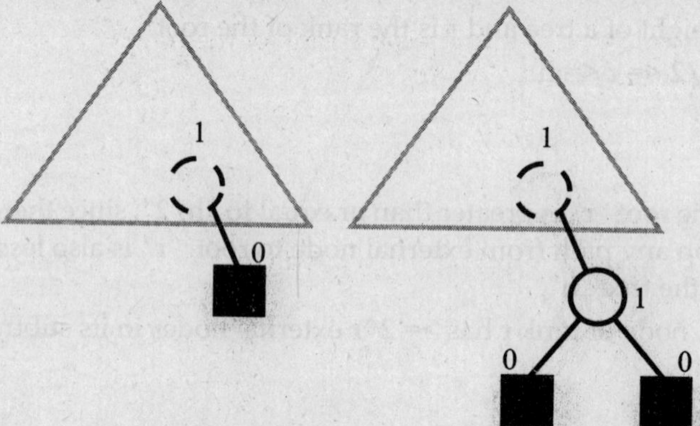

However, if the newly inserted node's parent is red we will have two consecutive red nodes in a path, which is not allowed. So, we have to fix the tree.

Phase II

While x is in case 2a and x is not root and p[x] is not root do:

Increase rank of p[p[x]] by one

(this makes p[x] and u[x] black and p[p[x]] red).

x <- p[p[x]].

If x is in case 1 or x is root or p[x] is root then stop.

else [x is not root and p[x] is not root and x is in case 2b]

Perform rotation as shown below and stop.

Case 1: p[x] is black.

Insert node x is red and its parent p[x] is black then we can terminate the insertion.

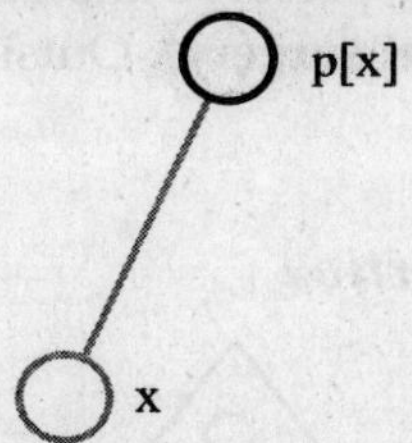

Case 2a: p[x] is red and u[x] is red.

x, p[x] and u[x] are all red, then we can recolor u[x] and p[x] to black and move x toward the root of the tree to recheck. There are four symmetric cases to case 2a, and the graph below show only one of the cases.

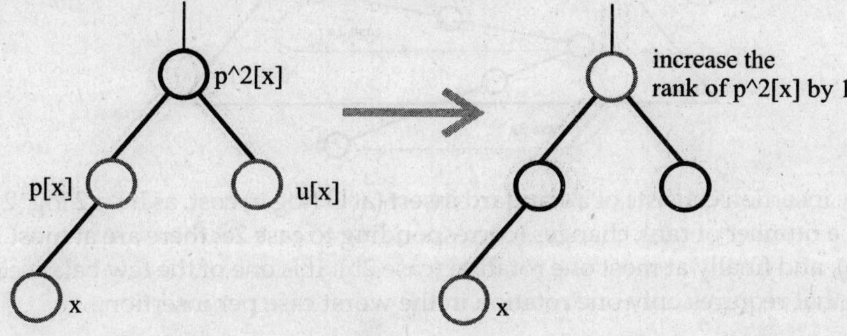

Case 2b: p[x] is red and u[x] is black.

x and p[x] are red and u[x] is black.

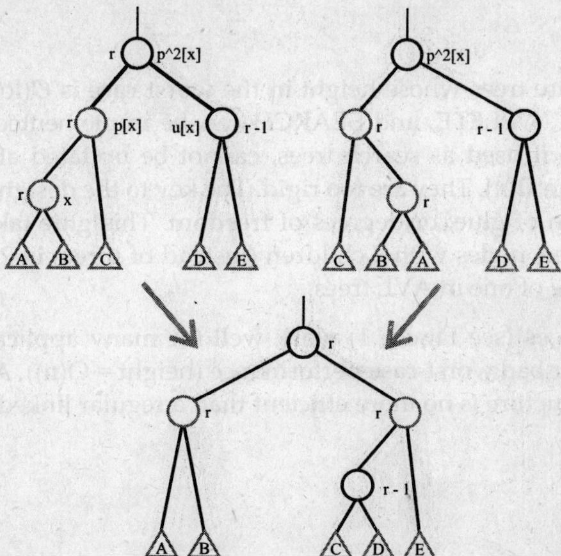

The keys of the nodes fall naturally into place.

In above picture the tree above and subtree below this portion of tree are consider as outside world. In order to preserve the red-black tree properties, one must perform a little changing **(local surgery)**. Outside world must not see this change after surgery.

Analysis of the algorithm for insertion

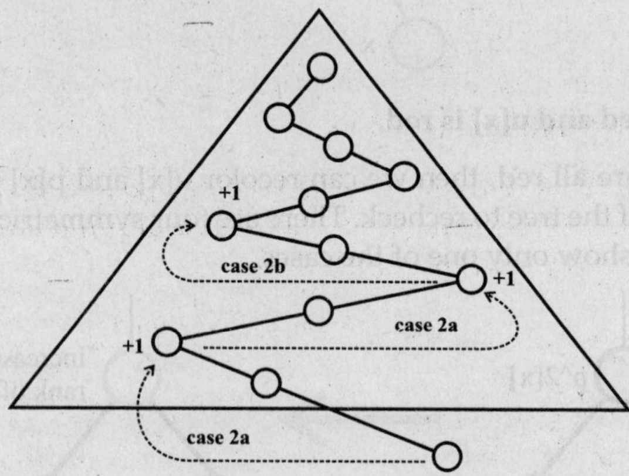

Every insertion consists of a standard insert (at O (log n) cost, as h <= 2 log_2 (n + 1)), followed by a number of rank changes (corresponding to case 2a: there are at most log_2 (n + 1) of these), and finally at most one rotation (case 2b). It is one of the few balanced binary search trees that requires only one rotation in the worst case per insertion.

The time for Phase I in insertion takes O (lg n). The time for Phase II in insertion takes O (lg n) for changing the rank and O (1) for rotation.

2.8 BALANCED SEARCH TREES

Introduction

Balanced search trees are trees whose height in the worst case is $O(\log n)$ and for which the operations INSERT, DELETE, and SEARCH can be implemented in $O(\log n)$ time. Complete binary trees, if used as search trees, cannot be updated after an insertion or deletion in time less than $\Omega(n)$. They are too rigid. The key to the design of balanced search trees is the introduction of glue, or degrees of freedom. This glue takes the form of red nodes in a red-black tree, nodes with 2 children (instead of three) in 2-3 trees, and nodes with a height-imbalance of one in AVL trees.

Binary search trees (see Figure 1) work well for many applications but they are limiting because of their bad worst-case performance (height = O(n)). A binary search tree with this worst-case structure is no more efficient than a regular linked list.

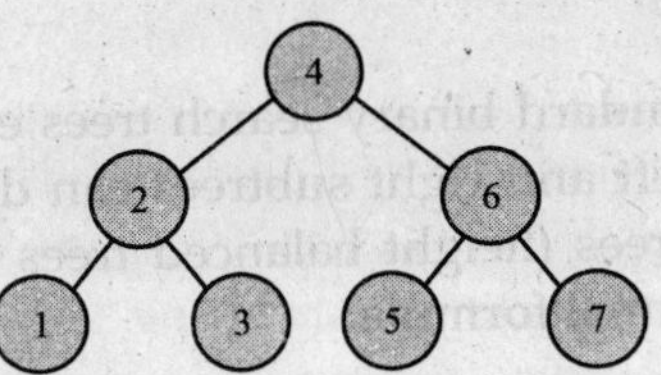

Figure 1: Binary search tree

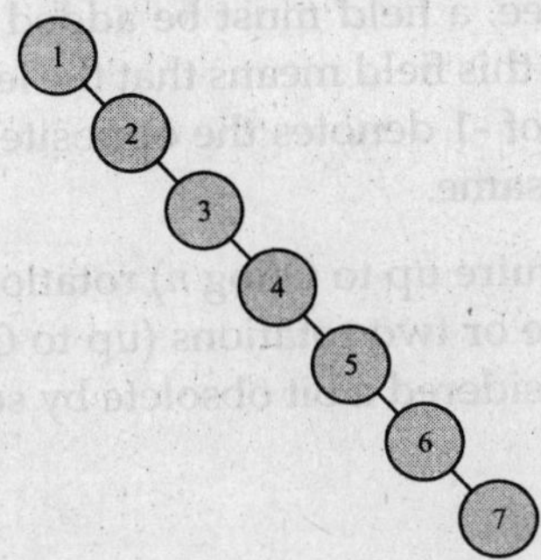

Figure 2: Worst case binary search tree

Types of Balanced Search Trees

There exist over one hundred types of balanced search trees. Some of the more common types are: AVL trees, B-trees, and red-black trees. B-trees are a category of tree designed to work well on magnetic disks and other direct-access secondary storage devices

Heights of balanced search trees

red-black tree: (height $\leq 2 \log_2(n + 1)$)

AVL tree: (height $\leq (1.44042\ldots) \times \log_2 n$)

2-3 tree: (height $\leq 1 \times \log_2 n$

AVL tree

AVL trees were invented by two computer chess specialists in Russia, Adelson-Velskii and Landis in 1962 (hence the acronym AVL). See next section for detailed information regarding AVL trees.

B-tree

A B-tree of order m is a tree exhibiting the following properties:

1. the root is either a leaf or has between 2 and m children
2. all nonleaf nodes (except the root) have between [m/2]and m children
2. all leaves are at the same depth

B-trees of order 4 are known as 2-3-4 trees, and a B-tree of order 3 is known as a 2-3 tree.

Properties of AVL Trees

AVL trees are identical to standard binary search trees except that for every node in an AVL tree, the height of the left and right subtrees can differ by at most 1 (Weiss, 1993, p:108). AVL trees are HB-k trees (height balanced trees of order k) of order HB-1. The following is the height differential formula:

$$\text{Height}(T_L) - \text{Height}(T_R) \le k$$

When storing an AVL tree, a field must be added to each node with one of three values: 1, 0, or -1. A value of 1 in this field means that the left subtree has a height one more than the right subtree. A value of -1 denotes the opposite. A value of 0 indicates that the heights of both subtrees are the same.

Updates of AVL trees require up to $O(\log n)$ rotations, whereas updating red-black trees can be done using only one or two rotations (up to $O(\log n)$ color changes). For this reason, they (AVL trees) are considered a bit obsolete by some.

Sparse AVL trees

Sparse AVL trees are defined as AVL trees of height h with the fewest possible nodes. Figure 3 shows sparse AVL trees of heights 0, 1, 2, and 3.

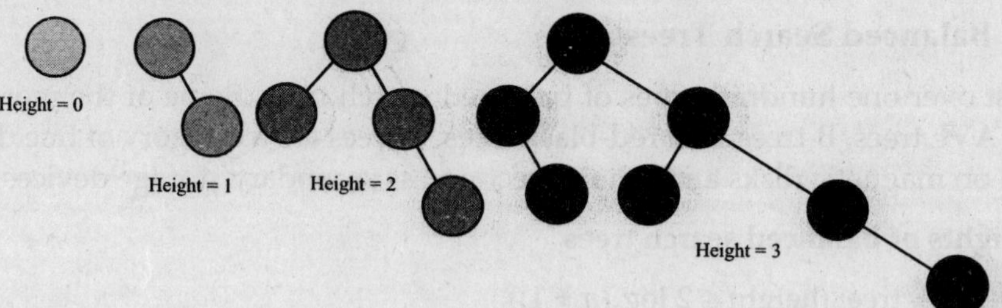

***Figure 3:** Structure of an AVL tree*

Analysis of AVL tree organizations

We first analyze the number of nodes n_k in a sparse AVL tree of height *k*.

From Figure 3, we can deduce the following recurrence relation:

$$\begin{cases} n_k = n_{k-1} + n_{k-2} + 1, \ \forall k \ge 2 \\ n_0 = 1 \\ n_1 = 2 \end{cases}$$

which looks like the Fibonacci sequence given by:

$$0, 1, 1, 2, 3, 5, 8, 13, 21, 34, 55, \ldots$$

Adding **1** on both sides of the equalities we obtain:

$$\begin{cases} (n_k + 1) = (n_{k-1} + 1) + (n_{k-2} + 1) \\ (n_0 + 1) = 2 \\ (n_1 + 1) = 3 \end{cases}$$

Taking a_k to be $n_k + 1$, we rewrite the recurrence relation as:

$$\begin{cases} a_k = a_{k-1} + a_{k-2} \\ a_0 = 2 \\ a_1 = 3 \end{cases}$$

which is the usual Fibonacci recurrence relation.

By inspecting the Fibonacci sequence, one suspects that it grows somehow "exponentially" i.e. that it is of the form: $a_k = Ac^k$, for some suitable constants **A** and **c** that we have to find.

Replacing a_k by Ac^k in the Fibonacci recurrence relation, we get:

$$Ac^k = Ac^{k-1} + Ac^{k-2}$$

After cancelling **A**, dividing by c^{k-2} on both sides, the following quadratic equation:

$$c^2 = c + 1$$

is solved with the usual method, and:

$$c = \frac{1 \pm \sqrt{5}}{2}$$

The theory for *linear homogeneous recurrence relations* (cf: *Rosen, K. "Discrete Mathematics and its Applications", third edition.*) says that the general solution of such a recurrence relation is given by:

$$a_k = A_1\left(\frac{1+\sqrt{5}}{2}\right)^k + A_2\left(\frac{1-\sqrt{5}}{2}\right)^k$$

Note that: a^k is an integer. Also:

since $\left|\frac{1-\sqrt{5}}{2}\right| < 1$, we have $A_2\left(\frac{1-\sqrt{5}}{2}\right)^k \to 0$ fast.

We still have to find the two unknowns A_1 and A_2. Using the initial conditions in the recurrence relation, we know that $a_0 = 2$ and $a_0 = 3$, so the constants are extracted from:

$$\begin{cases} 2 = A_1 = A_2 \\ 3 = A_1\left(\frac{1+\sqrt{5}}{2}\right) + A_2\left(\frac{1-\sqrt{5}}{2}\right) \end{cases}$$

Solving we get: $A_1 = 1 + \frac{2}{\sqrt{5}}$ and, $A_1 = 1 - \frac{2}{\sqrt{5}}$

Hence, a sparse AVL tree of height **k** has:

$$n_k = a_k - 1 \geq A_1\left(\frac{1+\sqrt{5}}{2}\right)^k - A_2 - 1 \text{ nodes}$$

If an AVL tree in general has height **k**, and **n** nodes, then:

$$n \geq n_k \geq A_1\left(\frac{1+\sqrt{5}}{2}\right)^k - A_2 - 1$$

and therefore, after trivial operations,

$$k \le \frac{\log_2((n+A_2+1)/A_1)}{\log_2((1+\sqrt{5})/2)}$$
$$= 1.44\ldots \times \log_2 n + O(1)$$

Note: $\frac{1+\sqrt{5}}{2}$ is known under the name *golden ratio* and powers of it are very close to be integers.

Analysis of 2-3 Trees

In the worst case, a 2-3 tree is a complete binary tree. Complete binary tree of height h has:

1 + 2 + 4 + ... + 2^h
= (2^(h+1) - 1)/(2 - 1)
= 2^(h+1) - 1 nodes.

Therefore, the height of such a tree with n nodes can be computed as:

n = 2^(h+1) - 1,

2^(h+1) = n + 1,

h + 1 = $\log_2$(n+1),

h = $\log_2$ (n+1) - 1 ~ = $\log_2 n$. (n >>)

The best case of a 2-3 tree is a complete ternary tree. A complete ternary tree of height h has:

1 + 3 + 9 + ... + 3^h
= (3^(h+1) - 1)/(3 - 1)
= (3^(h+1) - 1)/2 nodes.

Thus, the height of such a tree with n node can be calculated in the same way.

n = (3^(h+1) - 1)/2,

3^(h+1) = 2n + 1,

h + 1 = $\log_3$ (2n+1) (base 3),

h = $\log_3$ (2n+1) - 1 ~= $\log_3$ (n>>)

Therefore, the height of a 2-3 tree is sandwiched between $\log_2 n$ and $\log_3 n$, thus, always beats a complete binary tree which has a height ~= $\log_2 n$.

Structure of 2-3 Trees

Internal structure of a 2-3 tree (see Figure 4)

the internal(non-terminal) nodes have two or three children

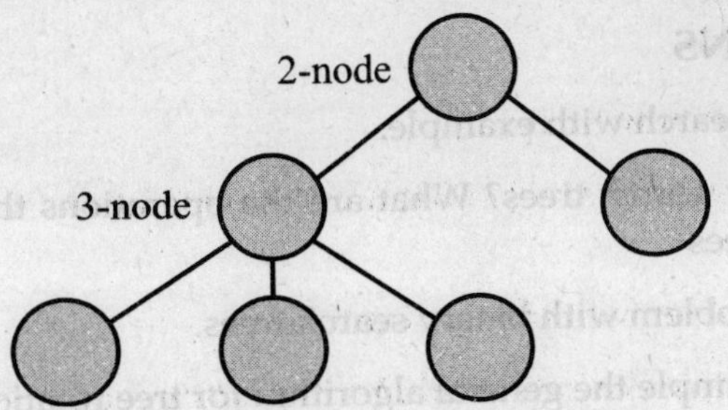

Figure 4: Internal structure of a 2-3 tree

3 possible 2-3 organizations

- the 2-3 tree is an empty tree
- the tree has a root node with a single data item and each of its children are 2-3 trees
- the tree has a root node with two data items and three children, each of which is a 2-3 tree

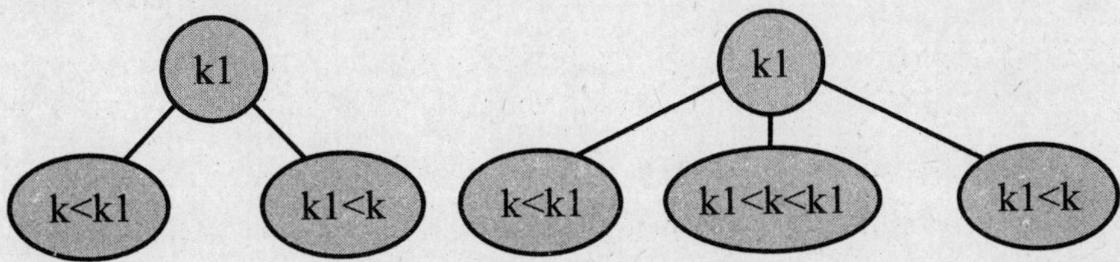

Figure 5: Possible 2-3 organizations

Although searching operations on a 2-3 balanced search tree are guaranteed a very good worst case, this property comes at the expense of sometimes costly insertions. Figure 6 illustrates such a situation and the Java applet below performs the insertion.

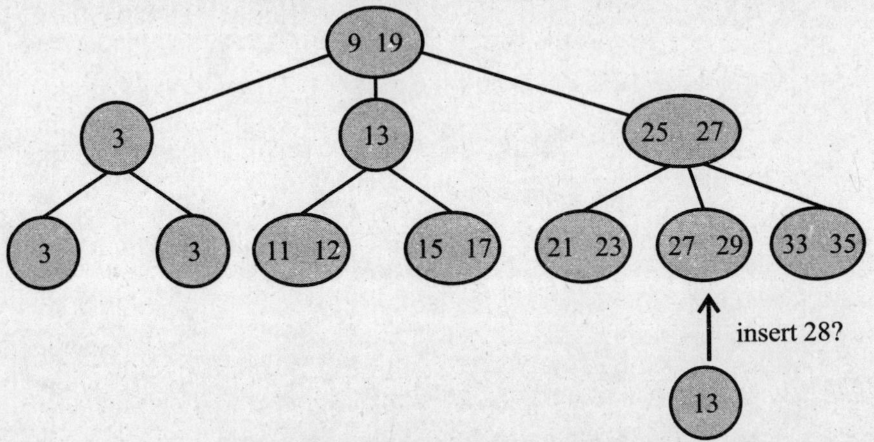

Figure 6: Insertion into a 2-3 tree

REVIEW QUESTIONS

1. Explain binary search with example.
2. What are binary search trees? What are the operations that can be performed on binary search trees
3. Elaborate the problem with binary search trees.
4. Explain with example the general algorithm for tree rotation.
5. Explain how different operations can be performed on AVL and RED BLACK TREES.

DISJOINT SETS

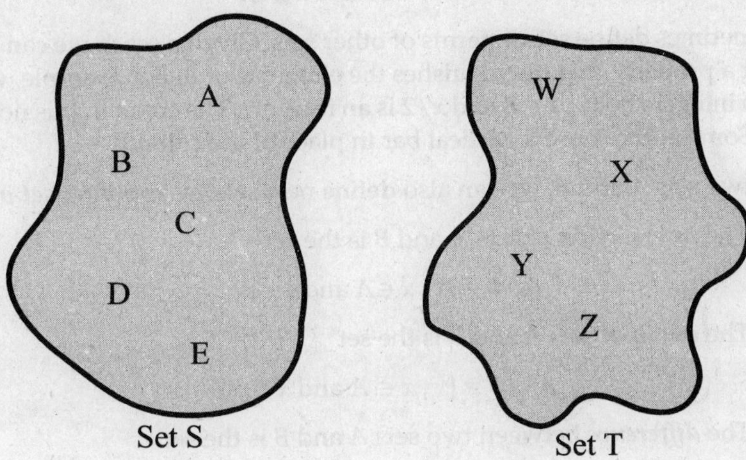

3.1 INTRODUCTION TO SETS

We know a ***set*** is a collection of distinguishable objects, called its ***members*** or ***elements.*** If an object x is a member of a set S, we write $x \in S$ (read "x is a member of S" or, more briefly, "x is in S"). If x is not a member of S, we write $x \notin S$. We can describe a set by explicitly listing its members as a list inside braces. For example, we can define a set S to contain precisely the numbers 1, 2, and 3 by writing $S = \{1, 2, 3\}$. Since 2 is a member of the set S, we can write $2 \in S$, and since 4 is not a member, we have $4 \notin S$. A set cannot contain the same object more than once, and its elements are not ordered. Two sets A and B are ***equal***, written $A = B$, if they contain the same elements. For example, $\{1, 2, 3, 1\} = \{1, 2, 3\} = \{3, 2, 1\}$.

- We adopt special notations for frequently encountered sets.
- ø denotes the ***empty set***, that is, the set containing no members.
- **Z** denotes the set of ***integers***, that is, the set $\{\ldots, 2, -1, 0, 1, 2, \ldots\}$.
- **R** denotes the set of ***real numbers***.
- **N** denotes the set of ***natural numbers***, that is, the set $\{0, 1, 2, \ldots\}$.[1]

[1]Some authors start the natural numbers with 1 instead of 0. The modern trend seems to be to start with 0.

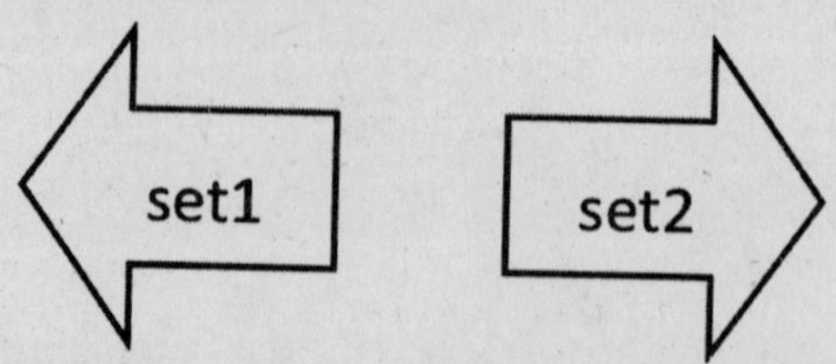

If all the elements of a set A are contained in a set B, that is, if $x \in A$ implies $x \in B$, then we write $A \subseteq B$ and say that A is a ***subset*** of B. A set A is a ***proper subset*** of B, written $A \subset B$, if $A \subseteq B$ but $A \neq B$. (Some authors use the symbol "$\subset$ to denote the ordinary subset relation, rather than the proper-subset relation.) For any set A, we have $A \subseteq A$. For two sets A and B, we have $A = B$ if and only if $A \subseteq B$ and $B \subseteq A$. For any three sets A, B, and C, if $A \subseteq B$ and $B \subseteq C$, then $A \subseteq C$. For any set A, we have $\emptyset \subseteq A$.

We sometimes define sets in terms of other sets. Given a set A, we can define a set $B \subseteq A$ by stating a property that distinguishes the elements of B. For example, we can define the set of even integers by $\{x : x \in \mathbf{Z}$ and $x/2$ is an integer$\}$. The colon in this notation is read "such that." (Some authors use a vertical bar in place of the colon.)

Given two sets A and B, we can also define new sets by applying ***set operations:***

- The ***intersection*** of sets A and B is the set

$$A \cap B = \{x : x \in A \text{ and } x \in B\}.$$

- The ***union*** of sets A and B is the set

$$A \cup B = \{x : x \in A \text{ and } x \in B\}.$$

- The ***difference*** between two sets A and B is the set

$$A - B = \{x : x \in A \text{ and } x \notin B\}.$$

Set operations obey the following laws.

Empty set laws:

$$A \cap \emptyset = \emptyset,$$
$$A \cap \emptyset = A.$$

Idempotency laws:

$$A \cap A = A,$$
$$A \cup A = A.$$

Commutative laws:

$$A \cap B = B \cap A,$$
$$A \cup B = B \cup A.$$

Associative laws:

$$A \cap (B \cap C) = (A \cap B) \cap C,$$
$$A \cup (B \cup C) = (A \cup B) \cup C.$$

Distributive laws:

$$A \cap (B \cup C) = (A \cap B) \cup (A \cap C),$$

$$A \cup (B \cap C) = (A \cup B) \cap (A \cup C).$$

Absorption laws:

$$A \cap (A \cup B) = A,$$

$$A \cup (A \cap B) = A.$$

DeMorgan's laws:

$$A - (B \cap C) = (A - B) \cup (A - C),$$

$$A - (B \cup C) = (A - B) \cap (A - C).$$

A − (B ∩ C) = A − (B ∩ C) = (A ∩ B) ∪ (A − C)

Figure: A Venn diagram illustrating the first of DeMorgan's laws .

Often, all the sets under consideration are subsets of some larger set U called the ***universe.*** For example, if we are considering various sets made up only of integers, the set Z of integers is an appropriate universe. Given a universe U, we define the ***complement*** of a set A as $\overline{A} = U - A$. For any set $A \subseteq U$, we have the following laws:

$$\overline{\overline{A}} = A,$$

$$A \cap \overline{A} = \phi$$

$$A \cap \overline{A} = U.$$

DeMorgan's laws can be rewritten with complements. For any two sets A, $B \subseteq U$, we have

$$\overline{A \cap B} = \overline{A} \cup \overline{B},$$

$$\overline{A \cap B} = \overline{A} \cap \overline{B}.$$

Two sets A and B are ***disjoint*** if they have no elements in common, that is, if $A \cap B = \emptyset$.

A collection $S = \{S_i\}$ of nonempty sets forms a ***partition*** of a set S if

- the sets are ***pairwise disjoint***, that is, $S_i, S_j \in S$ and $i \neq j$ imply $S_i \cap S_j = \emptyset$, and
- their union is S, that is,

$$S = \bigcup_{S_i \in S} S_i$$

In other words, S forms a partition of S if each element of S appears in exactly one $S_i \in S$.

The number of elements in a set is called the ***cardinality*** (*or* ***size***) of the set, denoted $|S|$. Two sets have the same cardinality if their elements can be put into a one-to-one correspondence. The cardinality of the empty set is $|\emptyset| = 0$. If the cardinality of a set is a natural number, we say the set is ***finite***; otherwise, it is ***infinite***. An infinite set that can be put into a one-to-one correspondence with the natural numbers **N** is ***countably infinite***; otherwise, it is ***uncountable***. The integers **Z** are countable, but the reals **R** are uncountable.

For any two finite sets A and B, we have the identity

$$|A \cup B| = |A| + |B| - |A \cap B|,$$

from which we can conclude that

$$|A \cup B| \leq |A| + |B|.$$

If A and B are disjoint, then $|A \cap B| = 0$ *and thus* $|A \cup B| = |A| + |B|$. If $A \subseteq B$, then $|A| \leq |B|$.

A finite set of n elements is sometimes called an ***n-set***. A 1-set is called a ***singleton***. A subset of k elements of a set is sometimes called a ***k-subset***.

The set of all subsets of a set S, including the empty set and the set S itself, is denoted 2^S and is called the ***power set*** of S. For example, $2^{\{a,b\}} = \{\emptyset, \{a\}, \{b\}, \{a,b\}\}$. The power set of a finite set S has cardinality $2|S|$.

We sometimes care about setlike structures in which the elements are ordered. An ***ordered pair*** of two elements a and b is denoted (a, b) and can be defined formally as the set $(a, b) = \{a, \{a, b\}\}$. Thus, the ordered pair (a, b) is *not* the same as the ordered pair (b, a).

The ***Cartesian product*** of two sets A and B, denoted $A \times B$, is the set of all ordered pairs such that the first element of the pair is an element of A and the second is an element of B. More formally,

$$A \times B = \{(a,b) : a \in A \text{ and } b \in B\}.$$

For example, $\{a, b\} \times \{a, b, c\} = \{(a, a), (a, b), (a, c), (b, a), (b, b), (b, c)\}$. When A and B are finite sets, the cardinality of their Cartesian product is

$$|A \times B| = |A| \times |B|.$$

The Cartesian product of n sets $A_1, A_2, \ldots, A_n$ is the set of ***n-tuples***

$$A_1 \times A_2 \times \cdots \times A_n = \{(a_1, a_2, \ldots, a_n) : a_i \in A_i, i = 1, 2, \ldots, n\},$$

whose cardinality is

$$|A_1 \times A_2 \times \cdots \times A_n| = |A_1| \cdot |A_2| \cdots |A_n|$$

if all sets are finite. We denote an n-fold Cartesian product over a single set A by the set

$$A^n = A \times A \times \cdots \times A,$$

whose cardinality is $|A^n| = |A|^n$ if A is finite. An n-tuple can also be viewed as a finite sequence of length n (see page 84).

Disjoint Set

A collection of nonempty *disjoint* sets S = *S*1, *S*2, ..., *Sk* , i.e., each *Si* is a nonempty set that has *no* element in common with any other *Sj* .

Each set is identified by a *unique element* called its *representative.*

Operations

MAKE-SET(x): *Given an element x that does not already belong to one of the sets,*

FIND-SET(x): *Given an element x,*

UNION(x,y):

- *Given two distinct elements x and y*
- *let Sx be the set that contains x and Sy be the set that contains y.*
- UNION(x,y) *is an operation that results in a new set consisting of Sx and Sy.*

Applications

- Maintaining the set of *connected components* of a graph.
- Maintain lists of *duplicate copies of webpages.*
- Constructing a *minimum spanning tree* for a graph (Kruskal).

Finding connected components:

For all v in V do
MAKE-SET(v)
For all (u,v) in E do
UNION(u,v)

3.2 KRUSKAL'S ALGORITHM FOR MSTS

Intuition: Grow an MST *A* by repeatedly adding the *"lightest"* edge from *E* that does *not* create a *cycle.*

Example

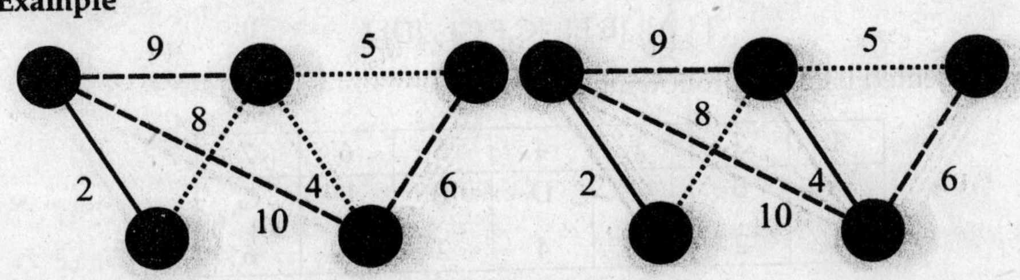

Order of edges in priority queue: 2,4,5,6,8,9,10

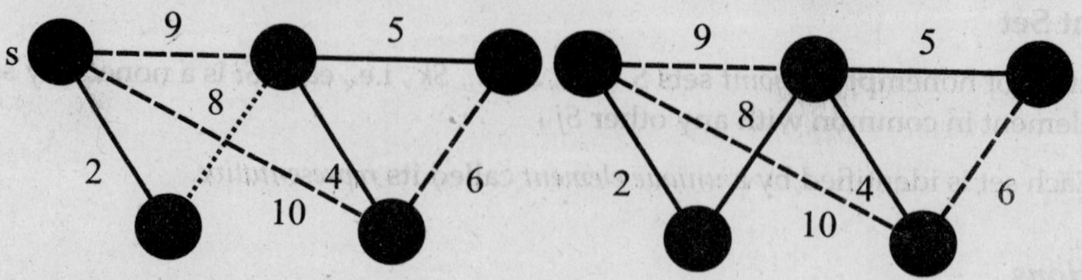


```
KRUSKAL-MST(G=(V,E),w:E->Z)
A := {};
insert the edges into a priority queue Q;
for each vertex v in V
        MAKE-SET(v);
while (Q not empty)
        e = EXTRACT-MIN(Q);    \* e = (u,v) *\
        if FIND-SET(u) =/= FIND-SET(v) then
            UNION(u,v);
            A := A U {e};
        end if
    end while
END KRUSKAL-MST
```

1.3 DATA STRUCTURES FOR DISJOINT SETS

1. Arrays
2. Linked lists
3. Trees

Arrays

One position for each element.Each position stores *the element* and an *index* to the *set representative*. For example, the collection of sets

{ { A}, {B,E}, {C,F,G} , {D} }

could be represented using the following array:

1	2	3	4	5	6	7
A	B	C	D	E	F	G
1	2	6	4	2	6	6

Operations

MAKE-SET(x): store *x* in the next available location.

FIND-SET(x): the *index value* stored with *x* indicates the *representative* of the *set containing x*, so FIND-SET(x).

It takes time O(1).

Trees

Represent each set by a tree, where each element points to its parent and the root points back to itself.

The *representative* of a set is the *root*.

Note that the *trees* are *not* necessarily *binary trees*:

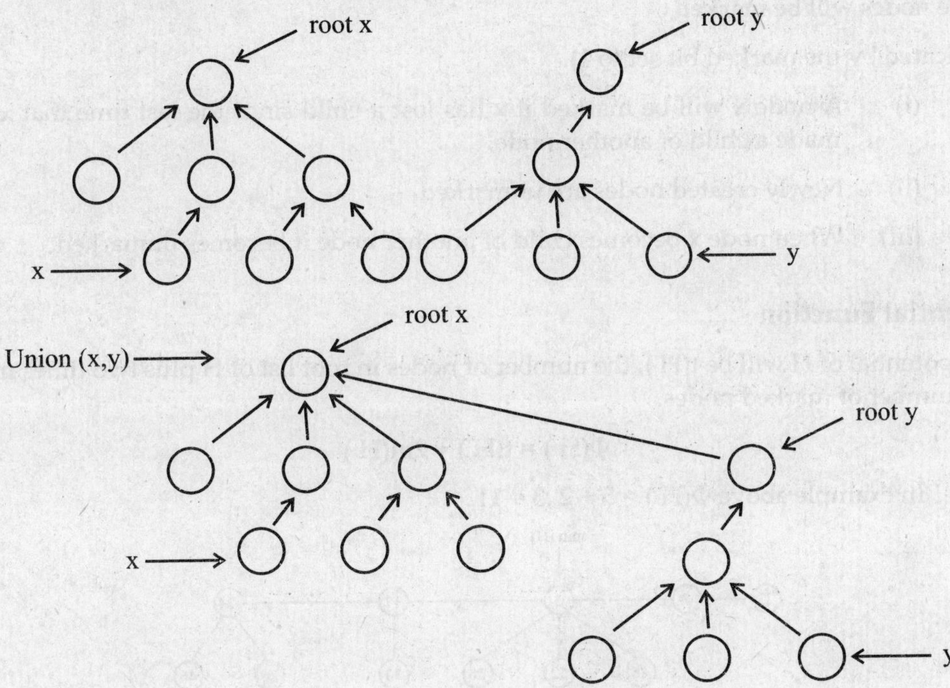

Fibonacci heaps

Fibonacci heaps, like Binomial heaps, are a collection of heap-ordered trees.

Some properties:

1. Nodes in a F.H are **not** ordered (by degree) in the root list or as siblings.
2. Root and sibling lists kept as circularly-linked lists.

   Allows constant time deletion/insertion/concatenation.

   Each node stores its degree (number of children).

   min[H] is a pointer to minimum root in root list.

   N (H) keeps number of nodes currently in H .

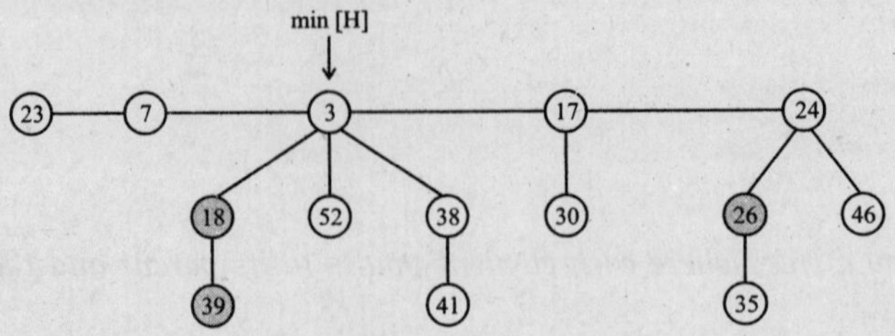

Marked Nodes

Some nodes will be **marked**

(indicated by the marked bit set to 1).

(i) A node x will be marked if x has lost a child since the last time that x was made a child of another node.

(ii) Newly created nodes are unmarked

(iii) When node x becomes child of another node it becomes unmarked.

Potential Function

The potential of H will be t(H), the number of nodes in root list of H plus two times m(H), the number of marked nodes.

$$\Phi(H) = t(H) + 2m(H)$$

In example above $\Phi(H) = 5 + 2.3 = 11$.

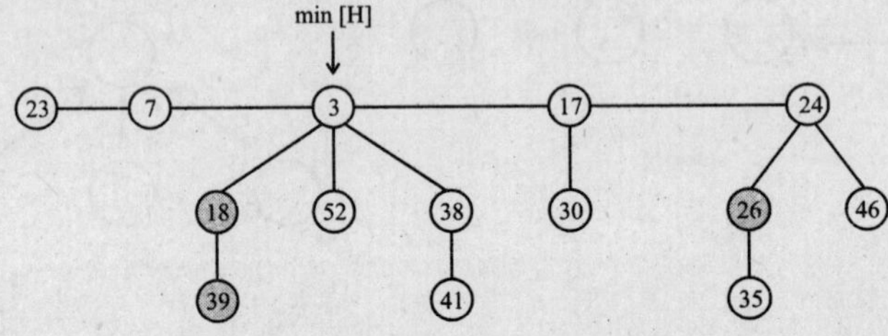

Assumption: There is a maximum degree D(n) on the degree of any node in an n-node Fibonacci heap. We will prove later that D(n) = O(log n).

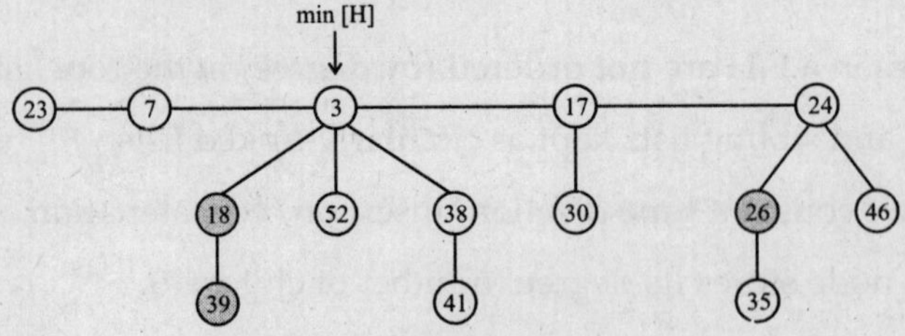

Make-Heap():

This is a very easy O(1) (both amortized and actual) operation.

Minimum(H): Return the node pointed to by min[H]. This takes O(1) actual time. The heap does not change before and after this operation so difference in potential is 0. Amortized cost is then also O(1).

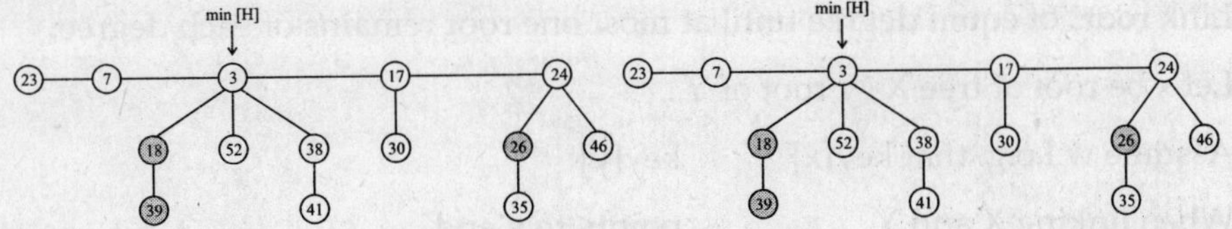

H′=Insert(H, x):

Create new tree containing x & add it to root list.
M in[H] = min(M in[H], x). Update pointers appropriately

Do not combine items in the root list.
Clean up will be done during Extract-Min(H).
If k nodes inserted into H , then H becomes a linked list with k single nodes.

Actual cost c of operation is O(1).

$$t(H') = t(H) + 1;\ m(H') = m(H) \text{ so}$$

$$\Phi(H')-\Phi(H) = ((t(H')+2m(H'))-(t(H)+2m(H))) = 1$$

and amortized cost satisfies

$$\hat{c} = c + 1 = O(1).$$

H=Union(H1, H2):

Just concatenate the two root lists of H1 and H2.

Do not combine items in the root list.
Set min[H] = min(min[H1], min[H2]). Actual cost of this operation is c = O(1).

Concatenating the root lists does not change the total number of items in the root lists or the total number of marked nodes so change in potential is

$$\begin{aligned}\Phi(H) &- (\Phi(H1) + \Phi(H2)) \\ &= (t(H) + 2m(H)) \\ &= ((t(H1) + 2m(H1)) + (t(H2) + 2m(H2)) \\ &= 0\end{aligned}$$

and amortized cost is

$$\hat{c} = c + 0 = O(1).$$

Extract-Min(H):

This is the most complicated operation.
It is here where we clean-up large root lists.
At the end of this operation, root list will contain at most one root of each possible degree. This implies that root list contains less then D (n-1) +1 nodes.

UNIT 2

Extract-Min(H) is quite similar to same operation in binomial heaps.

Let A be tree with root min[H]. Extract A from H .

Remove the root of A; reinsert remaining trees back into root list of heap. update min[H] during this procedure.

Link roots of equal degree until at most one root remains of each degree.

Let x be root of tree X , y root of Y .

Assume w.l.o.g. that key[x] key[y]

When linking X and Y point≤ to x and

increment degree(x) and set mark(y)=0.

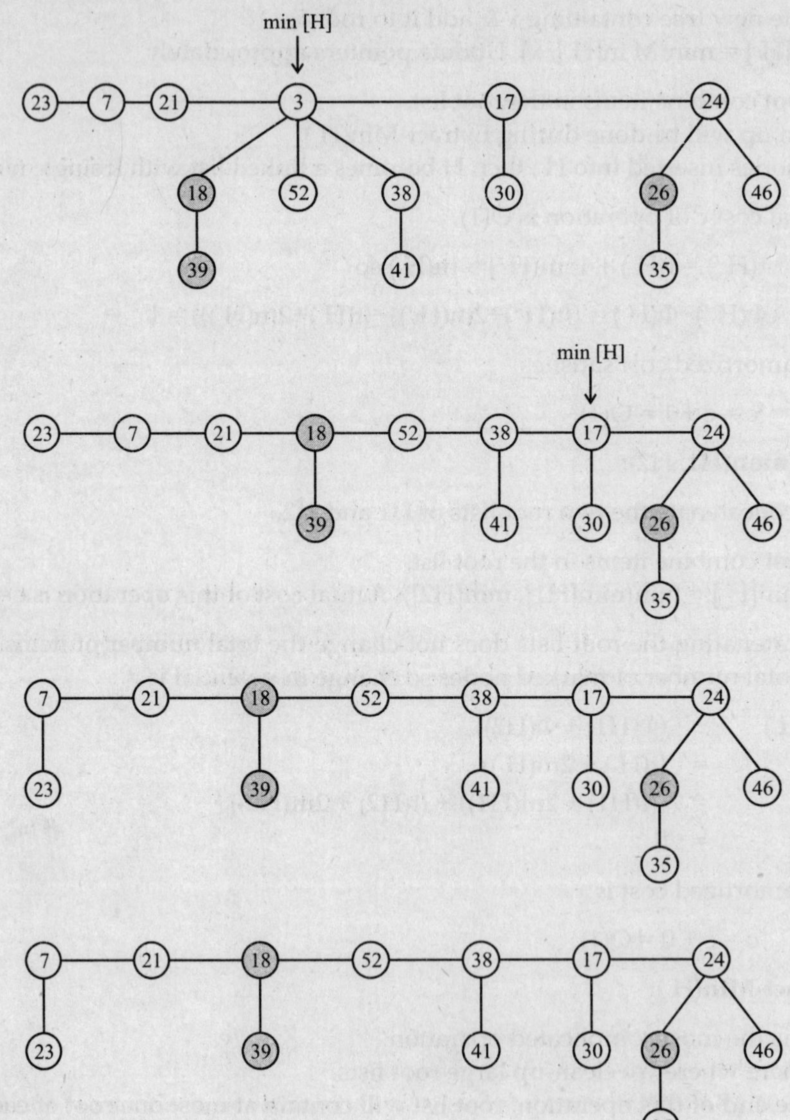

UNIT 2

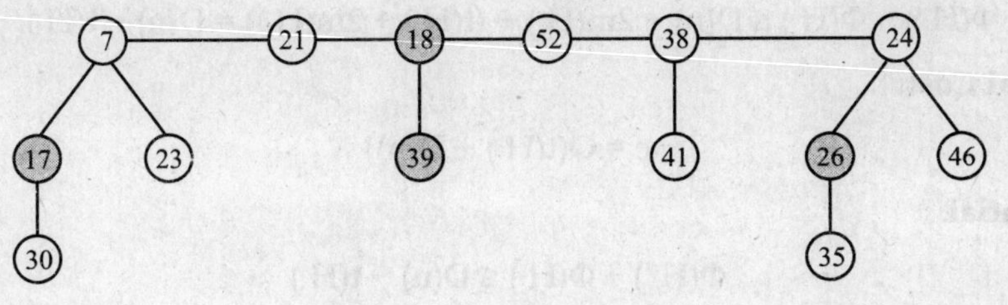

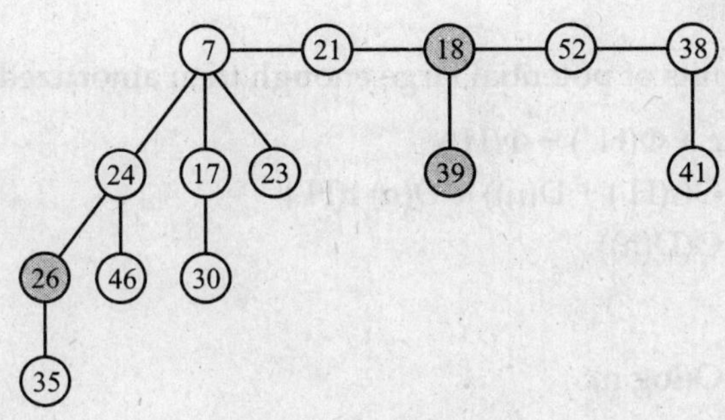

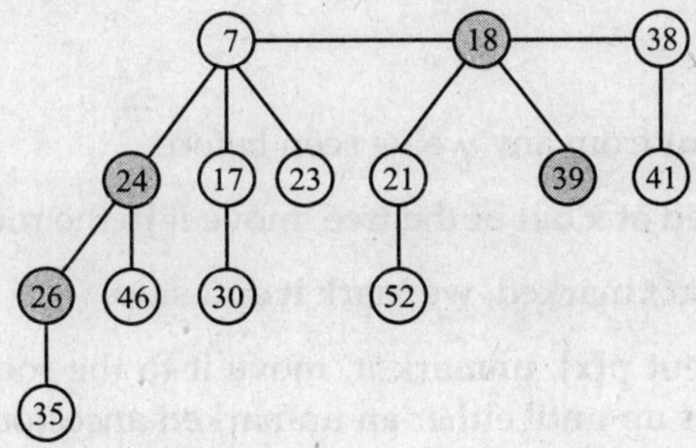

Actual Cost:

A has at most D(n) children.

After concatenation there will be at most 1 nodes on root list.

$$t(H) + D(n)$$

Linking any two tr − requires O(1).

Total cost of concatinating, linking and updating min[H] is O(t(H) + D(n)).

Actual cost is then c = O(t(H) + D(n)).

Potential:

Original potential is $\Phi(H) = t(H) + 2m(H)$.

Final potential is then

$$\Phi(H') = t(H') + 2m(H') \leq D(n) + 2m(H)$$

and

$$\Phi(H') - \Phi(H) \le D(n) + 2m(H) - (t(H) + 2m(H)) = D(n) - t(H).$$

Actual Cost:

$$c = O(t(H) + D(n))$$

Potential:

$$\Phi(H') - \Phi(H) \le D(n) - t(H)$$

Amortized Cost:

If we scale the units of potential large enough then amortized cost is

$$\begin{aligned} \hat{c} &= c + \Phi(H') - \Phi(H) \\ & O(t(H) + D(n)) + D(n)\ t(H) \\ &= O(D(n)) \end{aligned}$$

so

$$\hat{c} = O(\log n).$$

Decrease-Key(*H, x, k*):

Let p[x] = parent[x].

This operation is very different from any we've seen before.

We actually Cut subtree rooted at x out of the tree, move it to the root list and unmark x.

We then look at p[x]; if it wasn't marked, we mark it and stop.

If it was marked, we cut p[x], unmark it, move it to the root list, and then check p[p[x]], cascading this process up until either an unmarked ancestor or the root is found.

Decrease-Key(H, x, k)

(i) First check if k < key[p[x]]. If not, do nothing.

(ii) Otherwise

Cut(H, x, p[x]) CascadingCut(H, p[x])

(iii) If k < key[min[H]] then

min[H] = x

Cut(H, x, y):

(i) Move tree rooted at x to root list;

decrement degree[y].

(ii) set mark[x] = false

CascadingCut(H, y)

If y not in root list

then if mark[y] == false **then** mark[y] = true **else** Cut(H, y, p[y])

CascadingCut(H, p[y])

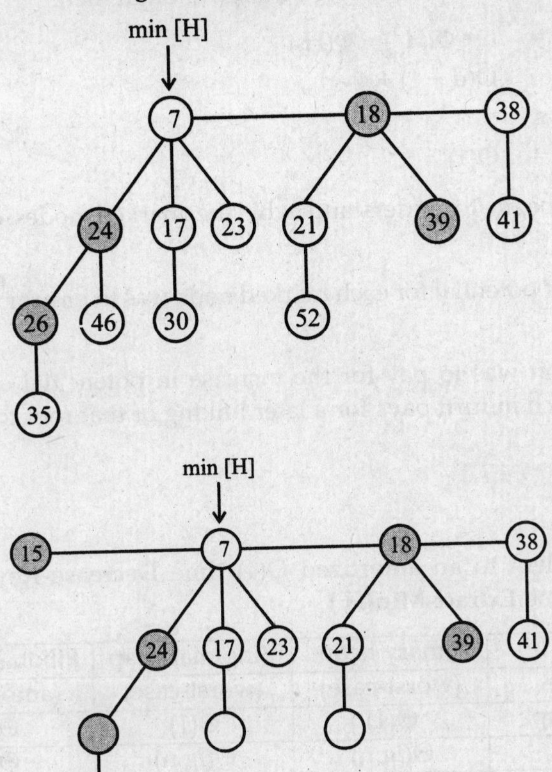

Node containing 46, has key decreased to 15.

Decrease-Key(H, x, k): Run Time

Actual Cost:

If CascadingCut is recursively called d times,

$$c = O(d + 1)$$

Potential:

Original potential is $\Phi = t(H) + 2m(H)$.

After operation there are $t(H) + d$ trees in root list and at most

$$m(H)\ (d\ 1) + 1 = m(H)\ d + 2$$

marked− node−s. Then

$$\Phi(H') - \Phi(H) \leq 4 - d$$

UNIT 2

Amortized Cost:

If we scale the units of potential to be large enough then

$$\hat{c} = c + \Phi(H') - \Phi(H)$$
$$O(d + 1) + 4 - d$$
$$\leq -$$
$$= O(1)$$

We can now begin to understand why the marked nodes contribute 2m(H) to potential.

The first unit of potential for each marked node was to pay for a step in the cascaded cut.

The second unit was to pay for the increase in poten- tial caused by a cut node becoming a root, which in turn pays for a later linking of that root to another root during a Decrease-Key.

Delete(*H, x*):

This is equivalent to an amortized O(1) time **Decrease-Key** (H, x, −∞) and an amortized O(log n) time **Extract-Min(H)**

Procedure	Binary heap (worst-case)	Binomial heap (worst-case)	Fibonacci heap (amortized)
Make-Heap	Θ(1)	Θ(1)	Θ(1)
Insert	Θ(lg n)	O(lg n)	Θ(1)
Minimum	Θ(1)	O(lg n)	Θ(1)
Extract-Min	Θ(lg n)	Θ(lg n)	O(lg n)
Union	Θ(n)	O(lg n)	Θ(1)
Decrease-Key	Θ(lg n)	Θ(lg n)	Θ(1)
Delete	Θ(lg n)	Θ(lg n)	O(lg n)

We have demonstrated that Fibonacci Heaps satisfy the stated amortized running times under the assumption that D(n) = O(log n) where D(n) is the maxi- mum degree of a tree in a Fibonacci Heap containing n nodes.

REVIEW QUESTIONS

1. What are disjoint sets? What are the operation and applications of disjoint sets?
2. Explain the Kruskal's Algorithm for MSTS.
3. What are Fibonacci heap? Elaborate with examples.
4. Prove that Fibonacci Heaps satisfy the amortized running times under the assumption that D(n) = O(log n) where D(n) is the maxi- mum degree of a tree in a Fibonacci Heap containing n nodes.

UNIT 3

ADVANCED ALGORITHM ANALYSIS AND DESIGN

CHAPTER 1

DYNAMIC PROGRAMMING

UNIT 3

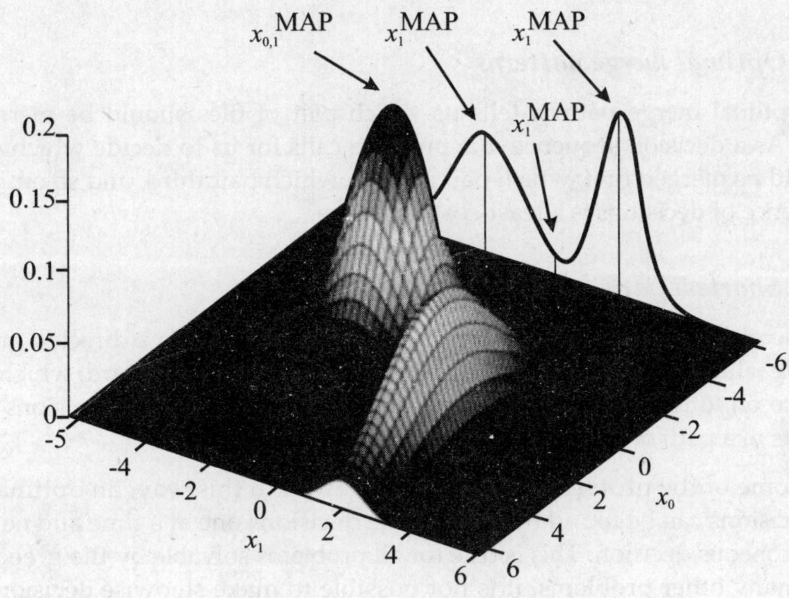

1.1 INTRODUCTION

Dynamic programming is a strategy of algorithm design that can be used when the solution to a problem can be viewed as the result of a sequence of decisions. In computation problems many questions can be solved by dynamic programming.

Example 1. Knapsack

The famous knapsack problem can be viewed as the result of a sequence of decisions. We have to decide the values x_1, $1 \leq i \leq n$. First we make a decision on x_1, then on x_2, then on x_3, and so on. An optimal sequence of decisions maximizes the objective function $\sum p_i x_i$ (It also satisfies the constraints $\sum w_i x_i t \leq m$ and $0 \leq x_i \leq 1$.)

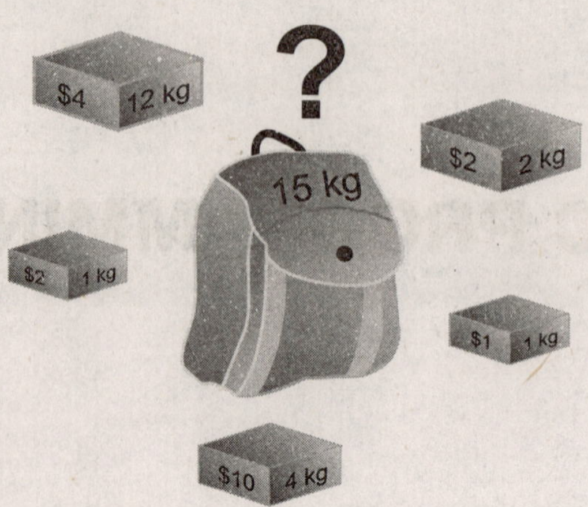

Example 2.Optimal merge patterns

An optimal merge pattern tells us which pair of files should be merged at each step. As a decision sequence, the problem calls for us to decide which pair of files should be merged first, which pair second, which pair third, and so on. An optimal sequence of decisions is a least-cost sequence.

Example 3. Shortest path

One way to find a shortest path from vertex i to vertex j in a directed graph G is to decide which vertex should be the second vertex, which the third, which the fourth, and so on, until vertex j is reached. An optimal sequence of decisions is one that results in a path of least length.

For some of the problems that may be viewed in this way, an optimal sequence of decisions can be found by making the decisions one at a time and never making an erroneous decision. This is true for all problems solvable by the greedy method. For many other problems, it is not possible to make stepwise decisions in such a manner that the sequence of decisions made is optimal.

Example 4.

Suppose we wish to find a shortest path from vertex *i* to vertex *j*. Let A_i be the vertices adjacent from vertex *i*. Which of the vertices in A_i should be the second vertex on the path? There is no way to make a decision at this time and guarantee that future decisions leading to an optimal sequence can be made. If on the other hand we wish to find a shortest path from vertex i to all other vertices in G, then at each step, a correct decision can be made .

One way to solve problems for which it is not possible to make a sequence of stepwise decisions leading to an optimal decision sequence is to try all possible decision sequences. We could enumerate all decision sequences and then pick out the best. But the time and space requirements may be prohibitive. Dynamic programming often drastically reduces the amount of enumeration by avoiding the enumeration of some decision sequences that cannot possibly be optimal. In dynamic programming an optimal sequence of decisions is obtained by making explicit appeal to the principle of optimality.

1.2 PRINCIPLE OF OPTIMALITY

The principle of optimality states that an optimal sequence of decisions has the property that whatever the initial state and decision are, the remaining decisions must constitute an optimal decision sequence with regard to the state resulting from the first decision.

Thus, the essential difference between the greedy method and dynamic programming is that in the greedy method only one decision sequence is ever generated. In dynamic programming, many decision sequence a may be generated. However, sequences containing suboptimal subsequences cannot be optimal (if the principle of optimality holds) and so will not generated.

Example 5. Shortest path with principle of optimality

Let us again Consider the shortest-path problem of Example 3. Assume that $i, i_1, i_2, \ldots, i_k, j$ is a shortest path from i to j. Starting with the initial vertex i, a decision has been made to go to vertex i_1. Following this decision, the problem state is defined by vertex i_1 and we need to find a path from i_1 to j. It is clear that the sequence $i, i_1, i_2, \ldots, i_k, j$ must constitute a shortest i_1 to j path. If not, let $i_1, r_1, r_2, \ldots, r_q, j$ be a shortest i_1 to j path. Than $i, i_1, r_1, \bullet\bullet\bullet, r_q, j$ is an i to j path that is shorter than the path $i; i_1, i_2, \ldots, i_k, j$. Therefore the principle of optimality applies for this problem.

Example 6. 0/1 knapsack

The 0/1 knapsack problem is similar to the knapsack problem except that the x_i's are restricted to have a value of either 0 or 1. Using KNAP($_1$, j, y) to represent the problem

$$\text{maximize } \sum_{1<i<j} p_i x_i$$
$$\text{subject to } \sum_{l<i<j} w_i x_i \leq y \qquad (1)$$
$$xi = 0 \text{ or } 1, 1 \leq i \leq j$$

The knapsack problem is KNAP(1, n, m). Let $y_1, y_2, \ldots, y_n$ be an optimal squence of 0/1 values for $x_1, x_2, \ldots, x_n$, respectively. If $y_1 = 0$, then $y_1, y_2, \ldots, y_n$ must constitute an optimal sequence for the problem KNAP(2, n,m). If it does not, then $y_1, y_2, \ldots, y_n$ is not an optimal sequence for for the problem KNAP(2,n,m $-w_1$) if it isn't, then there is another 0/1 sequence $z_2, z_3, \ldots z_n$ such that $\sum_{2 \leq I \leq n} w_i z_i \leq m - w1$ and $\sum_{2 \leq I \leq n} p_i z_i > \sum_{2 \leq I \leq n} p_i y_i$ Hence, the sequence $y_1, z_2, z_3, \ldots z_n$ is a sequence for (1)With greater value. Again the principle of optimality applies.

UNIT 3

Let S_0 be the initial problem state. Assume that n decisions d_i, $1 \leq i \leq n$, have to be made. Let D_1 $\{r_1, r_2, ..., r_j\}$ be the set of possible decision. values for d_i. Let S_i be the problem state following the choice of decision. r_i $1 \leq i \leq j$. Let p_i be an optimal sequence of decisions with respect to the problem state S_i. Then, when the principle of optimality holds, an optimal -sequence of decisions with respect to S_o is the best of the decision sequences r_i, p_i, $1 \leq i \leq j$.

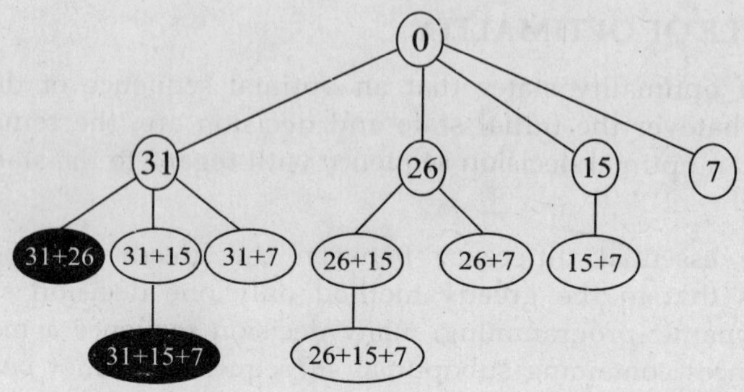

Example 7

Let A, be the set of vertices adjacent to vertex For each vertex $k \in A_i$, let p_k be a shortest path from k to j. Then, a shortest i to j path is the shortest of the paths {i,pk | $k; \in$ Ai}.

Example 8

Let $g_j(y)$ be the value of an optimal solution to KNAP(j + 1, n, y). Clearly, $g_o(m)$ is the value of an optimal solution to KNAP(1, n, m). The possible decisions for x_i are 0 and 1(Di ={0, 1}). from the principle of optimality it follows that

$$g_o(m) = \max\{g_1(m),\ g_1(m - w_1) + pi\} \tag{2}$$

While the principle of optimality has been stated only with respect to the initial state and decision, it can be applied equally well to intermediate states and decisions. The next two examples show how this can be done.

Example 9

Let k be an intermediate vertex on a shortest i to j path i, i_1, i_2, ..., k, p_1, p_2, ..., j. The paths $i, i_1, ..., k$ and $k, p_1, ..., J$ must, respectively, be shortest i to k and k to j paths.

Example 10

Let $y_1, y_2, ..., y_n$ be an optimal solution to KNAP(1, n, m). Then, for each j, $1 \leq j \leq n$, $y_1, ..., y_j$, and $y_{j+1}, ... y_n$ must be optimal solutions to the problems KNAP(1,j, $\Sigma_{2 \leq I \leq n}$ $w_i y_i$) and KNAP($j+1, n, m-\Sigma_{2 \leq I \leq n}$ $w_i y_i$) respectively. This observation allows us to generalize (2) to

$$g_i=(y) = \max \{g_{i+1}(y), g_{i+1}(y-w_{i+1}) + P_{i+1}\} \quad (3)$$

The recursive application of the optimality principle results in a recurrence equation of type (3). Dynamic programming algorithms solve this recurrence to obtain a solution to the given problem instance. The recurrence (3) can be solved using the knowledge $g_n(y) = 0$ for all $y \geq 0$ and $g_n(y) = -\infty$ for $y < 0$. From $g_n(y)$, one can obtain $g_{n-1}(y)$ using (3) with $i = n-1$. Then, using $g_{n-1}(y)$, one can obtain $g_{n-2n}(y)$. Repeating in this way, one can determine $g_1(y)$ and finally $g_o(m)$ using (3) with $i = 0$.

Example 11

0/1 knapsack for the case in which $n = 3$, $w_1 = 2, w_2 = 3, W_3 = 4$, $p_j = 1, p_2 = 2 P_3 = 5$, and $m = 6$.

We have to compute $g_o(6)$. The value of $g_o(6) = \max \{g_1(6), g_1(4) + 1\}$.

In turn, $g_1(6) = \max \{g_2(6), g_2(3)+2\}$.

But $g_2(6) = \max \{g_3(6), g_3(2)+5\} = \max \{0, 5\} = 5$.

And $g_2(3) = \max \{g_3(3), g_3(3-4) + 5) = \max \{0, -\infty\} = 0$.

Thus $g_1(6) = \max \{5, 2\} = 5$.

Similarly, $g_1(4) = \max \{g_2(4), g_2(4-3) + 2\}$.

But $g_2(4) = \max \{g_3(4), g_3(4-4) + 5\} = \max \{0, 5\} = 5$.

The value of $g_2(1) = \max \{g_3(1)\ g_3(1-4) + 5\} = \max \{0 - \infty\} = 0$.

Thus, $g_1(4) = \max\{5, 0\} = 5$.

Therefore, $g_o(6) = \max \{5, 5 + 1\} = 6$.

Example 12

Let *Pj* be the set of vertices adjacent to vertex j(that is, $k \in Pj$ *if* $(k, j) \in E(G)$*]*. For each *k E.Pj*, let *tk* be a shortest *i* to *k* path. The principle of optimality holds and a shortest i to *j path in* the shortest of the paths $\{P_k, j \mid k \in Fj\}$.

To obtain this formulation, we started at vertex j and looked at the last decision made. The last decision was to use one of the edges *(k, j)*, $k \in Pj$ In a sense, we are looking backward on the i to j path.

Example 13

Looking backward on the sequence of decisions $x_i, x_{2i}, ..., x_n$, we see that

$$fj(y) = \max\{f_{j-i}(y), f_{j-1}(y - w_j) + p_j\} \quad (4)$$

where $fj(y)$ is the value of an optimal solution to KNAP(1, j, y).

The value of an optimal solution to KNAP(1, n, m) *is* $f_n(m)$. Equation (4) can be solved by beginning with $f_o(y) = 0$ for all y, $y \geq 0$, and $f_o(y) = -\infty$, for all y, $y < 0$. From this, $f_1, f_2, ..., f_n$ can be successively obtained.

The solution method outlined in Examples 12 and 13 may indicate that one has to look at all possible decision sequences to obtain an optimal decision sequence using dynamic programming. This is not the case. Because of the use of the principle of optimality, decision sequences containing subsequences that are sub optimal are not considered. Although the total number of different decision sequences is exponential in the number of decisions (if there are *d* choices for each of the n decisions to be made then there are d^n possible decision sequences), dynamic programming algorithms often have a polynomial complexity.

Another important feature of the dynamic programming approach is that optimal solutions to sub problems are retained so as to avoid re computing their values. The use of these tabulated values makes it natural to recast the recursive equations into an iterative algorithm. Most of the dynamic programming algorithms in this chapter are expressed in this way.

The remaining part of this chapter apply dynamic programming to a variety of problems. These examples should help you understand the method better and also realize the advantage of dynamic programming over explicitly enumerating all decision sequences.

1.3 MULTISTAGE GRAPHS

A multistage graph G = *(V, E)* is a directed graph in which the vertices are partitioned into k≥ 2 disjoint sets *Vi*, $1 \le i < k$. Inaddition, if (u, v) is an edge in E, then **u** ∈ *Vi* and v ∈ V_{i+1} for some i, $1 \le i < k$. The sets Vi and V_k are such that $|V_1| = |Vk|$ I= 1. Let s and t, respectively, be the vertices in V_1 and V_k. The vertex s is the source, and *t* the *sink*. Let *c(i, j)* be the cost of edge *(i, j)*. The cost of a path from s to *t* is the sum of the costs of the edges on the path. The multistage graph problem is to find a minimum-cost path from s to t. Each set *Vi* defines a stage in the graph. Because of the constraints on E, every path from s to t starts in stage 1, goes to stage 2. then to stage 3, then to stage 4, and so on, and eventually terminates in stage k. Figure 1. shows a five-stage graph. A minimum-cost s to t path is indicated by the broken edges.

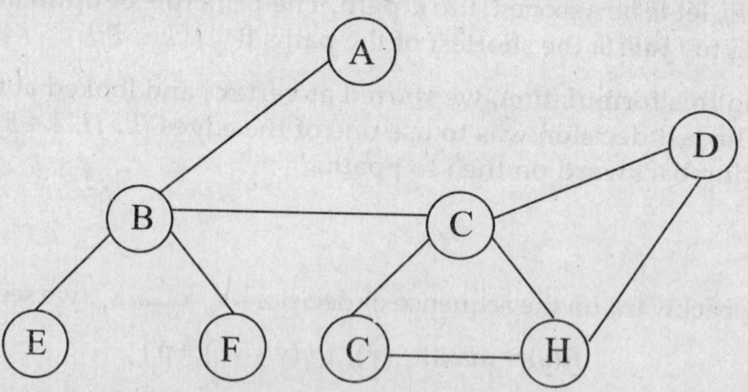

Many problems can be formulated as multistage graph problems. We give only one example. Consider a resource allocation problem in which *n* units of resource are to be allocated to *r* projects. If *j*, $0 \le j \le n$, units of the resource are allocated to project *i*, then the resulting net profit is *N(i, j)*. The problem is to allocate the resource to the r projects in such a way as to maximize total net profit. This problem can be formulated as an r +

1 stage graph problem as follows. Stage i, $1 \leq i \leq r$, represents project i. There are $n + 1$ vertices $V(i, j)$, $0 \leq j \leq n$, associated with stage i, $2 \leq i \leq r$. Stages 1 and r + 1 each have one vertex, fV(1, 0) = s and $V(r + 1, n) = t$, respectively. Vertex $V(i, j)$, $2 \leq i \leq r$, represents the state in which a total of j units of resource have been allocated to -projects 1, 2, ..., i - 1. The edges in G are of the form (V(i, j), $V(i + 1, 1)$) for all $j \leq$ I and $1 \leq i < r$.

The edge $(V(i, j), V(i + 1, l))$, $j \leq l$, *is* assigned a weight or cost of $N(i, l - j)$ and corresponds to allocating $l - j$ units of resource to project i, $1 \leq i \leq r$. In addition, G has edges of the type $(V(r, j), V(r + 1, n))$. Each such edge is assigned a weight of $\max_{o<p<n-j}\{N(r,p)\}$. The resulting graph for a three project problem with n = 4 is shown in Figure 2. It should be easy to see that an optimal allocation of resources is defined by a maximum cost s to t path. This is easily converted into a minimum-cost problem by changing the sign of all the edge costs.

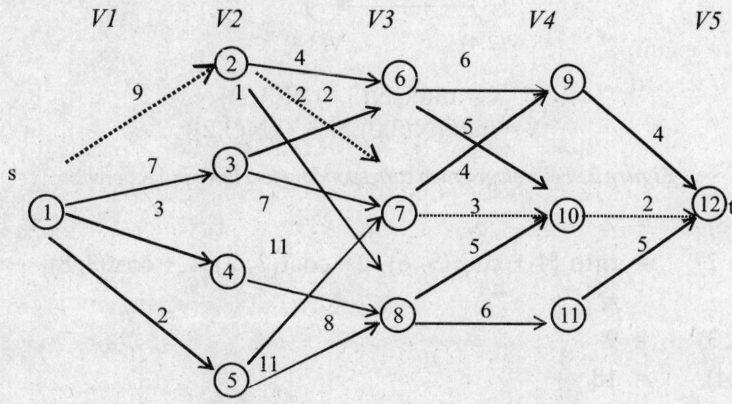

Figure 1. Five-stage graph

A dynamic programming formulation for a k-stage graph problem is obtained by first noticing that every s to t path is the result of a sequence of k– 2 decisions. The ith decision involves determining which vertex in V_{i+1}, $1 \leq i \leq k - 2$, is to be on the path. It is easy to see that the principle of optimality holds. Let $p(i, j)$ be a minimum-cost path from vertex j in Vi to vertex t. Let *cost(i, j)* be the cost of this path. Then, using the forward approach, we obtain

$$cost(i,j) = \min_{\substack{l \in v_{i+1} \\ (j,l) \in E}} \{C(j, l) + cost(i + 1, l)\} \quad (5)$$

Since, $cost(k - 1, j) = c(j,t)$ if $(j,t) \in E$ and $cost(k - 1, j) = \infty$ if $(j,t) \notin E$. *(5.)* may be solved for *cost (1, s)* by first computing *cost(k - 2, j) for* all $j \in Vk{-}2$, then cost(k- 3,j) for all $j \in Vk{-}3$, and so on, and finally *cost (1, s)*. Trying this out on the graph of Figure 1., we obtain

cost(3, 6) = min {6 + *cost*(4, 9), 5+ *cost*(4,10)}
= 7

cost(3,7) = min {4 + cost(4,9), 3 + *cost(4,10)*}
= 5

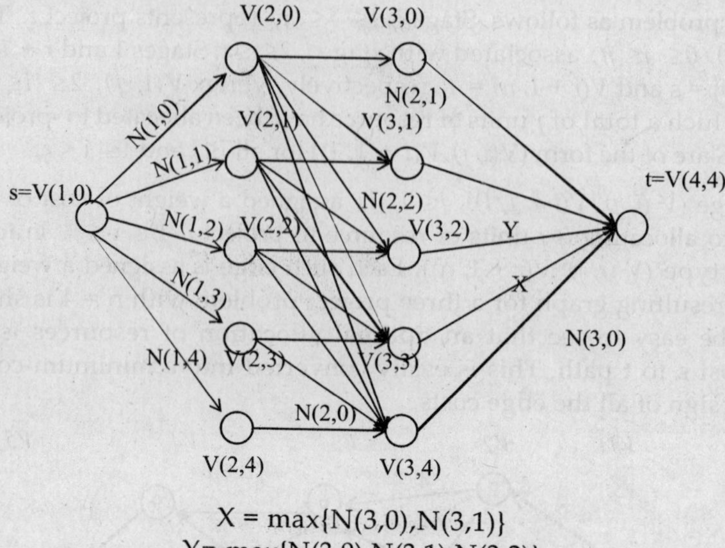

***Figure 2.** Four-stage graph corresponding to a three-project problem*

$$
\begin{aligned}
\text{cost}(3, 8) &= 7\\
\text{cost}(2, 2) &= \min\{4 + \text{cost}(3, 6), 2 + \text{cost}(3, 7), 1 + \text{cost}(3, 8)\}\\
&= 7\\
\text{cost}(2, 3) &= 9\\
\text{cost}(2,4) &= 18\\
\text{cost}(2, 5) &= 15\\
\text{cost}(1,1) &= \min\{9 + \text{cost}(2, 2), 7 + \text{cost}(2, 3), 3 + \text{cost}(2, 4), 2 + \text{cost}(2,5)\}\\
&= 16
\end{aligned}
$$

Note that in the calculation of cost(2, 2), we have reused the values of cost(3, 6), cost(3, 7), and cost(3, 8) and so avoided their recomputation. A minimum cost s to t path has a cost of 16. This path can be determined easily if we record the decision made at each state (vertex). Let $d(i, j)$ be the value of l(where l is a node) that minimizes $c(j,1) + cost(i + 1, l)$ (using Eq 5.).

From the Figure 1 we obtain

$d(3,6) = 10; d(3,7) = 10; d(3,8) = 10;$

$d(2, 2) = 7;$ $d(2, 3) = \mathbf{6};$ $d(2, 4) = 8;$ $d(2, 5) = \mathbf{8};$

$d(1,1) = 2$

Let the minimum-cost path be $s = 1, v_2, v_3, \ldots, v_{k-i}\ t$. It is easy to see that $\boldsymbol{v2 = d(1,1) = 2, v3 = d(2,d(1,1)) = 7}$, **and** $\boldsymbol{v4 = d(3,d(2, d(1,1))) = d(3,7) = 10}$.

Now to solve Eq (5) for a general k-stage graph, let us impose an ordering on the vertices in V. This ordering makes it easier to write the algorithm. We require that the n vertices in V are indexed 1 through n. Indices are assigned in order of stages. First, s is assigned index 1, then vertices in V2 are assigned indices, then vertices from V_3, and so on. Vertex t has index n. Hence, indices assigned to vertices in V_{i+1} are bigger than those assigned to vertices in V_i (see Figure 1).

As a result of this indexing scheme, cost and *d* can be computed in the order n–1, n–2,..., 1. The first subscript in cost, p, and d only identifies the stage number and is omitted in the algorithm. The resulting algorithm, in pseudocode, is FGraph (Algorithm 1.).

The complexity analysis of the function FGraph is fairly straightforward. If G is represented by its adjacency lists, then r in line 9 of Algorithm 1 can be found in time proportional to the degree of vertex *j*. Hence, if G has $|E|$ edges, then the time for the for loop of line 7 is $\Theta(|V| + |E|)$. *The* time for the for loop of line 16 is $\Theta(k)$. Hence, the total time is $\Theta(|V| + |E|)$. In addition to the space needed for the input, space is needed for cost[ ], *d[ ]*, and p[ ].

```
1.  Algorithm FGraph(G, k., n,p)
2.      // The input is a k-stage graph G=(V, E) with n vertices
3.          // indexed in order of stages. E is a set of edges and c[i, j]
4.  // is the cost of (i, j). p[1 : k] is a nuuimum-cost path.
5.  {
6.  cost[n] := 0.0;
7.          for j:= n - 1 to 1 step -1 do
8.  Compute cost[j].
9.  Let r be a vertex such that (j, r) is an edge
10. of G and c[j, r]  + cost[r] is minimum;
11. cost[j] := c[j, r] + cast[r];
12. d[j] := r;
13. }
14. // Find a minimum-cost path.
15. p[1] := 1; p[k] := n;
16. for j:= 2 to k-1 do p[j] :- d[p[j -1]];
17. }
```

Algorithm 1. Multistage graph (Forward Approach)

The multistage graph problem can also be solved using the backward approach. Let bp(i, j) be a minimuin-cost path from vertex s to a vertex *j* in tit. Let ***bcost(i, j)*** be the cost of ***bp(i, j)***. From the backward approach we obtain

$$bcost(i,j) = \min_{\substack{l \in V_{i-1} \\ (l,j) \in E}} \{bcost(i-1, l) + c(l,j)\} \qquad (6)$$

Since ***bcost(2, j) = c(1, j) if (1,j)*** $\in$ E and ***bcost(2, j)*** = ∞ if $(1, j) \notin$, *bcost(i, j)* canbe computed using (6) by first computing *bcost* for *i*= 3, then for i = 4, and so on. For the graph of Figure 1, we obtain

bcost(3, 6) = min {bcost(2, 2) + c(2,6), bcost(2, 3) + c(3,6)}
= min {9+4,7+2}
= 9

bcost(3,7) = 11
bcost(3,8) = 10
bcost(4,9) = 15
bcost(4,10) = 14
bcost(4,11) = 16
bcost(5,12) = 16

The corresponding algorithm, in pseudocode, to obtain a minimum-cost *s- t* path is BGraph (Algorithm 2). The first subscript on *bcost, p,* and *d* are omitted for the same reasons as before. This algorithm has the same complexity as FGraph provided G is now represented by its inverse adjacency lists (i.e., for each vertex *v* we have a, list of vertices *w* such that *(w, v) ∈ E).*

```
Algorithm BGraph(G, k, n, p)
Same function as FGraph
{
bcost[1] := 0.0;
for j:= 2 to ri do
{ // Compute bcost[j].
Let r be such that (r, j) is an edge of
G and bcost[r] + c[r, j] is minimum;
bcost[j] := bcost[r] + c[r, j];
d[j] := r;
}
// Find a minimum-cost path.
p[l] := 1; p[k] := n;
for j:= k - 1 to 2 do p[j] := d[p[j + 1]];
}
```

Algorithm 2. Multistage graph (backward approach)

It should be easy to see that both FGraph and BGraph work correctly even on a more generalized version of multistage graphs. In this generalization, the graph is permitted to have edges **(u, v)** such **that** *u* ∈Vi, **v** ∈ Vj, **and i** < j.

Note: In the pseudocodes **FGraph and BGraph, bcost(i,** j) is set to ∞ for *any (i, j) ∉E.* When programming these pseudocodes, one could **use** the maximum allowable floating point number for ∞. If the weight of any such edge is added to some other costs, a floating point overflow might occur. Care should be taken to avoid such overflows.

8.4 ALL-PAIRS SHORTEST PATHS

Let $G = (V, E)$ be a directed graph with n vertices. Let cost be a cost adjacency matrix for G such that cost(i, i) = 0, $1 < i \leq n$. Then cost(i, j) is the length (or cost) of edge *(i, j)* if $(i, j) \in E(G)$ and $cost(i, j) = \infty$ if $i \neq j$ and $(i, j) \notin E(G)$. The all-pairs shortest-path problem is to determine a matrix *A* such that *A(i, j)* is the length of a shortest path from i to *j*. Since each application of this procedure requires $O(n^2)$ time, the matrix *A* can be obtained in $O(n^3)$ time.

We obtain an alternate $O(n^3)$ solution to this problem using the principle of optimality. Our alternate solution requires a weaker restriction on edge costs than required by ShortestPaths. Rather than require $cost(i, j) \geq 0$, for every edge *(i, j)*, we only require that G have no cycles with negative length. Note that if we allow G to contain a cycle of negative length, then the shortest path betweem any two vertices on this cycle has length $-\infty$

Let us examine a shortest *i* to *j* path in G, $i \neq j$. This path originates at vertex i and goes through some intermediate vertices (possibly none) and terminates at vertex j. We can assume that this path contains no cycles for if there is a cycle, then this can be deleted without increasing the path length (no cycle has negative length). If *k* is an intermediate vertex on this shortest path, then the subpaths from i to *k* and from *k* to j must be shortest paths from *i* to k and *k* to j, respectively. Otherwise, the i to g path *is* not of minimum length. So, the principle of optimality holds. This' alerts, us to. the prospect of using dynamic programming. If *k* is the intermediate vertex with highest index, then the *i* to *k* path is a shortest i to *k* path in G going through no vertex with index greater than *k* - 1. Similarly the *k* to j path Ls a shortest k to j path in G going through no vertex of index greater than *k - 1*. We can regard the construction of a shortest *i* to *j* path as first requiring a decision as to which is the highest indexed intermediate vertex k. Once this decision has been made, we need to find two shortest paths, one from *i* to k and the other from *k* to *j*. Neither of these may go through a vertex with index greater than k- 1. Using A^k *(i., j)* to represent the length of a shortest path from *i* to *j* going through no vertex of index greater than *k*, we obtain

$$A(i, j) = \min\{ \min_{1 \leq k \leq n} \{A^{k-1}(i, k) + A^{k-1}(k, j)\}, cost,(i, j)\} \quad (7)$$

Clearly, $A^\circ(i, j) = cost(i, j)$, $1 \leq i \leq n$, $1 \leq j \leq n$. We can obtain a recurrence for , $A^k(i, j)$ using an argument similar to that used before. A shortest path from *i* to *j* going through no vertex higher than *k* either goes through vertex *k* or it does not. If it does, $A^k(i, j) = Ak^{-1}(i, k) + A^{k-1}(k, j)$.

If it does not then no intermediate vertex has index greater than k – 1. Hence $A^k(i, j) = A^{k-1}(i, j)$. Combining, we get

$$A^k(i,j) = \min\{A^{k-1}(i, j), A^{k-i}(i\ k) + A^{k-1}(k,j)\}, k \geq 1 \quad (8)$$

The following example shows that (8) is not true for graphs with cycles of negative length.

Example 14. Figure 3 shows a digraph together with its matrix A°. For this graph $A^2(1,3) \neq \min\{A^1(1, 3), A^1(1, 2) + A^1(2, 3)\} = 2$. Instead we see that $A^2(1, 3) = -\infty$. The length of the path

1,2,1,2,1,2,...,1,2,3

can be made arbitrarily small. This is so because of the presence of the cycle *1 2 1* which has a length of -1.

Recurrence (8) can be solved for A^n by first computing A^1, thenA^2, then A^3,, and so on. Since there is no vertex in G with index greater than n, $A(i, j) = A^n(i, j)$. Function AllPaths computes ,$A^n(i, j)$: The computation is done inplace so the superscript on *A is* not needed. The reason this computation can be carried out in-place is that $A^k(i, k) = A^{k-1}(i, k)$ and $A^k(k, j) = A^{k-1}(k, j)$. Hence, when A^k *is* formed, the kth column and row do not change. Consequently, when $A^k(i, j)$ *is* computed in line 11 of Algorithm 3, $A(i, k) = A^{k-1}(i, k) = A^k(i, k)$ and $A(k, j) = A^{k-1}(k, j) = A^k(k, j)$.

So, the old values on which the new values are based do not change on this iteration.

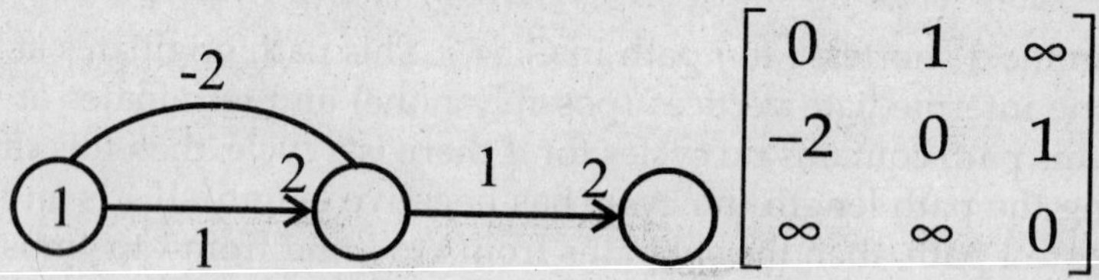

Figure 3. Graph with negative cycle

0 Algorithm AllPaths(cost, A, n)

```
1.  // cost[1 : n, l: n] is the cost adjacency matrix of a graph with
2.  // n vertices; A[i, j] is the cost of a shortest path from vertex
3.  // i to vertex j. cost[i, i] = 0.0, for 1≤ i≤ n.
4.  {
5.  for i:=l to n do
6.  for j:= 1 to n do
7.  A[i, j] := cost.[i, j]; // Copy cost into A.
8.  for k:= 1 to n do
9.  for i:=l to n do
10. for j:=ltondo
11. A[i,j]      min(A[i, j], A[i, k] + A[k, j]);
12. }
```

Algorithm 3. Function to compute lengths of shortest paths

Example 15. The graph of Figure 4(a) has the cost matrix of Figure 4(b). The initial A matrix, $A^{(0)}$, plus its values after 3 iterations $A^{(1)}$, $A^{(2)}$, and $A^{(3)}$ are given in Figure 4.

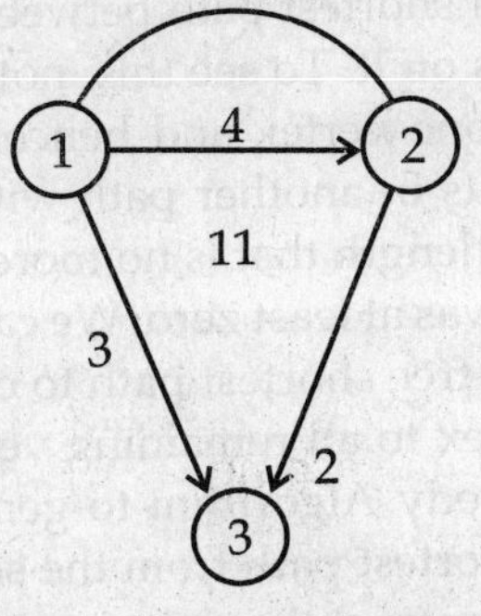

A°	1	2	3
1	0	4	11
2	6	0	2
3	3	∞	0

A'	1	2	3
1	0	4	11
2	6	0	2
3	3	7	0

(a) ***Example digraph***

A^2	1	2	3
1	0	4	6
2	6	0	2
3	3	7	0

A^3	1	2	3
1	0	4	6
2	5	0	2
3	3	7	0

Figure 4. Directed graph with associated matrices

Let M = max *{cost(i, j(i, j)* ∈ E(G)j- It is easy to see that $A^n(ij) \le (n - 1)M$. From the working of **AIPaths,** it is clear that if (i, *j*) ∉ *(G)* and i≠ *j*, then we can initialize cost(i, *j*) to any number greater than (n– *1)M* (rather than the maximum allowable floating point number). If at termination, *A(i, j)* > *(n - 1)M,* then there is no directed path from i w *j* in G. Even for this choice of ∞, care should be taken to avoid any floating point overflows.

Complexity of **AIIPaths is Θ(n³).**

1.5 SINGLE-SOURCE SHORTEST PATHS: GENERAL WEIGHTS

To see this, consider the graph of Figure 5. Let *v*= 1 be the source vertex. Here *n* = 3.The loop of lines 12 to 22 of *Greedy Algorithm to Generate Shortest Path* is iterated just once. Also *u* = 3 in lines 15 and 16, and so no changes are made to ***dist[ ].*** The algorithm terminates with ***dist[2]*** = 7 and ***dist[3]*** = 5. The shortest path from 1 to 3 is 1,2,3. This path has length 2, which is less than the computed value of ***dist*[3].**

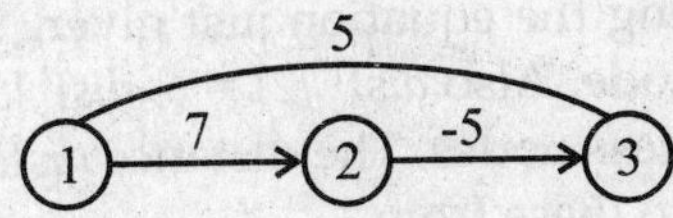

Figure 5. Directed graph with a negative-length edge

When negative edge lengths are permitted, we require that the graph have no cycles of negative length. This is necessary to ensure that shortest paths consist of a finite number of edges. For example, in the graph of Figure 5, the length of the shortest path from vertex 1 to **vertex 3** is –∞. The length of the path 1,2,1,2,1.2,…,1,2,3 can be made arbitrarily small as was shown in Example 14.

When there are no cycles of **negative length, there is** a shortest path between any two vertices of an n-vertex graph that has at most n – 1 edges on it. To see this, note that a path that has more than n –1 edges must repeat at least one vertex and hence must contain a cycle. Elimination of the cycles from the path results in another path with the same source and destination. This path is cycle-free and has a length that is no more than that of the original path, as the length of the eliminated cycles was at least zero. We can use this observation on the maximum number of edges on a cycle-free shortest path to obtain an algorithm to determine a shortest path from a source vertex to all remaining vertices in the graph. As in the case of ShortestPaths (Algorithm Greedy Algorithm to generate Shortest Parhs), we compute only the length, *dist[u,]*, of the shortest path from the source vertex v to u. An exercise examines the extension needed to construct the shortest paths.

Let $dist^{\ell}[zi]$ be the length of a shortest path from the source vertex v to vertex u under the constraint that tho shortest path contains at most ℓ edges. Then, *(list' [u.] =cost[v,u].* $1 \leq a \leq n$. As noted earlier, when there are no cycles of negative length, we can limit our search for shortest paths to paths with at most n– 1 edges. Hence, $dist^{n-1}[u]$ is the length of an unrestricted shortest path from v to u.

Our goal then is to compute $dist^{n-1}[u]$ for all *u*. This can be done using the dynamic programming methodology. First, we make the following observations:

1. If the shortest path from v to u with at most *k, k* > *1*, edges has no more than k - 1 edges, then $di,,t^{k}[u] = dist^{k-1}[u]$.

2. If the shortest path from *v* to *u* with at most *k, k* > 1, edges has exactly k edges, then it is made up of a shortest path from v to some vertex *j* followed by the edge (j, u). The path from *v* to *j* has *k - 1* edges, and its length is $dist^{k-1}[j]$. All vertices *i* such that the edge *(i, u)* is in the graph are candidates for *j*. Since we are interested in a shortest path, the i that minimizes $dist^{k-1}[i] + cost[i, u]$ *is* the correct value for j.

These observations result in the following recurrence for *dist:*

$dist^{k}[u] = \min \{dist^{k-1}[u], \min \{dist^{k-1}[i] + cost[i,u]\}\}$

This recurrence can be used to compute $dist^{k}$ from $disk^{k-1}$, for $k= 2,3,\dots,n-1$

Example 16.

Figure 6. gives a seven-vertex graph, together with the *arrays* $dist^{k}$, $k = 1, \dots, 6$. These arrays were computed using the equation just given. For instance, $dist^{k}[1] = 0$ for all *k* since 1 is the source node. Also $dist^{1}[2] = 6$, $dist^{1}[3] = 5$, and $dist^{1}[4] = 5$, since there are edges from 1 to these nodes. The distance *distl[]* is ∞ for the nodes 5,6, and 7 since there are no edges to these from 1.

$$\mathbf{dist^2[2]} = \mathbf{\min \{dist^1 [2], min}i \mathbf{\ distl [i] + cost[i, 2] \}}$$

$$= \min \{6, 0+ 6, 5- 2, 5+ \infty, \infty + \infty, \infty + \infty, \infty + \infty\} = 3$$

Here the terms 0 + 6, 5 – 2, 5 + ∞, ∞ + ∞, ∞ + ∞, and ∞ + ∞ correspond to a, choice of i= 1, 3, 4, 5, 6, and 7, respectively. The rest of the entries are computed it). an analogous manner,

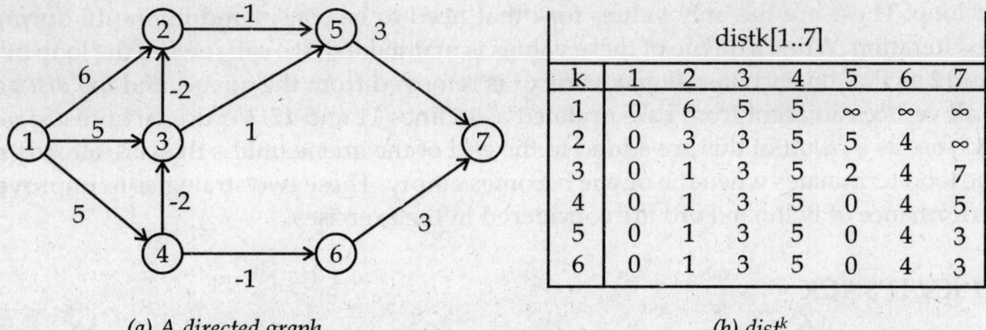

k	1	2	3	4	5	6	7
	distk[1..7]						
1	0	6	5	5	∞	∞	∞
2	0	3	3	5	5	4	∞
3	0	1	3	5	2	4	7
4	0	1	3	5	0	4	5
5	0	1	3	5	0	4	3
6	0	1	3	5	0	4	3

(a) A directed graph *(b) $dist^k$*

***Figure 6.** Shortest paths with negative edge lengths*

An exercise shows that if we use the same memory location *dist[ul* for $dist^k[u]$, $k= 1,...,n-1$, then the final value of *dist[u] is* still $dist^{n-1}[u]$. Using this fact and the recurrence for *dist* shown above, we arrive at the pseudocode of Algorithm 5.4 to compute the length of the shortest path from vertex v to each other vertex of the graph. This algorithm is referred to as the Bellman and Ford algorithm.

Each iteration of the for loop of lines 7 to 12 takes $O(n^2)$ time if adjacency matrices are used and $O(e)$ time if adjacency lists are used. Here e is the number of edges in the graph. The overall complexity is $O(n^3)$ when adjacency matrices are used and $O(ne)$ when adjacency lists are used. The observed complexity of the shortest-path algorithm can be reduced by noting that if none of the *dist* values change on one iteration of the for loop of lines 7 to 12, then none will change on successive iterations. So, this loop can be rewritten to terminate either after n– 1 iterations or after the -

```
1.  Algorithm BellmanFord(v, cost, dist,, n)
2.  // Single-source/all-destinations shortest
3.  // paths with negative edge costs
4.  {
5.  for i := 1 to n do //Initialize dist.
6.  dist[i] := cost[v, i];
7.  for k:=2 to n-l do
8.  for each u such that u ≠ v and u has
9.  at least one incoming edge do
10. for each (i, u) in the graph do
11. if dist[u] > dist[i] + cost[i, u] then
12. dist[u] := dist[i] + cost[i,u]
13. }
```

Algorithm 4. Bellman and Ford algorithm to compute shortest paths

First iteration in which no *dist* values, whichever occurs first. Another possibility is to maintain a queue of vertices *i* whose *dist* values changed on the previous iteration of the for loop. These are the only values for i that need to be considered in line 10 during the next iteration. When a queue of these values is maintained, we can rewrite the loop of lines 7 to 12 so that on each iteration, a vertex i is removed from the queue, and the *dist* values of all vertices adjacent from i are updated as in lines 11 and *12*. Vertices whose *dist* values decrease as a result of this are added to the end of the queue unless they are already on it. The loop terminates when the queue becomes empty. These two strategies to improve, the performance of Bellman Ford are considered in the exercises.

0/1 KNAPSACK

Now we consider 0/1 knapsack problem. A solution to the knapsack problem can be obtained by making a sequence of decisions on the variables $x_1, x_2, ..., x_n$. A decision on variable x_i involves determining which of the values 0 or 1 is to be assigned to it. Let us assume that decisions on the *xi* are made in the order $x_n, x_{n-1}, ..., x_1$. Following a decision on x_n, we may be in one of two possible states: the capacity remaining in the knapsack is m and no profit has accrued or the capacity remaining is m- w_n and a profit of $\mathbf{p_n}$ has accrued. It is clear that the remaining decisions $x_{n-1}, ..., x_1$ must be optimal with respect to the problem state resulting from the decision on x_n. Otherwise, $x_n, ..., x_1$ will not be optimal. Hence, the principle of optimality holds.

Let f_j *(y)* be the value of **an** optimal solution to **KNAP(1,** *j, y*). Since the principle of optimality holds, we obtain

$$f_n(m) = \max\{f_{n-1}(m), f_{n-1}(m - w_n) + P_n\} \qquad (9)$$

For arbitrary $f_j = (y)$, i > 0, Equation 9 generalizes to

$$fi(y) = \max\{f_{i-1}(y), f_{i-1}(y - w_i) + p_i\} \qquad (10)$$

Equation 9 can be solved for $f_n(m)$ by beginning with the knowledge $fo(y) = 0$ for all *y* and f_i (y) $= -\infty$, y< 0. Then $f_1, f_2, ..., f_n$ can be successively computed using (10). When the w_i's are integer, we need to compute *fi(y)* for integer y, $0 \leq y \leq m$. Since $fi(y) = -\infty$ for y < 0, these function values need not be computed explicitly. Since each f_i can be computed from *fi–1* in 0(m) it takes $\Theta(mn)$ time to compute f_n When the w_i's are real numbers, *fi(,y)* is needed for real numbers y such that $0 \leq y \leq m$. So, *fi* cannot be explicitly computed for all y in this range. Even when the w_i's are integer, the explicit $\Theta(mn)$ computation of f_n may not be the most efficient computation. So. i we explore an alternative method for both cases.

Notice that *fi(y)* is an ascending step function; i.e., there are a finite number of y's, $0 = y_1 < Y_2 < ... < y_k$, such that $fi(y_1) < fi(y2) < ... < fi(y_k) > fi(y) - \infty\ y \leq yi; fi(y) = f(yk), y \geq yk$; and $fi(y) = fi(yj).\ 'y_j \leq y \leq y_{j+1}$.

So, we need to compute only *fi(yj)*, $1 \leq j \leq k$.

We use the ordered set $S^1 = \{(f(yj), y_j) | 1 \leq j \leq k\}$ to represent $f_1(y)$. Each member of

Si is a pair *(P, W)*, where P = *fi*(yj) and *W*= y_j. Notice that $S^\circ = \{(0, 0)\}$. We can compute S^{1+1} from S^1 by first computing

$$S^i_1 = \{(P, W) | (P - pi, W - w_i) \in S^i\} \qquad (11)$$

Now, S^{i+i} can be computed by merging the pairs in S^i and S^i together. Note that if S^{i+1} contains two pairs *(Pj, Wj)* and *(Pk, Wk)* with the property that $P_J \leq P_k$ and $w_j \geq W_k$, then the pair *(P_j, Wj)* can be discarded because of (10). Discarding or purging rules such as this one are also known as dominance rules. Dominated tuples get purged. In the above,. *(Pk , Wk.* dominates *(Pj, Wj)*.

Interestingly, the strategy we have come up with can also be derived by attempting to solve the knapsack problem via a systematic examination of the up to $2^{n'}$ possibilities for $x_1, x_2, ..., x_n$, Let S' represent the possible states resulting from the $2i$ decision sequences for $x_1,...,x_i$. A state refers to a pair *(Pj, Wj)*, *Wj* being the total weight of objects included in the knapsack and P. being the corresponding profit. To obtain S^{i+1}, we note " that the possibilities for x_{i+1} are $x_{i+1} = 0$ or $x_{i+1} = 1$. When $x_{i+i} = 0$, the resulting states are the same as for S^i. When $x_{i+1} = 1$, the resulting states are obtained by adding $(p_{i+1}w_{i+i})$ to each state in *Si*. Call the set of these additional states S^i_1. The S^i_1 is the same as in Equation 11. Now, S^{i+1} can be computed by merging the states in S^i and S^i_1 together.

Example 21

Consider the knapsack instance n = 3, (w_1, w_2, w_3) =(2, 3, 4),(p_1, p_2, p_5)=(1,2,5) and m = 6. For these data we have

S° = {(0,0)};S° = *{(1,2)}*

S^1 ={*(0, 0)*, (1, 2)}; Si ={(2, 3), (3, 5)}

S^2 = {(0, 0), (¹,2), (2, 3), (3, 5)}; S^2_1 = {(5, 4), (6, s), (7, 7), (8, 9)}

S^3 = {(o, o)> (1, 2), (2, 3), (5, 4), (s, 6), (7, 7), (8, 9)}

Note that the pair (3, 5) has been eliminated from S^3 as a result of the purging rule.

When generating the S^is, we can also purge all pairs *(P, W)* with W > *m* as these pairs determine the value of $f_n(x)$ only for x > m. Since the knapsack capacity is m, we are not interested in the behavior of f_n for x > m. when all pairs *(Pj,Wj)* with W_j > m are purged from the S^is, f_n(m) is given by the P value of the last pair in S^n (note that the S^is are ordered sets). Note also that by computing S^n, we can find the solutions to all the knapsack problems, KNAP(1, n, x), 0≤ x≤ m, and not just KNAP(1, n, m). Since, we want only a solution to KNAP(1, n, m), we can dispense with the computation of S^n. The last pair in S^n is either the last one in S^{n-1} or it is $P_j + p_n, W_j + w_n$), where *(Pj, Wj)* $\in S^{n-1}$ such that $W_j + w_n \leq$ m and W_j *is* maximum.

If *(P1, WI)* is the last tuple in S^n, a set of 0/1 values for the x_i's such that $\Sigma pixi$ = P1 and $\Sigma wixi = W1$ can be determined by carrying out a search through the *S's*. We can set x_n = 0 if *(P1, Wl)* $\in S^{n-1}$ If *(P1, W1)* $\notin S'^{n-1}$, then *(P1 - p_n, W1 - w_n)* $\in S'^{n-1}$ and we can set x_n = *1*.

This leaves us to determine how either *(P1, W1)* or *(P1 - p_n, W1- Wn,)* was obtained in S'^{n-1}. This can be done recursively.

Example 22

With m= 6, the value of $f_3(6)$ is given by the tuple (6, 6) S^3 (Example 21). The tuple (6, 6) $\notin S^2$, and so we must set *x3* = 1. The pair (6, 6) came from the pair (6 – *p3* 6 – *w3*) _(1, 2). Hence (1, 2) $\in S^2$. Since (1,2) $\in S_1$, we can set $x_2 = 0$. Since (1, 2) $\notin S^{\circ}$, we obtain x_1.= 1. Hence an optimal solution is $(x_1, x2, x3)$=(1, 0, 1).

We can sum up all we have said so far in the form of an informal algorithm DKP (Algorithm 4). To evaluate the complexity of the algorithm, we need to specify how the sets S^i and S^i_1 are to be represented; provide an algorithm to merge S^i and S^i_1 and specify an algorithm that will trace through S^{-n-1}, ..., S^1 and determine a set of 0/1 values for *xn,...x1*

```
Algorithm DKP(p, w, n, m)
{
S°:= 1(0,0)};
for i:=l to n-l do
{
S^(i-1) := {(P,W) | (P-pi,W -wi) ∈ S^(i-1) and W≤ m};
S^i := MergePurge(S^(i-1), Si-1);
}
(PX, WX ):=last pair in S^(i-1);
(PY, WY) := (P' + p_n W' + w_n where W' is the largest W in
any pair in S^(n-1) such that W + w_n,≤ m;
// Trace back for x_n, x_(n-1,...,) x_1.
if (PX > PY) then x_n := 0;
else x_n := 1;
Trace BackFor(x_(n-1,....,) x_1);
}
```

Algorithm 5. Infermal knapsack algorithm,

We can use an array *pair[ ]* to represent all the pairs *(P, W)*. The *P* values are stored in *pair[ ].p* and the *W* values in *pair[ ].w*. Sets S°, *Sl* , S^{n-1} can be stored adjacent to each other. This requires the use of pointers b[i], 0,≤ i ≤ *n*, where *b[i]* is the location of the first element in S^1, $0 \le i \le n$, and *b[n]* is one more than the location of the last element in S^{n-1} .

Example 23

Using the representation above, the sets S°, S^1, and S^2 of Example 21 appear as

1	2	3	4	5	6	7		
pair[ ].p	0	0	1	0	1	2	3	
pair[ ].w	0	0	2	0	2	3	5	
		b[0]		b[1]		b[2]		b[3]

The merging and purging of S^{i-1} and S^{i-1}_1 can be carried out at the same time that S^{i-1}_i is generated. Since the pairs in S^{i-1} are in increasing order of P and *W*, the pairs for S^i are generated in this order, If the next pair, generated for S^{i-1}_i is *(PQ; WQ)*, then we can merge into S^i all pairs from S^{i-1} with *W* value ≤ *WQ*. The purging rule can be used to decide whether any pairs get purged. Hence, no additional space is needed in which to store S^{i-1}_i

DKnap (Algorithm 5) generates S^i from S^{i-1} in this way. The S^is are generated in the for loop of lines 7 to 42 of Algorithm 5. At the start of each iteration t = b[i – 1] and h is the index of the last pair in S^{i-1} The variable k points to the next tuple in S^{i-1} that has to be merged into S^i In line 10, the function Largest determines the largest q, t ≤ q ≤ h 'for which pair[q].w + w[i] ≤ *m*. This can be done by performing a binary search. The code for this function is left as an exercise. Since u′ is set such that for all **Wj, h ≥ j > u, Wj + wi > m**, the pairs for S^{i-1} are *(P(j)+ p_1, W((j) wi),* 1≤ j≤ u. The for loop of lines 11 to 33 generates these pairs. Each time a pair *(pp, u7w)* is generated, all pairs *(P, W)* in S^{i-1} with *W< ww* not yet purged or merged into S^i are merged into S^i Note that none of these may be purged. Lines 21 to 25 handle the case when the next pair in S^{i-1} has a W value equal to *ww*. In this case the pair with lesser P value gets purged. In case *pp > P(next - 1)*, then the pair *(pp, ww)* gets purged. Otherwise, *(pp, ww)* is added to S^i. The while loop of lines 31 and 32 purges all unmerged pairs in S^{i-1} that can be purged at this time. Finally, following the merging of S^{i-1}_i into S^i there may be pairs remaining in S^{i-1} to be merged into S^i. This is taken care of in the while loop of lines 35 to 39. Note that because of lines 31 and 32, none of these pairs can be purged. Function TraceBack (line 43) implements the if statement and trace-back step of the function DKP (Algorithm 4).

If $|S^i|$ is the number of pairs in S^i, then the array *pair* should have a minimum dimension of $d=\sum_{0\le i\le n-1}|S^i|$. Since it is not possible to predict the exact space needed, it is necessary to test for *next > d* each time *next* is incremented. Since each S^i, *i > 0*, is obtained by merging S^{i-1} and S^{i-1}_i and $|S^{i-1}_i| \le |S^{i-1}|$, it follows that $|S^i| \le 2|S^{i-1}|$. In the worst case no pairs will get purged and

$$\sum_{0\le i\le n-1} |S^i| = \sum_{0\le i\le n-1} 1^i = n^n - 1$$

The time needed to generate S^i from S^{i-1} is $\Theta(|S^{i-1}|)$. Hence, the time needed to compute all the S^is, 0≤ i< n, is $\Theta(\sum|S^{i-1}|)$. Since $|S^i| \le 2^i$, the time needed to compute all the S^i's is. $O(2^n)$. If the pj's are integers, then each pair *(P, W)* in *S′* has an integer P and $P\le \sum_{1\le j\le i} P_j$

Similarly, if the wj's are integers, each *W* is an integer and *W≤ m*. In any S^i the pairs have distinct W values and also distinct P values. Hence,

$$|S^i| \le 1 + \sum_{i\le i\le j} p_i$$

when the p_j's are integers and

$$|S^i| \le 1 + 1 + \min\left\{\sum_{i\le i\le j} w_j, m\right\}$$

```
PW = record {float p; float w; }
Algorithm DKnap(p, w, x, n, m)
{
        //pair[ ] is an array of PWs.
        b[0] := 1; pair[1].p := pair[1].w := 0.0; // S°
t:= 1; h:= 1; // Start and end of S°
b[1] := next := 2; // Next free spot in pair[ ]
for i:=l to n – 1 do
{// Generate S^i.
k:=t;
u:= Largest(pair, w, t, h, i, m);
for j:= t to u do
{// Generate S_1^{i-1} and merge.
pp := pair[j].p + p[i]; ww := pair[j].w + w[i];
// (pp,ww)) is the next element in S_1^{i-1}
while ((k ≤ h) and (pair[k].w ≤ ww)) do
{
        pair[next].p := pair[k].p;
        pair[next].w := pair[k].w;
        next := next + 1; k:= k+ 1;
        }
if{((k ≤ h.) and (pair[k].w = ww)) then
        {
if pp < pair[k].p then pp := pair[k].p;
k:=k+1;
}
if pp > pair[next – 1].p then
        {
pair[next].p := pp; pair[next].w := ww;
next := next + 1 ;
}
while ((k ≤ h) and (pair[k].p ≤ pair[next - 1].p))
do k:= k+ 1;
}
// Merge in remaining terms from S^{i-1}
while (k ≤ h) do
{
pair[next].p := pair[k].p; pair[next].w := pair[k].w;
next := next + 1; k:= k+ 1;
}
```

```
// Initialize for S^{i+1}
t:= h+ 1; h:= next – 1; b[i + 1] := next;
}
TraceBack(p, w, pair, x, m, n);
}
```

Algorithm 6. Algorithm for 0/1 knapsack problem

When the w_j's are integers. When both the *pj's* and *wj's* are integers, the time and space complexity of DKnap (excluding the time for TraceBack) is O(min{2^n, $n\Sigma_{1 \le i \le n} P_i$,nm } In this bound $\Sigma_{1 \le i \le n} P_i$ can be replaced *by* $\Sigma_{1 \le i \le n} P_i$ / gcd ($p_{i....}$ p_n) and m by gcd (w_1, w_2, . . , w_n, m) (see the exercises). The exercises indicate how TraceBack may be implemented so as to have a space complexity O(1) and a time complexity $O(n^2)$.

Although the above analysis may seem to indicate that DKnap requires too much computational resource to be practical for large n, in practice many instances of this problem can be solved in a reasonable amount of time. This happens because usually, all the p's and *w*'s are integers and m is much smaller than 2^n. The purging rule is effective in purging most of the pairs that would otherwise remain in the S^is.

Algorithm Dkanp can be speeded up by the use of heuristics. Let L be an estimate on the value of an optimal solution such that $f_n(m) \ge L$. Let PLEFT(i) $\Sigma_{1 \le i \le n} pj$. If S^i contains a tuple *(P, W)* such that P + PLEFT(i) < *L*, then (P, *W*) can be purged from S^i. To see this, observe that *(P, W)* can contribute at best the pair $(P + \Sigma_{i<j<n} p_j, W + \Sigma_{i<j\le n} w)$ to S_1^{n-1}. Since $P + \Sigma_{i<j\le n} p_j = P$ + PLEFT(i) < L, it follows that this pair cannot lead to a pair with value at least *L* and so cannot determine an optimal solution. A simple way to estimate *L* such that $L \le f_n(m)$ is to consider the last pair *(P, W)* in S^i. Then, $P \le f_n(m)$ .A better estimate is obtained by adding some of the remaining objects to *(P, W)*. Example 24 illustrates this. Heuristics for the knapsack problem are discussed in greater detail in the chapter on branch-and-bound. The exercises explore a divide and-conquer approach to speed up **DKnap** so that the worst case time is $O(2^{n/2})$.

Example 24

Consider the following instance of the knapsack problem:

n = 6,(p_1, p_2 , p_3 ,p_4, p_5, p_6) = (w_1,w_2, w_3,w_4, w_5,w_6) =(100, 50, 20, 10, 7,3), and m = 165. Attempting to fill the knapsack using objects in the order 1, 2, 3, 4, 5, and 6, we see that objects 1, 2, 4, and 6 fit in and yield a profit of 163 and a capacity utilization of 163. We can thus begin with ***L*** = 163 as a value with the property $L \le f_n(m)$. Since pi = *wi*, every pair **(P, W)** ∈ *Si*,0≤ i≤ 6 has P = *W*. Hence, each pair can be replaced by the singleton P or W. PLEFT(0) = 10, PLEFT(1) = 90, PLEFT(2) = 40, PLEFT(3) = 20, PLEFT(4) = 10, PLEFT(5) = 3, and PLEFT(6) = 0. Eliminating from each S^i any singleton P such that P+ PLEFT(i) < *L*, we obtain

S^o = {0}; S^o_1 = {100}

S^1. = {100}; S^1_1 = {150}

S^2 = {150}; S^2_1 = ϕ

UNIT 3

$S^3 = \{150\}; S^3_1 = \{160\}$

$S^4 = \{160); S^4_1 = \phi$

$S^5 = \{160\}$

The singleton 0 is deleted **from** S^i as 0+ PLEF'I'(1)< 163. The set S^2_1 does not contain the singleton 150 + 20 = 170 as m< 170. S^3 does not contain the 100 or the 120 as each is less than L – PLEFT(3). And so on. The value $f_6(165)$ can be determined from S^5. In this example, the value of L did not change. In general, L will change if a better estimate is obtained as a result of the computation of some S^i. If the heuristic wasn't used, then the computation would have proceeded as

$S^0 = \{0\}$

$S^1 = \{0,100\}$

$S^2 = \{0, 50,100,150\}$

$S^3 = \{0, 20, 50, 70,100,120,150\}$

$S^4 = \{0,10,20,30,50,60,70,80,100,110,120,130,150,160\}$

$S^5 = \{0,7,10,17,20,27,30,37,50,57,60,67,70,77,80,87,100, 107,110,117,120,127,130,137,150,157,160\}$

The value $f_6(165)$ can now be determined from S^5, using the knowledge (p_6, w_6) = (3, 3).

1.6 TRAVELING SALESPERSON PROBLEM

We Just applied dynamic programming to a subset selection problem 0/1 knapsack. Let we turn our attention to a permutation problem. Note that permutation problems usually are much harder to solve than sub, problems as there are n! different permutations of n objects Whereas there are only 2^n different subsets of n objects $(n! > 2^n)$. Let $G = (V, E)$ be a directed graph with edge costs c_{ij}. The variable c_{ij} is defined such that $cij > 0$ for all i and j and $c_{ij} = \infty$ if $(i, j) \notin E$. Let $|V| = n$ and assume $n > 1$. A tour of G is a directed simple cycle that includes every vertex in V. The cost of a tour is the sum of the cost of the edges on the tour. The **traveling salesperson problem** is to find a tour of minimum cost.

The traveling salesperson problem finds application in a variety of situations. Suppose we have to route a postal van to pick up mail from mailboxes located at n different sites. An n + 1 vertex graph can be used to represent the situation. One vertex represents

the post office from which the postal van starts and to which it must return. Edge *(i, j)* is assigned a cost equal to the distance from site *i* to site *j*. The route taken by the postal van is a tour, and we are interested in finding a tour of minimum length.

As a second example, suppose we wish to use a robot arm to tighten the nuts on some piece of machinery on an assembly line. The arm will start from its initial position (which is over the first nut to be tightened), successively move to each of the remaining nuts, and return to the initial position. The path of the arm is clearly a tour on a graph in which vertices represent the nuts. A minimum-cost tour will minimize the time needed for the arm to complete its task (note that only the total arm movement time is variable; the nut tightening time is independent of the tour).

Let us take example from a production environment in which several commodities are manufactured on the same set of machines. The manufacture proceeds in cycles. In each production cycle, n different commodities are produced. When the machines are changed from production of commodity *i* to commodity *j*, a change over cost c_{ij} is incurred. It is desired to find a sequence in which to manufacture these commodities. This sequence should minimize the sum of change over costs (the remaining production costs are sequence independent). Since the manufacture proceeds cyclically, it is necessary to include the cost of starting the next cycle. This is just the change over cost from the last to the first Commodity. Hence, this problem can be regarded as a traveling salesperson problem on an *n* vertex graph with edge cost c_{ij}*s* being the changeover cost from commodity *i* to commodity *j*.

In the following discussion we shall, without loss of generality, regard a tour to be a simple path that starts and ends at vertex 1. Every tour consists of an edge (1, k) for some $k \in V - \{1\}$ and a path from vertex *k* to vertex 1. The path from vertex *k* to vertex 1 goes through each vertex in V−{1, *k*} exactly once. It is easy to see that if the tour is optimal, then the path from *k* to 1 must be a shortest *k* to 1 path going through all vertices in $V - \{1, k\}$. Hence, the principle of optimality holds. Let *g(i, S)* be the length of a shortest path starting at vertex i, going through all vertices in S, and terminating at vertex 1. The function $g(1, V\text{-}\{1\})$ is the length of an optimal salesperson tour. From the principal of optimality it follows that

$$g(1, V-\{1\}) = \min\{c_{1k} + g(k, v-\{1, k\})\} \qquad (12)$$

Generalizing (12), we obtain (for $i \notin S$)

$$(g(i, S) = \min_{j \in S}\{c_{ij} \pm g(j, S\text{-}\{j\})\} \qquad (13)$$

Equation 12 can be solve for g (1, V− { 1}) if we know $g(k, V - \{1, k\})$ for all choices of *k*. The g values can be obtained by using (13).

Clearly, $g(i,\phi) = c_{i1}$, $1 \le i \le n$. Hence, we can use (13) to obtain *g(i,S)* for all S of size 1. Then we can obtain *g(i, S)* for *S* with $|S| = 2$ and so on. When $|S| < n - 1$, the values of *i* and S for which *g(i, S)* is needed are such that $i \ne 1, 1 \notin S$, and $i \notin S$.

Example 25

Consider the directed graph of Figure 7(a). The edge lengths are given by matrix c of Figure 7(b).

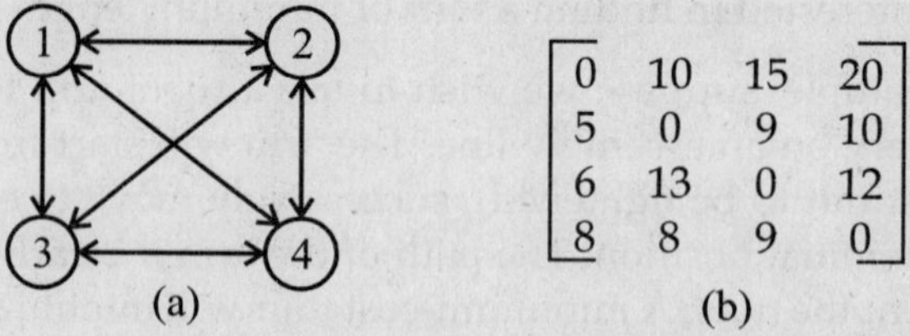

Figure 7. Directed graph and edge length matrix

Thus g(2,ϕ) = c_{21} = 5, g(3, ϕ) = c_{31} = 6, and 9(4, ϕ) = c_{41} = 8. Using (13), we obtain

g(2,{3}) = C_{23} + g(3, ϕ) = 15 g(2, {4,}) = 18

g(3, {2}) = 18 g(3,{4}) = 20

g(4,{2}) = 13 g(4,{3}) = 15

Next, we compute g(i, S) with | S| = 2, i≠ 1, 1∉ S and *i*∉ *S.*

g(2, {3,,4}) = min {c_{23} + g(3,{4}), c_{24} +g(4,{3})} = 25

g(3, {2,4}) = min {c_{32} +g(2, {4}),c_{34}+g(4, {2})} = 25

gC4, {2, 3}) = min {$c_4$2 + g(2,{3}), c_{43} + g(3, {2})} = 23

Finally, from **(12)** we obtain

g(1,{2,3,4}) = **min** {c_{12} + **g(2, {3, 4}), c_{13}+ g(3, {2, 4}), c_{14} + g(4, {2, 3}) }**

= **min {35,40,43}**

= **35**

An optimal tour of the graph of Figure 7(a) has length 35. A tour of this length can be constructed if we retain with each *g(i, S)* the value of *j* that minimizes the right-hand side of (13). Let *J(i, S)* be this value. Then, J(1, {2, 3,4}) = 2. Thus the tour starts from 1 and goes to 2. The remaining tour can be obtained from g(2, {3, 4}). So J(2, {3, 4}) = 4. Thus the next edge is (2, 4). The remaining tour is for g(4, {3}). So J(4, {3}) = 3. The optimal tour is 1, 2, 4, 3, 1.

Let N be the number of *g(i, S)*'s that have to be computed before (12) can be used to compute g(1, V–{1}). For each value of | S | there are n–1 choices for i. The number of distinct sets S of size k not including 1 and I is

$$\binom{n-2}{k}$$

$$N = \sum_{K=0}^{n-2} (n-1)\binom{n-2}{k} = (n-1)n^{n-2}$$

An algorithm that proceeds to find an optimal tour by using (12) and (13) will require Θ($n^2 2^n$) time as the computation of g(i, S) with | S | = ***k*** requires *k* – 1 comparisons when solving (13). This is better than enumerating all n! different tours to find the best one.

The most serious drawback of this dynamic programming solution is the space needed, $O(n2^n)$. This is too large even for modest values of n.

REVIEW QUESTIONS

1. List the problems that can be solved by Dynamic programming.
2. Explain multistage graph in detail.
3. Write a note on all pairs shortest path.
4. Explain single source shortest path problem in detail.
5. Write a note on 0/1 knapsack problem.
6. What is difference between knapsack and 0/1 knapsack problem?
7. What is traveling salesman problem? How we can solve it. Explain.

UNIT 3

CHAPTER 2

THE GREEDY METHOD

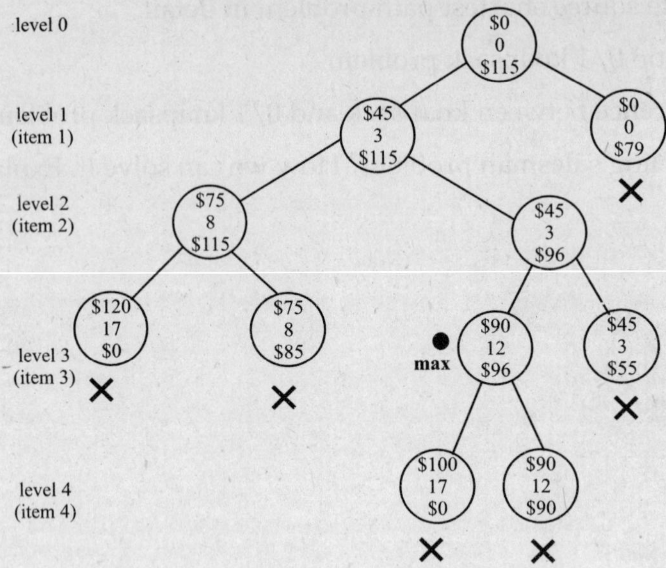

2.1 INTRODUCTION

The greedy method strategy very efficient and straight forward design technique for algorithms. It finds its applications to a wide variety of problems. Most of these problems have n inputs and require us to obtain a subset that satisfies some constraints. Any subset that satisfies these constraints is termed as a feasible solution. We need to find,a feasible solution that either, maximizes or minimizes a given objective_function.

A feasible solution that does this is called an optimal solution. There is usually an obvious way to determine a feasible, solution but not necessarily an optimal solution.

By greedy method we can devise an algorithm that works in stages, considering one input at a time. At each stage, a decision is made regarding whether a particular input is in an optimal solution. This is done by considering the inputs in an order determined by some selection procedure. If the inclusion of the next input into the partially constructed optimal solution will result in an infeasible solution, then this input is not added to the partial solution. Otherwise, it is added. The selection procedure itself is based on some optimization measure. This measure may be the objective function. In fact, several different optimization measures may be plausible for a given problem. Most of these, however, will result in algorithms that generate sub optimal solutions. This version of the greedy technique is called the *subset paradigm.*

We can describe the subset paradigm abstractly, but more precisely than above, by considering the control abstraction in Algorithm 1.

The function Select selects an input from a[ ] and removes it. The selected input's value is assigned to x. Feasible is a Boolean-valued function that determines whether x can be included into the solution vector.

```
Algorithm Greedy(a, n)
// a[1 : n] has the n inputs.
{
        solution := θ; // Initialize the solution to problem.
        for i:=l to n do
        {
        x := Select(a);
        if Feasible(solution, x) then
        solution := Union(solution, x);
        }
    return solution;
}
```

Algorithm 1. Greedy method

The function Union combines x with the solution and updates the objective function. The function Greedy describes the essential way that a greedy algorithm will look, once a particular problem is chosen and the functions Select, Feasible, and Union are properly implemented.

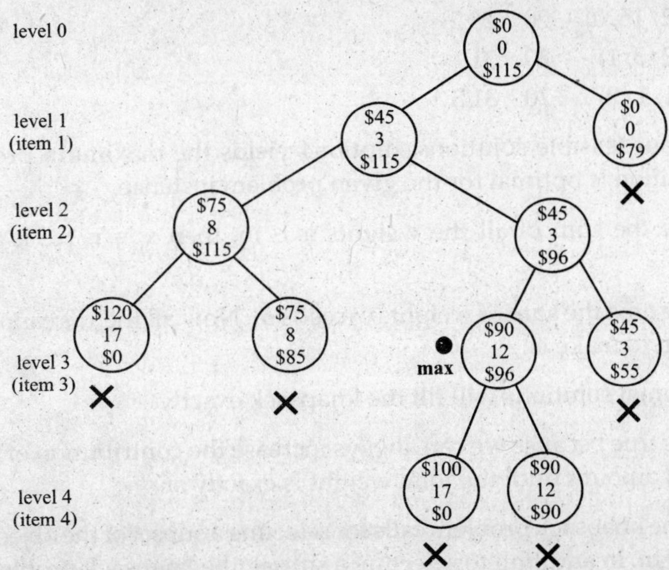

For problems that do not call for the selection of an optimal subset, in the greedy method we make decisions by considering the inputs in some order. Each decision is made using an optimization criterion that can be computed using decisions already made. Call this version of the greedy method the ordering paradigm.

2.2 KNAPSACK PROBLEM

Let us try to apply the greedy method to solve the knapsack problem. We are given n objects and a knapsack or bag. Object i has a weight ωi and the knapsack has a capacity *m*. If a fraction x_i, $0 \le x_i \le 1$ object *i* is placed into the knapsack, then a profit of $p_i x_i$ is earned. The objective is to obtain a filling of the knapsack that maximizes the total profit earned. Since the knapsack capacity is m, we require the total weight of all chosen objects-to be at most m. Formally, the problem can be stated as

$$\text{maximize} \sum_{1 \le i \le n} p_i x_i \quad (1)$$

$$\text{subject to} \sum_{1 \le i \le n} w_i x_i + \le m \quad (2)$$

and $0 \le x_i \le 1, 1 \le i \le n$ (3)

The profits and weights are positive numbers.

A feasible solution (or filling) is any set $(x_1, \ldots, x_n)$ satisfying (2) and (3) above. An optimal solution is a feasible solution for which (1) is maximized

For example consider the following instance of the knapsack problem: n = 3, m = 20. (p_1, p_2, p_3) =(25, 24,15), and $(w_1, w_2, w3)$=(18,15,10). Four feasible solutions are:

	(x1, x2, x3)	$\Sigma w_i x_i$	$\Sigma p_i x_i$
1.	(1/2, 1/3, 1/4)	16.5	24.25
2.	(1, 2/15, 0)	20	28.2
3.	(0, 2/3, 1)	20	31
4.	(0, 1, 1/2)	20	31.5

Of these four feasible solutions,solution4 yields the maximum profit. As we shall soon see, this solution is optimal for the given problem instance.

Lemma 1. In case the sum of all the weights is ≤ m, then x_i = i, 1≤ i≤ n is an optimal solution.

So let us assume the sum of weights exceeds m. Now all the *xi's* cannot be 1. Another observation to make is:

Lemma 2. All optimal solutions will fill the knapsack exactly.

Lemma 2 is true because we can always increase the contribution of some object *i* by a fractional amount until the total weight is exactly *m*.

Note that the knapsack problem calls for selecting a subset of the objects and hence fits the subset paradigm. In addition to selecting a subset, the knapsack problem also involves the selection of an x_i for each object. Several simple greedy strategies to obtain feasible solutions whose Sums are identically ***m*** suggest themselves. First, we can try to fill the knapsack by including next the object with largest profit. If an object under consideration doesn't fit, then a fraction of it is included to fill the knapsack. Thus each time an object is included (except possibly when the last object is included) into the knapsack, we obtain the largest possible increase in profit value. Note that if only a fraction of the last object is included, then it may he possible to get a bigger increase by using a different object. For example, if we have two units of space left and two objects with ($p_i = 4$, $w_i = 4$) and ($pj = 3$, $w_j = 2$) remaining, then using *j* is better than using half of *i*. Let us this selection strategy on the data of first example .

Object one has the largest profit value ($p_1 = 25$). So it is placed into the knapsack first. Then $x_1 = 1$ and a profit of 25 is earned. Only 2 units of knapsack capacity are left. Object two has the next largest profit ($P_2 = 24$). However, $w_2 = 15$ and it doesn't fit into the knapsack. Using $x_2 = 2/15$ fills the knapsack exactly with part of object 2 and the value of the resulting solution is 28.2 This is solution 2 and it, is readily seen to be suboptimal. The method used to obtain this solution is termed to be a gready methodbecause at each step we chose to introduce that object which would increase the objective function value the most. However, this greedy method did not yield an optimal solution. Note that even if we change the above strategy so that in the last step the objective function increases by as much as possible, an optimal solution is not obtained for Example .

By the preceding example, we note that considering objects in order of nonincreasing profit values does not yield an optimal solution because even though the objective function value takes on large increases at each step, the number of steps is few as the knapsack capacity is used lip at a rapid rate. So. let us try to be greedy with capacity and use it up as slowly as possible. This requires us to consider the objects in order of nondecreasing weights w_i, Using Example 4.1, solution 3 results· This too is suboptimal. This time, even though capacity is used slowly, profits aren't coming in rapidly enough.

Thus, our next attempt is an algorithm that strives to achieve a balance between the rate at which profit increases and the rate at which capacity is used. At each step we include that object which has *the maximum profit per unit of capacity used. This means that objects are considered in order of the ratio pi/wi. Solution 4 of example is produced by this strategy. If the objects have already been sorted into non-increasing order of p_i/w_i, then function GreedyKnapsack (Algorithm 2) obtains solutions corresponding to this strategy. Note that solutions corresponding to the first two strategies can be obtained using this algorithm if the objects are initially in the appropriate order. Disregarding the time to initially sort the objects, each of the three strategies outlined above requires only O(n) time.

```
Algorithm GreedyKnapsack(m, n)
//p[1 : n] and w[1 : n] contain the profits and weights respectively
    // of the n objects ordered such that p[i] /w[i] ≥ p[i + 1]/w[i + 1].
//m is the knapsack size and x[1 : n] is the solution vector.
    {
    for i:= 1 to n do x[i] := 0.0; // Initialize x.
```

```
        U:=m;
        for i:=l to n do
        {
    if (w[i] > U) then break;
        x[i] := 1.0; U:= U – W[i];
        }
    if (i ≤ n) then x[i] := U/w[i];
    }
```

Algorithm 2. Greedy method for the knapsack problem

We have seen that when one applies the greedy method to the solution of the knapsack problem, there are at least three different measures one can attempt to optimize when determining which object to include next. These measures are total profit, capacity used, and the ratio of accumulated profit to capacity used. Once an optimization measure has been chosen, the greedy method suggests choosing objects for inclusion into the solution in such a way that each choice optimizes the measure at that time. Thus a greedy method using profit as its measure will at each step choose an object that increases the profit the most. If the capacity measure is used, the next object included will increase this the least. Although greedy-based algorithms using the first two measures do not guarantee optimal solutions for the knapsack problem, Theorem below shows that a greedy algorithm using strategy 3 always obtains an optimal solution. This theorem is proved using the following technique:

Compare the greedy solution with any optimal solution. If the two solutions differ, then find the first x_i at which they differ. Next, it is shown how to make the x_i in the optimal solution equal to that in the greedy solution without any loss in total value. Repeated use of this transformation shows that the greedy solution is optimal.This technique of proving solutions optimal is used often in this text. Hence, you should master it at this time.

Theorem . If $p_l/w1 \geq p2/w2 \ldots \geq p_n/w_n$, then Greedy Knapsack generates an optimal solution to the given instance of the knapsack problem.

Proof: Let $x=(x_i \ldots, x_n)$ be the solution generated by Greedy Knapsack . If all the x_1 equal one, then clearly the solution is optimal.

So, let j be the least index such that $x_j \neq 1$.

From the algorithm it follows that $xi = 1$ for $1 \leq i \leq j$, $x_i = 0$ for $j < i \leq n$, and $0 < x_j < 1$.

Let $y=(y_i \ldots, y_n)$ be an optimal solution. From Lemma 2, we can assume that $\sum wiyi = m$. Let k be the least index such that $y_k \leq x_k$. Clearly, such a k must exist. It also follows that $y_k \leq x_k$. To see this, consider the three possibilities $k < j$,

$k= j$,or $k > j$.

1. If $k < j$, then $x_k = 1$. But, $y_k \neq xk$, and so $y_k < x_k$.
2. If k= j, then since $\sum wixi = m$ and $yi = xi$ for $1 \leq i < j$, it follows that either $y_k < xk$ or $\sum wiyi > m$

3. If $k > j$, then $\Sigma wiyi > m$, and this is not possible.

Now suppose we increase, Yk to Xk and decrease as, many of $(y_{k+1}, \ldots, y_n)$ as necessary so that the total capacity used is still m. This results in a new Solution $z = (z_1, \ldots z_n)$with $z_1 = x_1, 1 \le 1 \le k$, and $\Sigma_{k, i \le n}\ \omega I(yi\text{-}zi) = w_{k(} zk - yk)$. Then, for z we -have

$$\sum_{1 \le i \le n} Pi\,zi = \sum_{1 \le i \le n} Pi\,yi + (zk - yk)wk\ Pk / wk - \sum_{k < i \le n} (yi - zi)wi\ pi / wi$$

$$\ge \sum_{1 \le i \le n} Pi\,yi + \left[(zk - yk)wk\ Pk / wk - \sum_{1 \le i \le n} (yi - zi)wi\right] pi / wi$$

$$\sum piyi$$

If $\Sigma pizi > \Sigma piyi$, then y could not have been an optimal solution. *If* these sums are equal, then either $z = x$ and x is optimal, or $z \neq x$. In the latter case, repeated use *of* the above argument will either show that y is not optimal, or transform y into x and thus show that x too is optimal.

2.3 SINGLE-SOURCE SHORTEST PATHS

Graph finds their application in almost each and every situation of real life. Graphs can be used to represent the highway structure of a state or country with vertices representing cities and edges representing sections of highway. The edges can then be assigned weights which may be either the distance between the two cities connected by the edge or the average time to drive along that section of highway. A motorist wishing to drive from city *A* to *B* would be interested in answers to the following questions:

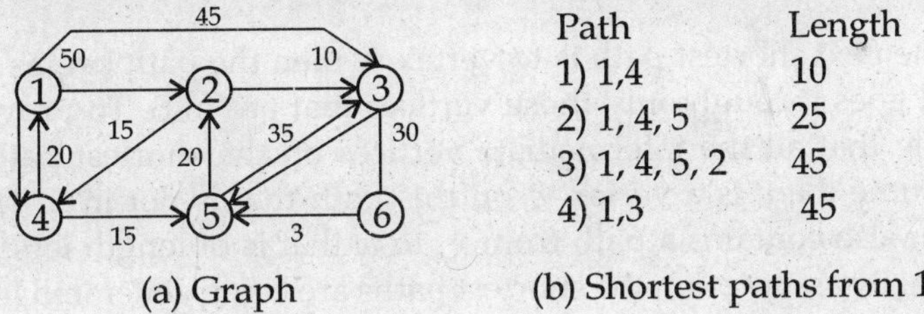

Figure 1. *Graph and shortest paths from vertex 1 to all destinations*

- Is there a path from *A* to *B*?
- If there is more than one path from A to B, which is the shortest path?

The problems defined by these questions are special cases of the path problem we study in this section. The length of a path is now defined to be the sum of the weights of the edges on that path. The starting vertex of the path is referred to as the ***source,*** and the last vertex the ***destination.*** The graphs are digraphs to allow for one-way streets. In the problem we consider, we are given a directed graph G=(V, E), a weighting function *cost* for the edges of G, and a source vertex v_o. The problem is to determine the shortest paths from v_o to *all* the remaining vertices of G. It is assumed that all the weights are positive. The shortest path between v_o and some other node v is an ordering among a subset of the edges. Hence this problem fits the ordering paradigm.

For example Consider the directed graph of Figure 1.(a). The numbers on the edges are the weights. If node 1 is the source vertex, then the shortest path from 1 to 2 is 1, 4, 5, 2. The length of this path is 10 + 15 + 20 = 45. Even though there are three edges on this path, it is shorter than the path 1; 2 which is of length 50. There is no path from 1 to 6. Figure 1.(b) lists the shortest paths from node 1 to nodes 4, 5, 2, and 3, respectively. The paths have been listed in nondecreasing order of path length.

To formulate a greedy-based algorithm to generate the shortest paths. we must conceive of a multistage solution to the problem and also of an optimization measure. One possibility is to build the shortest paths one by one. As an optimization measure we can use the sum of the lengths of all paths so far generated. For this measure to be minimized, each individual path must be of minimum length. If we have already constructed i shortest paths, then using this optimization measure, the next path to be constructed should be the next shortest minimum length path. The greedy way (and also a systematic way) to generate the shortest paths from v_o to the remaining vertices is to generate these paths in non decreasing order of path length. First, a shortest path to the nearest vertex is generated. Then a shortest path to the second nearest vertex is generated, and so on. For the graph of Figure 1.(a) the nearest vertex to v_o = 1 is 4(cost[1, 4] = 10). The path 1, 4 is the first path generated. The second nearest vertex to node 1 is 5 and the distance between 1 and 5 is 25. The path 1, 4, 5 is the next path generated. In order to generate the shortest paths in this order, we need to be able to determine (1) the next vertex to which a shortest path must be generated and (2) a shortest path to this vertex. Let S denote the set of vertices (including v_o) to which the shortest paths have already been generated. For *w* not in S, let ***dist[w]*** be the length of the shortest path starting from v_o, going through only those vertices that are in S, and ending at w. We observe that:

1. If the next shortest path is to vertex u, then the path begins at v_o, ends at u, and goes through only those vertices that are in S. To prove this, we must show that all the intermediate vertices on the shortest path to u, are in S. Assume there is a vertex w on this path that is not in S. Then, the v_o to u path also contains a path from v_o to *w* that is of length less than the v_o to u path. By assumption the shortest paths are being generated in nondesreasing order of path length, and so the shorter path v_o to w must already have been generated. Hence, there can be no intermediate vertex that is not in S.

2. The destination of the next path generated must be that of vertex u which has the minimum distance, *dist[u]*, among all vertices not in S. This follows from the definition of dist and observation 1. In case there are several vertices not in S with the same *dist*, then any of these may be selected.

3. After being selected a vertex it as in observation 2 and generated the shortest v_o to u path, vertex u becomes a member of S. At this point the length of the shortest paths starting at v_o, going though vertices only in S, and ending at a vertex w not in S may decrease; that is, the value of *dist[w]* may change. If it does change, then it must be due to a shorter path starting at v_o and going to u and then to w. The intermediate vertices on the v_o to u path and the u to to path must all be in S. Further, the v_o to u path must be the shortest such path; otherwise *dist[w]* is not defined properly. Also, the u to to path can be chosen

so as not to contain any intermediate vertices. Therefore, we can conclude that if *dist[w]* is to change (i.e., decrease), then it is because of a path from v_0 to u to w, where the path from v_0 to u is the shortest such path and the path from u to w is the edge (u, w). The length of this path is ***dist[u] + cost[u, w].***

The above observations lead to a simple Algorithm 3 for the singlesource shortest path problem. This algorithm (known as Dijkstra's algorithm) only determines the lengths of the shortest paths from v_0 to all other vertices in G. The generation of the paths requires a minor extension to this algorithm and is left as an exercise. In the function **ShortestPaths** (Algorithm 3) it is assumed that the *n* vertices of G are numbered 1 through *n*. The set *S* is maintained as a bit array with *S[i]* = 0 if vertex *i* is not in *S* and S[i] = 1 if it is. It is assumed that the graph itself is represented by its cost adjacency matrix with cost[i, j]'s being the weight of the edge *(i, j)*. The weight *cost[i, j]* is set to some large number, ∞, in case the edge *(i, j)* is not in E(G). For *i* = *j*, *cost[i, j]* can be set to any nonnegative number without affecting the outcome of the algorithm.

From our earlier discussion, it is easy to see that the algorithm is correct. The time taken by the algorithm on a graph with *n* vertices is $O(n^2)$. To see this, note that the for loop of line 7 in Algorithm 3 takes $\Theta(n)$ time. The for loop of line 12 is executed *n*– 2 times. Each execution of this loop requires *O(n)* time at lines 15 and 16 to select the next vertex and again at the for loop of line 18 to update *dist*. So the total time for this loop is $O(n^2)$. In case a list t of vertices currently not in s is maintained, then the number of nodes on this list would at any time be n – *num*. This would speed **tip** lines 15 and 16 and the for loop of line 18, but the asymptotic time would remain $O(n^2)$. This and other variations of the algorithm are explored in the exercises.

Any shortest path algorithm must examine each edge in the graph at least once since any of the edges could be in a shortest path. Hence, the minimum possible time for such an algorithm would be $\Omega(|E|)$. Since cost adjacency matrices were used to represent the graph, it takes $O(n^2)$ time just to determine which edges are in G, and so any shortest path algorithm using this representation must take $\Omega(n^2)$ time. For this representation then, algorithm **ShortestPaths is** optimal to within a constant factor. If a change to adjacency lists is made, the overall frequency of the for loop of line 18 can be brought down to $O(|E|)$ (since dist can change only for vertices adjacent from u). If V–S is rnaintained as a red-black tree , each execution of lines 15 and 16 takes O(log n) time. Note that a red-black tree supports the following operations in O(log n) time: insert, delete (an arbitrary element), find-min, and search (for an arbitrary element). Each update in line 21 takes O(log n) time as well (since an update can be done using a delete and an insertion into the red-black tree).

Thus the overall run. time is $O((n + |E|) \log n)$.

```
1    Algorithm ShortestPaths(v, cost, dist, n)
2    //dist [j], 1≤ j≤ n, is set to the length of the shortest
3    // path from vertex v to vertex j in a digraph G with n
4    // vertices. dist[v] is set to zero. G is represented by its
5    // cost adjacency matrix cost[1 : n, l: n].
6    {
```

```
7    for i:= 1 to n do
8    {// Initialize S.
9    S[i] := false; dist[i] := cost[v, i];
10   }
11   S[v] := true; dist[v] := 0.0; // Put v in S.
12   for num := 2 to n– 1 do
13   {
14   // Determine n – 1 paths from v.
15   Choose u from among those vertices not
16   in S such that dist[u] is minimum;
17   S[u] := true; // Put u in S.
18   for (each w adjacent to u with S[w] = false) do
19   // Update distances.
20   if (dist[w] > dist[u] + cost[u, w])) then
21   dist[w] := dist[u] + cost [U, w];
22   }
23   }
```

Algorithm 3. Greedy algorithm for shortest paths

For example let us see the eight vertex digraph of Figure 2(a) with cost adjacency matrix as in Figure 2(b). The values of *dist* and the vertices selected at each iteration of the for-loop of line 12 in Algorithm 3 for finding all the shortest paths from Boston are shown in Figure 3. To begin with, S contains only Boston. In the first iteration of the for loop (that is, for *num* = 2), the city *u* that is not in *S* and whose *dist[u] is* minimum is identified to be New York. New York enters the set S. Also the *dist[ ]* values of Chicago, Miami, and New Orleans get altered since there are shorter paths to these cities via New York. In the next iteration of the for loop, the city that enters S is Miami since it has the smallest *dist[ ]* value from among all the nodes not in *S.* None of the *dist[ ]* values are altered. The algorithm continues in a similar fashion and terminates when only seven of the eight vertices are in S. By the definition of *dist,* the distance of the last vertex, in this case Los Angeles, is correct as the shortest path from Boston to Los Angeles can go through only the remaining six vertices.

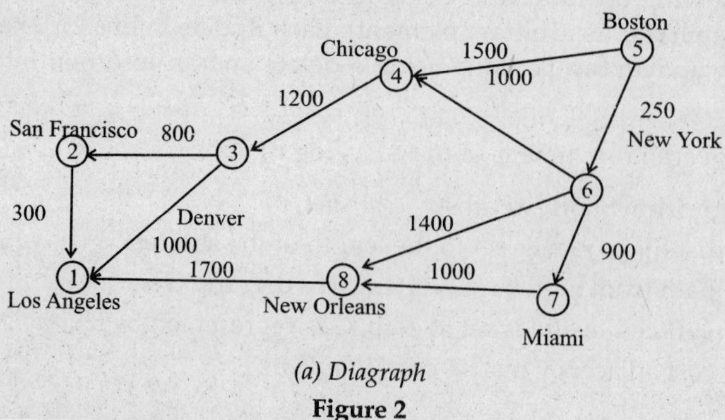

(a) Diagraph

Figure 2

	1	2	3	4	5	6	7	8
1	0							
2	300	0						
3	100	800	0					
4			1200	0				
5				1500	0	250		
6				1000		0	900	1400
7							0	1000
8	1700							0

(b) Length-adjacency matrix

One can easily verify that the edges on the shortest paths from a vertex v to all remaining vertices in a connected undirected graph G form a spanning tree of G. This spanning tree is called ***a shortest-path spanning tree***. Clearly, this spanning tree may be different for different root vertices v.

Iteration	S	Vertex selected	Distance							
			LA	SF	DEN	CHI	BOST	NY	MIA	NO
			[1]	[2]	[3]	[4]	[5]	[6]	[7]	[8]
Initial	--	----	+∞	+∞	+∞	1500	0	250	+∞	+∞
1	(5)	6	+∞	+∞	+∞	1250	0	250	1150	1650
2	{5,6}	7	+∞	+∞	+∞	1250	0	250	1150	1650
3	{5,6,7}	4	+∞	+∞	2450	1250	0	250	1150	1650
4	{5,6,7,4}	8	3350	+∞	2450	2450	0	250	1150	1650
5	{5,6,7,4,8}	3	3350	3250	2450	1250	0	250	11.50	1650
6	{5,6,7,4,8,3}	2	3350	3250	2450	1250	0	250	1150	1650
I	{5,6,7,4,8,3,2}									

REVIEW QUESTIONS

1. What you know about greedy method?
2. What kinds of problems can be solved by greedy method?
3. Solve knapsack problem by greedy method.
4. Write greedy algorithm for shortest path problem.
5. Explain shortest path problem as a greedy method problem.

UNIT 3

CHAPTER 3

BACKTRACKING

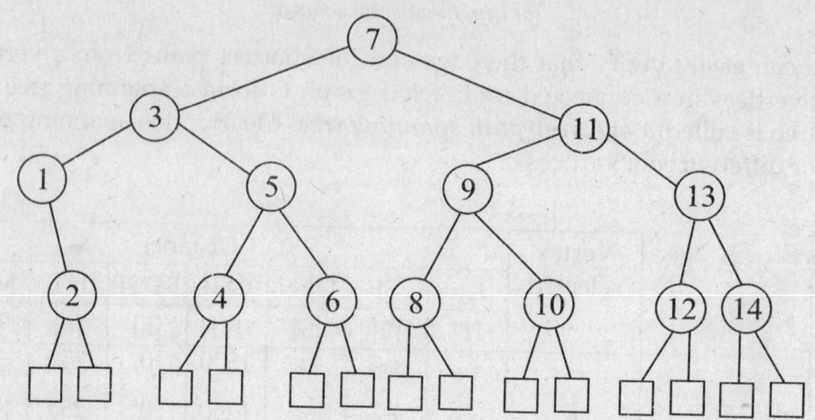

3.1 INTRODUCTION

Now we will talk about another design principle namely Backtracking. It is one of the fundamental principle of algorithm design, backtracking represents one of the most general techniques. Many problems which deal with searching for a set of solutions or which ask for an optimal solution satisfying some constraints can be solved using the backtracking formulation. The name backtrack was first coined by D. H. Lehmer. Early workers who studied the process were R. J. Walker, who gave an algorithmic account of the technique. The technique is applicable to a variety of applications.

In many applications of the backtrack method, the desired solution is expressible as an n-tuple $(x_1, ..., x_n)$, where the x*i* are chosen from some finite set S_i. Often the problem to be solved calls for finding one vector that maximizes (or minimizes or satisfies) a criterion function $P(x_1, \ldots, x_n)$. Sometimes it seeks all vectors that satisfy P. For example, sorting the array of integers in a[1 : n] is a problem whose solution is expressible by an *n*tuple, where x_i is the index in a of the ith smallest element. The criterion function P is the inequality $a[x_i] < a[x_{i+1}]$ for $1 \leq i < n$. The set S_i is finite and includes the integers 1-through n. Though sorting is not usually one of the problems solved by backtracking, it is one example of a familiar problem whose solution can be formulated as an n-tuple. In this chapter we study a collection of problems whose solutions are best done using backtracking.

Suppose m_i is the size of set S_i. Then there are $m = m_1 m_2 \cdots m_n$ ntuples that are possible candidates for satisfying the function *P*. The brute force approach would be to form all these n-tuples, evaluate each one with P, and save those which yield the optimum.

The backtrack algorithm has as its virtue the ability to yield the same answer with far fewer than m trials. Its basic idea is to build up the solution vector one component at a time and to use modified criterion functions *Pi* $(x_1, ..., x_i)$ (sometimes called bounding functions) to test whether the vector being formed has any chance of success. The major advantage of this method is :if it is realized that the partial vector$(x_1, x_2, ..., x_i)$ can in to way lead to an optimal solution, then mi+1...mn possible test vectors can be ignored entirely.

Many of the problems we solve using backtracking require that all the solutions satisfy a complex set of constraints. For any problem these constraints can be divided into two categories: explicit and implicit.

Explicit constraints are rules that restrict each x_i *to take on values only from a given set.*

Common examples of explicit constraints are

$x_i \geq 0$	or	S_i ={all nonnegative real numbers}
$x_i = 0$ or 1	or	$S_i = \{0,1\}$
$l_i \leq x_i \leq u_i$	or	$S_i = \{a : l_i \leq a = u_i\}$

The explicit constraints depend on the particular instance I of the problem being solved. All tuples that satisfy the explicit constraints define a possible ***solution space*** for I.

The implicit constraints are rules that determine which of the tuples in the solution space of I satisfy the criterion function. Thus implicit constraints describe the way in which the x_i *must relate to each other.*

Example

Eight queens problem.

A classic combinatorial problem is to place eight queens on an 8 x 8 chessboard so that no two "attack," that is, so that no two of them are on the same row, column, or diagonal. Let us number the rows and columns of the chessboard 1 through 8 (Figure 1). The queens can also be numbered 1 through 8. Since each queen must be on a different row, we can without loss of generality assume queen i is to be placed on row i. All solutions to the 8-queens problem can therefore be represented as 8-tuples $(x_1, ..., x_8)$, where x_i is the column on which queen *i* is placed. The explicit constraints using this formulation are S_i ={1, 2,3,4,5,6,7,8}, $1 \leq i \leq 8$. Therefore the solution space consists of 8^8 8-tuples. The implicit constraints for this problem are that no two x_i's can be the same (i.e., all queens must be on different columns) and no two queens can be on the same diagonal. The first of these two constraints implies that all solutions are permutations of the 8-tuple (1, 2, 3, 4, 5, 6, 7, 8). This realization reduces the size of the solution space from 8^8 tuples to 8! tuples. We see later how to formulate the second constraint in terms of the x_i. Expressed as an 8-tuple, the solution in Figure 1 is (4, 6, 8, 2, 7, 1, 3, 5).

	1	2	3	4	5	5	6	8
1				Q				
2						Q		
3								Q
4		Q						
5							Q	
6	Q							
7			Q					
8					Q			

Figure 1. A Solution To The 8-Queens Problem

Example

Sum of subsets problem.

Given positive numbers w_i, $1 \leq i \leq n$, and m, this problem calls for finding all subsets of the w_i whose sums are m. For example, if $n = 4$, $(w_1, w_2, w_3, w_4) = (11, 13, 24, 7)$, and m= 31, then the desired subsets are (11, 13, 7) and (24, 7). Rather than represent the solution vector by the w_i which sum to m, we could represent the solution vector by giving the indices of these w_i. Now the two solutions are described by the vectors (1, 2, 4) and (3, 4). In general, all solutions are k-tuples $(x_1, x_2, \ldots, x_k)$, $1 \leq k \leq n$, and different solutions may have different-sized tuples. The explicit constraints require $x_i \in \{j \mid j$ is an integer and $1 \leq j \leq n\}$. The implicit constraints require that no two be the same and that the sum of the corresponding w_i's be m. Since we wish to avoid generating multiple instances of the same subset (e.g., (1, 2, 4) and (1, 4, 2) represent the same subset), another implicit constraint that is imposed is that $x_i < x_{i+1}$, $1 \leq i \leq k$.

In another formulation of the sum of subsets problem, each solution subset is represented by an n-tuple $(x_1, x_2 ..., x_n)$ such that $x_i \in \{0.1\}$, $1 \le i \le n$. Then $x_i = 0$ if w_i is not chosen and $x_i = 1$ if w_i is chosen. The solutions to the above instance are (1, 1, 0, 1) and (0, 0, 1, 1). This formulation expresses all solutions using a fixed-sized tuple. Thus we conclude that there may be several ways to formulate a problem so that all solutions are tuples that satisfy some constraints. One can verify that for, both of the above formulations, the solution space consists of 2^n distinct tuples.

Backtracking algorithms determine problem solutions by systematically searching the solution space for the given problem instance. This search is facilitated by using a ***tree organization*** for the solution space. For a given solution space many tree organizations may be possible. The next two examples examine some of the ways to organize a solution into a tree.

Example 3

n-queens problem

The n-queens problem is a generalization of the 8queens problem of Example 1. Now n queens are to be placed on an *n x n* chessboard so that no two attack; that is, no two queens are on the same row, column, or diagonal. Generalizing our earlier discussion, the solution space consists of all ***n!*** permutations of the n-tuple (1, 2, ..., n*)*. Figure 2 shows a possible tree organization foi the case n = 4. A tree such as this is called ***a permutation tree.*** The edges are labeled by possible values of x_i. Edges from level 1 to level 2 nodes specify the values for x_1. Thus, the leftmost subtree contains all solutions with $x_1 = 1$; its leftmost subtree contains all solutions with $x_1 = 1$ and $x_2 = 2$, and so on. Edges from level *i* to level i + *1* are labeled with the values of *xi*. The solution space is defined by all paths from the root node to a leaf node. There are 4! = 24 leaf nodes in the tree of Figure 2.

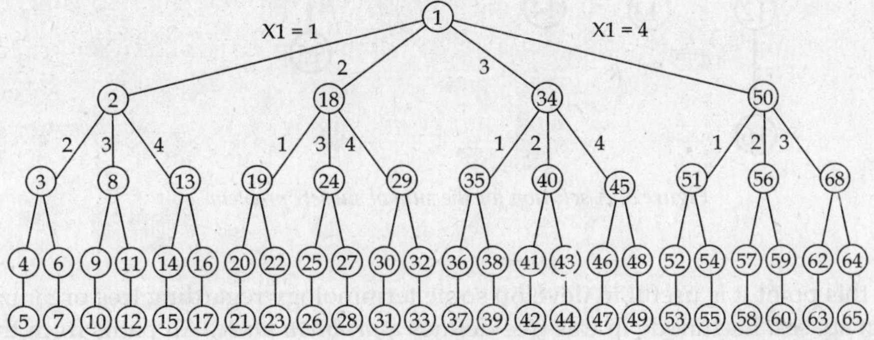

Figure 2. Tree organization of the 4-queens, solution space. Nodes are numbered as in depth first search.

Example

Sum of subsets problem

Earlier we gave two possible formulations of the solution space for the sum of subsets problem. Figures 3 and 4 show a possible tree organization for each of these formulations for the case n = 4. The tree of Figure 3 corresponds to the variable tuple size formulation. The edges are labeled such that an edge from a level i node to a level i + 1 node represents a value for x_i. At each node, the solution space is partitioned into subsolution spaces. The solution space is defined by all paths from the root node to any node in the tree, since any such path corresponds to a subset satisfying the explicit constraints. The possible paths are () (this corresponds to the empty path from the root to itself), (1), (1, 2), (1, 2, 3), (1, 2, 3, 4), (1, 2, 4), (1, 3, 4), (2), (2, 3), and so on. Thus, the leftmost subtree defines all subsets containing w_1, the next subtree defines all subsets containing w_2 but not w_1, and so on.

The tree of Figure 4 corresponds to the fixed tuple size formulation. Edges from level *i* nodes to level i + *1* nodes are labeled with the value of x_i, which is either zero or one. All paths from the root to a leaf node define the solution space. The left subtree of the root defines all subsets containing w_1, the right subtree defines all subsets not containing wl, and so on. Now there are 2^4 leaf nodes which represent 16 possible tuples.

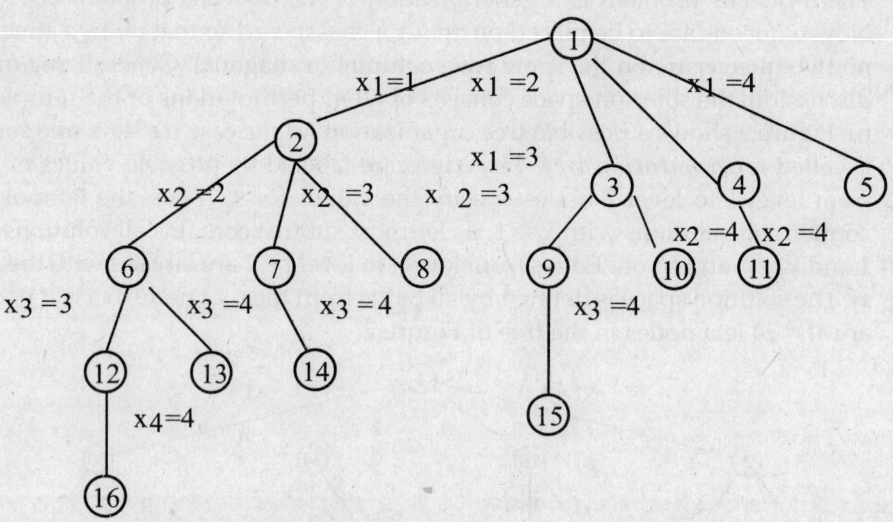

Figure 3. A solution for the sum of subsets problem.

At this point it is useful to develop some terminology regarding tree organizations of solution spaces. Each node in this tree defines a ***problem state.*** All paths from the root to other nodes define the ***state space*** of the problem. ***Solution states*** are those problem states s for which the path from the root to s defines a tuple in the solution space. In the tree of Figure3 all nodes are solution states whereas in the tree of Figure 4 only leaf nodes are solution states. ***Answer states*** are those solution states s for which the path from the root to s defines a tuple that is a member of the set of solutions (i.e., it satisfies the implicit constraints) of the problem. The tree organization of the solution space is referred to as the ***state space tree.***

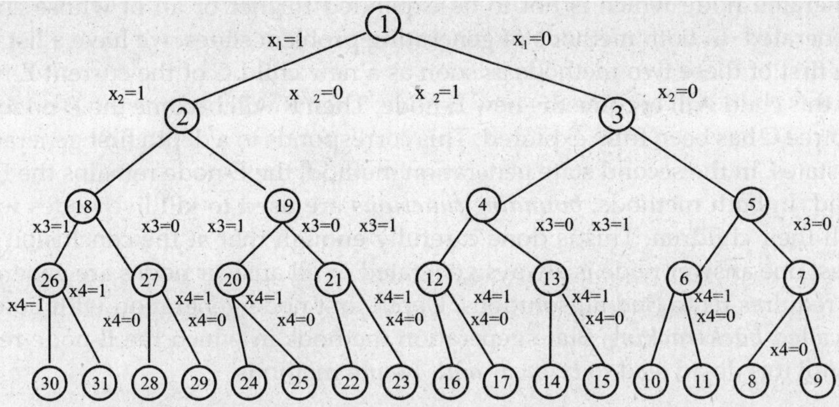

Figure 4. Another solution for the sum of subsets problems. Nodes are numbered as in D-search.

At each internal node in the space tree of Examples 3 and 7.4 the solution space is partitioned into disjoint sub-solution spaces. For example, at node 1 of Figure 2 the solution space is partitioned into four disjoint sets. Subtrees 2, 18, 34, and 50 respectively represent all elements of the solution space with x_1 = 1, 2, 3, and 4. At node 2 the sub-solution space with x_1 = 1 is further partitioned into three disjoint sets. Subtree 3 represents all solution space elements with x_1 = 1 and x_2 = 2. For all the state space trees we study in this chapter, the solution space is partitioned into disjoint sub-solution spaces at each internal node. It should be noted that this is not a requirement on a state space tree. The only requirement is that every element of the solution space be represented by at least one node in the state space tree.

The state space tree organizations described in Example 4 are called ***static trees***. This terminology follows from the observation that the tree organizations are independent of the problem instance being solved. For some problems it is advantageous to use different tree organizations for different problem instances. In this case the tree organization is determined dynamically as the solution space is being searched. Tree organizations that are problem instance dependent are called ***dynamic trees***. As an example, consider the fixed tuple size formulation for the sum of subsets problem (Example 4). Using a dynamic tree organization, one problem instance with n= 4 can be solved by means of the organization given in Figure 4. Another problem instance with n = 4 can be solved by means of a tree in which at level 1 the partitioning corresponds to x_2 = 1 and x_2 = 0. At level 2 the partitioning could correspond to x_1 = 1 and x_1 = 0, at level 3 it could correspond to x_3 = 1 and x_3 = 0, and so on.

Once a state space tree has been conceived of for any problem, this problem can be solved by systematically generating the problem states, determining which of these are solution states, and finally determining which solution states are answer states. There are two fundamentally different ways to generate the problem states. Both of these begin with the root node and generate other nodes. A node which has been generated and all of whose children have not yet been generated is called a ***live node***. The live node whose children are currently being generated is called the E-node (node being expanded). *A **dead node*** is a generated node which is not to be expanded further or all of whose children have been generated. In both methods of generating problem states, we have a list of live nodes. In the first of these two methods as soon as a new child C of the current E-node R is generated, this child will become the new E-node. Then R will become the E-node again when the subtree C has been fully explored. This corresponds to a depth first generation of the problem states. In the second state generation method, the E-node remains the E-node until it is dead. In both methods, ***bounding functions*** are used to kill live nodes without generating all their children. This is done carefully enough that at the conclusion of the process at least one answer node is always generated or all answer nodes are generated if the problem requires us to find all solutions. Depth first node generation with bounding functions is called ***backtracking.*** State generation methods in which the E-node remains the E-node until it is dc-ad lead to ***branch- and- bound*** methods.

The nodes of Figure 2 have been numbered in the order they would be generated in a depth first generation process. The nodes in Figures 3 and 4 have been numbered according to two generation methods in which the E-node remains the E-node until it is dead. In Figure 3 each new node is placed into a queue. When all the children of the current E-node have been generated, the next node at the front of the queue become the new E-node. In Figure 4 new nodes are placed into a stack instead of a queue. Current terminology is not uniform in referring to these two alternatives. Typically the queue method is called breadth first generation and the stack method is called D-search (depth search).

Example 5

4-queens problem

Let us see how backtracking works on the 4-queens problem. As a bounding function, we use the obvious criteria that if $(x_1, x_2, \ldots, x_i)$ is the path to the current E-node, then all children nodes with parent-child labelings x_{i+1} are such that $(x_1,\ldots,x_{i+1})$ represents a chessboard configuration in which no two queens are attacking. We start with the root node as the only live node. This becomes the E-node and the path is (). We generate one child. Let us assume that the children are generated in ascending order. Thus, node number 2 of Figure 2 is generated and the path is now (1). This corresponds to placing queen 1 on column 1. Node 2 becomes the E-node. Node 3 is generated and immediately killed. The next node generated is node 8 and the path becomes (1, 3). Node 8 becomes the E-node. However, it gets killed as all its children represent board configurations that cannot lead to an answer node. We backtrack to node 2 and generate another child, node 13. The path is now (1, 4). Figure 5 shows the board configurations as backtracking proceeds. Figure 5 shows graphically the steps that the backtracking algorithm goes through as it tries to find a solution. The dots indicate placements of a queen which were tried and rejected because another queen was attacking. In Figure 5(b) the second queen is placed on columns 1 and 2 and finally settles on column 3. In Figure 5(c) the algorithm tries all four columns and is unable to place the next queen on a square. Backtracking now takes place. In Figure 5(d) the second queen is moved to the next possible column, column 4 and the third queen is placed on column 2. The boards in Figure 5 (e), (f), (g), and (h) show the remaining steps that the algorithm goes through until a solution is found.

Figure 6 shows the part of the tree of Figure 2 that is generated. Nodes are numbered in the order in which they are generated. A node that gets killed as a result of the bounding function has a B under it. Contrast this tree with Figure 2 which contains 31 nodes.

With this example completed, we are now ready to present a precise formulation of the backtracking process. We continue to treat backtracking in a general way. Vie assume that all answer nodes are to be found and not just one. Let $(x_1, x_2, \ldots, x_i)$ be a path from the root to a node in a state space tree. Let $T(x_1, x_2, \ldots, x_i)$ be the set of all possible values for x_{i+1} such that$(x_1, x_2, \ldots x_{i+1})$ is also path to a problem state. $T(x_1, x_2, \ldots, x_n)=\theta$

We assume the existence of bounding function B_{i+1} (expressed as predicates) such that if $B_{i+1}(x_1, x_2, \ldots, x_{i+1})$ is false for a path $(x_1, x_2, \ldots, x_{i+1})$ from the root node to a problem state, then the path, cannot be extended to reach an answer node. Thus the candidates for position i + 1 of the solution vector $(x_1, \ldots, x_n)$ axe those values which are generated by T and satisfy $B_{i+1.}$ Algorithm 1 presents a recursive formulation of the backtracking technique. It is natural to describe backtracking in this way since it is essentially a postorder traversal of a tree . This recursive version is initially invoked by

Backtrack(1);

```
Algorithm Backtrack(k)
// This schema describes the backtracking process using
// recursion. On entering, the first k – 1 values
    / / x[1], x[2], ... , x[k – 1] of the solution vector
// x[1 : n] have been assigned. x[ ] and n are global.
{
for (each x[k] ∈ T(x[1], ... , x[k - 1]) do
{
if (Bk(x[1], x[2], ... , x[k]) ≠ 0) then
{
if (x[1], x[21,..., x[k] is a path to an answer node)
then write (x[1 : k]);
if (k < n) then Backtrack(k + 1);
}
}
}
```

Algorithm 1 Recursive backtracking algorithm

The solution vector $(x_1, \ldots, x_n)$, is treated as a global array *x[1 : n]*. All the possible elements for the k th position of the tuple that satisfy ***Bk*** are generated, one by one, and adjoined to the current vector ($x_1,...,x_{k-1}$). Each time x_k is attached, a check is made to determine whether a solution has been found. Then the algorithm is recursively invoked. When the for loop of line 7 is exited, no more values for x_k exist and the current copy of Backtrack ends. The last unresolved call now resumes, namely, the one that continues to examine the remaining elements assuming only k – 2 values have been set.

Note that this algorithm causes all solutions to be printed and assumes that tuples of various sizes may make up a solution. If only a single solution is desired, then a flag can be added as a parameter to indicate the first occurrence of success.

```
1.   Algorithm | Backtrack(n)
2.   // This schema describes the backtracking process.
3.   // All solutions are generated in x[1 : n] and printed
4.   // as soon as they are determined.
5.   {
6.       k := 1;
7.       while (k ≠ 0) do
8.       {
9.       if (there remains an untried x[k] ∈ T(x[1], x[2],...,
10.      x[k - 1]) and Bk(x[1], ..., x[k]) is true) then
11.      {
12.      if (x[1]; ..., x[k] is a path to an answer node)
13.      then write (x[1 : k]);
14.      k := k + 1; // Consider the next set.
15.      }
16.      else k:= k - 1; // Backtrack to the previous set.
17.      } 18 }
```

Algorithm 2: General iterative backtracking method

An iterative version of Algorithm 1 appears in Algorithm 2. Note that T( ) will yield the set of all possible values that can be placed as the first component x_1 of the solution vector. The component x_1 will take on those values for which the bounding function $B_1 (x\ 1)$ is true. Also note how the elements are generated in a depth first manner. The variable k is continually incremented and a solution vector is grown until either a solution is found or no untried value of x_k remains. When k is decremented, the algorithm must resume the generation of possible elements for the k th position that have not yet been tried. Therefore one must develop a procedure that generates these values in some order. If only one solution is desired, r6placing write (x[1 : k]); with **{write** (x[1 : k]); **return;}** suffices.

The efficiency of both the backtracking algorithms we've just seen depends very much on four factors: (1) the time to generate the next x_k, (2) the number of x_k satisfying the explicit constraints, (3) the time for the bounding functions B_k, and (4) the number of x_k satisfying the B_k. Bounding functions are regarded as good if they substantially reduce the number of nodes that are generated. However, there is usually a trade-off in that bounding functions that are good also take more time to evaluate. What is desire-' is a reduction in the overall computing time and not just a reduction ii, the number of nodes generated. For many problems, the size of the state space tree is too large to permit the generation of all nodes. Bounding functions must be used and hopefully at least one solution is found in a reasonable time span. Yet for many problems (e.g., n-queens) no sophisticated bounding methods are known.

One general principle of efficient searching is called rearrangement. For many problems the sets S_i can be taken in any order. This suggests that all other things being equal, it is more efficient to make the next choice from the set with the fewest elements. This strategy doesn't pay off for the *n* queens problem, and examples can be constructed that prove this principle won't always work. The potential value of this heuristic is exhibited in Figure 7 by the two backtracking search trees for the same problem. If we are able to remove a node on level twc of Figure 7(a), then we are effectively removing 12 possible 4-tuples from consideration. If we remove a node from level two of the tree in Figure 7(b), then only eight tuples are eliminated. More-sophisticated rearrangement strategies are studied in conjunction with dynamic state space trees.

As stated previously, there are four factors that determine the time required by a backtracking algorithm. Once a state space tree organization, is selected, the first three of these are relatively independent of the problem instance being solved. Only the fourth, the number of nodes generated, varies from one problem instance to another. A backtracking algorithm on one problem instance might generate only O(n) nodes whereas on a different (and even closely related) instance it might generate almost all the nodes in the state space tree. If the number of nodes in the solution space is 2^n or n!, the worst-case time for a backtracking algorithm will generally he $O(p(n)\ 2^n)$ or $O(q(n)\ n!$ respectively. The $p(n)$ and $q(n)$ are polynomials in n. The importance of backtracking lies in its ability to solve some instances with large n in a very small amount of time. The only difficulty is in predicting the behavior of a backtracking algorithm for the problem instance we wish to solve.

We can estimate the number of nodes- that will be generated by a backtracking algorithm working on a certain instance by using Monte Carlo methods. The general idea in the estimation method is to generate a random path in the state space tree. Let X be a node on-this random path. Assume that X is at level i of the state space tree. The bounding functions are used at node X to determine the number m_i of its children that do not get bounded. The next node on the path is obtained by randomly selecting one of these m_i children that do not get bounded. The path generation terminates at a node which is a leaf or all of whose children get bounded. Using these m_i's,

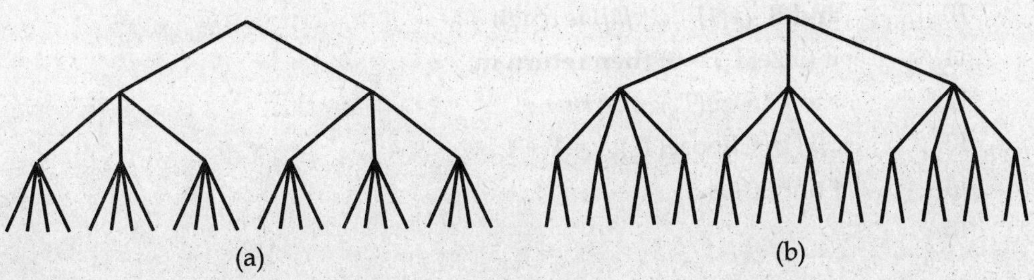

We can estimate the total number m of nodes in the state space tree that will not get bounded. This number is particularly useful when all answer nodes are to be searched for. In this case all unbounded nodes need to be generated. When only a single solution is desired, m may not be such a good estimate for the number of nodes generated as the backtracking algorithm may arrive at a solution by generating only a small fraction of the m nodes. To estimate m from the m_i's, we need to make an assumption on the bounding functions. We shall assume that these functions are static; that is, the backtracking algorithm does not change its bounding functions as it gathers information during its execution. Moreover, exactly the same function is used for all nodes on the same level of the state space tree. This assumption is not true of most backtracking algorithms. In most cases the hounding functions get stronger as the search proceeds. In these cases our estimate for m is higher than one that could be obtained if the change in the bounding functions were taken into consideration.

Continuing with the assumption of static bounding functions, we see that the number of unbounded nodes on level 2 is m_1. If the search tree is such that nodes on the same level have the same degree, then we would expect each level 2 node to have on the average m_2 unbounded children. This yields a total of m_1m_2 nodes on level 3. The expected number of unbounded nodes on level 4 is $m_1m_2m_3$. In general, the expected number of nodes on level i + 1 is $m_1m_2 \ldots m_i$. Hence, the estimated number m of unbounded nodes that will be generated in solving the given problem instance *I* is $m = 1 + m_i + m_1m_2 + m_1m_2m_3 + \ldots$.

Function Estimate (Algorithm 3) determines the value m. It selects a random path from the root of the state space tree. The function Size returns the size of the set T_k. The function Choose makes a random choice of an element in T_k. The desired sum is built using fhe variables *m* and *r*.

```
Algorithm Estimate()
// This algorithm follows a random path
// in a state space tree and produces an
// estimate of the number of nodes in the tree.
{
    k:= 1; m:= l; r:= l;
    repeat
    {
        Tk := {x[k] I x[k] E T(x[1], x[2],. . . , x[k - 1])
        and B_k (x[1], ..., x[k]) is true};
        if (5ize(T_k) = 0) then return m;
        r := r * Size(T_k); m:= rn + r;
        x[k] := Choose(T_k); k:= k + 1;
    } until (false);
}
```

Algorithm 3: Estimating the efficiency of backtracking

We use this estimator in later sections as we examine backtracking solutions to various problems. A better estimate of the number of unbounded nodes that will be generated by a backtracking algorithm can be obtained by selecting several different random paths (typically no more than 20) and determining the average of these values.

3.2 THE 8-QUEENS PROBLEM

Now we are ready to tackle the 8-queens problem via a backtracking solution. In fact we trivially generalize the problem and consider an n x n chessboard and try to find all ways to place n nonattacking queens. We observed from the 4-queens problem that we can let $(x_1, ..., x_n)$ represent a solution in which x_i is the column of the ith row where the ith queen is placed. The x_i's will all be distinct since no two queens can be placed in the same column. Now how do we test whether two queens are on the same diagonal?

If we imagine the chessboard squares being numbered as the indices of the two-dimensional array a[1 : n, l: n], then we observe that every element on the same diagonal that runs from the upper left to the lower right has the same row-column value. For example, in Figure 1, consider the queen at a[4,2]. The squares that are diagonal to this queen (running from the upper left to the lower right) are a[3,1], a[5,3], a[6,4), a[7,5], and a[8,6). All these squares have a row-column value of 2. Also, every element on the same diagonal that goes from the upper right to the lower left has the same row + column value. Suppose two queens are placed at positions *(i, j)* and *(k,* 1). Then by the above they are on the same diagonal only if

$$i - j = k - l \text{ or } i + j = k + l$$

The first equation implies

$$J - l = i - k$$

The second implies

$$j - l = k - i$$

Therefore two queens lie on the same diagonal if and only -if $|j - l| = |i - k|$.

Place(k, i) (Algorithm 4) returns a boolean value that is true if the k th queen can be placed in column i. It tests both whether i is distinct from all previous values x[1], ..., *x[k -1]* and whether there is no Other queen on the same diagonal. Its computing time is O(k – 1).

Using Place, we can refine the general backtracking method as given by Algorithm 1 and give a precise solution to the n-queens problem (Algorithm 5). The array *x[ ]* is global. The algorithm is invoked by NQueens(1,n).

```
Algorithm Place(k, i)
// Returns true if a queen can be placed in kth row and
// ith column. Otherwise it returns false. x[ ] is a
// global array whose first (k– 1) values have been set.
```

```
//Abs(r) returns the absolute value of r.
{
    for j:=l to k-l do
    if ((x[j] = i) ;// Two in the same column
    or (Abs(x[j] – i) = Abs(j - k)))
    // or in the same diagonal
    then return false;
    return true; }
```

Algorithm 4: Can a new queen be placed?

```
Algorithm NQueens(k, n)
// Using backtracking, this procedure prints all
    [possible placements of n queens on an n x n
    // chessboard so that they are nonattacking.
{
    for i:= 1 to n do
    {
    if Place(k, i) then
    {
    x[k] := i;
    if. (k = n) then write (x[1 : n]);
    else NQueens(k + 1, n);
    }
    }
}
```

Algorithm 5: All solutions to the n-queens problem

At this point we might wonder how effective function **NQueens** is over the brute force approach. For an 8 x 8 chessboard there are (8^4) possible ways to place 8 pieces, or approximately 4.4 billion 8-tuples to_examine. However, by allowing only placements of queens on distinct rows and columns, we require the examination of at most 8!, or only 40,320 8-tuples.

We can use **Estimate** to estimate the number of nodes that will be generated by **NQueens.** Note that the assumptions that are needed for **Estimate** do hold for **NQueens.** The bounding function is static. No change is made to the function as the search proceeds. In addition, all nodes on the same level of the state space tree have the same degree. In Figure 7.8 we see five 8 x 8 chessboards that were created using **Estimate.**

As required, the placement of each queen on the chessboard was chosen randomly. With each choice we kept track of the number of columns a queen could legitimately be placed on. These numbers are listed in the vector beneath each chessboard. The number following the vector represents the value that function **Estimate** would produce from these sizes. The average of these five trials is 1625. The total number of nodes in the 8-queens state space tree is

$$1+\sum_{j=0}^{7}\{\Pi^{j}{}_{I=0}(8-i)\}=69,281$$

So the estimated number of unbounded nodes is only about 2.34% of the total number of nodes in the 8-queens state space tree. (See the exercises for more ideas about the efficiency of **NQueens.)**

3.3 SUM OF SUBSETS

Suppose we are given n distinct positive numbers (usually called weights) and we desire to find all combinations of these numbers whose sums are m. This is called the ***sum of subsets*** problem. Examples 2 and 4 showed how we could formulate this problem using either fixed- or variable-sized tuples. We consider a backtracking solution using the fixed tuple size strategy. In this case the element x_i of the solution vector is either one or zero depending on whether the weight w_i is included or not.

The children of any node in Figure 4 are easily generated. For a node at level i the left child corresponds to $x_i = 1$ and the right to $x_i = 0$.

A simple choice for the bounding functions is $Bk(x_1, ,..., xk)$ = true iff

$$\sum_{i-1}^{k} wixi+\sum_{i=k+1}^{n} wi \geq m$$

Clearly $x_1, ..., x_k$ cannot lead to an answer node if this condition is not satisfied. The bounding functions can be strengthened if we assume the w_i's are initially in non decreasing order. In this case $x_1, ..., x_k$ cannot lead to an answer node if

$$\sum_{i=1}^{k} wixi+W_{k+1} \geq m$$

The bounding functions we **use are therefore**

$$Bk(x_1,\dots,X_k)=true\ if \sum_{i=1}^{k} W_iX_i+\sum_{i=k=1}^{n} W_k \leq m$$

$$\text{and} \sum_{i=1}^{k} W_iX_i+W_{k=1} \leq m \quad (1)$$

Since our algorithm will not make use of B_n, we need not be concerned by the appearance of w_{n+1} in this function. Although we have now specified all that is needed to directly use either of the backtracking schemas, a simpler algorithm results if we tailor either of these schemas to the problem at hand. This simplification results from the realization that if $x_k = 1$, then

$$\sum_{i=1}^{k} W_i X_i + \sum_{i=k+1}^{n} W_i > m$$

For simplicity we refine the recursive schema. The resulting algorithm is SumOfSub (Algorithm 6).

Algorithm SumOfSub avoids computing $\Sigma^k_{i=1} w_i x_i$ and $\Sigma^n_{k+1} w_i$ each time by keeping these values in variables s and r respectively. The algorithm assumes $w_1 \leq m$ and $\Sigma^n_{i=1} w_i \geq m$. The initial call is SumOfSub(0,1, $\Sigma^n_{i=1} w_i$). It is interesting to note that the algorithm does not explicitly use the test k > n to terminate the recursion. This test is not needed as on entry to the algorithm, $s \neq m$ and $s + r \geq m$. Hence, $r \neq 0$ and so k can be no greater than n. Also note that in the else if statement (line 11), since $s + w_k < m$ and $s + r \geq m$, it follows that $r \neq w_k$ and hence $k + 1 \leq n$. Observe also that if $s + w_k = m$(line 9), then $x_{k+1}, ..., x_n$ must be zero. These zeros are omitted from the output of line 9. In line 11 we do not test for $\Sigma^k_{i=1} w_i x_i + \Sigma^n_{k+1} w_i \geq m$, as we already know $s + r \geq m$ and $x_k = 1$.

```
1.   Algorithm SumOfSub(s, k, r)
2.   //Find all subsets of u+[1 : n] that sum to m. The values of x[j],
3.   //1 ≤ j< k, have already been determined. s= Σj=1 w[j] * x(jj
4.   //and Σj=k w[j]. The w[j]'s are in nondecreasing order.
5.       //It is assumed that w[1] ≤ m and   Σ n I=1 w[i] ≥ m.
6.   {
7.   // Generate left child. Note: s + w[k] ≤ m since Bk-1 is true.
8.   x[k] :=1
9.   if (s+w[k] = m,) then write (x(1 : k,]); //Subset found
10.      //There is no recursive call here as w[J] > 0. 1 ≤ j ≤ n.
11.      else if (s + w[k] + w[k + 1] ≤ m)
12.      then SumOfSub(s + w[k], k+ 1, r- w[k]);
13.      // Generate right child and evaluate Bk.
14.      if ((s + r - w[k] ≥ m) and (s + w[k + 1] ≤ m)) then
15.      {
16.      x[k] := 0;
17.      SumOfSub(s, k + 1, r - w[k]);
18.  }
19.  }
```

Algorithm 6: Recursive backtracking algorithm for sum of subsets problem.

REVIEW QUESTIONS

1. What is backtracking? Explain the eight queens example in details.
2. Explain the algorithm for
   (a) 4-queens problem.
   (b) n-queens problem.
3. Explain the working of recursive backtracking algorithm
4. Explain the working of algorithm for estimating the efficiency of backtracking
5. Write and explain the recursive backtracking algorithm for sum of subsets problem.

UNIT 3

DIVIDE AND CONQUER

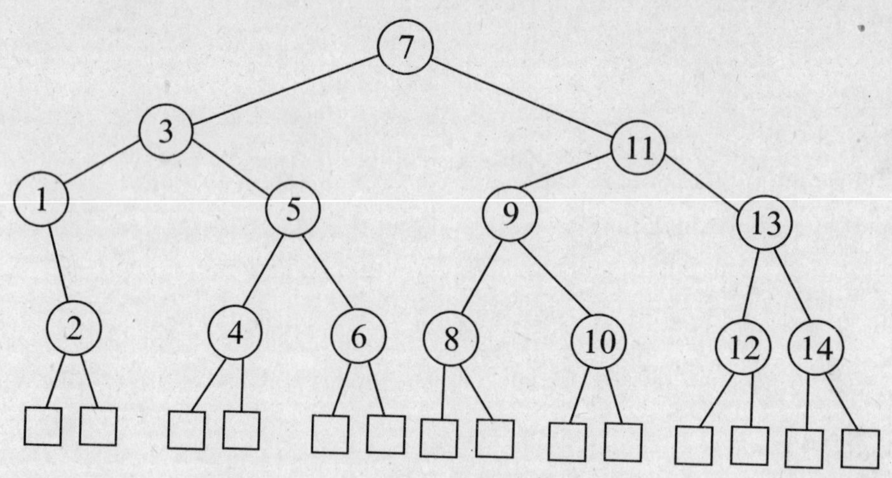

4.1 INTRODUCTION TO GENERAL METHOD

Given a function to compute on n inputs the ***divide-and-conquer*** strategy suggests splitting the inputs into k distinct subsets, $1 < k \leq n$, yielding k subproblems. These subproblems must be solved, and then a method must be found to combine subsolutions into a solution of the whole. If the subproblems are still relatively large, then the divide-and-conquer strategy can possibly be reapplied. Often the subproblems resulting from a divide-and conquer design are of the same type as the original problem. For those cases the reapplication of the divide-and-conquer principle is naturally expressed by a recursive algorithm. Now smaller and smaller subproblems of the same kind are generated until eventually subproblems that are small enough to be solved without splitting are produced.

To be more precise, suppose we consider the divide-and-conquer strategy when it splits the input into two subproblems of the same kind as the original problem. This splitting is typical of many of the problems we examine here. We can write a control, abstraction that mirrors the way an algorithm based on divide-and-conquer will look. By a ***control abstraction*** we mean a procedure whose flow of control is clear but whose primary operations are specified by other procedures whose precise meanings are left undefined. D and C is initially invoked as D and C(P), where P is the problem to be solved.

Small(P) is a Boolean-valued function that determines whether the input size is small enough that the answer can be computed without splitting. If this is so, the function S is invoked. Otherwise the problem P is divided into smaller subproblems. These subproblems $P_1, P_2, \ldots, P_k$ are solved by recursive applications of DAndC. Combine is a function that determines the solution to *P* using the solutions to the *k* subproblems. If the size of P is n and the sizes of the k subproblems are $n_1, n_2 \ldots, n_k$, respectively, then the computing time of DAndC is described by the recurrence relation ***T(n).***

```
Algorithm DAndQP
{
    if Small(P) then return S(P);
    else
    {
        divide P into smaller instances P1, P2, ..., Pk, k≥ 1;
    Apply DAndC to each of these subproblems;
    return Combine(DAndC(P1),DAndC(P2),...,DAndC(Pk));
    }
}
```

Algorithm 1: General Method for divide-and-conquer(Control Abstraction)

$$T(n) = \begin{vmatrix} gn \\ T(n_1) + T(n_2) + + T(n_k) + f(n) \end{vmatrix} \quad \text{n small otherwise} \qquad (1)$$

Where *T(n) is* the time for DAndC on any input of size *n* and *g(n)* is the time to compute the answer directly for small inputs. The function *f(n)* is the time for dividing P and combining the solutions to subproblems. For divideand-conquer-based algorithms that produce subproblems of the same type as the original problem, it is very natural to first describe such algorithms using recursion.

The complexity of many divide-and-conquer algorithms is given by recurrences of-the form

$$T(n) = \begin{vmatrix} T(1) & n = 1 \\ aT(n/b) + f(n) & n > 1 \end{vmatrix} \qquad (2)$$

where a and *b* are known constants: We assume that T(1) is known and *n* is a power of b(i.e., $n = 6^k$).

One of the methods for solving any such recurrence relation is **called the *substitution method.*** This method repeatedly makes substitution for each occurrence of the function T in the right-hand side until all such occurrences disappear.

UNIT 3

Example 1

Consider the case in which a= 2 and 6= 2. Let T(1) = 2 and $f(n) = n$. We have

$$
\begin{aligned}
T(n) &= 2T(n/2) + n \\
&= 2[2T(n/4 + n/2] + n \\
&= 4T(n/4) + 2n \\
&= 4[2T(n/8) + n/4] + 2n \\
&= 8T(n/8) + 3n
\end{aligned}
$$

Thus, we see that $T(n) = 2^iT(n/2^i) + in$, for any $\log_2 n \geq i \geq 1$. In particular, then, $T(n) = 2^{\log_2 n}T(n/2^{\log_2 n}) + n \log_2 n$, corresponding to the choice of $i = \log_2 n$. Thus, $T(n) = nT(1) + n \log_2 n = n \log_{2n} + 2n$.

Beginning with the recurrence (2) and using the substitution method, it can be shown that

$$T(n) = n^{\log_b a\, 4}[T(^1) + n(n)]$$

where $u(n) = \sum^k_{j=1} h(b^j)$ and $h(n) = f(n) / n^{\log_b a}$.

Table 1 tabulates the asymptotic value of u(n) for various values of h(n). This table allows one to easily obtain the asymptotic value of T(n) for many of the recurrences one encounters when analyzing divide-and-conquer algorithms. Let us consider some examples using this table.

***Table 1.** u(n) values for various h(n) values*

h(n)	u(n)
O(nr), r < 0	O(1)
$\Theta((\log n)^i), i \geq 0$	$\Theta((\log n)^{i+1} / (i+1))$
$\Omega(n^r), r > 0$	$\Theta(h(n))$

Example 2

Look at the following **recurrence when n** is **a** power of 2:

$$T(n) = \begin{cases} T(1) & n = 1 \\ T(n/2) + c & n > 1 \end{cases}$$

Comparing with (2), we see that $a = 1$, $b = 2$, and $f(n) = c$. So, $\log_b(a) = 0$ and $h(n) = f(n)/n^{\log_b a} = c = c(\log n)^\circ = \Theta((\log n)^\circ)$. From Table 1, *we* obtain $u(n) = \Theta(\log n)$. So, $T(n) = n^{\log_b a}[c + \Theta(\log n)] = \Theta(\log n)$.

Example 3

Next consider the case in which $a= 2$, $b = 2$, and $f(n) = cn$. For this recurrence, $\log_b a= 1$ and $h(n) = f(n)/n = c = \Theta((\log n)^\circ)$. Hence, $u(n)= \Theta(\log n)$ and $T(n)= n[T(1) + \Theta(\log n)] = \Theta(n \log n)$.

Example 4

As another example, consider the recurrence $T(n) = 7T(n/2)+ 18n^2$, $n \geq 2$ and a power of 2. We obtain $a = 7$, $b= 2$, and $f(n) = 18n^2$. So, $\log_b a = \log_2 7 \approx 2.81$ and $h(n) = 18n^2/n^{\log_2 7} = 18n^{2-\log_2 7} = O(n^r)$, where $r= 2 - \log_2 7 < 0$. So, $u(n) = O(1)$. The expression for $T(n)$ is

$$T(n) = n^{\log_2 7}[T(1) + O(1)]$$
$$= \Theta(n^{\log_2 7})$$

as T(1) is assumed to be a constant.

Example 5

As a final example, consider the recurrence $T(n) = 9T(n/3)+4n^6$, $n \geq 3$ and a power of 3. Comparing with (2), we obtain $a = 9$, $b = 3$,and $f(n) -4n^6$. So, $\log_b a = 2$ and $h(n) = 4n^6/n^2 = 4n^4 = \Omega(n^4)$. From Table 1, we see that $u(n) = \Theta(h(n)) = \Theta(n^4)$. So,

$$T(n) = n^2[T(1) + O(n^4)] = E)(n^6)$$

as T(1) can be assumed constant.

4.2 BINARY SEARCH

Let a_i, $1 \leq i \leq n$, be a list of elements that are sorted in non-decreasing order. Consider the problem of determining whether a given element x is present in the list. If x is present, we are to determine a value j such that $a_j = x$. If x is not in the list, then j is to be set to zero. Let $P = (n, a_i, \ldots, a_l, x)$ denote an arbitrary instance of this search problem (n is the number of elements in the list, $a_i, \ldots, a_l$ is the list of elements, and x is the element searched for).

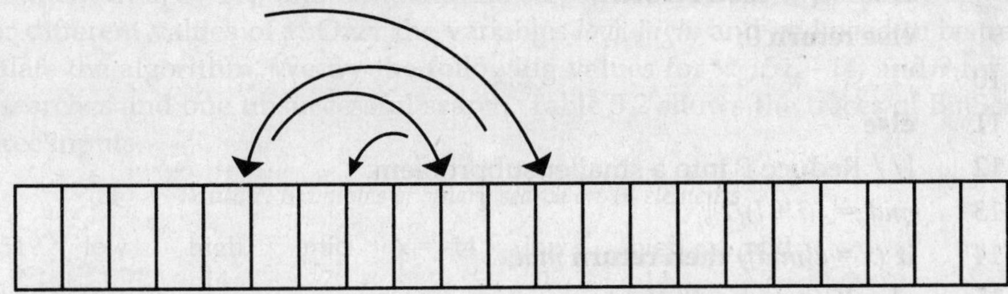

Divide-and-conquer can be used to solve this problem. Let Small(P) be true if $n = 1$. In this case, S(P) will take the value i if $x = a_i$; otherwise it will take the value 0. Then $g(1) = \Theta(1)$. If P has more than one element, it can be divided (or reduced) into a new subproblexn as follows. Pick an index q (in the range [i, l]) and compare x with a_q.

There are three possibilities:

$x = a_q$: In this case the problem P is immediately solved.

$x < a_q$: In this case x has to be searched for only in the sublist $a_i, a_{i+1}, \ldots, a_{q-1}$ Therefore, P reduces to $(q - i, a_i, \ldots, a_{q-1}\, x)$.

$x > a_q$: In this case the sublist to be searched is $a_{q+1}, \ldots, a_l$. P reduces to $(l-q, a_{q-1}, \ldots, a_l,$

x).

In this example, any given problem P gets divided (reduced) into one new subproblem. This division takes only Θ(1) time. After a comparison with a_q, the instance remaining to be solved (if any) can be solved by using this divide-and-conquer scheme again. If *q* is always chosen such that a_q is the middle element (that is, $q = \lfloor (n+1)/2 \rfloor$), then the resulting search algorithm is known as binary search. Note that the answer to the new subproblem is also the answer to the original problem P; there is no need for any combining. Algorithm 2 describes this binary search method, where **BinSrch** has four inputs a[], *i, l,* and *x*. It is initially invoked as **BinSrch(a,** 1, n, x).

A nonrecursive version of **BinSrch is** given in Algorithm 3. **BinSearch** has three inputs *a, n,* and *x*. The **while** loop continues processing as long as there are more elements left to check. At the conclusion of the procedure 0 is returned if x is not present, or *j* is returned, such that *a[j]* = *x*.

Is **BinSearch** an algorithm? We must be sure that all of the operations such as comparisons between *x* and *a[mid]* are well defined. The relational operators carry out the comparisons among elements of a correctly if these operators are appropriately defined.

```
Algorithm BinSrch(a, i, l, x)
// Given an array a[i : l] of elements in nondecreasing
// order, 1≤ i≤ l, determine whether x is present, and
// if so, return j such that x= a[j]; else return 0.
{
if (l = i) then // If Small(P)
{
if (x = a[i]) then return i;
else return 0;
}
else
{// Reduce P into a smaller subproblem.
mid :=⌊ (i + l)/2⌋;
if (x = a[mid]) then return mid;
else if (x < a[mid]) then
return BinSrch(a, i, mid - 1, x);
else return BinSrch(a, mid + 1, l, x);
}
}
```

Algorithm 2: Recursively defined binary search

```
Algorithm BInSearch(a,n,x)
// Given an array a[1 : n] of elements in nondecreasing
// order, n≥ 0, determine whether x is present, and
```

```
// if so, return j such that x = a[j]; else return 0.
{
low := 1; high := n;
    while (low ≤ high) do
    {
    mid := ⌊(low + high)/2⌋;
    if (x < a[mid]) then high := mid - 1;
else if (x > a[mid]) then low := mid + 1;
else return mid;
    }
    return 0;
}
```

Algorithm 3: Iterative Version of binary search

Note that *low* and *high* are integer variables such that each time through the loop either *x* is found or *low* is increased by at least one or *high* is decreased by at least one. Thus we have two sequences of integers approaching each other and eventually low becomes greater than *high* and causes termination in a finite number of steps if x is not present.

Example 6

Let us select the 14 entries

−15,−6,0, 7, 9, 23, 54, 82, 101, 112, 125, 131, 142, 151

Place them in a[1 : 14], and simulate the steps that BinSearch goes through as it searches for different values of *x*. Only the variables *low, high,* and *mid* need to be traced as we simulate the algorithm. We try the following values for x: 151, −14, and 9 for two successful searches and one unsuccessful search. Table 3.2 shows the traces of BinSearch on these three inputs.

Table 2. Examples of binary search on 14 elements

x= 151	low	high	mid	x = -14	low	high	mid
	1	14	7		1	14	7
	8	14	11		1	6	3
	12	14	13		1	2	1
	14	14	14		2	2	2
			found		2	1	not found

x = 9	low	high	mid
	1	14	7
	1	6	3
	4	6	5
			found

These examples may give us a little more confidence about Algorithm 3.3, but they by no means prove that it is correct. Proofs of algorithms are very useful because they establish the correctness of the algorithm for *all* possible inputs, whereas testing gives much less in the way of guarantees. Unfortunately, algorithm proving is a very difficult process and the complete proof of an algorithm can be many times longer than the algorithm itself.

We content ourselves with an informal "proof" of BinSearch.

Theorem 1

Algorithm BinSearch(a, n, x) works correctly

Proof:

We assume that all statements work as expected and that comparisons such as x > a[mid] are appropriately carried out. Initially low = *1, high = n, n*≥ 0, and a[1] ≤ *a[2]* ≤...≤a[n]. If n = *0,* the while loop is not entered and 0 is returned. Otherwise we observe that each time through the loop the possible elements to be checked for equality with *x* are *a[low], a[low + 1], ..., a[mid], ..., a[high].* If *x = a[mid],* then the algorithm terminates successfully. Otherwise the range is narrowed by either increasing *low* to *mid + 1* or decreasing *high* to *mid - 1.* Clearly this narrowing *of* the range does not affect the outcome *of* the search. *If low* becomes greater than *high,* then *x* is not present and hence the loop is exited.

Notice that to fully test binary search, we need not concern ourselves with the values of *a[1 : n]. By* varying *x* sufficiently, we can observe all possible computation sequences of BinSearch without devising different values for *a.* To test all successful searches, *x* must take on the *n* values in *a.* To test all unsuccessful searches, x need only take on *n*+ 1 different values. Thus the complexity of testing BinSearch is *2n + 1* for each *n.*

Now let's analyze the execution profile of BinSearch. The two relevant characteristics of this profile are the frequency counts and space required for the algorithm. For BinSearch, storage is required for the n elements of the array plus the variables *low, high, mid,* and *x,* or *n + 4* locations. As for the time, there are three posibilities to consider: the best, average, and worst cases.

Suppose we begin by determining the time for BinSearch on the previous data set. We observe that the only operations in the algorithm are comparisons and some arithmetic and data movements. We concentrate on comparisons between x and the elements in *a[ ],* recognizing that the frequency count of all other operations is of the same order as that for these comparisons. Comparisons between *x* and elements of *a[ ]* are referred to as element comparisons. We assume that only one comparison is needed to determine which of the three possibilities *of* the if statement holds. The number of element comparisons needed to find each *of* the *14* elements is

a:	[1]	[2]	[3]	[4]	[5]	[6]	[7]	[8]	[9]	[10]	[11]	[12]	[13]	[14]
Elements:	−15	−6	0	7	9	23	5	82	101	112	125	131	142	151
Comparisons:	3	4	2	4	3	4	1	4	3	4	2	4	3	4

No element requires more than *4* comparisons to be found. The average is obtained by summing the comparisons needed to find all *14* items and dividing by *14;* this yields *45/14*, or approximately 3.21, comparisons per successful search on the average. There are 15 possible ways that an unsuccessful search may terminate depending on the value of *x*. If $x < a[1]$, the algorithm requires 3 element comparisons to determine that x is not present. For all the remaining possibilities, the **BinSearch** requires 4 element comparisons. Thus the average number of element comparisons for an unsuccessful search is

$$(3 + 14 * 4)/15 = 59/15 \approx 3.93.$$

The analysis just done applies to any sorted sequence containing *14* elements. But the result we would prefer is a formula for *n* elements. A good way to derive such a formula plus a better way to understand the algorithm is to consider the sequence of values for mid that are produced by **BinSearch** for all possible values of x. These values are nicely described using a binary decision tree in which the value in each node is the value of mid. For example, if n = 14, then Figure 3.1 contains a binary decision tree that traces the way in which these values are produced by BinSearch.

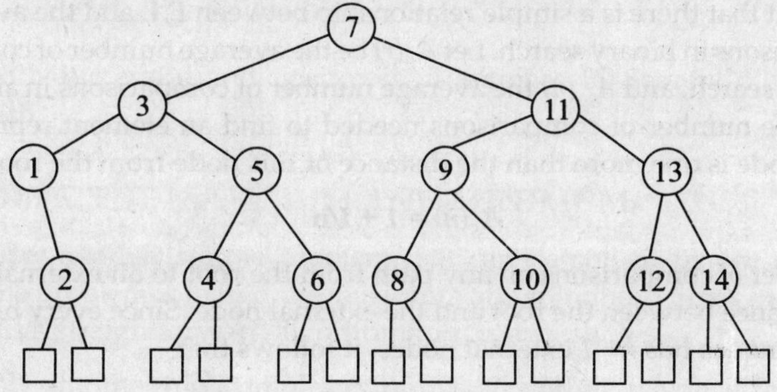

***Figure 1.** Binary decision tree for binary search, n= 14*

The first comparison is x with a[7]. If $x <$ a[7], then the next comparison is with a[3]; similarly, if $x >$ a[7], then the next comparison is with a[ll]. Each path through the tree represents a sequence of comparisons in the binary search method. If x is present, then the algorithm will end at one of the circular nodes that lists the index into the array where x was found. If x is not present, the algorithm will terminate at one of the square nodes. Circular nodes are called internal nodes, and square nodes are referred to as external nodes.

Theorem 2

If *n* is in the range $[2^{k-1}, 2^k)$, then BinSearch makes at most k element comparisons for a successful search and either k–1 or *k* comparisons for an unsuccessful search. (In other words the time for a successful search is O(log *n*) and for an unsuccessful search is Θ(log n)).

Proof:

Consider the binary decision tree describing the action of **BinSearch** on *n* elements. All successful searches end at a circular node whereas all unsuccessful searches end at a square node. If $2^{k-1} \leq n \leq, 2^k$, then all circular nodes are at levels 1, 2, ..., *k* whereas all square nodes are at levels k and k + 1 (note "hat the root is at level 1). The number of element comparisons needed to terminate at a circular node on level *i* is *i* whereas the number of element comparisons needed to terminate at a square node at level *i* is only i – 1. The theorem follows.

The theorem 2 defines the worst-case time for binary search. To determine the average behavior, we need to look more closely at the binary decision tree and equate its size to the number of element comparisons in the algorithm. The distance of a node from the root is one less than its level. The ***internal path length*** I is the sum *of* the distances of all internal nodes from the root. Analogously, the ***external path length*** E is the sum *of* the distances *of* all external nodes from the root. It is easy to show by induction that for any binary tree with *n* internal nodes, E and *I* are related by the formula

$$E=I+2n$$

It turns out that there is a simple relationship between *E,I,* and the average number of comparisons in binary search. Let $A_S(r)$ be the average number of comparisons in a successful search, and $A_u(n)$ the average number of comparisons in an unsuccessful search. The number of comparisons needed to find an element represented by an internal node is one more than the distance of this node from the root. Hence,

$$A_S(n) = 1 + I/n$$

The number *of* comparisons on any path from the root to an external node is equal to the distance between the root and the external node. Since every binary tree with *n* internal nodes has *n*+ *1* external nodes, it follows that

$$A_u(n)=E/(n+1)$$

By Using these three formulas for *E*, A_s, (n), and A_u (n), we find that

$$A_s(n) = (1 + 1/n)A_u(n) - 1$$

From this formula we see that $A_s(n)$ and $A_u(n)$ are directly related. The minimum value of $A_S(n)$ (and hence $A_u(n)$) is achieved by an algorithm whose binary decision tree has minimum external and internal path length. This minimum is achieved by the binary tree all of whose external nodes are on adjacent levels, and this is precisely the tree that is produced by binary search. From Theorem 2 it follows that E is proportional to n log n. Using this in the preceding formulas, we conclude that $A_s(n)$ and $A_u(n)$ are both proportional to log n. Thus we conclude that the average- and worst-case numbers of comparisons for binary search are the same to within a constant factor. The best-case analysis is easy. For a successful search only one element comparison is needed. For an unsuccessful search, Theorem 2 states that I log nj element comparisons are needed in the best case.

In conclusion we are now able to completely describe the computing time of binary search by giving formulas that describe the best, average, and worst cases:

successful searches	unsuccessful searches
$\Theta(1)$, $\Theta(\log n)$, $\Theta(\log n)$	$\Theta(\log n)$

best, average, worst best, average, worst

Can we expect another searching algorithm to be significantly better than binary search in the worst case. The method for proving such an assertion is to view the binary decision tree as a general model for any searching algorithm that depends on comparisons of entire elements. Viewed in this way, we observe that the ***longest*** path to discover any element is minimized by binary search, and so any alternative algorithm is no better from this point of view.

Before we end this section, there is an interesting variation of binary search that makes only one comparison per iteration of the **while** loop.

BinSearch will sometimes make twice as many element comparisons as BinSearch l (for example, when x > a[n]). However, for successful searches BinSearch l may make ***(logn)/2*** more element comparisons than BinSearch (for example, when x = a[mid]. The analysis of BinSearch l is left as an exercise. It should be easy to see that the best-, average-, and worst-case times for BinSearch l are Θ(logn) for both successful and unsuccessful searches.

For both successful and unsuccessful searches BinSearchl did marginally better than BinSearch.

4.3 FINDING THE MAXIMUM AND MINIMUM

Let us consider another simple problem that can be solved by the divideand-conquer technique. The problem is to find the maximum and minimum items in a set of n elements. Algorithm 4 is a straightforward algorithm to accomplish this.

In analyzing the time complexity of this algorithm, we once again concentrate on the number of element comparisons. The justification for this is that the frequency count for other operations in this algorithm is of the same order as that for element comparisons. More' importantly, when the elements in a[1 : n] are polynomials, vectors, very large numbers, or strings of characters, the cost of an element comparison is much higher than the cost of the other operations. Hence the time is determined mainly by the total cost of the element comparisons.

StraightMaxMin requires 2(n – 1) element comparisons in the best, average, and worst cases. An immediate improvement is possible by realizing

```
Algorithm StraightMaxMin(a, n, max, min)
// Set max to the maximum and min to the minimum of a[1 : n].
{
    max := min := a[1];
    for i:= 2 to n do
    {
        if (a[i] > max) then max := a[i];
        if (a[i] < min) then min := a[i];
    }
}
```

Algorithm 4: Straightforward maximum and minimum

That the comparison *a[i] < min is* necessary only when *a[i] > max is* false. Hence we can replace the contents of the for loop by

```
if (a[i] > max) then max := a[i];
else if (a[i] < min) then min := a[i];
```

Now the best case occurs when the elements are in increasing order. The number of element comparisons is $n - 1$. The worst case occurs when the elements are in decreasing order. In this case the number of element comparisons is $2(n - 1)$. The average number of element comparisons is less than $2(n - 1)$. On the average, *a[i] is* greater than *max* half the time, and so the average number of comparisons is $3n/2 - 1$.

A divide-and-conquer algorithm for this problem would proceed as follows: Let P = *(n, a[i],..., a[j])* denote an arbitrary instance of the problem. Here n is the number of elements in the list a[i],..:, *a[j]* and we are interested in finding the maximum and minimum of this list. Let Small(P)/ be true when $n \leq 2$. In this case, the maximum and minimum are *a[i]* if $n = 1$. If $n = 2$, the problem can be solved by making one comparison.

If the list has more than two elements, P has to be divided into smaller instances. For- example, we might divide P into the two instances P1 = $(\lfloor n/2 \rfloor$, a[1],..., a$[\lfloor n/2 \rfloor])$ and P2 = $(n - \lfloor n/2 \rfloor, a[\lfloor n/2 \rfloor + 1], \ldots, a[n])$. After having divided P into two smaller subproblems, we can solve them by recursively invoking the same divide-and-conquer algorithm. How can we combine the solutions for Pl and P2 to obtain a solution for P? If MAX(P) and MIN(P) are the maximum and minimum of the elements in P, then MAX(P) is the larger of MAX(P_1) and MAX(P2). Also, MIN(P) is the smaller of MIN(P_1) and MIN(P_2).

Algorithm 5. results from applying the strategy just described. MaxMin is a recursive algorithm that finds the maximum and minimum of the set of elements {a(i),a(i + 1),...,a(j)}. The situation of set sizes one (i = *j*) and two (*i = j- 1*) are handled separately. For sets containing more than two elements, the midpoint is determined (just as in binary search) and two new subproblems are generated. When the maxima and minima of these subproblems are determined, the two maxima are compared and the two minima are compared to achieve the solution for the entire set.

```
Algorithm MaxMin(i, j, max, min)
// a[1 : n] is a global array. Parameters i and j are integers,
// 1≤ i≤ j≤ n. The effect is to set max and min to the
// largest and smallest values in a[i : j], respectively.
{
    if (i = j) then max := min := a[i]; // Small(P)
    else if (i =i– 1) then // Another case of Small(P)
    {
    if (a[i] < a[j]) then
    {
        max := a(j]; min := a[i];
    }
```

```
else
{
max := a[i]; min := a[j];
}
}
else
{ // If P is not small, divide P into subproblems.
// Find where to split the set.
mid := ⌊(i + j)/2⌋;
// Solve the subproblems.
MaxMin(i, mid, max, min);
MaxMin(mid + 1, j, maxl, min 1);
// Combine the solutions.
if (max < maxl) then max := maxl;
if (min > minl) then min := minl;
}
}
```

Algorithm 5: Recursively finding the maximum and minimum

The procedure is initially invoked by the statement

MaxMin(1, *n*, *x*, *y*)

Suppose we simulate **MaxMin** on the following nine elements:

a:	[1]	[2]	[3]	[4]	[5]	[6]	[7]	[8]	[9]

22 13 –5 –8 15 60 17 31 47

A good way of keeping track of recursive calls is to build a tree by adding a node each time a new call is made. For this algorithm each node has four items of information ***i***, ***j***, ***max***, and ***min***. On the array a[ ] above, the tree of Figure 2. is produced.

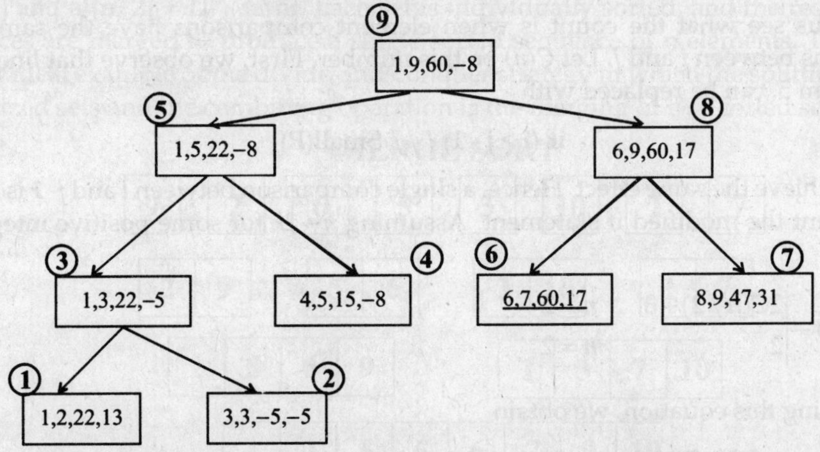

Figure 2. *Description of Trees of recursive calls of* **MaxMin.**

Carefull look at Figure 2 , we see that the root node contains 1and 9 as the ' values of *i* and *j* corresponding to the initial call to **MaxMin. This** execution produces two new calls to **MaxMin,** where *i* and *j* have the values 1, 5 and 6, 9, respectively, and thus split the set into two subsets of approximately, the same size. From the tree we can immediately see that the maximum depth of recursion is four (including the first call). The circled numbers in the upper left corner of each node represent the orders in which ***max*** and ***min*** are assigned values.

Now what is the number of element comparisons needed for MaxMin? If *T(n)* represents this number, then the resulting recurrence relation is

$$T(n) = \begin{vmatrix} T((n/21) + T(rn/21) + 2 & n > 2 \\ 1 & n = 2 \\ 0 & n = 1 \end{vmatrix}$$

When *n* is a power of two, $n = 2^k$ for some positive integer k, then

$$\begin{aligned} T(n) &= 2T(n/2) + 2 \\ &= 2(2T(7)/.4) +. 2) \\ &= 2^{k-i}T(2) + \sum 1 \leq i \leq k-12^i \\ &= 2^{k-1} + 2^k - 2 = 3n/2 - 2 \end{aligned} \quad (3)$$

Remember that $3n/2 - 2$ is the best-, average-, and worst-case number of comparisons when *n is* a power of two.

Compared with the $2n - 2$ comparisons for the straightforward method, this is a saving of 25% in comparisons. It can be shown that no algorithm based on comparisons uses less than 3n/2 - 2 comparisons. So in this sense algorithm **MaxMin** is optimal . But does this imply that MaxMin is better in practice? Not necessarily. In terms of storage, **MaxMin is** worse than the straightforward algorithm because it requires stack space for ***i, j, max, min, maxl,*** and ***min1*** Given *n* elements, there will be $\lfloor \log_2 n \rfloor + 1$ levels of recursion and we need to save seven values for each recursive call (don't forget the return address is also needed).

Let us see what the count is when element comparisons have the same cost as comparisons between *i* and *j*. Let *C(n)* be this number. First, we observe that lines 6 and 7 in Algorithm 5. can be replaced with

if (i > j - 1) { // Small(P)

to achieve the same effect. Hence, a single comparison between *i* and *j- 1* is adequate to implement the modified if statement. Assuming *n= 2k* for some positive integer k, we get

$$C(n) = \begin{vmatrix} 2C(n/2) + 3 & n > 2 \\ 2 & n = 2 \end{vmatrix}$$

Solving this equation, we obtain

$$C(n) = 2C(n/2) + 3$$

UNIT 3

$= 4C(n/4) + 6 + 3$

$= 2^{k-1}C(2) + 3\sum_{0}^{k-2} 2^{i}$

$= 2^{k} + 3*2^{k-1} - 3$

$= 5n/2 - 3$

The comparative figure for **StraightMaxMin** *is 3(n - 1)* (including the comparison. needed to implement the for loop). This is larger than *5n/2 - 3*. Despite this, MaxMin will be slower than **StraightMaxMin** because of the overhead of stacking *i, j, max,* and *min* for the recursion.

Algorithm 5 makes several points. If comparisons among the elements of a[ ] are much more costly than comparisons of integei variables, then the divide-and-conquer technique has yielded a more efficient (actually an optimal) algorithm. On the other hand, if this assumption is not true, the technique yields a less-efficient algorithm. Thus the divide-and-conquer strategy is seen to be only a guide to better algorithm design which may not always succeed. Also we see that it is sometimes necessary to work out the constants associated with the computing time bound for an algorithm. Both **MaxMin** and **StraightMaxMin** are 9(n), *so* the use of asymptotic notation is not enough of a discriminator in this situation. Finally, see the exercises for another way to find the maximum and minimum using only 3n/2 - 2 comparisons.

Note: In the design of any divide-and-conquer algorithm, typically, it is a straightforward task to define **Small(P)** and S(P). So, from now on, we only discuss how to divide any given problem P and how to combine the solutions to subproblems.

4.4 MERGE SORT

As another example of divide-and-conquer, we investigate a sorting algorithm that has the nice property that ill the worst case Its complexity *is*

O(n log n). This algorithm is called merge sort. We assume throughout that the elements are to be sorted in non decreasing order. Given a sequence of *n* elements (also called keys) a[l],... , a[n], the general idea is to imagine them split into two sets a[1]..... a[[n/2]] and a[[n/2] + 1], .., a[n]. Each set is individually sorted, and the resulting sorted sequences are merged to produce a single sorted sequence of n elements. Thus we have another ideal example of the divide-and-conquer strategy in which the splitting is into two equal-sized sets and the combining operation is the merging of two sorted sets into one.

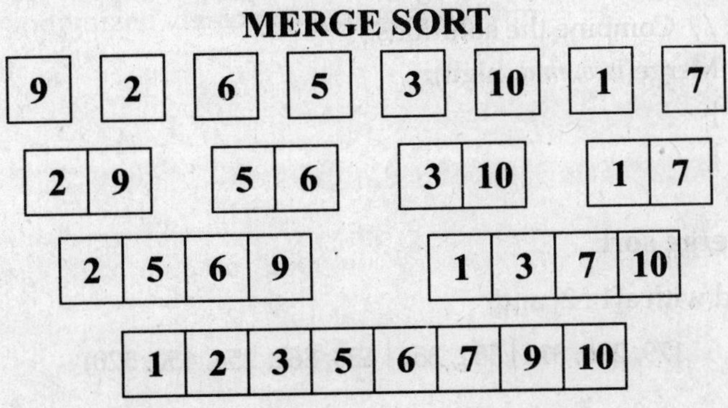

MergeSort (Algorithm 6) describes this process very, succinctly using recursion and a function **Merge** (Algorithm 7) which merges two sorted sets. Before executing **MergeSort,** the *n* elements should be placed in a[1 : n]. Then **MergeSort(l,n)** causes the keys to be rearranged into non decreasing order in a.

Example 7

Consider the array of ten elements a[1 : 10] =(311, 286, 179, 652, 351, 423, 861, 254, 450, 520). Algorithm **MergeSort** begins by splitting a[ ] into two subarrays each of size five (a[1 : 5] and a[6 : 10]). The elements in a[1 : 5] are then split into two subarrays of size three (a[1 : 3]) and two (a [4: 5]). Then the items in a[1 : 3] are split into subarrays of size two (a[l : 2]) and one (a[3 : 3]). The two values in a[1 : 2] are split a final time into one-element subarrays, and now the merging begins. Note that no movement of data has yet taken place. A record of the subarrays,is implicitly maintained by the recursive mechanism. Pictorially the file can now be viewed as

(311 1286 1 179 1652, 351 1423, 861, 254, 450, 520)

where vertical bars indicate the boundaries of subarrays. Elements *a[1]* and a[2] are merged to yield

(286, 311 1179 1652, 351 1423, 861, 254, 450, 520)

```
Algorithm MergeSort(low, high)
// a[law : high] is a global array to be sorted.
// Small(P) is true if there is only one element
        to sort. In this case the list is already sorted.
{
        if (low < high) then//If there are more than one element
        {
        // Divide P into subproblems.
        //Find where to split the set.
        mid := ⌊(law + high)/2⌋;
        // Solve the subproblems.
        MergeSort(low, mid);
        MergeSort(mid + 1, high);
        // Combine the solutions.
        Merge(low, mid, high);
        }
        }
```

Algorithm 6: Merge sort

Then a[3] is merged with a[1 : 2] and

179, 286, 311 | 652, 351 | 423, 861, 254, 450, 520)

is produced. Next, elements a[4] and a[5] are merged:

(179, 286, 311 | 351, 652 | 423, 861, 254, 450, 520)

and then a[1 :31 and a[4 : 5]:

(179, 286, 311; 351, 652 | 423, 861, 254, 460, 520)

At this point the algorithm has returned to the first invocation of MergeSort and is about to process the second recursive call. Repeated recursive calls are invoked producing the following subarrays:

(179, 286, 311, 351, 652 1423 18611254 1450, 520)

Elements a[6] and a[7] are merged. Then a[8] is merged with a[6: 7]:

```
Algorithm 1Vlerge(low, mid, high)
// a[low :high, is a global array containing two sorted
// subsets in a[low : mid] and in a[mid + 1: high]. The goal
// is to merge these two sets into a single set residing
// in a[low : high]. b[ ] is an auxiliary global array.
{
    h:= low; i:= low; j:= mid + 1;
    while ((h ≤ mid) and (j ≤ high)) do
    {
        if (a[h] ≤ a[j]) then
        {
            b[i] := a[h];h := h +1;
        }
        else
        {
            b[i] := a[j]; j:= j + 1;
        }
        i:=i+1;
    }
    if (h > mid) then
        for k:= j to high do
        {
            b[i] := a[k]; i:= i + 1;
        }
    else
        for k:= h to mid do {
            b[i] := a[k]; i:= i + 1;
        }
    for k:= low to high do a[k] := b[k];
}
```

Algorithm 7: Merging two sorted subarrays using auxiliary storage

(179, 286, 311, 351, 652 | 254, 423, 861 | 450, 520)

Next a[9] and a[10] are merged, and then a[6 : 8] and a[9 : 10]:

(179, 286, 311, 351, 652 | 254, 423, 450, 520, 861)

At this point there are two sorted subarrays and the final merge produces the fully sorted result

(179, 254, 286, 311, 351, 423, 450, 520, 652, 861)

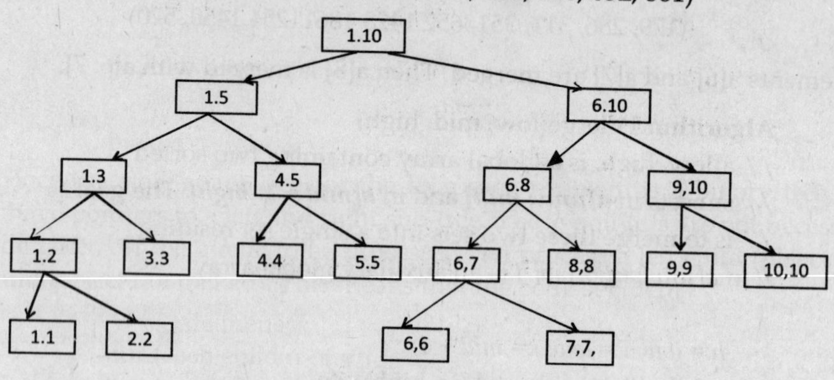

Figure 3. Tree of calls of MergeSort(1,10)

The Figure 3. is a tree that represents the sequence of recursive calls that are produced by **MergeSort** when it is applied to ten elements. The pair of values in each node are the values of the parameters *low* and *high.* Notice how the splitting continues until sets containing a single element are produced. Figure 4. is a tree representing the calls to procedure **Merge** by **MergeSort.** For example, the node containing 1, 2, and 3 represents the merging of a[1 : 2] with a[3].

If the time for the merging operation is proportional to n, then the computing time for merge sort is described by the recurrence relation

$$T(n) = \begin{cases} a & n = 1, \text{a a constant} \\ 2T(n/2) + cn & n = 2, \text{ c a constant} \end{cases}$$

When *n*,is a power of 2, n= 2k, we can solve this equation by successive substitutions:

$$\begin{aligned} T(n) &= 2(2T(n/4) + cn/2) + cn \\ &= 4T(n/4) + 2cn \\ &= 4(2T(n/8) + cn/4) + 2cn \\ &= 2^kT(1) + kcn \\ &= an + cn \log n \end{aligned}$$

It is easy to see that if $2^k < n \leq 2^{k+1}$, then $T(n) \leq T(2^{k+1})$. *Therefore*

$$T(n) \quad = \quad O(n \log n)$$

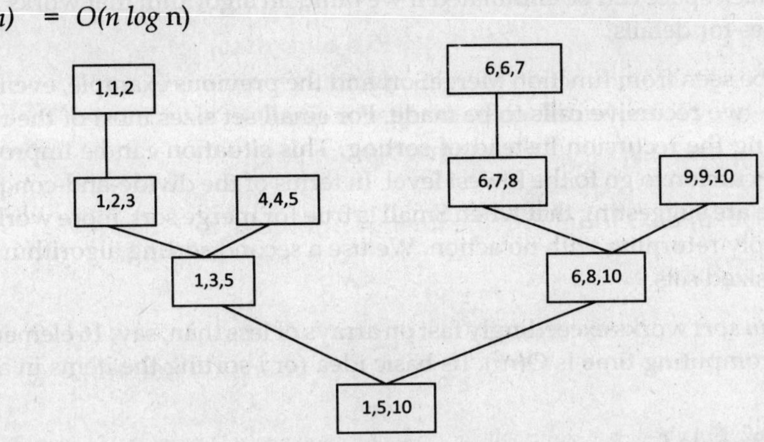

***Figure 4.** Tree of calls of Merge*

It is clear that Algorithm 6 nicely captures the divide-and-conquer nature of merge sort, there remain several inefficiencies that can and should be eliminated. We present these refinements in an attempt to produce a version of merge sort that is good enough to execute. Despite these improvements the algorithm's complexity remains $O(n \log n)$.

One complaint we might raise concerning merge sort is its use of **2n** locations. The additional n locations were needed because we couldn't reasonably merge two sorted **sets** in place. But despite the use of this space the algorithm still work hard and copy the result placed into b[low : high] back into *a[low : high]*, on each call of Merge. An alternative to this copying is to associate a new field of information with each key. (The elements in a[ ] are called keys.) This field is used to link the keys and any associated information together in a sorted list (keys and related information are called records). Then the merging of the sorted lists proceeds by changing the link values, and no records need be moved at all. A field that contains only a link will generally be smailer than an entire record, so less space will be used.

Along with the original array a[ ], we define an auxiliary array *link[1 : n]* that contains integers in the range [0, n]. These integers are interpreted as pointers to elements of a[ ]. A list is a sequence of pointers ending with a zero. Below is one set of values for *link* that contains two lists: Q and R. Tile integer Q =2 denotes the start of one list and R= 5 the start of the other.

link:	[1]	[2]	[3]	[4]	[5]	[6]	[7]	[8]
	6	4	7	1	3	0	8	0

The two lists are Q = (2, 4, 1, 6) and R=(5, 3, 7, 8). Interpreting these lists as describing sorted subsets of a[1 : 8], we conclude that $a[2] \leq a[4] \leq a[1] \leq a[6]$ and $a[5] \leq a,[3] \leq a[7] \leq a[\&]$.

Another complaint we could raise about MergeSort is the stack space that is necessitated by the use of recursion. Since merge sort splits each set into two approximately equal-sized subsets, the maximum depth of the stack is proportional to log n. The need for stack space seems indicated by the topdown manner in which this algorithm was devised. The need for stack space can be eliminated if we build an algorithm that works bottom-up; see the exercises for details.

As can be seen from function MergeSort and the previous example, even sets of size two will cause two recursive calls to be made. For small set sizes most of the time will be spent processing the recursion instead of sorting. This situation can be improved by not allowing the recursion to go to the lowest level. In terms of the divide-and-conquer control abstraction, we are suggesting that when Small is true for merge sort, more work should be done than simply returning with no action. We use a second sorting algorithm that works well on small-sized sets.

Insertion sort works exceedingly fast on arrays of less than, say, 16 elements, though *for* large *n* its computing time is O(n²). Its basic idea for i sorting the items in a[1 : n] *is* as follows:

for j:=2 to n do {

place *a[j]* in its correct position in the sorted set *a[1 : j - 1];*

}

Though all the elements in a[1 : j–1] may have to be moved to accommodate a[j]), for small values of *n* the algorithm works well. Algorithm 8. has the details.

```
Algorithm InsertionSort(a, n)
// Sort the array a[1 : n] into nondecreasing order, n ≥ 1.
{
    for j := 2 to n do 5
    {
        // a[1 : j – 1] is already sorted.
        item := a[j]; i := j – 1;
        while ((i ≥ 1) and (item < a[i])) do
        {
            a[i + 1] := a[i]; i := i – 1;
        }
        a[i + 1] := item;
    }
}
```

Algorithm 8: Insertion sort

The statements within the while loop can be executed zero up to a maximum of j times. Since *j* goes from 2 to *n*, the worst-case time of this procedure is bounded by

$$\sum_{2\le j\le n} j = n(n+1)/2-1 = \Theta(n^{2)}$$

Its best-case computing time is Θ(n) under the assumption that the body of the while loop is never entered. This will be true when the data is already in sorted order.

We are now ready to present the revised version of merge sort with the inclusion of insertion sort and the links. Function MergeSortl (Algorithm 9) is initially invoked by placing the keys of the records to be sorted in a[1 : n] and setting link[1 : n] to zero. Then one says MergeSortl(l,n). A pointer to a list of indices that give the elements of a[ ] in sorted order is returned. Insertion sort is used whenever the number of items to be sorted is less than 16. The version of insertion sort as given by Algorithm 8 needs to be altered so that it sorts *a[low : high]* into a linked list. Call the altered version **Insertion5ortl.**

```
Algorithm MergeSortl(low, high)
// The global array a[low : high] is sorted in non decreasing order
// using the auxiliary array link[low : high]. The values in link
// represent a list of the indices low through high giving a[ ] in
// sorted order. A pointer to the beginning of the list is returned.
{
    if ((high – low < 15) then
        return insertionSortl(a, link, low, high);
    else
    {
        mid := ⌊(low + high)/2⌋;
        q:= MergeSortl(low, mid);
        r:= MergeSortl (mid + 1, high);
        return Mergel(q,r);
    }
}
```

Algorithm 9: Merge sort with links

Example 8

As an aid to understanding this new version of merge sort, suppose we simulate the algorithm as it sorts the eight-element sequence (50, 10, 25, 30, 15, 70, 35, 55). We ignore the fact that less than 16 elements would normally be sorted using InsertionSort. The link array is initialized to zero. On each row the value of p points to the list in link that was created by the last completion of Mergel. To the right are the subsets of sorted elements that are represented by these lists. For example, in the last row p = 2 which begins the list of links 2, 5, 3, 4, 7, 1, 8, and 6; this implies a[2] ≤ a[5] ≤ a[3] ≤ a[4] ≤ a[7] ≤ a[1] ≤ a[8] ≤ a[6].

4.5 QUICKSORT

The divide-and-conquer approach from merge sort. In merge sort the file a[1:n] was divided at its midpoint into sub arrays which were independently sorted and later merged. In quicksort, the division into two sub arrays is made so that the sorted sub arrays do not need to be merged later. This is accomplished by rearranging the elements in a[1 : n] such that a[i] ≤ a[j] for all *i* between 1 and *m* and-all j between m+ 1 and n for some m, 1≤ m≤ n.

Thus, the elements in a[1 : in] and a[m + 1: n] can be independently sorted. No merge is needed. The rearrangement of the elements is accomplished by picking some element of a[ ], say **t** = ***a[s],*** and then reordering the other element . so that all elements appearing before t in a[l : n] are less than or equal to t and all elements appearing after t are greater than or equal to t. This rearranging is referred to as ***partitioning.***

Function Partition of Algorithm 10 accomplishes an in-place partitioning of the elements of a[m : p - 1]. It is-assumed that $a[p] \geq a[m]$ and that a[m] is the partitioning element. If m = 1 and p–1 = n, then a[n + 1] must be defined and must be greater than or equal to all elements in a[1 : n]. The assumption that a[m] is the partition element is merely for convenience; other choices for the partitioning element than the first item in the set are better in practice. "The function **Interchange (a,** i, j) exchanges a[i] with a(j].

Example 9

As an example of how **Partition** works, consider the following array of nine elements. The function is initially invoked as **Partition (a,** 1, 10). The ends of the horizontal line indicate those elements which were interchanged to produce the next row. The element a[1] = 65 is the partitioning element and it is eventually (in the sixth row) determined to be the fifth smallest element of the set. Notice that the remaining elements are unsorted but partitioned about a[5] = 65.

(1)	(2)	(3)	(4)	(5)	(6)	(7)	(8)	(9)	(10)	*i*	*p*
65	70	75	80	85	60	55	50	45	+∞	2	9
65	45	75	80	85	60	55	50	70	+∞	3	**8**
65	45	50	80	85	60	55	75	70	+∞	4	7
65	45	50	55	85	**60**	**80**	75	70	+∞	**5**	**6**
65	45	50	55	60	**85**	**80**	75	70	+∞	**6**	**5**
60	45	50	55	65	85	80	75	70	+∞		

By the application of Hoare's clever method of partitioning a set of elements about a chosen element, we can directly devise a divide-and-conquer method for completely sorting n elements. By a call to the function Partition, two sets S1 and S2 are produced. All elements in S1 are less than or equal to the elements in S_2. Hence S_1 and S_2 can be sorted independently. Each set is sorted by reusing the function ***Partition.*** Algorithm 11 describes the complete process.

```
Algorithm Partition(a, m, p)
// Within a[m], a[m + 1], ..., a(p – 1] the elements are
// rearranged in such a manner that if initially t= a[m],
// then after completion a[q] = t for some q between m
//and p–1,a[k] ≤t for m≤k<q,anda[k]≥t
// for q < k < p. q is returned. Set a[k]= ∞
{
v:= a[m]; i:= m; j.= p;
repeat
{
```

```
        repeat
            i :=i+1;
        until (a[i] ≥ v);
        repeat
            j:=j–1;
        until (a(j] ≤ v);
        if (i < j) then Interchange(a,i, j);
    } until (i ≥ j);
    a[m] := a(j]; a[j] := v; return j;
}
```

```
Algorithm Interchange(a, i, j)
Exchange a[i] with a(j].
{
    p:= a[i];
    a[i] := a[i]; a[j] := p;
}
```

Algorithm 10: The Partition of array *a[m : p - 1]* about a(m)

```
Algorithm QuickSort(p, q)
// Sorts the elements a[p],..., a[q] which reside in the global
// array a[1 : n] into ascending order; a[n + 1] is considered to
// be defined and must be > all the elements in a[1 : n].
{
    if (p < q) then //- If there are more than one element
    {
    // divide P into two subproblems.
        j := Partition (a, p, q + 1);
    //j is the position of the partitioning element.
    // Solve the subproblems.
    QuickSort(p, j - 1);
    QuickSort( j+ 1,q);
    // There is no need for combining solutions.
    }
}
```

Algorithm 11: For Sorting by partitioning

In analyzing Quick Sort, we count only the number of element comparisons C(n). It is easy to see that the frequency count of other operations is of the same order as C(n). We make the following assumptions: the *n* elements to be sorted are distinct, and the input distribution is such that the partition element v = a[m] in the call to Partition(a, m, p) has an equal probability of being the ith smallest element, $1 \le i \le p - m$, in a[m : p- 1].

Swaping

12	9	4	10	120	1	3	99	13

↑ Finding Lower Value ←

12	9	4	10	120	1	3	99	13

Swaping

3	9	4	10	120	1	12	99	13

Finding Greater Value → ↑

3	9	4	10	120	1	12	99	13

Swaping

3	9	4	10	12	1	120	99	13

↑ Finding Lower Value ←

3	9	4	10	12	1	120	99	13

Swaping

First, let us obtain the worst-case value $C_w(n)$ of C(n). The number of element comparisons in each call of ***Partition*** is at most p – m + *1*. Let *r* be the total number of elements in all the calls to Partition at any level of recursion. At level one only one call, Partition(a, l, n+l), is made and r = n; at level two at most two calls are made *and* r = *n - 1;* and so on. At each level of recursion, *O(r)* element comparisons are made by Partition. At *each* level, *r* is at least one less than the *r* at the previous level as the partitioning elements of the previous level are eliminated. Hence $C_\omega(n)$ is the sum on *r* as r varies from 2 to n, or $O(n^2)$.

The average value $C_A(n)$ of *C(n)* is much less then Cω(n). Under the assumptions made earlier, the partitioning element v has an equal probability of being the ith-smallest element, $1 \le i \le p - m$, in a[m : p – 1]. Hence the two subarrays remaining to be sorted are **a[m : j]** and **a[j + 1: p - 1]** with probability 1/(p – m), $m \le j < p$. From this we obtain the recurrence

$$C_A(n) = n+1+1/n \sum_{1 \le k \le n} C_A(k-1) + C_A(n-k)\} \quad (5)$$

The number of element comparisons required by partition on its first call *is n* + 1. Note that $C_A(O) = C_A(1) = 0$ Multiplying both sides of (5) by n, we obtain

$$nC_A(n) = n(n+1) + 2[C_A(O) + C_A(l) + \ldots + C_A(n-1)) \quad (6)$$

Replacing n by n – 1 in (6) gives

$$(n-1)\,C_A(n-1) = -\,n(n-1) + 2(C_A(0) + \ldots + C_A(n-2)]$$

Subtracting this from (6), we get

$$nC_A(n) - (n-1)\,C_A(n-1) = 2n + 2C_A(n-1)$$

or

$$C_A(n)/(n+1) = C_A(n-1)/n + 2/(n+1)$$

Repeatedly using this equation to substitute for $C_A(n-1)$, $C_A(n-2)$, ..., we get

$$\frac{C_A(n)}{n+1} = \frac{C_A(n-2)}{n-1} + \frac{2}{n} + \frac{2}{n+1}$$
$$= \frac{C_A(n-3)}{n-2} + \frac{2}{n-1} + \frac{2}{n} + \frac{2}{n+1}$$
$$= \frac{C_A(1)}{2} + 2\sum 3 \le k \le n+1\ 1/k$$
$$= 2\sum 3 \le k \le n+1\ 1/k \quad (7)$$

Since

$$\sum_{3 \le k < n+1} 1/k \le \int_2^{n+1} 1/x\,dx = \log_e(n+1) = \log_e 2$$

The Eq (7) yields

$$C_A(n) \le 2(n+1)[\log_e(n+2) - \log_e 2] = O(n \log n)$$

Here the worst-case time is $O(n^2)$, the average time is only O(n log n). Let us now look at the stack space needed by the recursion. In the worst case the maximum depth of recursion may be *n*–1. This happens, for example, when the partition element on each call to **Partition** is the smallest value in a[m : p – 1]. The amount of stack space needed can be reduced to O(log *n)* by using an iterative version of quick sort in which the smaller of the two sub arrays a[p : j – 1] and a(j + 1: *q]* is always sorted first. Also, the second recursive call can be replaced by some assignment statements and a jump to the beginning of the algorithm. With these changes, Quick Sort takes the form of Algorithm 12.

We call now verify that the maximum stack space- needed (log n). Let *S(n)* be the maximum stack space needed. Then it follows that

$$S(n) \le \begin{vmatrix} 2 + S(\lfloor (n-1)/2 \rfloor) & n > 1 \\ 0 & n \le 1 \end{vmatrix}$$

which is less than 2 log n.

InsertionSort is exceedingly fast for n less than about 16. Hence **InsertionSort** can be used to speed up QuickSort2 whenever $q-p < 16$. The exercises explore various possibilities for selection of the partition clement.

Performance Analysis

QuickSort and **MergeSort** were evaluated on a SUN workstation 10/30. In both cases the recursive versions were used. For **QuickSort** the **Partition** function was altered to carry out the median of three rule (i.e. the partitioning **element vas** the median of a[m], a[⌊(m+p-1)/2⌋] and a[p-1]). Each data set consisted of random integers in the range (0, 1000). Tables 2 and 3 **record the** actual computing times in milliseconds. Table 2 displays the **average** computing times. For each n, 50 random data sets were used. Table 3 shows the worst-case computing times for the 50 data sets.

Scanning the tables, we immediately see that QuickSort is faster than **MergeSort** for all values. Even though both algorithms require O(n log *n)* time on the average, **QuickSort** usually performs well in practice. The exercises discuss other tests that would make useful comparisons.

4.6 RANDOMIZED SORTING ALGORITHMS

Though algorithm **QuickSort** has an average time of $O(n \log n)$ on n elements, its worst-case time is $O(n^2)$. On the other hand it does not make use of any

```
Algorithm QuickSort2(p, q)
// Sorts the elements in a[p : q].
{
      // stack is a stack of size 2 log(n).
      repeat
      {
      while (p < q) do
      {
      j:= Partition (a, p, q+ 1);
      if ((j - p) < (q - j)) then
      {
      Add(j + 1); // Add j + 1 to stack.
      Add(q); q:= j – 1; // Add q to stack
      }
      else
      {
      Add(p); // Add p to stack.
      Add(j – 1); p:= j + 1; // Add j – 1 to stack
      }
      }//Sort the smaller subfile.
      if stack is empty then return;
      Delete(q); Delete(p); // Delete q and p from stack.
      } until (false);
}
```

Algorithm 12: Iterative version of QuickSort

Additional memory as does MergeSort. A possible input on which QuickSort displays worst-case behavior is one in which the elements are already in sorted order. In this case the partition will be such that there will be only one element in one part and the rest of the elements will fall in the other part. The performance of any divide-and-conquer algorithm will be good if the resultant subproblems are as evenly sized as possible. Can QuickSort be modified so that it performs well on every input? The answer is yes. Is the technique of using the median of the three elements a[p], $a[\lfloor (q+p)/2 \rfloor]$, and *a[q]* the solution? Unfortunately it is possible to construct inputs for which even this method will take $\Omega(n^2)$ time, as is explored in the exercises.

The solution is the use of a randomizer. While sorting the array a[p : q], instead of picking a[m], pick a random element (from among a[p], ... ,a[q]) as the partition element. The resultant randomized algorithm (RQuickSort)

Table 2. The Average computing times

n	1000	2000	3000	4000	5000
MergeSort	72.8	167.2	275.1	378.5	500.6
QuickSort	36.6	85.1	138.9	205.7	269.0
n	6000	7000	8000	9000	10000
MergeSort	607.6	723.4	811.5	949.2	1073.6
QuickSort	339.4	411.0	487.7	556.3	645.2

***Table 3.** Worst-case computing times*

n	1000	2000	3000	4000	5000
MergeSort	105.7	206.7	335.2	422.1	589.9
QuickSort	41.6	97.1	158.6	244.9	397.8
n	6000	7000	8000	9000	10000
MergeSort	691.3	794.8	889.5	1067.2	1167.6
QuickSort	383.8	497.3	569.9	616.2	738.1

Works on any input and runs in an expected *O(n log n)* time, where the expectation is over the space of all possible outcomes for the randomizer (rather than the space of all possible inputs). The code for RQuickSort is given in Algorithm 13. Note that this is a Las Vegas algorithm since it will always output the correct answer. Every call to the randomizer Random takes a certain amount of time. If there are only a very few elements to sort, the time taken by the randomizer may be comparable to the rest of the computation). For this reason, we invoke the randomizer only if (q – p) > 5. But 5 is not a, magic number; in the machine employed, this seems to give the best, results. In general this number should be determined empirically.

```
Algorithm RquickSort(p,q)
// Sorts the elements a[p],...,a[q] which roside in the global
// array a[1 :n] into ascending order. a[n + 1] is considered to
// be defined and must be ≥ all the elements in a[1 : n].
{
if (p < q) then
{
if ((q - p) > 5) then
Interchange (a, Randorn() mod (q – p + 1) + p,p);
j:= Partitioro(a, p, q+ 1);
// j is the position of the partitioning element.
RQuickSort(p, j – 1);
RQuickSort( j+ 1, q);
}
}
```

13. Quick sort algorithm (Randomized Version)

The proof of the fact that RQuickSort has an expected O(*n* ***log*** **n) time** is the same as the proof of the average time of QuickSort. Let *A(n)* be the average time of RQuickSort on ***any input*** of *n* elements. Then the number of elements in the second part will be 0, 1, 2,….,n–2 or n –1, all with an equal probability of 1/n (in the probability space of outcomes for the randomizer).

Thus the recurrence relation for *A(n)* will be

$$A(n) = 1/n \sum_{1<k<n} (a(k-1) + A(n-k)) + n + 1$$

This is the same as Equation (4) and hence its solution is *O(n* log n).

RQuickSort and QuickSort (without employing the median of three elements rule) were evaluated on a SUN **10/30** workstation. Table 4 displays the times for the two algorithms in milliseconds averaged over 100 runs. For each n, the input considered was the sequence of numbers 1, 2, ..., n. As we can see from the table, RQuickSort performs much better than QuickSort. Note that the times shown in this table for QuickSort are much more than the corresponding entries in Tables 3.5 and 3.6. The reason is that QuickSort makes $\Theta(n^2)$ comparisons on inputs that are already in sorted order. However, on random inputs its average performance is very good.

Table 4. *A Comparison of QuickSort and RQuickSort on the input a[i] = i, 1 ≤ i ≤ n; times are in milliseconds.*

n	1000	2000	3000	14000	5000
QuickSort	195.5	759.2	1728	3165	4829
RQuickSort	9.4	21.0	30.5	41.6	52.8

The performance of RQuickSort can be improved in various ways. For example, we could pick a small number of the elements in the array a[] randomly and use the median of these elements as the partition element. These randomly chosen elements form a random sample of the array elements. We would expect that the median of the sample would also be an approximate median of the array and hence result in an-approximately even partitioning of the array.

An even more generalized version of the above random sampling technique is shown in Algorithm 14. Here we choose a random sample S of s elements (where s is a function of *n)* from the input sequence *X* and sort them using

HeapSort, MergeSort, or any other sorting algorithm. Let $\ell 1, \ell 2, \ldots, \ell s$ be the sorted sample. We partition X into s+ 1 parts using the sorted sample as partition keys. In particular Xl $=\{x \in X \mid x \le \ell_1\}$; **Xi** $=\{x \in X \mid \ell_{i-1} < x \le \ell i\}$, for i = 2,3,... s; and $X_{s+1} = \{x \in X \mid x > \ell_s\}$. After having partitioned X into s+ 1 parts, we sort each part recursively. For a proper choice of s, the number of comparisons made in this algorithm is only *n* log n + o(n log *n)*. Note the constant 1 before *n* log *n*.

$s=n/\log^2 n$. The sample can be sorted in O(s logs) = O(n/logn) time and comparisons if we use HeapSort or MergeSort. If we store the sorted sample elements in an array, say b[ ], for each $x \in X$, we can determine which part Xi it belongs to in ≤ log n comparisons using binary search on *b[ ]*. Thus the partitioning process takes *n* log n + ***O(n)*** comparisons. In the **exercises** you are asked to show that with high probability the cardinality

```
Algorithm RSort(a, n)
// Sort the elements a[1:n]
    {
    Randomly sample s elements from a[ ];
    Sort this sample;
    Partition the input using the sorted sample as partition keys;
    Sorteach part separately;
}
```

Algorithm 14: A randomized Version of sorting algorithm.

Of each .Xi, is no more than *O(n/s* logn) = O($\log^3 n$). Using HeapSort or MergeSort to sort each of the Xi's (without employing recursion on any of them), the total cost of sorting the X_i's is

$$\sum_{i=1}^{s+1})(|Xi|\log|Xi|) = \max_{1\le l}\{\log|Xi|\}\sum_{s=1}\sum_{i=1}^{s+1} O(|Xi|)$$

Since each | Xi | is O($\log^3 n$), the cost of sorting the s+l parts is *O(n log log n) = o(n log n)*. In summary, the number of comparisons made in this randomized sorting algorithm is n log ***n*** + *0(n* log n).

REVIEW QUESTIONS

1. Explain divide and conquer method in details.
2. Write a note on all binary decision trees for binary search.
3. Differentiate between iterative and randomized version of quick sort algorithm.
4. Explain the algorithm for straightforward and recursive maximum and minimum
5. Explain the randomized version of sorting algorithm.

UNIT 3

CHAPTER 5

BRANCH AND BOUND

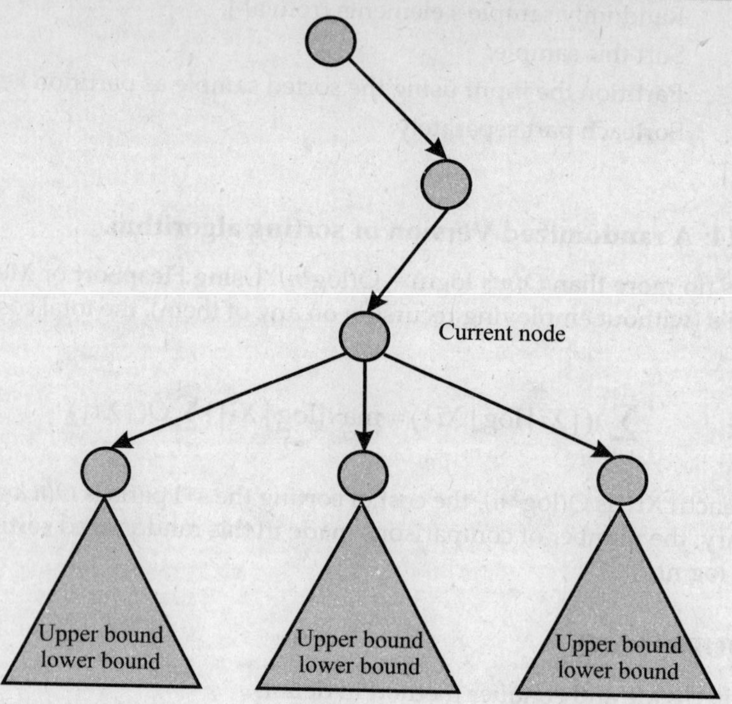

5.1 INTRODUCTION

Like backtracking, branch-and-bound searches the set of all possible solutions embedded in a state space tree for a solution to some problem whose solution set is exponential in size. Also like backtracking, the complexity of a branch-and-bound is, in its worst case, exponential, gain, like backtracking, a branch and bound algorithm can significantly decrease execution time by use of a 'promising' function that prevents the algorithm from searching sub-trees of the state space tree that have been branded as 'non-promising' by the promising function. There are, however, three significant differences between backtracking and branch-and-bound algorithms.

First, the branch-and-bound technique is restricted to optimization problems. The second difference relates to how the state space tree can be traversed. A backtracking problem must do a pre-order depth first search of the state space tree. A branch-and-bound attack is not restricted to a depth first search of the state space tree, but it may use a depth first search if it needs to. The third difference is that a branch-and- bound must completely search the state space tree. All branch-and-bound algorithms search for an optimum value. If the entire state-space tree is not searched, then the possibility exists that the optimum value is located in the un-searched portion of the state space tree. This would imply that the found solution is not the optimum.

The nQueens backtracking algorithm searched the state space tree until it found a solution. For some values of n, the nQueens problem has many solutions, but only one was needed because all satisfy the nQueens problem criteria.

The restriction of the branch-and-bound technique to optimization problems has consequences for the design of the promising function. Optimal means smallest or largest depending on the problem. Some random possible solution mechanism generates a possible candidate solution.

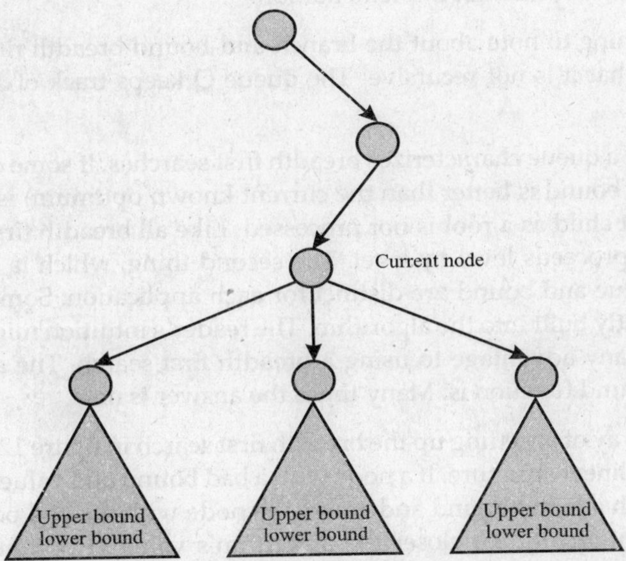

As the traversal of the state space tree proceeds, the 'pre-solution' at the current node is assessed. If it can be determined that it is worse than the current candidate optimum, that search down the entire subtree whose root is that node is abandoned. If the current candidate solution has a chance of being a more optimum solution than the candidate solution, the search proceeds. If the current node is a leaf, the candidate optimum solution is updated if necessary. After the entire state space tree is searched, the optimum solution will be the remaining solution. There may in fact be several equivalent optimum solutions but none will be 'more optimum' than the returned solution.

The issue of traversal order is much more complex. Most readers know that there are two basic methods to search a graph. These two methods are the depth first search and the breadth first search. When searching a state space tree of embedded solutions, or any tree for that matter, the depth first search tries to go from the root to a leaf as quickly as possible. The breadth first search of a tree searches the tree level by level. The breadth first search processes every node in level k before processing any node in level k+1. This continues until every leaf is searched and then the breadth first search stops. Like the un-modified depth first search, the breadth first search will exhaustively visit every node in the tree. If the tree being searched is a state space tree of solutions that contains an exponential, in terms of input size, number of nodes, then the search by either method has exponential complexity.

In the previous section, the backtracking algorithm used its promising function to stop the depth first search of any sub-tree whose root node was not found promising. Branch-and- bound algorithms search for optimums, so a promising node in a branch-and-bound setting has a different meaning. Essentially a node in a branch-and-bound application is promising if it still has potential to lead to an optimum solution. Just as in the case of backtracking, the breadth first search in a branch-and-bound algorithm stops searching a particular sub-tree when it is clear that to search further down, in a breadth first manner, of that sub-tree is pointless. Figure figure 12..1 lists the general pattern for a branch-and-bound breadth first implementation.

The first thing to note about the branch-and-bound breadth first search algorithm in figure 12.1 is that it is not recursive. The queue Q keeps track of all currently known promising nodes.

This use of a queue characterizes breadth first searches. If some child of a promising node (one whose bound is better than the current known optimum) is not promising, the sub-tree with that child as a root is not processed. Like all breadth first based searches of trees, the search proceeds level by level. The second thing, which is obvious, is that the two functions value and bound are distinct for each application. Sometimes the function of value is implicitly built into the algorithm. The reader's intuition might lead them to ask whether there is any advantage to using a breadth first search. The answer depends on how sharp the bound function is. Many times the answer is no.

Is there a way of speeding up the breadth first search in figure 12.1? A basic queue is a first-in-first-out linear structure. If a node with a bad bound and value is put on the queue before a node with a better bound and value, the node with the bad bound would still be processed first. Intuitively the closer the algorithm's value of optimum is to the actual optimum, the more nodes v (in the 'for' loop of algorithm figure 12..1) will have fewer and perhaps no children that are enqueued into the queue Q. This would lessen the number of state space tree nodes placed on Q and decrease execution time. If, however, the node with the best bound and value is the next node removed from the queue and processed, then fewer nodes will be processed and execution time should decrease. A queue that has this behavior is called a priority queue. Objects that are placed on the queue so that the object with highest priority is the object in the front position, which is the next object to be processed. This is called a 'best first' strategy. The outline of the 'best fit' strategy is listed in figure 12.2.

```
optimumType BranchAndBoundBreadthFirst (StateSpaceTree T){
    optimumType temp, optimum;
    queue<nodeType> Q;
    nodeType u, v;
    v = T.root(); // operation root() returns T's root// Q.enqueue(v);
    optimum = value(v);
```

```
    while(Q.length() is not zero){
      v = Q.dequeue();
        for (each child u of v){
            temp = value(u);
              if (temp is better than optimum){
                  optimum = temp;
              }
            if (bound(u) better than optimum){ Q.enqueue(u);
        }
      }
    }
    return optimum;
}
```

Figure 12.1: Outline for any branch-and-bound algorithm that uses a breadth first search.

This algorithm assumes the existence of a suitable structured state space tree and two functions value and bound which determine if the current node is still promising.

```
optimumType BranchAndBoundBestFirst (StateSpaceTree T){
        optimumType temp,
        optimum;
        priorityQueue<nodeType>
        PQ; nodeType u, v;
        v = T.root(); // operation root() returns T's root// PQ.AddInorder(v);
        optimum = value(v);
        while(PQ.length() is not zero){
          v = PQ.dequeue();
          if (bound(v) is better than optimum){
            for (each child u of v){
              temp = value(u);
                if (temp is better than optimum){
              optimum = temp;
              }
            if (bound(u) better than optimum){ PQ.AddInorder(u);
          }
        }
      }
    }
    return optimum;
}
```

Figure figure 12..2 Outline for any branch-and-bound algorithm that uses a best first search. Note

That a removed node is not even processed if its bound is not better than the current optimum bound. Like the breadth first version listed in figure 12..1, this algorithm assumes the existence of a suitable structured state space tree and two functions value and bound which determine if the current node is still promising, and in addition uses a priority queue instead of a standard queue.

This form of the branch-and-bound algorithm gets its name 'best first' from its use of a priority queue that puts the node with the best bound as the next to process. To improve efficiency and decrease execution time the bound of any node that is removed from the priority queue is checked again before any of node's children are processed. The reason for this additional check is simple to comprehend: maybe nodes down the queue would not have been added to the priority queue if the 'best first's' bound and value had been known earlier. Priority of nodes on the queue is done by which node has the best bound. There are several ways to implement a priority queue. The heap structure, which will be introduced in section 9.4, is a suitable mechanism where adding and removing an object both have complexity O(lg(n)) where n is the length of the queue.

The priority queue could also be implemented as a binary search tree where adding an object to the priority queue is the same as inserting an object in the tree and removing the object with highest priority is the same as descending from the root down along the right sub-tree pointer until the first tree node with null right pointer is found. This node has the highest priority so it is the one removed.

In section studied before the knapsack problem using a backtracking strategy was developed. In the remainder of this section the knapsack problem will be solved using both a breadth first and a best fit strategy. Three things are needed: a definition and mechanism for computing the bound function, a definition and mechanism for computing the value function, and an efficient way to represent the state space tree and its nodes. Recall that the knapsack problem is defined by n the number of objects, MaxWeight which is the maximum capacity of the knapsack and two vectors value[1..n] and weight[1..n]. Value[i] and weight[i] are the value and weight of the ith object respectively. The knapsack problem's goal is to maximize the value of the objects chosen and placed in knapsack subject to their total weight not exceeding MaxWeight. The entire object must be either taken or left.

An implicit requirement for the bound function is that the computation be efficient. At the root node of the state space tree, before any object has been chosen, the function bound returns a value that is always equal to or greater than the optimum value when the knapsack is finally loaded optimally. If it were possible to take a portion of an object, then the function bound can be converted using the greedy method.

If the objects in both the vectors value and weight have been sorted so that the ratio value[i]/weight[i] is non-increasing. The function bound is the value of the knapsack when all of the first objects that fit into the knapsack as well as the portion of the next object that fits. Thus the value in the knapsack can never exceed this value. The simple pseudo-code computes the value of bound for the entire problem. The value in the knapsack will always be less than or equal to this bound.

```
integer k=1, bound = 0, pickedWeight = 0;
```

```
while ((k≤n) and (pickedWeight<MaxWeight){
    if (weight[k]≤(MaxWeight – pickedWeight)){
      bound = bound + value[k];
        pickWeight = pickedWeight + weight[k];
      else {
        bound = bound +
          value[k]*(MaxWeight-pickedWeight)/weight[k];
        pickedWeight=MaxWeight;
      }
    k = k + 1;
}
```

This definition of bound is too restrictive. The function bound must be general enough to compute the bound after the first k objects have been processed, that is either chosen or not chosen. At that point the picked weight of the already picked objects and their value is known. Instead of starting picking the objects at the first object, objects would be picked starting at the next object. Figure figure 12..3 contains the pseudo-code for the bound function. The function bound assumes that the number of objects n, the knapsack's capacity maxWeight, and the two vectors weight[1..n] and value[1..n] are global to the function. Note that the computational complexity of the function bound is O(n) where n is the number of objects left to pick from.

```
float bound( integer level, integer pickedWgt, integer pickedVal){
  integer k=level+1, val=pickedVal;
  integer pickedWeight = pickedWgt;
while ((k≤n) and (pickedWeight<MaxWeight)){
  if (weight[k]≤(MaxWeight – pickedWeight)){
    val = val + value[k];
      pickedWeight = pickedWeight + weight[k];}
    else {
      val = val +
      value[k]*(MaxWeight-pickedWeight)/weight[k];
      pickedWeight=MaxWeight; }
    k = k + 1;
  }
return val;
}
```

Figure figure 12.3 The function bound computes a value equal to the maximum value of the objects

in the knapsack under the assumption that the first level objects have been processed and the weight and value of the picked objects are pickedWgt and pickedVal respectively.

The function value is not explicitly needed if the running total is kept inside the nodes of the state space tree. The state space tree node representation is done next. While the actual state space tree is never built, its binary structure is used. First note that by the design of the bound function, each node must maintain some information. Clearly the node must know everything needed in order to compute its level in order that the node knows which object is to be next picked. This implies that the minimum node structure is

```
structure
    node{
integer
    level;
        integer
pickedValue;
        integer
pickedWeight; }
```

Since the state space tree for the knapsack problem is a binary tree, every node should have pointers to a left and right sub-tree. These pointers are not necessary because any node taken off the queue to be processed can process a left child (object picked) and right child (object not picked). This means that the code segment

```
v = Q.dequeue();
for (each child u of v){
    temp = value(u);
    if (temp is better than optimum){
        optimum = temp; }
if (bound(u) better than
    optimum){ Q.enqueue(u);
    }
```

from the breadth first search pattern in figure 12.1 can be replaced by

```
v = Q.dequeue();
// Do left child of v, next object picked
// left.pickedValue
= v.pickedValue+value[v.level+1]; left.level
= v.level + 1;
left.pickedWeight=v.pickedWeigh
t+weight[v.level+1];
if ((left.pickedWeight≤MaxWeight) and (left.pickedValue>optimum)){
optimum = left.pickedValue;
}
if (bound(left.level, left.pickedWeight, left.pickedValue))> optimum){
Q.enqueue(left);
}
// Do right child, next object
not picked//
```

```
right.pickedValue=
v.pickedValue; right.level =
v.level + 1; right.pickedWeight=v.pickedWeight;
if (bound(right.level, right.pickedWeight, right.pickedValue) > optimum)
{ Q.enqueue(right);
}
```

Where left and right are of node type. The careful reader will have noted that the only difference between the right child and its parent is the level, so there is no need to check if right.pickedValue is greater than already known optimum value. The full knapsack problem using breadth first branch and bound is listed in figure 12.4.

```
integer breadthFirstKnapsack( integer n integer MaxWeight,
    vector <integer> value[1..n], vector<integer> weight[1..n]){
integer temp, optimum=0;
    structure node{
    integer level;
    integer pickedValue;
    integer pickedWeight;
    }
node v, left, right;
queue<node> Q;
v.level=0; // set root node of state space tree//
v.pickedValue = 0;
v.pickedWeight = 0;
Q.enqueue(v);
while(Q.length() is not
zero) { v =
Q.degueue();
// Do left child of v, next object
picked// left.pickedValue=
v.pickedValue+value[v.level+1];
left.level = v.level + 1;
left.pickedWeight=v.pickedWeight +
        weight[v.level+1];
if ((left.pickedWeight≤MaxWeight) and
(left.pickedValue>optimum)){
optimum = left.pickedValue;
}
if ((left.pickedWeight≤Maxweight) and
(bound(left.level, left.pickedWeight, left.pickedValue))> optimum)){
Q.enqueue(left);
```

```
}

// Do right child, next object not picked//
right.pickedValue= v.pickedValue; right.level = v.level + 1; right.
pickedWeight=v.pickedWeight;
if (bound(right.level, right.pickedWeight, right.pickedValue) > optimum)
{
Q.enqueue(right);
}
}
return optimum;
}
```

Figure 12..4 The knapsack problem implemented using a branch and bound breadth first strategy. The function bound was defined in figure 12.3.

Note that breadthFirstKnapsack only returns the optimum value, and does not which objects were picked. The algorithm can be easily modified to return which values were picked. This modification is left to the exercises. Figure figure 12..5 shows a simple application of breadthFirstKnapsck with n=5.

(a) value[1..5] = {12, 4, 12, 4, 5} weight[1..5] = { 3, 2, 4, 4, 1} MaxWeight = 7

(b) value[1..5] = {5, 12, 12, 4, 4} weight[1..5] = {1, 3, 4, 2, 4} MaxWeight = 7

(c)

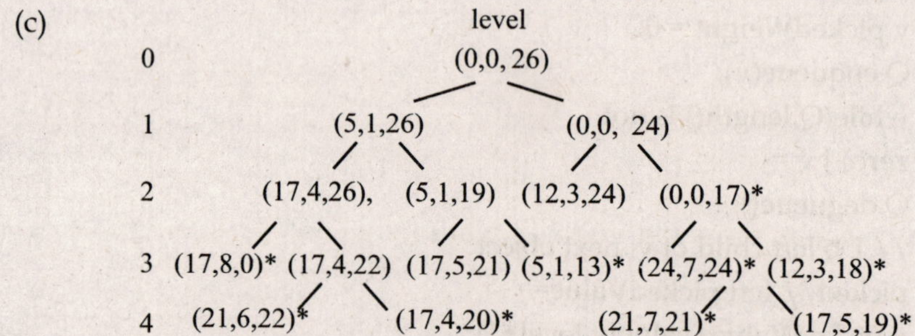

Figure figure 12..5 (a) A set of 5 objects with weights and value. (b) the set of objects in part (a) sorted so that value[i]/weight[i] is non-increasing. This is a requirement of the function bound. (c) State space tree where the 3 fields in the node are pickedValue, pickedWeight, and bound respectively. Only the nodes that are computed are listed. Nodes not put on the queue Q are flagged with an ''. Nodes with a '0' in the third or bound field were not put on the queue because they exceeded the weight. Nodes where the pickedValue equaled the bound were not put on the queue because their weight equaled MaxWeight of the knapsack. If the node's bound is less than the optimum value, it to is not placed on the queue. No node on level 5 was ever considered. Note that the maximum return is 24. From the state space tree it is clear that 'sorted' objects 2 and 3 were chosen. Note that 17 nodes are computed but only 8 are placed on the queue.*

Modifying the breadthFirstKnapsack algorithm to use a 'best first' strategy is simple now that all the work has been done in implementing Figure figure 12..4. The first modification is to the node structure, which becomes

```
structure node{
integer level;
integer pickedValue; integer pickedWeight; integer nodeBound; }
```

The field nodeBound is needed because the priority queue as nodes in non-increasing order by nodeBound. Intuitively, the node with the best chance of having a child where the optimum is achieved is the next node processed. Figure figure 12..6 is the best first version of the knapsack problem.

```
integer bestFirstKnapsack( integer n, integer MaxWeight,
vector <integer> value[1..n], vector<integer> weight[1..n]){
integer optimum=0;
structure node{
integer level;
integer pickedValue; integer pickedWeight; integer nodeBound; } node v,
    left, right; priorityQueue<node> Q;
v.level=0; // set root node of state space tree//
v.pickedValue = 0; v.pickedWeight = 0; v.nodeBound = bound(0,0,0);
    Q.AddInorder(v); while(Q.length() is not zero){ v = Q.dequeue();
if (v.nodeBound > optimum){
// Do left child of v, next object picked//
left.pickedValue= v.pickedValue + value[v.level+1]; left.level = v.level +
    1; left.pickedWeight=v.pickedWeight + weight[v.level+1];
left.nodeBound = bound(left.level, left.pickedWeight, left.pickedValue);
if ((left.pickedWeight≤MaxWeight) and (left.pickedValue>optimum)){
optimum = left.pickedValue;
}
if ((left.pickedWeight≤MaxWeight) and (left.nodeBound > optimum)){
    Q.AddInorder(left); }
// Do right child, next object not picked//
right.pickedValue= v.pickedValue;
right.level = v.level + 1;
right.pickedWeight=v.pickedWeight;
right.nodeBound = bound(right.level, right.pickedWeight, right.
    pickedValue);
if (right.nodeBound > optimum){ Q.AddInorder(right); }
}
}
return optimum;
}
```

Figure figure 12..6 The knapsack problem implemented using a branch and bound best first strategy.

The function bound was defined in figure 12.3.

Figure figure 12..7 contains the example first listed in figure 12.5 except that it is done using the best first strategy. Best fit usually processes significantly fewer nodes, especially as n gets larger.

(a) value[1..5] = {5, 12, 12, 4, 4} weight[1..5] = {1, 3, 4, 2, 4} MaxWeight = 7

(a) Best first state space tree

level 26,24,22,21

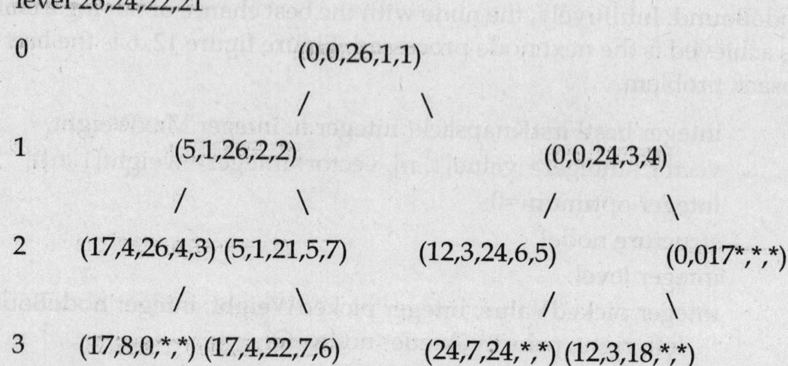

Figure 12.7 (a) The same set of 5 objects with weights and value from figure 12.5(b) after the set of objects in part were sorted so that value[i]/weight[i] is non-increasing. (b) State space tree. The five node fields are pickedValue, pickedweight, nodeBound, order-in and order-out respectively. Recall that nodes are placed in the priority queue by order of non-decreasing nodeBound.

The field order-in is the order nodes are placed on the priority queue, while order-out is the order nodes come off the priority queue. Only the nodes that are put on the queue Q are listed. Note no nodes on level four were ever computed or placed on the queue. The number that is above the node is the order that each node was placed on the priority queue. Eleven nodes were processed but only seven were placed on the priority queue.

While the best fit state space tree in figure 12.7 processed six fewer nodes and placed one node less on the priority queue than the breadth first tree in figure 12..4, the actual number for large n is more significant. Many of the un-processed nodes in best first would actually be roots of large sub-trees processed in the breadth first branch-and-bound search.

5.2 OTHER EXAMPLES OF THE BACKTRACKING TECHNIQUE

Suppose the nQueens problem had been rephrased to find all the board positions where n queens could be placed on the board. By simply rotating the board one-quarter, one-half, and three-quarters of a turn, a given solution will suggest three other solutions by symmetry. Can backtracking be modified to do this? The answeris yes and the implementation is left to the exercises.

The Sum-of-subsets problem is a classical computer science problem. There are three inputs: a positive integern, an integer valued vector with n components s[1..n], and an fixed integer value Sum. There are several related variations of the problem. The decision version of the sum-of-subset problem as whether or not there is any subset of s[1..n] whose total equals Sum. Or the goal of the sum-of-subset problem's goal would be to find some subset of s[1..n] whose total is Sum. Finally, one problem can be phrased to find all subsets of s[1..n] whose total is Sum. The state space tree of the sum-of-subsets problem is similar to the state space tree of the knapsack problem. In the knapsack problem the ith object is either picked or not. In the sum-of-subsets problem the ith number s[i] is either used or not used. A partial sum is associated any particular node of the state space tree. Since nothing is being optimized, this must be a backtracking problem. Figure figure 12..1 is a simple state space tree for n=4.

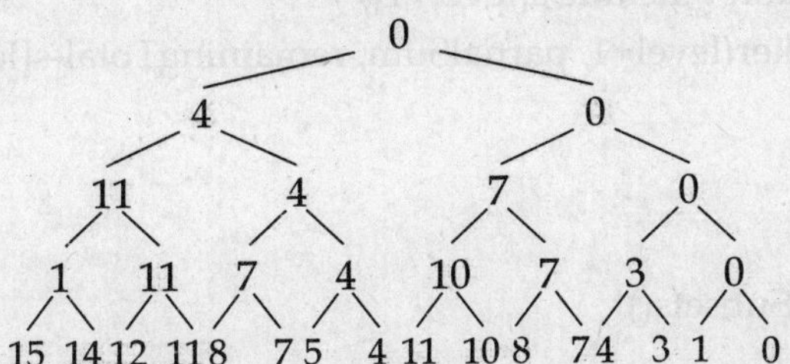

Figure 12.1 A simple state space tree for the sum-of-subsets problem with the four integers 4,7, 3, 1. The node values represent partial sums.

The version of the sum-of-subsets problem solved now is the decision version. Now that both the node structure and state space tree structure, the remaining task to be done is to derive a way of determining if a node is promising. Two strategies suggest themselves. If the set of numbers s[1..n] happens to be sorted in non- decreasing order then a node at the ith level of the state space tree is not promising if nodepartialSum + s[i+1] > Sum

Let S(i) denote the sum of the elements in s[1..n] starting from index i and ending at index n. Then the ith node is not promising if nodepartialSum + S(i+1) < Sum

The latter condition works whether of not the array is sorted. Either condition can work by itself but they can be combined. Figure figure 12..2 lists the pseudo-code for a promising function that combines both strategies.

```
boolean promising(integer level, integer partialSum, integer remainingTotal){
if ((partialSum + s[level+1])>Sum){
return false; }
else if ((partialSum + remainingTotal) < Sum){
return false; }
else {
return true; }
}
```

Figure 12.2 The promising function for the sum-of-subsets problem. This function assumes that s[1..n] is sorted. The parameter partialSum is the sum of the chosen numbers up to level while remainingTotal is the sum of the entries in s[1..n] from index level+1 through index n.

The rest of the algorithm is easy to implement. A certain amount of pre-processing is done. First the array s[1..n] is sorted. Chapter 9 has several sorting algorithms that have f(n*lg(n)) complexity. A value total equal to the sum of the elements is also computed which has (n) complexity. The pseudo-code is listed in figure 12..

```
boolean backtracker(integer level, integer partialSum, integer remaingTotal){
if (promising(level,partialSum,remainingTotal) equals true){
```

```
if ( partialSum equals Sum){
return true; }
else { // left child, pick s[level+1]//
return backtracker(level+1, partialSum+s[level+1],remainingTotal-s[level+1]);
// right child, don't include s[level+1]//
return backtracker(level+1, partialSum, remainingTotal-s[level+1]);
}
}


boolean SumOfSubsets(){
integer i, total=0;
Sort(s[1..n], non-decreasing);
for (i=1, i≤n; i++) {
total = total + s[i];
]
return backtracker(0, 0, total);
}
```

Figure 12.3. The Sum-of-subsets decision problem that uses a backtracking strategy. The number of objects in the set, the vector s[1..n] and the number Sum are assumed global to the procedure.

It is an easy task to determine which numbers add up to Sum. This will be done in the exercises.

The next problem considered is the Hamiltonian cycle problem. Given a graph the Hamiltonian problem is to determine whether or not the graph contains a maximal simple cycle, and if it does, output the cycle. A cycle is a path that starts and ends at the same vertex. A maximal cycle is one that visits every vertex. A maximal cycle is characterized by a sequence of n vertices with an edge joining each adjacent pair and an edge joining the first and last vertices. This is an exhaustive search problem and not an optimization problem, so it is a candidate for a backtracking attack. Figure figure 12..4a shows a simple graph without a Hamilton Cycle while figure 12.4b shows a simple graph with a Hamilton Cycle.

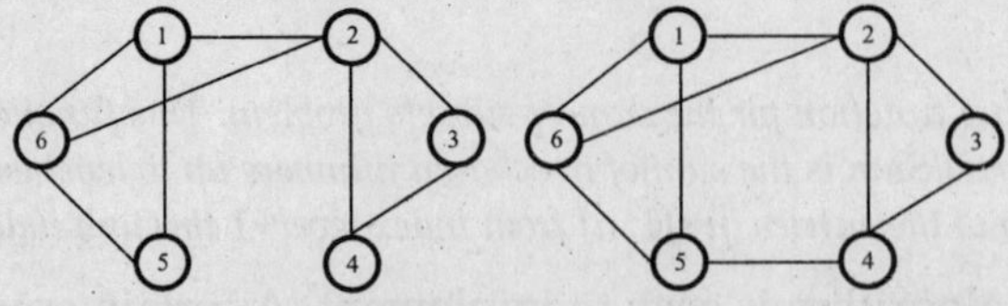

Figure 12..4(a) A graph with 6 vertices that does not contain a Hamilton Cycle and (b) agraph with 6 vertices that contains the Hamilton Cycle <1,2,3,4,5,6,1>

It does not make any difference which vertex is the start vertex in a cycle, so any vertex can serve as a start vertex. Determining a promising function is simple. At level i, i vertices have been picked. If edge from the ith vertex to the next or jth vertex exists, and the jth vertex has not been picked before, then the jth vertex is promising. Figure figure 12..5 lists a promising function for this problem where n is the number of vertices in the graph the global vector picked[1..n] is the list of vertices already picked.

```
boolean promising(integer level, integer i){
integer k;
for (k=1, k≤level; k++){ if (i equals picked[k]){ return false; }
}
return true;
}
```

Figure 12..5 This promising function returns true if the vertex i has not been picked before and false otherwise.

The backtracking algorithm Hamilton listed in figure 12.6 starts with a call to HamiltonCycle(1). At any stage it searches for all promising vertices and does a depth first search until level equals n. At that point it tries to determine if an edge exists joining picked[1] to picked[n]. It is assumed that picked[1]=1.

```
void HamiltonianCycle(integer level){
integer k, next;
if ((level equals n) and (G.edgeExists(1,picked[n]) equals true)){
output("Order of vertices in the cycle is");
for (k=1, k≤n; k++){
output (k, ", "); }
output(1);
}
else{
for(k=1; k≤G.outDegree(picked[level]); k++){
next = G.nextDest(picked[level]);
if    (promising(level,    next)    equals    true){    picked[level+1]    =    next;
      HamiltonCycle(level+1);    }
}
}
}
```

Figure 12.6 This backtracking implementation of the Hamiltonian Cycle problem is just an exhaustive search using a backtracking strategy.

Many exhaustive searches can be set up using a backtracking strategy. Exhaustive searches where something is being optimized are candidates for branch-and-bound attacks. Before a problem with exponential complexity can be solved using either backtracking or branch-and-bound, the structure of its state space tree, the structure of the nodes of the state space tree, and some way of determining if a node is promising or what its bounds andvalues are must be discerned. This is the hardest part of the implementation.Once these things are determined, the implementation is straightforward.

SUMMARY

Backtracking and branch-and-bound are two techniques based on traversing the state space tree of all possible solutions. The backtracking technique always traverses the state space tree using a depth first search. All backtracking algorithms are patterned after backtracker in figure 12.3. They are essentially optimized depth first searches. Branch-and-bound attacks are only applicable to optimization problems, but the state space tree can be traversed any way that checks all possible promising nodes.

The backtracking technique is designed to make a series of choices. Each choice is evaluated to see if it possibly leads to a solution. If it does, the next choice is made by a depth first search of the state space tree. If the choice was a bad one, then the choice is undone by 'backing up' or backtracking, and then making another choice.

The branch-and-bound technique is not restricted to how it traverses the state space tree. Two strategies are breadth first and best first. In both strategies the promising function from the backtracking strategy is replaced by a 'bound' function that tries to help with the optimization by making a better choice.

Both techniques are essentially exhaustive searches of the solution space embedded on a state space tree. For this reason, both the backtracking and branch-and-bound techniques are applied to problems that have exponential complexity. Even when the problem has been successfully implemented as either a backtracking or branch-and-bund, the implementation still has exponential complexity. However, whenever either one of these techniques is successfully applied, the execution time is considerable reduced.

REVIEW QUESTIONS

1. What is branch and bound technique .list the problems that can be solved by branch and bound technique.
2. Elaborate some examples of the backtracking technique
3. What are promising function and hamiltonian cycle
4. Explain backtracking implementation of the hamiltonian cycle problem

UNIT 4

GRAPH ALGORITHMS

CHAPTER 1

GRAPHS

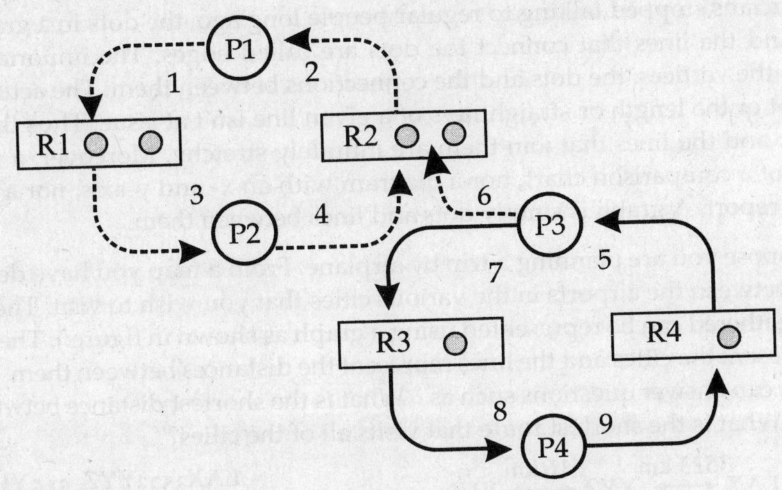

1.1 INTRODUCTION

A graph is an abstract data type (ADT) that consists of a set of nodes and a set of edges that establish relationships (connections) between the nodes. The graph ADT follows directly from the graph concept from mathematics. In practice, some information is associated with each node and edge. A graph is a generalization of the tree structure, where instead of a strict parent/child relationship between tree nodes, any kind of complex relationships between the nodes can be represented.

A graph G = <V, E> consists of a set of *vertices* (also known as nodes) V and a set of *edges* (also known as arcs) E. Graph is also defined as: A set of items connected by *edges*. Each item is called a *vertex* or node. Formally, a graph is a *set* of vertices and a *binary relation* between vertices, adjacency.

Graph is like a road map. Cities are vertices. Roads from city to city are edges. (How about junctions or branches in a road? You could consider junctions to be vertices, too. If you don't want to count them as vertices, a road may connect more than two cities. So strictly speaking you have *hyperedges* in a *hypergraph*. If you want to allow more than one road between each pair of cities, you have a *multigraph*, instead. It all depends on how you want to define it.)

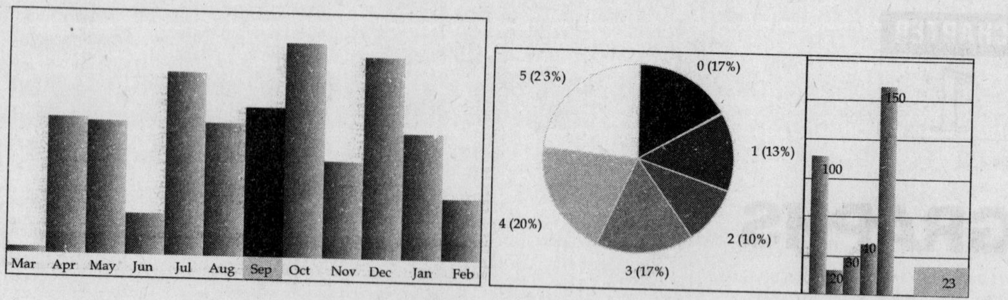

Another way to think of a graph is as a bunch of dots connected by lines. Because mathematicians stopped talking to regular people long ago, the dots in a graph are called vertices, and the lines that connect the dots are called edges. The important things are edges and the vertices: the dots and the connections between them. The actual position of a given dot or the length or straightness of a given line isn't at issue. Thus the dots can be anywhere, and the lines that join them are infinitely stretchy. Moreover, a mathematical graph is not a comparison chart, nor a diagram with an x- and y-axis, nor a squiggly line on a stock report. A graph is simply dots and lines between them.

Suppose you are planning a trip by airplane. From a map you have determined the distances between the airports in the various cities that you wish to visit. The information you have gathered can be represented using a graph as shown in figure:). The points in the graph represent the cities and the lines represent the distances between them. Given such a graph, you can answer questions such as ``What is the shortest distance between LAX and JFK?'' or ``What is the shortest route that visits all of the cities?''

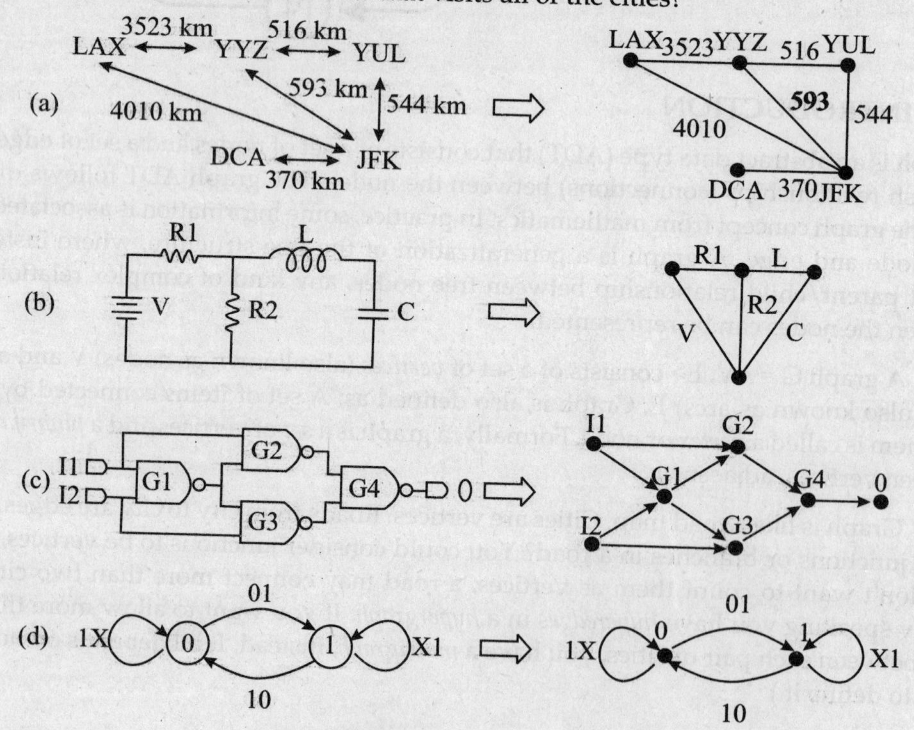

Figure: *Real-World Examples of Graphs*

An electric circuit can also be viewed as a graph as shown in figure:). In this case the points in the graph indicate where the components are connected (i.e., the wires) and the lines represent the components themselves (e.g, resistors and capacitors). Given such a graph, we can answer questions such as ``What are the mesh equations that describe the circuit's behavior?''

Similarly, a logic circuit can be reduced to a graph as shown in figure:). In this case the logic gates are represented by the points and arrows represent the signal flows from gate outputs to gate inputs. Given such a graph, we can answer questions such as ``How long does it take for the signals to propagate from the inputs to the outputs?'' or ``Which gates are on the critical path?''

Finally, figure:) illustrates that a graph can be used to represent a *finite state machine.* The points of the graph represent the states and labeled arrows indicate the allowable state transitions. Given such a graph, we can answer questions such as ``Are all the states reachable?'' or ``Can the finite state machine deadlock?''

1.2 GRAPH TERMINOLOGY

Undirected Graph - In an *undirected* graph, an edge has no sense of direction and is written as an unordered pair {u,v} or u<->v. An undirected graph can be represented by a directed graph if every undirected edge {u,v} is represented by two directed edges <u,v> and <v,u>.

Adjacent Nodes - If an edge connects two nodes u and v then u and v are said to be *adjacent* nodes

Neighbors – Adjacent nodes are also called neighbors.

Degree of a node – The degree of a node v (written as deg(v)) is the number of edges containing V.

Isolated Node - If deg(v) = 0 then v is called isolated node.

Path - A *path* in G is a sequence of vertices $\langle v_0, v_1, v_2, ..., v_n \rangle$ such that $\langle v_i, v_{i+1} \rangle$ (or $\{v_i, v_{i+1}\}$), for each i from 0 to n-1, is an edge in G.

Closed Path - If $v_0 = v_n$, then the path is called closed path

Cycle - The path is a *cycle* if $v_0=v_n$.

Simple Path - The path is *simple* if no two vertices are identical.

Simple Cycle - The path is a *simple cycle* if $v_0=v_n$ and no other two vertices are identical.

Acyclic Graph - A *graph* with no *path* that starts and ends at the same *vertex*

Complete Graph – A graph is complete if every node u in graph is adjacent to every node v. a complete graph with n nodes will have n(n-1)/2 edges.

Connected Graph – A graph is said to be connected if there is a path between any two of its nodes.

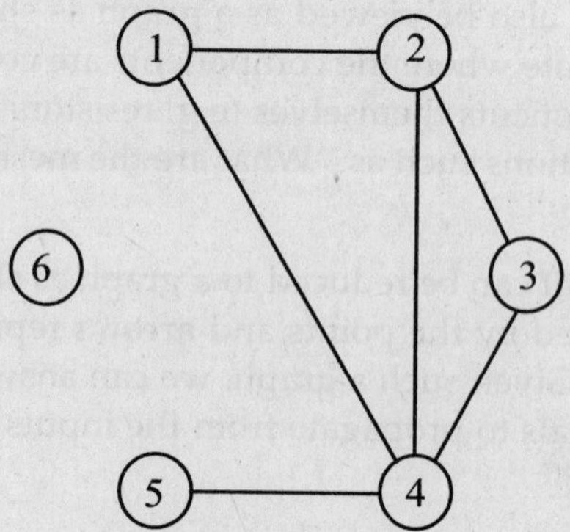

Figure: An example of undirected graph

In the above graph, we notice the following

- It contains 6 nodes and 6 edges.
- Nodes (1,2,4), (2,3,4), (4,5) are adjacent nodes or neighbors.
- Degree of node 1 is 2 and of 4 is 4.
- Node 6 is isolated node.
- (1,2,3,4) is a simple path of length 2.
- (1,2,3,4,1) is a closed path or simple cycle.
- The graph is not a complete graph
- The graph is Connected graph

Tree Graph – A connected graph without any cycle is called tree graph or simply tree. A finite tree graph with n node will have n-1 edges.

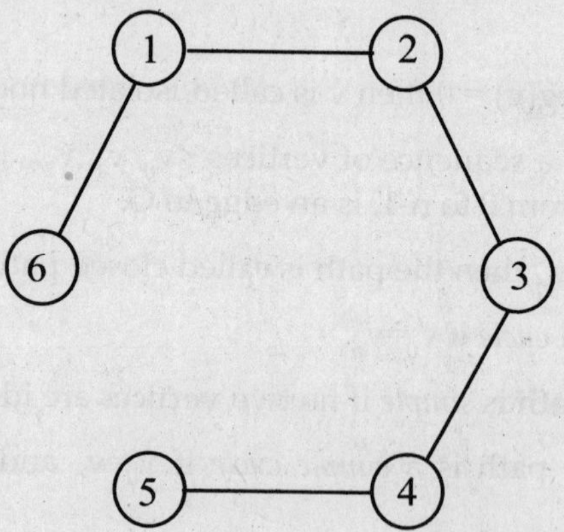

Figure: An example of Tree Graph

Multiple Edges – Distinct edges e_1 and e_2 are called multiple edges if they connect same nodes.

Loops – An edge e is called loop if it has identical endpoints.

Multigraph – A graph with multiple edges and loops.

Directed Graph - In a *directed* graph, each edge has a sense of direction from u to v and is written as an ordered pair <u,v> or u->v.

Outdegree – Number of edges begning at a node.

Indegree – Number of edges ending at a node.

Source- A node v is called source if it has positive outdegree but zero indegree.

Sink - A node v is called sink if it has positive indegree but zero outdegree.

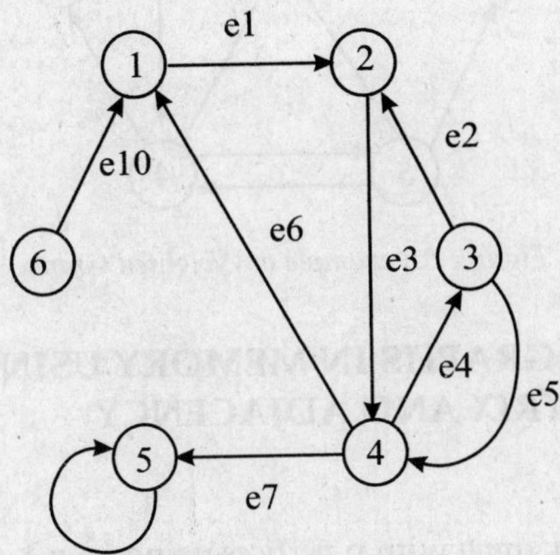

Figure: An example of Directed Graph

In the above graph, we notice the following

- Edges e4 and e5 are multiple edges.
- Edge e8 is a loop.
- The graph is multigraph
- Outdegree of node 4 is 2
- Indegree of node 4 is 2
- Node 6 is a source

Weighted Graphs - We may also want to associate some cost or weight to the traversal of an edge. When we add this information, the graph is called weighted graph.

Strongly Connected Components - A directed graph is strongly connected if for every two nodes u and v there is a path from u to v and one from v to u.

Bipartite Graph - An undirected graph G(V;E) is bipartite if it contains no cycle of odd length.

The vertex set of a bipartite graph can be divided into two sets V1 and V2 such that all edges in G go between V1 and V2.

Biconnected Components - An undirected graph is called biconnected if for every pair of nodes u and v there are two node disjoint paths between u and v. To disconnect a biconnected graph you need to delete at least two nodes. The biconnected components of an undirected graph are its maximal biconnected subgraphs.

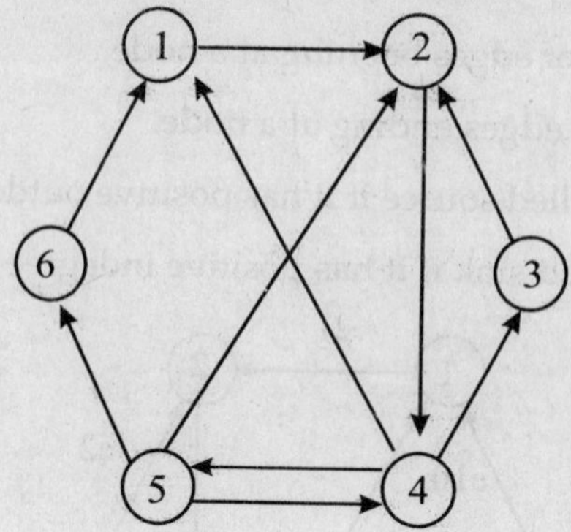

Figure: An example of Weighted Graph

1.3 IMPLEMENTING GRAPHS IN MEMORY USING ADJACENCY MATRIX AND ADJACENCY List

A representation of a *directed graph* with n *vertices* using an n × n *matrix*, where the entry at (i,j) is 1 if there is an *edge* from vertex i to vertex j; otherwise the entry is 0. A *weighted graph* may be represented using the weight as the entry. An *undirected graph* may be represented using the same entry in both (i,j) and (j,i) or using an *upper triangular matrix*.

An adjacency matrix is one of the two common ways to represent a graph. The adjacency matrix shows which nodes are adjacent to one another. Two nodes are adjacent if there is an edge connecting them. In the case of a directed graph, if node j is adjacent to node i, there is an edge from i to j. In other words, if j is adjacent to i, you can get from i to j by traversing one edge. For a given graph with n nodes, the adjacency matrix will have dimensions of $n \times n$. For an unweighted graph, the adjacency matrix will be populated with boolean values.

For any given node i, you can determine its adjacent nodes by looking at row $(i, [1 \,..\, n])$ of the adjacency matrix. A value of true at (i, j) indicates that there is an edge from node i to node j, and false indicating no edge. In an undirected graph, the values of (i, j) and (j, i) will be equal. In a weighted graph, the boolean values will be replaced by the weight of the edge connecting the two nodes, with a value of zero indicating no edge.

The memory use of an adjacency matrix is $O(n^2)$.

A representation of a *directed graph* with n *vertices* using an *array* of n *lists* of vertices. List i contains vertex j if there is an *edge* from vertex i to vertex j. A *weighted graph* may be represented with a list of vertex/weight pairs. An *undirected graph* may be represented by having vertex j in the list for vertex i and vertex i in the list for vertex j.

A graph G= can be represented by a $|V|*|V|$ *adjacency* matrix A. If G is directed, A_{ij}=true if and only if $<v_i,v_j>$ is in E. There are at most $|V|^2$ edges in E.

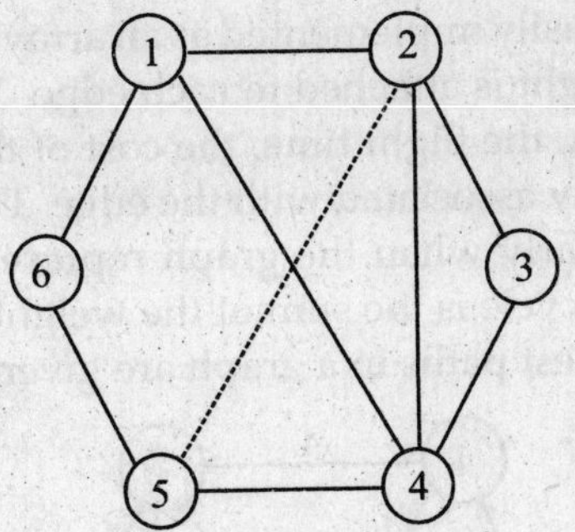

Figure:Directed Graph

	1	2	3	4	5	6
1		T				
2			T			
3		T				
4	T		T		T	
5		T		T		T
6	T					

Figure:Adjacency Matrix of Directed Graph in figure.

If G is undirected, $A_{ij}=A_{ji}$=true if $\{v_i,v_j\}$ is in E and $A_{ij}=A_{ji}$=false otherwise. In this case there are at most $|V|*(|V|+1)/2$ edges in E, A is symmetric and space can be saved by storing only the upper triangular part A_{ij} for i>=j.

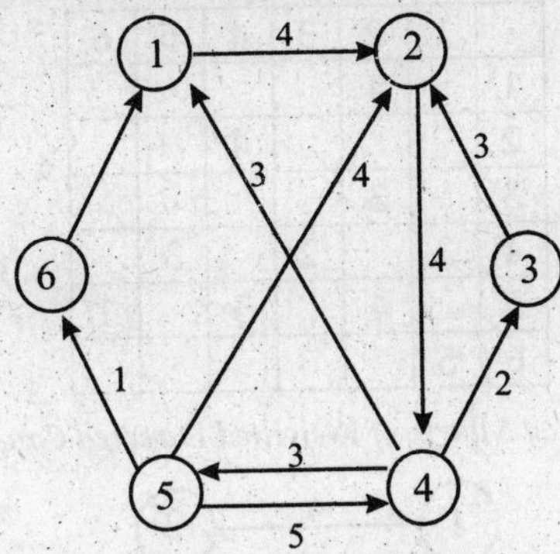

Figure: Undirected Graph

	1	2	3	4	5	6
1		T		T		T
2	T		T	T	T	
3		T		T		
4	T	T	T		T	
5		T		T		T
6	T				T	

Figure: Adjacency Matrix of Undirected Graph in figure.

An adjacency matrix is easily implemented as an array. Both directed and undirected graphs may be *weighted*. A weight is attached to each edge. This may be used to represent the distance between two cities, the flight time, the cost of the fare, the electrical capacity of a cable or some other quantity associated with the edge. The weight is sometimes called the *length* of the edge, particularly when the graph represents a map of some kind. The weight or length of a path or a cycle is the sum of the weights or lengths of its component edges. Algorithms to find shortest paths in a graph are given later.

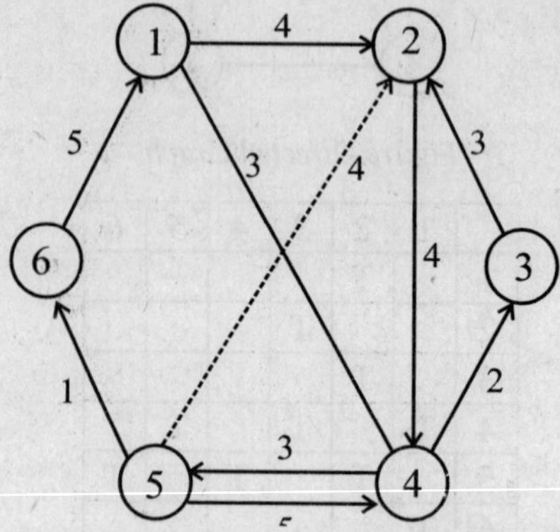

Figure: Weighed directed graph

The adjacency matrix of a weighted graph can be used to store the weights of the edges. If an edge is missing a special value, perhaps a negative value, zero or a large value to represent "infinity", indicates this fact.

	1	2	3	4	5	6
1		4				
2				4		
3		3				
4	3		2		3	
5		4		5		1
6	5					

Figure: Adjacency Matrix of Weighted Directed Graph in figure.

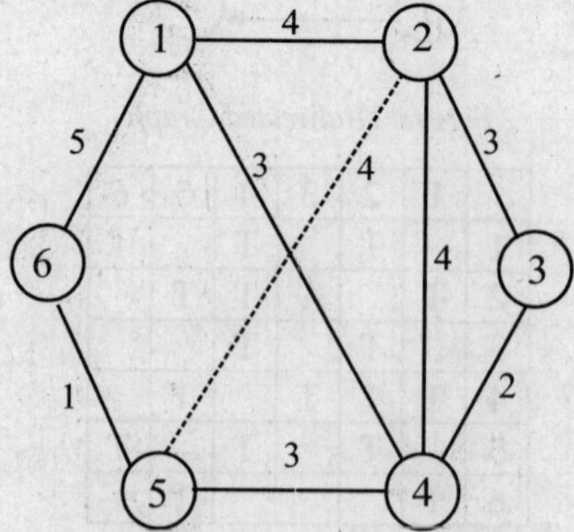

Figure: Weighed undirected graph

	1	2	3	4	5	6
1		4		3		5
2	4		3	4	4	
3		3		2		
4	3	4	2		3	
5		4		3		1
6		5			1	

Figure:Adjacency Matrix of Weighted Undirected Graph in figure: 2.

It is often the case that if the weights represent distances then the natural distance from v_i to itself is zero and the diagonal elements of the matrix are given this value.

A weighted adjacency matrix is easily defined in any imperative programming language.

A graph is *complete* if all possible edges are present. It is *dense* if most of the possible edges are present. It is *sparse* if most of them are absent, $|E| << |V|^2$. Adjacency matrices are space efficient for dense graphs but inefficient for sparse graphs when most of the entries represent missing edges. Adjacency lists use less space for sparse graphs.

Graphs can also be represented with the help of adjacency list. An Adjacency List is an array Adj[1:n] of pointers, where Adj[u] points to a linked list containing the vertices u

Example (Attention: A loop at vertex 2).

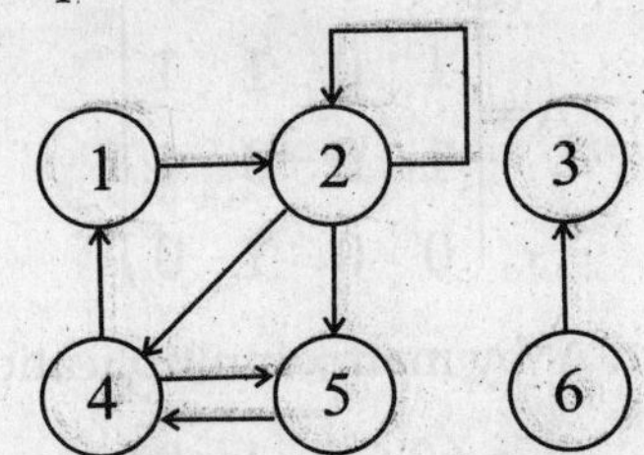

Figure: Example graph

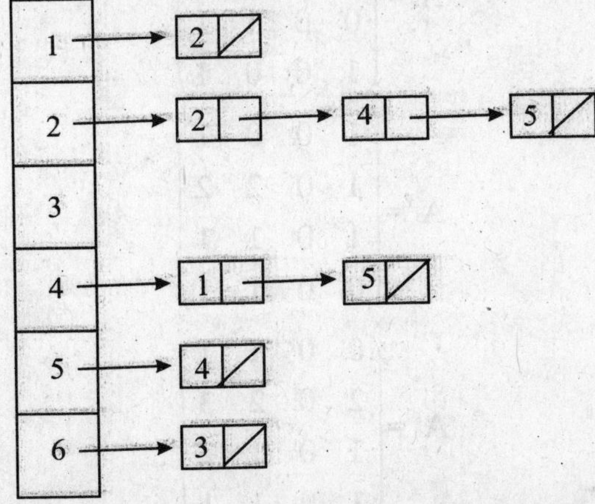

Figure: Linked list representation of graph in figure: 4

UNIT 4

1.4 PATH MATRIX

Let G be simple directed graph with m node $V_1, V_2, \ldots, V_m$. The path matrix or reachability matrix of G is the m-square matrix $P=(P_{ij})$ defined as follows:

$$P_{ij} = \begin{cases} 1, & \text{if there is a path from } V_i \text{ to } V_j \\ 0, & \text{otherwise} \end{cases}$$

Let A be the adjancy matrix and let $P = P=(P_{ij})$ be the path matrix of a digraph G. P_{ij} = 1 if and only if there is nonzero number in the ij entry of the matrix

$$B_M = A + A^2 + A^3 + \ldots\ldots\ldots + A^M$$

For example consider the following digraph

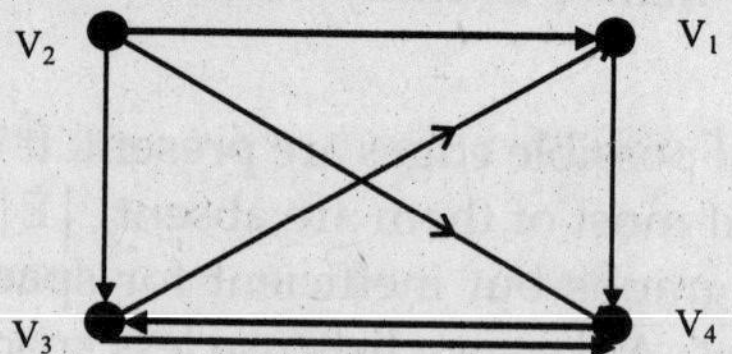

Figure: Example digraph

Here adjacency matrix A is

$$A=\begin{pmatrix} 0 & 0 & 0 & 1 \\ 1 & 0 & 1 & 1 \\ 1 & 0 & 0 & 1 \\ 0 & 0 & 1 & 0 \end{pmatrix}$$

We can find out A^2, A^3 and A^4 by matrix multiplications.

$$A^2=\begin{pmatrix} 0 & 0 & 1 & 0 \\ 1 & 0 & 1 & 2 \\ 0 & 0 & 1 & 1 \\ 1 & 0 & 0 & 1 \end{pmatrix}$$

$$A^3=\begin{pmatrix} 1 & 0 & 0 & 1 \\ 1 & 0 & 2 & 2 \\ 1 & 0 & 1 & 1 \\ 0 & 0 & 1 & 1 \end{pmatrix}$$

$$A^4=\begin{pmatrix} 0 & 0 & 1 & 1 \\ 2 & 0 & 2 & 3 \\ 1 & 0 & 1 & 2 \\ 1 & 0 & 1 & 1 \end{pmatrix}$$

UNIT 4

Now $B_4 = A + A^2 + A^3 + A^4$

$$A_4 = \begin{pmatrix} 1 & 0 & 2 & 3 \\ 5 & 0 & 6 & 8 \\ 3 & 0 & 3 & 5 \\ 2 & 0 & 3 & 3 \end{pmatrix}$$

The path matrix P can be find out by replacing non zero's by 1

$$p = \begin{pmatrix} 1 & 0 & 1 & 1 \\ 1 & 0 & 1 & 1 \\ 1 & 0 & 1 & 1 \\ 1 & 0 & 1 & 1 \end{pmatrix}$$

1.5 SHORTEST PATHS

Sometimes it's required to find out the shortest path between two nodes in a graph. One of the examples is traveling sales man problem.

Let G be weighted graph maintained as weighted matrix $W = (W_{ij})$ in memory. W_{ij} is defined as

$$W_{ij} = \begin{cases} W(e), \text{ if there is an edge e from } V_i \text{ to } V_j \\ 0, \text{ otherwise} \end{cases}$$

Matrix Q will be used to store shortest paths between nodes. Matrix $Q_k[i,j]$ is defined as

$$Q_k[i,j] = MIN(Q_{k-1}[i,j], Q_{k-1}[i,k] + Q_{k-1}[k,j])$$

$Q_k[i,j]$ is the smallest of length of the preceding path from V_i to V_j.

1.5.1 Shortest Path Algorithm

SHORTEST_PATH

```
1.    for i,j=1,2,......m
          if W[i,j]=0 then
              Q[i,j] = infinity;
          else
              Q[i,j] = w[i,j];
2.    repeat step 3 and 4 for k=1,2,....,m
3.    repeat step 4 for i=1,2,....,m
4.        repeat for j=1,2,....,m
              Qk[i,j] = MIN(Qk-1[i,j], Qk-1[i,k] + Qk-1[k,j]);
5.    exit
```

Example:

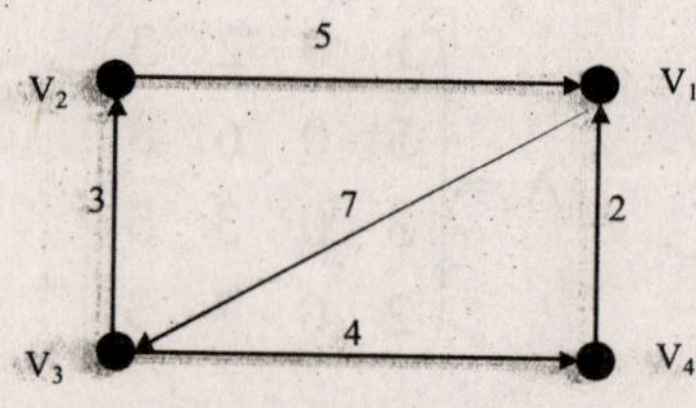

Figure: Example digraph

Fist we find Q_0

$$Q_0 = \begin{pmatrix} \infty & \infty & 7 & \infty \\ 5 & \infty & \infty & \infty \\ \infty & 3 & \infty & 4 \\ 2 & \infty & \infty & \infty \end{pmatrix}$$

Now with the help of SHORTEST_PATH algorithm we compute Q_1, Q_2 and Q_3

$$Q_1 = \begin{pmatrix} \infty & \infty & 7 & \infty \\ 5 & \infty & 12 & \infty \\ \infty & 3 & \infty & 4 \\ 2 & \infty & 9 & \infty \end{pmatrix}$$

$$Q_2 = \begin{pmatrix} \infty & \infty & 7 & \infty \\ 5 & \infty & 12 & \infty \\ 8 & 3 & 15 & 4 \\ 2 & \infty & 9 & \infty \end{pmatrix}$$

$$Q_3 = \begin{pmatrix} 15 & 10 & 7 & 11 \\ 5 & 15 & 12 & 16 \\ 8 & 3 & 15 & 4 \\ 2 & 12 & 9 & 13 \end{pmatrix}$$

1.6 GRAPH TRAVERSING ALGORITHMS

To traverse means to visit the vertices in some systematic order. We have already discussed following traversal methods for trees:

- preorder: visit each node before its children.
- postorder: visit each node after its children.
- inorder (for binary trees only): visit left subtree, node, right subtree.

Let us consider other traversals: breadth first search (BFS) and depth first search (DFS). Both of these construct spanning trees with certain properties useful in other graph algorithms.

1.6.1 Breadth First Search

A breadth-first search (BFS) is a tree search algorithm used for traversing or searching a tree, tree structure, or graph. The algorithm begins at the root node and explores all the neighboring nodes. Then for each of those nearest nodes, it explores their unexplored neighbor nodes, and so on, until it finds the goal.

Formally, BFS is an uninformed search method that aims to expand and examine all nodes of a graph systematically in search of a solution. In other words, it exhaustively searches the entire graph without considering the goal until it finds it. It does not use a heuristic.

Breadth First Search algorithm

1. Declare two empty lists: Open and Closed.
2. Add Start node to our Open list.
3. While our Open list is not empty, loop the following:
   a. Remove the first node from our Open List.
   b. Check to see if the removed node is our destination.
      i) If the removed node is our destination, break out of the loop, add the node to our Closed list, and return the value of our Closed list.
      ii) If the removed node is not our destination, continue the loop (go to Step c).
   c. Extract the neighbors of our above removed node.
   d. Add the neighbors to the end of our Open list, and add the removed node to our Closed list.
4. exit

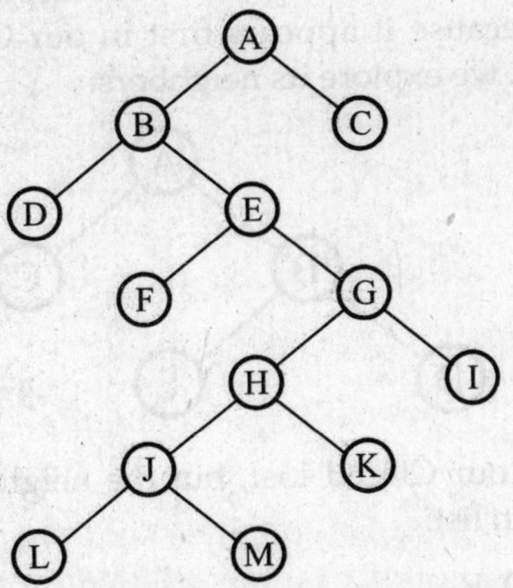

Figure: Example graph

Let's try to find a path between nodes A and E.

Step 0

Let's start with our root/goal node:

Like before, I will continue to employ the Open and Closed Lists to keep track of what needs to be done:

- Open List: A
- Closed List: <empty>

Step 1

Now, let's explore the neighbors of our A node. So far, we are following in depth first's foot steps:

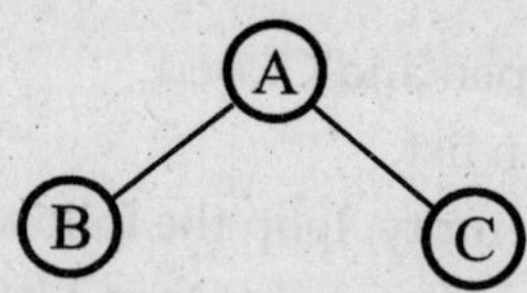

We remove A from our Open list and add A to our Closed List. A's neighbors, the B and C nodes, are added to our Open list. They are added to the end of our Open list, but since our Open list was empty (after removing A), it's hard to show that in this step.

Our current Open and Closed Lists contain the following data:

- Open List: B, C
- Closed List: A

Step 2

Here is where things start to diverge from our depth first search method. We take a look the B node because it appears first in our Open List. Because B isn't our intended destination, we explore its neighbors:

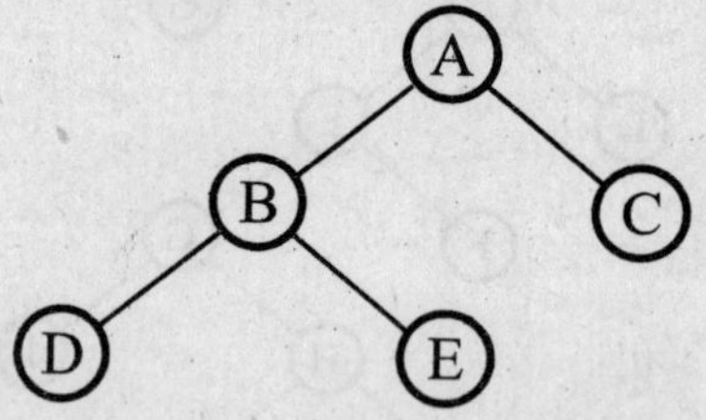

B is now moved to our Closed List, but the neighbors of B, nodes D and E are added to the end of our Open list:

- Open List: C, D, E
- Closed List: A, B

Step 3

We now expand our C node:

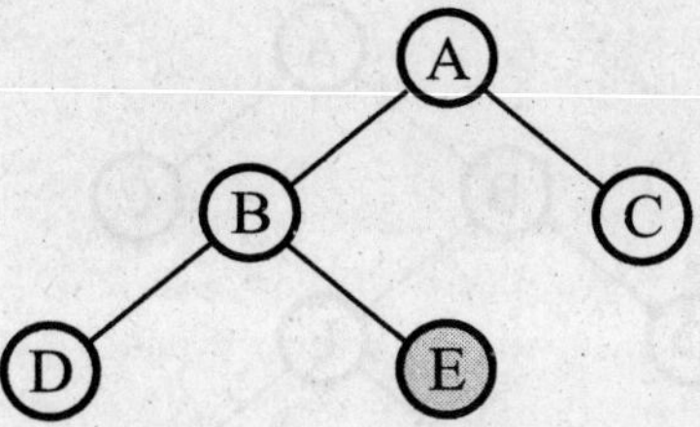

Since C has no neighbors, all we do is remove C from our Closed List and move on:

- Open List: D, E
- Closed List: A, B, C

Step 4

Similar to Step 3, we expand node D. Since it isn't our destination, and it too does not have any neighbors, we simply remove D from our to Open list, add D to our Closed List, and continue on:

- Open List: E
- Closed List: A, B, C, D

Step 5

Because our Open list only has one item, we have no choice but to take a look at node E. Since node E is our destination, we can stop here:

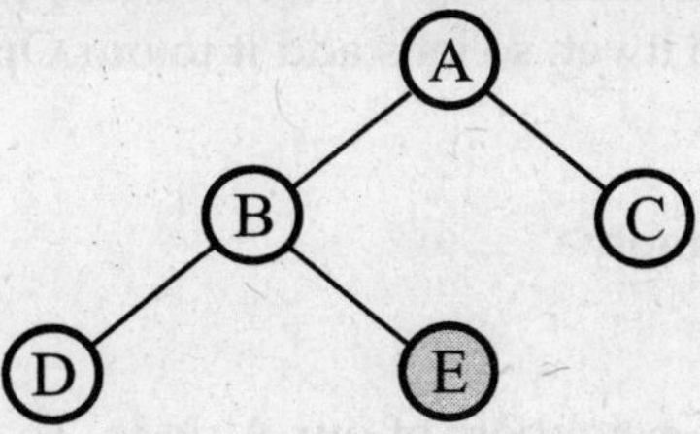

Our final versions of the Open and Closed Lists contain the following data:

- Open List: <empty>
- Closed List: A, B, C, D, E

Traveling from A to E takes you through B, C, and D using breadth first search.

1.6.2 Depth First Search

Depth first search works by taking a node, checking its neighbors, expanding the first node it finds among the neighbors, checking if that expanded node is our destination, and if not, continue exploring more nodes.

The above explanation is probably confusing if this is your first exposure to depth first search. We hope the following demonstration will help more. Using our same search tree, let's find a path between nodes A and F:

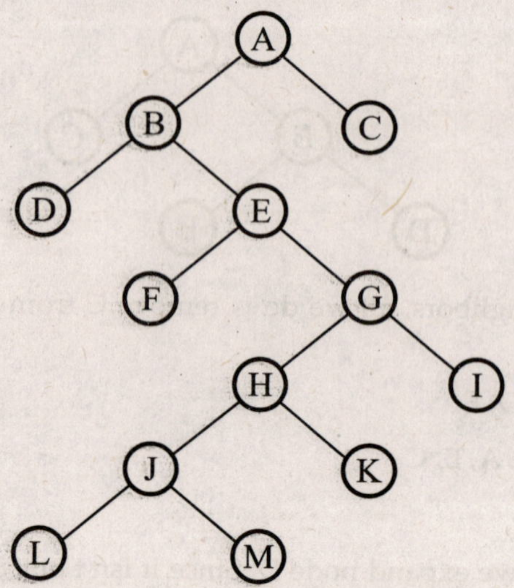

Step 0

Let's start with our root/goal node:

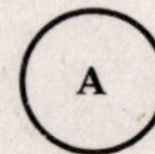

I will be using two lists to keep track of what we are doing - an Open list and a Closed List. An Open list keeps track of what you need to do, and the Closed List keeps track of what you have already done. Right now, we only have our starting point, node A. We haven't done anything to it yet, so let's add it to our Open list.

- Open List: A
- Closed List: <empty>

Step 1

Now, let's explore the neighbors of our A node. To put another way, let's take the first item from our Open list and explore its neighbors:

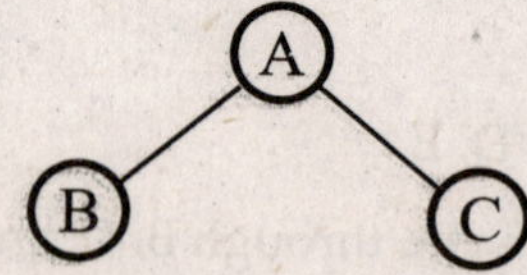

Node A's neighbors are the B and C nodes. Because we are now done with our A node, we can remove it from our Open list and add it to our Closed List. You aren't done with this step though. You now have two new nodes B and C that need exploring. Add those two nodes to our Open list.

Our current Open and Closed Lists contain the following data:

- Open List: B, C
- Closed List: A

Step 2

Our Open list contains two items. For depth first search and breadth first search, you always explore explore the first item from our Open list. The first item in our Open list is the B node. B is not our destination, so let's explore its neighbors:

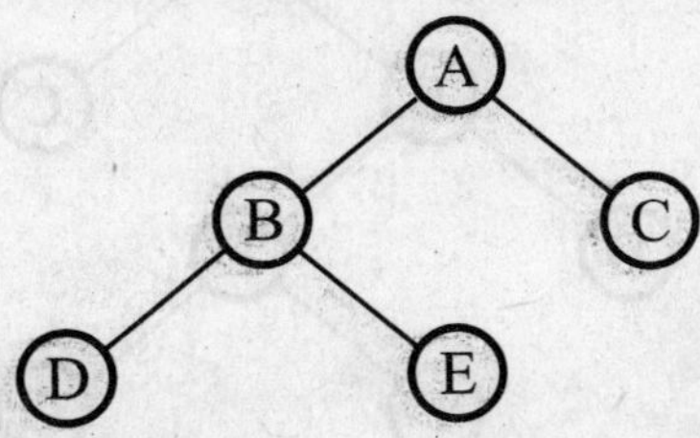

Because I have now expanded B, I am going to remove it from the Open list and add it to the Closed List. Our new nodes are D and E, and we add these nodes to the beginning of our Open list:

- Open List: D, E, C
- Closed List: A, B

Step 3

You should start to see a pattern forming. Because D is at the beginning of our Open List, we expand it. D isn't our destination, and it does not contain any neighbors. All you do in this step is remove D from our Open List and add it to our Closed List:

- Open List: E, C
- Closed List: A, B, D

Step 4

We now expand the E node from our Open list. E is not our destination, so we explore its neighbors and find out that it contains the neighbors F and G. Remember, F is our target, but we don't stop here though. Despite F being on our path, we only end when we are about to expand our target Node - F in this case:

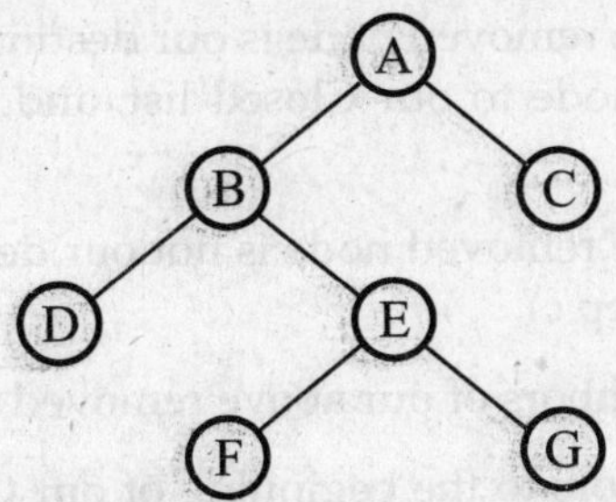

Our Open list will have the E node removed and the F and G nodes added. The removed E node will be added to our Closed List:

- Open List: F, G, C
- Closed List: A, B, D, E

Step 5

We now expand the F node. Since it is our intended destination, we stop:

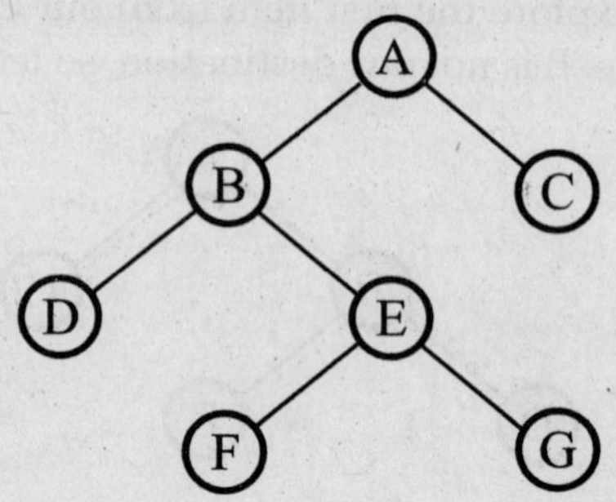

We remove F from our Open list and add it to our Closed List. Since we are at our destination, there is no need to expand F in order to find its neighbors. Our final Open and Closed Lists contain the following data:

- Open List: G, C
- Closed List: A, B, D, E, F

The final path taken by our depth first search method is what the final value of our Closed List is: A, B, D, E, F. Towards the end of this tutorial, I will analyze these results in greater detail so that you have a better understanding of this search method.

Depth First Search algorithm

1. Declare two empty lists: Open and Closed.
2. Add Start node to our Open list.
3. While our Open list is not empty, loop the following:
   a) Remove the first node from our Open List.
   b) Check to see if the removed node is our destination.
      i) If the removed node is our destination, break out of the loop, add the node to our Closed list, and return the value of our Closed list.
      ii) If the removed node is not our destination, continue the loop (go to Step c).
   c) Extract the neighbors of our above removed node.
   d) Add the neighbors to the beginning of our Open list, and add the removed node to our Closed list. Continue looping.
4. exit

GLOSSARY

Graph - abstract data type (ADT) that consists of a set of nodes and a set of edges that establish relationships (connections) between the nodes.

Adjacent Nodes - If an edge connects two nodes u and v then u and v are said to be *adjacent* nodes

Neighbors – Adjacent nodes are also called neighbors.

Degree of a node – The degree of a node v (written as deg(v)) is the number of edges containing V.

Isolated Node - If deg(v) = 0 then v is called isolated node.

Path - A *path* in G is a sequence of vertices $<v_0, v_1, v_2, ..., v_n>$ such that $<v_i,v_{i+1}>$ (or $\{v_i,v_{i+1}\}$), for each i from 0 to n-1, is an edge in G.

Closed Path - If $v_0 = v_n$, then the path is called closed path

Cycle - The path is a *cycle* if $v_0=v_n$.

Simple Path - The path is *simple* if no two vertices are identical.

Simple Cycle - The path is a *simple cycle* if $v_0=v_n$ and no other two vertices are identical.

Acyclic Graph - A *graph* with no *path* that starts and ends at the same *vertex*

Complete Graph – A graph is complete if every node u in graph is adjacent to every node v. a complete graph with n nodes will have n(n-1)/2 edges.

Connected Graph – A graph is said to be connected if there is a path between any two of its nodes.

Tree Graph – A connected graph without any cycle is called tree graph or simply tree. A finite tree graph with n node will have n-1 edges.

Multiple Edges – Distinct edges e_1 and e_2 are called multiple edges if they connect same nodes.

Loops – An edge e is called loop if it has identical endpoints.

Multigraph – A graph with multiple edges and loops.

Directed Graph - In a *directed* graph, each edge has a sense of direction from u to v and is written as an ordered pair <u,v> or u->v.

Outdegree – Number of edges begning at a node.

Indegree – Number of edges ending at a node.

Source- A node v is called source if it has positive outdegree but zero indegree.

Sink - A node v is called sink if it has positive indegree but zero outdegree.

Weighted Graphs - We may also want to associate some cost or weight to the traversal of an edge. When we add this information, the graph is called weighted graph.

Strongly Connected Components - A directed graph is strongly connected if for every two nodes u and v there is a path from u to v and one from v to u.

Bipartite Graph - An undirected graph G(V;E) is bipartite if it contains no cycle of odd length.

The vertex set of a bipartite graph can be divided into two sets V1 and V2 such that all edges in G go between V1 and V2.

Biconnected Components - An undirected graph is called biconnected if for every pair of nodes u and v there are two node disjoint paths between u and v. To disconnect a biconnected graph you need to delete at least two nodes. The biconnected components of an undirected graph are its maximal biconnected subgraphs.

SUMMARY

Adjancy matrix - A representation of a *directed graph* with n *vertices* using an n × n *matrix*, where the entry at (i,j) is 1 if there is an *edge* from vertex i to vertex j; otherwise the entry is 0. A *weighted graph* may be represented using the weight as the entry. An *undirected graph* may be represented using the same entry in both (i,j) and (j,i) or using an *upper triangular matrix*.

A breadth-first search (BFS) is a tree search algorithm used for traversing or searching a tree, tree structure, or graph. The algorithm begins at the root node and explores all the neighboring nodes. Then for each of those nearest nodes, it explores their unexplored neighbor nodes, and so on, until it finds the goal.

Depth first search works by taking a node, checking its neighbors, expanding the first node it finds among the neighbors, checking if that expanded node is our destination, and if not, continue exploring more nodes.

REVIEW QUESTIONS

1. Differentiate between closed path and cycle.
2. Represent the following graph with the help of adjacency matrix and adjacency list.

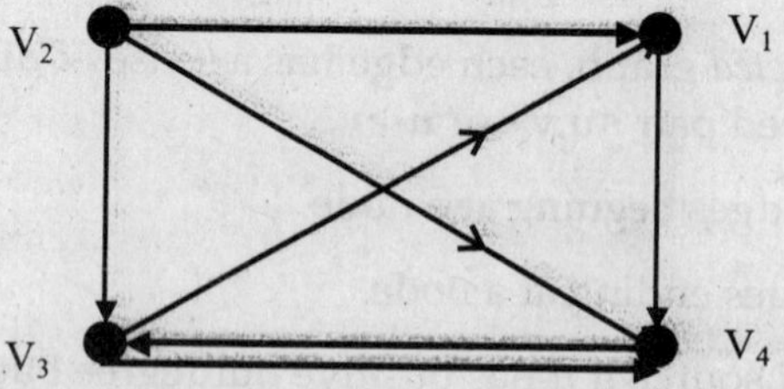

3. What is the usefulness of path matrix?
4. How path matrix and complete graph are related?
5. Explain Graph traversing algorithms in details.

CHAPTER

2

SINGLE–SOURCE SHORTEST PATH

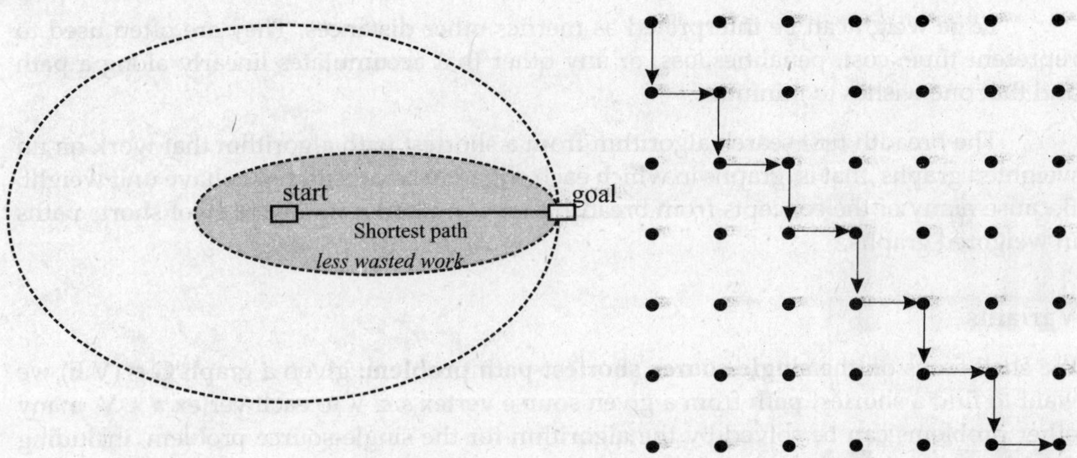

2.1 INTRODUCTION

Suppose some motorist want to move from Chicago to Boston. Every motorist wishes to find the shortest possible route from Chicago to Boston Given a road map of the United States on which the distance between each pair of adjacent intersections is marked. But the problem is how to determine this shortest route ?

One possible way is to enumerate all the routes from Chicago to Boston, add up the distances on each route, and select the shortest. It is easy to see, however, that even if we disallow routes that contain cycles, there are millions of possibilities, most of which are simply not worth considering. For example, a route from Chicago to Houston to Boston is obviously a poor choice, because Houston is about a thousand miles out of the way.

In a shortest-paths problem, we are given a weighted, directed graph G = (V,E), with weight function w : E → R mapping edges to real-valued weights. The weight of path p = $\{v_0, v_1, ..., v_k\}$ is the sum of the weights of its constituent edges:

$$W(p) = \sum_{i=1}^{k} w(\{v_i - 1, v_i$$

we define the shortest-path weight from *u* to *v* by

δ(*u*,*v*) = {min {w(p) : u v} if ther is a path from u to v,
∞ otherwise

A shortest path from vertex u to v is then defined as any path p with weight w(p) =δ(u,v).

In the Chicago-to-Boston example, we can model the road map as a graph: vertices represent road distances. Our goal is to find a shortest path from a given intersection in Chicago (say, clerk st.and Addison Ave) to a given intersection in Boston (say, Brookline Ave and yawkey Way).

Edge weightcan be interpreted as metrics other distances. They are often used to represent time, cost, penalities,loss, or any other that accumulates linearly along a path and that one wishes to minimize.

The breadth first search algorithm from a shortest path algorithm that work on un weighted graphs ,that is, graphs in which each edge can be considered to have unit weight. Because many of the concepts from breadth first search arise in the study of shorts paths in weighted graphs.

Variants

We shall focus on the **single-source shortest-path problem:** given a graph G = (V,E) we want to find a shortest path from a given sourse vertex *s* ∈ V to each vertex *v* ∈ V. many other problems can be solved by the algorithm for the single-source problem, including the following variants.

Single- destination shortest-path problem: find a shorts path to a given destination vertex t from each vertex *v*. by reversing the direction of each edge in the graph, we can reduce this problem to a single problem.

Single-pair shortest-path problem: find a shortest path from *u* to *v* for given vertices *u* and *v*. if we solve the single-source problem with source vertex u, we solve this problem also. Moreover, no algorithms for this problem are know that run asymptotically faster then the best single-source in the worst case.

All -pair shortest-path problem: find a shortest path from *u* to *v* for every pair of vertices *u* to *v*. although this problem can be solved by running a single-source algorithm once from each vertex, it can usually be solved faster. Additionally, its structure is of interest in its own right.

2.2 OPTIMAL SUBSTRUCTURE OF A SHORTEST PATH

Shortest-path algorithms typically rely on the property that a shortest path between two vertices contains other shortest paths within it.this optimal-substructure property is a hallmark of the applicability of both dynamic programming and the greedy method. Dijkstra's algorithm, is a greedy algorithm, and the floyd-warshall is a dynamic-programming algorithm. The following lemme ststesthe optimal substructure property of shortest paths more precisely.

Lemma (Subpaths of shortest paths are shortest paths)

Given a weighted, directed graph G = *(V, E)* with weight function $w : E \rightarrow R$, let p = (v_1, v_2, ... , v_k) be a shortest path from vertex v_1, to vertex v_k and, for any i and j such that $1 \leq i \leq j \leq k$, let p_{ij} = *(vi, v,+,, ..., v_j)* be the subpath of *p* from vertex v_i to vertex v_j. Then, *p,j is* a shortest path from v_i to v_j.

Proof If we decompose path p into $v_1 \overset{p1i}{\rightarrow} v_i \overset{pij}{\rightarrow} v_j \overset{pjk}{\rightarrow} v_k$ then we have that w(p) = w(p_{1i}) + w(p_{ij}) + w(p_{jk}). Now, assume that there is a path p_{ij} from v_i to v_j with weight *w(p,;) < w(p,j)*. Then, $v_1 \overset{p1i}{\rightarrow} v_i \overset{pij}{\rightarrow} v_j \overset{pjk}{\rightarrow} v_k$ is a path from v_i to v_k whose weight *w(p1i) + w(p_{ij}) + w(pjk)* is less than w(p), which contradicts the assumption that p is a shortest path from v_I to *vk.*

Negative-weight edges

In some instances of the single-source shortest-paths problem, there may be edges whose weights are negative. If the graph G = (V, E) contains no negative weight cycles reachable from the source s, then for all v *E* V, the shortest-path weight *8(s,* v) remains well defined, even if it has a negative value. If there is a negative-weight cycle reachable from s, however, shortest-path weights are not well defined. No path from s to a vertex on the cycle can be a shortest path-a lesser-weight path can always be found that follows the proposed "shortest" path and then traverses the negative-weight cycle. If there is a negative-weight cycle on some path from s to v, we define S(s, *v*)= -∞

Figure illustrates the effect of negative weights and negative-weight cycles on shortest-path weights. Because there is only one path from *s* to *a* (the path (s, a)), S(s, *a)* = *w(s, a)* = 3. Similarly, there is only one path from s to *b,* and so *S(s, b)* = *w(s, a)* + *w(a, b)* = 3 + (-4) =-1. There are infinitely many paths from s to c: *(s, c), (s, c, d, c), (s, c, d, c, d, c),* and so on. Because the cycle *(c, d, c)* has weight 6 + (-3) = 3 > 0, the shortest path from s to c is *(s, c),* with weight *8(s,* c) = 5. Similarly, the shortest path from s to *d is (s, c, d),* with weight S(s, *d)* = *w* (s, *c)* + *w (c, d)* = 11. Analogously, there are infinitely many paths from s to *e: (s, e), (s, e, f, e), (s, e, f, e, f, e),* and so on. Since the cycle *(e, f, e)* has weight 3 + (-6) --3 < 0, however, there is no shortest path from s to *e.* By traversing the negative-weight cycle *(e, f, e)* arbitrarily many times, we can find paths from s to *e* with arbitrarily large negative weights, and so *S(s, e)=-∞.* Similarly, *S(s, f)=-∞.* Because g is reachable from *f,* we can also find paths with arbitrarily large negative weights from s to g, and S(s, g)=-∞. Vertices *h, i,* and *j* also form a negative-weight cycle. They are not reachable from s, however, and *so S(s,h)=S(s,i)=S(s, j)=∞.*

Some shortest-paths algorithms, such as Dijkstra's algorithm, assume that all edge weights in the input graph are nonnegative, as in the road-map example. Others, such as the Bellman-Ford algorithm, allow negative-weight edges in the input graph and produce a correct answer as long as no negative-weight cycles are reachable from the source. Typically, if there is such a negative-weight cycle, the algorithm can detect and report its existence.

Cycles

Can a shortest path contain a cycle? As we have just seen, it cannot contain a negative-weight cycle. Nor can it contain a positive-weight cycle, since removing the cycle from the path produces a path with the same source and destination vertices and a lower path weight. That is, if p=(v_o, v_1, ..., v_k) is a path and c=(v_i, v_{i+1},..., v_j) is a positive-weight cycle on this path (so that $v_i = vj$ and $w(c) > 0$), then the path $p'=(v_o, v_1, \ldots, vi\ v_{i+1}, v_{j+2}, \ldots, V_k)$ has weight w(p') = $w(p) - w(c) <$ w(p), and so p cannot be a shortest path from v_o to v_k.

That leaves only 0-weight cycles. We can remove a 0-weight cycle from any path to produce another path whose weight is the same. Thus; if there is a shortest path from a source vertex s to a destination vertex v that contains a 0-weight cycle, then there is another shortest path from s to v without this cycle. As long as a shortest path has 0-weight cycles, we can repeatedly remove these cycles from the path until we have a shortest path that is cycle-free. Therefore, without loss of generality we can assume that when we are finding shortest paths, they have no cycles. Since any acyclic path in a graph G = (V, E) contains at most $|V|$ distinct vertices, it also contains at most $|v|$-1 edges. Thus, we can restrict our attention to shortest paths of at most $|v|$ - 1 edges.

2.3 REPRESENTING SHORTEST PATHS

We often wish to compute not only shortest-path weights, but the vertices on shortest paths as well. The representation we use for shortest paths is similar to the one we used for breadth-first trees in Section 22.2. Given a graph G=(V, *E)*, we maintain for each vertex $v \in V$ ***predecessor*** π *[v]* that is either another vertex or NIL. The shortest-paths algorithms in this chapter set the n attributes so that the chain of predecessors originating at a vertex v runs backwards along a shortest path from s to v. Thus, given a vertex v for which $\pi[v] \neq$ NIL, the procedure PRINT-PATH(G, s, v) can be used to print a shortest path from s to v.

During the execution of a shortest-paths algorithm, however, the π values need not indicate shortest paths. As in breadth-first search, we shall be interested in the ***predecessor subgraph*** $G\pi = (V_\pi, E\pi)$ induced by the π values. Here again, we define the vertex set V_π to be the set of vertices of G with non-NIL predecessors, plus the sources:

$V\pi = \{v \in V{:}\pi[v] \neq \text{NIL}\} \cup \{s\}$.

The directed edge set E, is the set of edges induced by the π values for vertices in V_n:

$E\pi = \{(\pi[u], v) \in E{:} v \in V\pi - \{s\}\}$.

We shall prove that the n values produced by the algorithms in this chapter have the property that at termination $G\pi$ is a "shortest-paths tree"-informally, a rooted tree containing a shortest path from the source s to every vertex that is reachable from s. A shortest-paths tree is like the breadth-first tree, but it contains shortest paths from the source defined in terms of edge weights instead of numbers of edges. To be precise, let G = (V, E) be a weighted, directed graph with weight function w : $E \rightarrow R$, and assume that G contains no negative-weight cycles reachable from the source vertex $s \in V$, so that shortest paths are well defined. *A* ***shortest paths tree*** rooted at s is a directed subgraph G' =(V', E'), where $V' \subseteq V$ and $E' \subseteq E$, such that

1. V' is the set of vertices reachable from s in G,
2. G' forms a rooted tree with root s, and
3. for all $v \in V'$, the unique simple path from s to v in G' is a shortest path from s to **v** ***in G.***

Shortest paths are not necessarily unique, and neither are shortest-paths trees. For example, Figure shows a weighted, directed graph and two shortest-paths trees with the same root.

Relaxation

The algorithms in this chapter use the technique of ***relaxation.*** For each vertex v∈ V, we maintain an attribute d[v]; which is an upper bound on the weight of a shortest path from source s to v. We call d*[v} **a shortest-path estimate.*** We initialize the shortest-path estimates and predecessors by the following Θ(V)-time procedure.

```
INITIALIZE- SINGLE-SOURCE (G, s)
for each vertex v ∈ V[G]
do d∈v← ∞
π[V]← NIL
d[s]← 0
```

After initialization, π[v] = NIL for all v ∈ *V, d[s]* = 0, and *d[v]* = ∞ for v∈V-{S}.

The process of ***relaxing'*** an edge *(u, v)* consists of testing whether we can improve the shortest path to v found so fat by going through u and, if so, updating d[v] and π [v]. A relaxation step may decrease the value of the shortest-path estimate d[v] and update v's predecessor field π[v]. The following code performs a relaxation step on edge *(u, v)*.

```
RELAX (U, V, W)
if d[v] > d[u] + w(u, v)
then d[v]← d[u] + w(u, v)
π[v] <<← u
```

Figure shows two examples of relaxing an edge, one in which a shortest-path estimate decreases and one in which no estimate changes.

Each algorithm in this chapter calls INITIALIZE-SINGLE-SOURCE and then repeatedly relaxes edges. Moreover, relaxation is the only means by which shortestpath estimates and predecessors change. The algorithms in-this chapter differ in how many times they relax each edge and the order in which they relax edges. In Dijkstra's algorithm and the shortest-paths algorithm for directed acyclic graphs, each edge is relaxed exactly once. In the Bellman-Ford algorithm, each edge is relaxed many times.

2.4 PROPERTIES *OF* SHORTEST PATHS AND RELAXATION

To prove the algorithms in this chapter correct, we shall appeal to several properties of shortest paths and relaxation. We state these properties here, and proves them formally. For your reference, each property stated here includes the appropriate lemma or corollary number. The latter five of these properties, which refer to shortest-path estimates or the predecessor subgraph, implicitly assume that the graph is initialized with a call to INITIALIZE-SINGLE-SOURCE(G, s) and that the only way that shortest-path estimates and the predecessor subgraph change are by some sequence of relaxation steps.

Triangle inequality (Lemma)
For any edge $(u, v) \in E$, we have $\delta(s, v) \leq \delta(s, u) + w(u, v)$.

Upper-bound property (Lemma)
We always have $d[v] \geq \delta(s, v)$ for all vertices $v \in V$, and once $d[v]$ achieves the value $\delta(s, v)$, it never changes.

No-path property (Corollary)
If there is no path from s to v, then we always have $d[v] = \delta(s, v) = \infty$.

Convergence property (Lemma)
If $s \sim u \rightarrow v$ is a shortest path in G for some $u, u \in V$, and if $d[u] = \delta(s, u)$ at any time prior to relaxing edge (u, v), then $d[v] = \delta(s, v)$ at all times afterward.

Path-relaxation property (Lemma)
If $p = (v_o, v_i, ..., v_k)$ is a shortest path from s = vo to *vk*, and the edges of *p* are relaxed in the order $(v_o, v_1), (v_1, v_2), \ldots, (v_{k-1}, v_k)$, then $d[v_k] = \delta(s, v_k)$. This property holds regardless of any other relaxation steps that occur, even if they are intermixed with relaxations of the edges of p.

Predecessor-subgraph property (Lemma)
Once $d[v] = \delta(s, v)$ for all $v \in V$, the predecessor subgraph is a shortest-paths tree rooted at s.

2.5 BELLMAN-FORD ALGORITHM

The ***Bellman-Ford algorithm*** solves the single-source shortest-paths problem in the general case in which edge weights may be negative. Given a weighted, directed graph $G = (V, E)$ with source s and weight function $w : E \rightarrow R$, the Bellman-Ford algorithm returns a Boolean value indicating whether or not there is a negative-weight cycle that is reachable from the source. If there is such a cycle, the algorithm indicates that no solution exists. If there is no such cycle, the algorithm produces the shortest paths and their weights. ,

The algorithm uses relaxation, progressively decreasing an estimate d[v] on the weight of a shortest path from the source s to each vertex $v \in V$ until it achieves the actual shortest-path weight $\delta(s, v)$. The algorithm returns TRUE if and only if the graph contains no negative-weight cycles that are reachable from the source.

```
BELLMAN=FORD(G, w, s)
1.   INITIALIZE-SINGLE-SOURCE(G, s)
2.   for i ←1to| V[G]| -1
3.   do for each edge (u, v) ∈ E[G]
4..  do RELAX(u, v, w)
5.   for each edge (u, v) ∈ E[G]
6.   do if d[v] > d[u] + w(u, v)
7.   then return FALSE
8.   return TRUE
```

Figure shows the execution of the Bellman-Ford algorithm on a graph with 5 vertices. After initializing the d and π values of all vertices in line 1, the algorithm makes

| V | - 1 passes over the edges of the graph. Each pass is one iteration of the **for** loop of lines 2-4 and consists of relaxing each edge of the graph once. Figures show the state of the algorithm after each of the four passes over the edges. After making | V | -1 passes, lines 5-8 check for a negative weight cycle and return the appropriate Boolean value. (We'll see a little later why this check works.)

The Bellman-Ford algorithm runs in time O(VE), since the initialization in line I takes O(V) time, each of the I V I -1 passes over the edges in lines 2-4 takes O (E) time, and the for loop of lines 5-7 takes O(E) time.

To prove the correctness of the Bellman-Ford algorithm, we start by showing that if there are no negative-weight cycles, the algorithm computes correct shortest-path weights for all vertices reachable from the source.

Lemma

Let G = *(V, E)* be a weighted, directed graph with source s and weight function w : *E*→ R, and assume that G contains no negative-weight cycles that are reachable from s. Then, after the | V | - 1 iterations of the for loop of lines 2-4 of BELLMAN-FORD, we have *d[v]* =δ*(s, v)* for all vertices v that are reachable from s.

Proof We prove the lemma by appealing to the path-relaxation property. Consider any vertex v that is reachable from s, and let p = (v_o, v_1, ... , v_k), where v_o = s and v_k = v, be any acyclic shortest path from s to v. Path p has at most | V | - 1 edges, and so *k* ≤ | V | - 1. Each of the | **V** | - 1 iterations of the for loop of lines 2-4 relaxes all .*E* edges. Among the edges relaxed in the i th iteration, for *i* = 1, 2, ..., *k, is* (v_{i-1}, v_i). By the path-relaxation property, therefore, $d[v] = d[v_k] = \delta(s, v_k) = \delta(s, v)$.

Corollary

Let G = *(V, E)* be a weighted, directed graph with source vertex s and weight function ω: *E*→ *R*. Then for each vertex v ∈ V, there is a path from s to v if and only if BELLMAN-FORD terminates with *d[v]* <∞ when it is run on G.

Proof

Theorem (Correctness of the Bellman-Ford algorithm)

Let BELLMAN-FORD be run on a weighted, directed graph G=*(V, E) with* source s and weight function ω: *E*→*R*. If G contains no negative-weight cycles that are reachable from s, then the algorithm returns TRUE, we have *d[v]* =δ *(s, v)* for all vertices v ∈ V, and the predecessor subgraph Gπ is a shortest-paths tree rooted at s. If G does contain a negative-weight cycle reachable from s, then the algorithm returns FALSE.

Proof Suppose that graph G contains no negative-weight cycles that are reachable from the source s. We first prove the claim that at termination, *d[v]* = δ*(s, v)* for all vertices *v* ∈ V. If vertex v is reachable from s, then Lemma proves this claim. If v is not reachable from s, then the claim follows from the no-path property. Thus, the claim is proven. The predecessor-subgraph property, along with the claim, implies that G, is a shortest-paths tree. Now we use the claim to show that BELLMAN-FORD returns TRUE. At termination, we have for all edges (u, v) ∈ E,

$$\begin{aligned} d[v] &= \delta(s, v) \\ &\leq \delta(s, u) + \omega(u, v) \text{ (by the triangle inequality)} \\ &= d[u] + w(u, v), \end{aligned}$$

and so none of the tests in line 6 causes BELLMAN-FORD to return FALSE. It therefore returns TRUE.

Conversely, suppose that graph G contains a negative-weight cycle that is reachable from the source s; let this cycle be c=(v_o, v_1, ..., v_k), where $v_o = v_k$. Then,

$$\sum_{i=1}^{k} \omega(v_{i-1}, v_1) < 0$$

Assume for the purpose of contradiction that the Bellman-Ford algorithm returns TRUE. Thus, $d[v_i] \leq dfv_{i-1}] + w(v_{i-1}, v_i)$ for $i = 1, 2, ..., k$. Summing the inequalities around cycle c gives us

$$\sum_{i=1}^{k} d[vi] \leq \sum_{i=1}^{k} (d[v_{i-1}] + w(v_{i-1}, v_i)$$
$$= \sum_{i=1}^{k} d[v_{i-1}] + \sum_{i=1}^{k} w(v_{i-1}, v_i)$$

Since $V_O = vk$, each vertex in c appears exactly once in each of the summations $\Sigma^k{}_{i=1}$ $d[v_i]$ and $\Sigma^k{}_{i=1}$ $d[v_{i-1}]$, and so

$$\sum_{i=1}^{k} d[v_i] = \sum_{i=1}^{k} d[v_{i-1}]$$

Moreover, by Corollary d [vi] is finite for $i = 1, 2, ..., k$, Thus,

$$0 \leq \sum_{i=1}^{k} w(v_{i-1}, v_i)$$

which contradicts inequality. We conclude that the Bellman-Ford algorithm returns TRUE if graph G contains no ,negative-weight cycles reachable from the source, and FALSE otherwise.

2.6 SINGLE-SOURCE SHORTEST PATHS IN DIRECTED ACYCLIC GRAPHS

By relaxing the edges of a weighted dag (directed acyclic graph) G = (V, E) according to a topological sort of its vertices, we can compute shortest paths from a single source in Θ(V + E) time. Shortest paths are always well defined in a dag, since even if there are negative-weight edges, no negative-weight cycles can exist.

The algorithm starts by topologically sorting the dag to impose a linear ordering on the vertices. If there is a path from vertex u to vertex v, then u precedes v in the topological sort. We make just one pass over the vertices in the topologically sorted order. As we process each vertex, we relax each edge that leaves the vertex.

```
DAG-SHORTEST-PATHS (G, w, s)
1.    topologically sort the vertices of G
2.    INITIALIZE- SINGLE -SOURCE (G, s)
3.    for each vertex u, taken in topologically sorted order
4.    do for each vertex v∈= Adj[u]
5.    do RELAX(u, v, w)    ,
```

Figure shows the execution of this algorithm.

The running time of this algorithm is easy to analyze. As shown in Section, the topological sort of line 1 can be performed in Θ(V+ *E)* time. The call of INITIALIZE-SINGLE-SOURCE in line 2 takes Θ(V) time. There is one iteration per vertex in the **for loop** of lines 3-5. For each vertex, the edges that leave the vertex are each examined exactly once. Thus, there are a total of| E| iterations of the inner **for loop** of lines 4-5. (We have used an aggregate analysis here.) Because each iteration of the inner **for loop** takes Θ(1) time, the total running time *is*Θ(*V + E)*, which is linear in the size of an adjacency-list representation of the graph.

The following theorem shows that the DAG-SHORTEST-PATHS procedure correctly computes the shortest paths.

Theorem

If a weighted, directed graph G=(V, E) has source vertex s and no cycles, then at the termination of the DAG-SHORTEST-PATHS procedure, d[v] = δ(s, v) for all vertices v∈ *V*, and the predecessor subgraph Gπ is a shortest-paths tree.

Proof We first show that *d[v]* = δ*(s, v)* for all vertices v ∈*V* at termination. If *v* is not reachable from s, *then d[v]* =δ*(s, v)* =∞ *by* the no-path property. Now, suppose that v is reachable from s, so that there is a shortest path p=(v_o, v_1, ..., v_k), where v_o = s and v_k = v. Because we process the vertices in topologically sorted order, the edges on p are relaxed in the order (v_o, v_1}, (v_1, v_2), ...,(u_{k-1}, u_k). The path-relaxation property implies that *d[v*]-= S(s, *vi)* at termination for *i* = 0, 1, . . . , *k*. Finally, by the predecessor sub graph property, Gπ is a shortest-paths tree.

An interesting application of this algorithm arises in determining critical paths *in **PERT chart***[2] analysis. Edges represent jobs to be performed, and edge weights represent the times required to perform particular jobs. If edge (u, v) enters vertex v and edge (v, x) leaves v, then job (u, v) must be performed prior to job (v, x). A path through this dag represents a sequence of jobs that must be performed in a particular order. *A **critical path*** is *a longest* path through the dag, corresponding to the longest time to perform an ordered sequence of jobs. The weight of a critical path is a lower bound on the total time to perform all the jobs. We can find a critical path by either negating the edge weights and running DAG-SHORTEST-PATHS, or running DAG-SHORTEST-PATHS, with the modification that we replace "∞" by "-∞" in line 2 of INITIALIZE-SINGLE-SOURCE and ">" by "<" in the RELAX procedure.

RIVIEW QUESTIONS

1. What are the variants of shortest path problems.
2. What is the optimal substructure of a shortest path?
3. Prove: Given a weighted, directed graph G = *(V, E)* with weight function $w : E \to R$, let p = (v_1, v_2, ... , v_k) be a shortest path from vertex v_1, to vertex v_k and, for any i and j such that $1 \le i \le j \le k$, let p_{ij} = *(vi, v,+,, ..., v_j)* be the subpath of *p* from vertex v_i to vertex v_j. Then, *p,j is* a shortest path from v_i to v_j.
4. Explain how shortest paths are represented.
5. Elaborate all the Properties *of* shortest paths and relaxation.
6. Explain and prove Bellman-Ford algorithm.
7. Explain Single-source shortest paths in directed acyclic graphs.

CHAPTER

3

UNIT 4

ALL-PAIRS SHORTEST PATHS

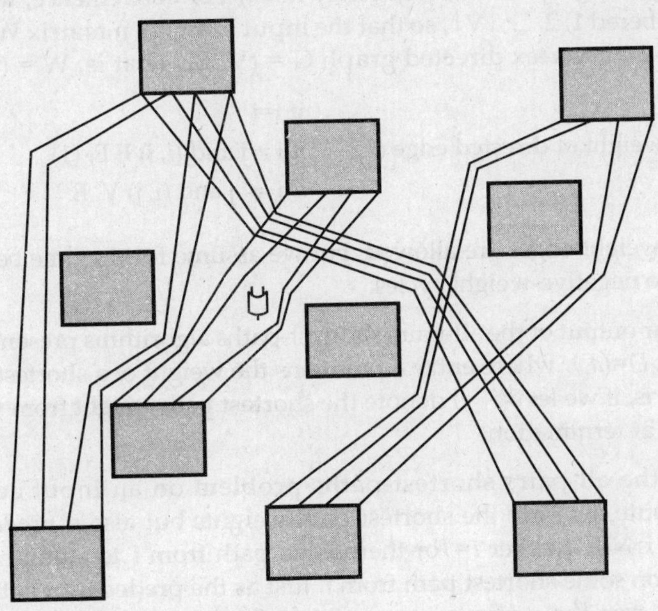

3.1 INTRODUCTION

The theme of this chapter is centered on the problem of finding shortest paths between all pairs of vertices in a graph. This kind of problem might arise in making a table of distances between all pairs of cities for a road atlas. We are given a weighted, directed graph G = (V, *E)* with a weight function V : E → R that maps edges to real-valued weights. We wish to find, for every pair of vertices u, v ∈ V, a shortest (least-weight) path from u to v, where the weight of a path is the sum of the weights of its constituent edges. We typically want the output in tabular form: the entry in u's row and v's column should be the weight of a shortest path from u to v.

Generally we solve an all-pairs shortest-paths problem by running a single-source shortest-paths algorithm | V | times, once for each vertex as the source. If all edge weights are nonnegative, we can use Dijkstra's algorithm. If we use the linear-array implementation of the min-priority queue, the running time is $O(V^3 + V E) = O - (V^3)$. The binary min-heap implementation of the min-priority queue yields a running time of O $(V E \lg V)$, which is an improvement if the graph is sparse. Alternatively, we can implement the min-priority queue with a Fibonacci heap, yielding a running time of O $(V^2 \lg V + VE)$.

If negative-weight edges are allowed, Dijkstra's algorithm can no longer be used. Instead, we must run the slower Bellman-Ford algorithm once from each vertex. The resulting running time is $O(V^2E)$, which on a dense graph is $O(V^4)$. In the following topics we shall see how to do better. We shall also investigate the relation of the all-pairs shortest-paths problem to matrix multiplication and study its algebraic structure the single-source algorithms, which assume an adjacency-list representation of the graph, most of the algorithms in this chapter use an adjacency-matrix representation. (Johnson's algorithm for sparse graphs uses adjacency lists.) For convenience, we assume that the vertices are numbered 1, 2, ... , $|V|$, so that the input is an n x n matrix W representing the edge weights of an n-vertex directed graph G = (V, E). That is, $W = (w_{ij})$, where

$$w_{ij} = \begin{cases} 0 & \text{if } i=j \\ \text{the weight of directed edge } (i,j) & \text{if } i \neq j \text{ and } (i, j) \text{ E E}, \ (1) \\ \infty & \text{if } i \neq j \text{ and } (i, j) \text{ V E} \end{cases}$$

Negative-weight edges are allowed, but we assume for the time being that the input graph contains no negative-weight cycles.

The tabular output of the all-pairs shortest-paths algorithms presented in this chapter is an $n \times n$ matrix $D=(d_{ij})$, where entry d_{ij} contains the weight of a shortest path from vertex i to vertex j. That is, if we let $\delta(i, j)$ denote the shortest path weight from vertex i to vertex j, then $d_{ij} = \delta(i, j)$ at termination.

To solve the all-pairs shortest-paths problem on an input adjacency matrix, we need to compute not only the shortest-path weights but also ***a predecessor matrix*** $\Pi = (\pi_{ij})$, where $n_{,j}$ is NIL if either $i=j$ or there is no path from i to j, and otherwise π_{ij} is the predecessor of j on some shortest path from i. Just as the predecessor subgraph G_n from is a shortest-paths tree for a given source vertex, the subgraph induced by the i th row of the Π matrix should be a shortest-paths tree with root i. For each vertex $i \in V$, we define the ***predecessor subgraph*** of G for i as $G_{\pi,i} = (V_{\pi,i}, E_{\pi,i})$, where

$$V_{\pi,i} = \{ j \in V : \pi_{ij} \neq \text{NIL}) \cup \{i\}$$

and

$$E_{\pi,i} = \{(\pi_{ij}, J) : J \in V_{\pi,i} - \{i\}\}$$

If $G_{\pi,i}$ is a shortest-paths tree, then the following procedure, which is a modified version of the PRINT-PATH procedure, prints a shortest path from vertex i to vertex j.

PRINT-ALL-PAIRS-SHORTEST-PATH(Π, i, j)

```
if i = j
then print i
else if π_ij = NIL
then print "no path from" i "to" j "exists".
else PRINT-ALL-PAIRS-SHORTEST-PATH(Π, iπ_ij )
print j
```

In order to highlight the essential features of the all-pairs algorithms in this chapter, we won't cover the creation and properties of predecessor matrices as extensively as we dealt with predecessor subgraphs . The basics are covered by some of the exercises.

Shortest Paths and Matrix Multiplication

This section presents a dynamic-programming algorithm for the all-pairs shortestpaths problem on a directed graph G = (V, *E*). Each major loop of the dynamic program will invoke an operation that is very similar to matrix multiplication, so that the algorithm will look like repeated matrix multiplication. We shall start by developing a$\Theta(V^4)$-time algorithm for the all-pairs shortest-paths problem and then improve its running time to $\Theta(V^3 \lg V)$.

Before proceeding, let us briefly recap the steps given for developing a dynamic-programming algorithm.

1. Characterize the structure of an optimal solution.
2. Recursively define the value of an optimal solution.
3. Compute the value of an optimal solution in a bottom-up fashion.

(The fourth step, constructing an optimal solution from computed information, is dealt with in the exercises.)

The structure of a shortest path

We start by characterizing the structure of an optimal solution. For the all-pairs shortest-paths problem on a graph G=(V, E), we have proven that all subpaths of a shortest path are shortest paths. Suppose that the graph is represented by an adjacency matrix $W=(w_{ij})$. Consider a shortest path p from vertex i to vertex j, and suppose that p contains at most m edges. Assuming that there are no negative-weight cycles, m is finite. If i = j, then p has weight 0 and no edges. If vertices i and j are distinct, then we decompose path p into i~k→j, where path p' now contains at most m – 1 edges. By p' is a shortest path from i to k, and so $\delta(i, j) = \delta(i, k) + w_{kj}$.

A recursive solution to the all-pairs shortest-paths problem

Now, let l_{ij} be the minimum weight of any path from vertex i to vertex j that contains at most m edges. When m = 0, there is a shortest path from i to j with no edges if and only if i = j. Thus,

$$l^{(m)}_{ij} = \begin{cases} 0 & \text{if } i = j, \\ \infty & \text{if } i \neq j \end{cases}$$

For $m \geq 1$, we compute $l^{(m)}_{ij}$ as the minimum of $l^{(m-1)}_{ij}$ (the weight of the shortest path from i to j consisting of at most m–1 edges) and the minimum weight of any path from i to j consisting of at most m edges, obtained by looking at all possible predecessors k of j. Thus, we recursively define

$$1^{(m)}_{ij} = \min(1^{(m+1)}_{ij}, \min_{1\le k\le n}\{1^{(m-1)}_{kj} + \omega_{kj}\})$$
$$= \min_{1\le k\le n}\{1^{(m-1)}_{kj} + \omega_{kj}\})$$

The latter equality, follows since $w_{ij} = 0$ for all j.

What are the actual shortest-path weights δ(i, j)? If the graph contains no negative-weight cycles, then for every pair of vertices i and j for which δ(i, j) < ∞, there is a shortest path from i to j that is simple and thus contains at most n – 1 edges. A path from vertex i to vertex j with more than n – 1 edges cannot have lower weight than a shortest path from i to j. The actual shortest-path weights are therefore given by

$$\delta(i, j) = 1^{(n-1)}_{ij} = 1^{(n)}_{ij} = 1^{(n-1)}_{ij} = \dots \dots \qquad (3)$$

Computing the shortest-path weights bottom up

Taking as our input the matrix $W=(\omega_{ij})$, we now compute a series of matrices $L^{(1)}$, $L^{(2)}$, ..., $L^{(n-1)}$, where for m= 1, 2, ..., n-- 1, we have $L^{(m)} = 1^{(n)}_{ij}$

The final matrix $L^{(n-1)}$ contains the actual shortest-path weights. Observe that $1^{(n)}_{ij} = w_{ij}$ for all vertices $i, j \in V$, and so $L^{(1)} = W$.

The heart of the algorithm is the following procedure, which, given matrices $L^{(m-1)}$ and W, returns the matrix $L^{(m)}$. That is, it extends the shortest paths computed so far by one more edge.

```
EXTEND-SHORTEST-PATHS (L, W )
n ← rows[L]
let L′ = l_ij be an n x n matrix
for i = 1 to n
do for j ← 1 to n
do l_ij ← ∞
for k ← 1 to n
do l_ij ← min(l_ij , l_kj + w_kj)
return L′
```

The procedure computes a matrix $L' = (1'_{ij})$, which it returns at the end. It does so by computing equation (.2) for all i and j, using L for $L^{(m-1)}$ and L' for $L^{(m)}$.

(It is written without the superscripts to make its input and output matrices independent of m.) Its running time is Θ(n^3) due to the three nested **for loops.**

Now we can see the relation to matrix multiplication. Suppose we wish to compute the matrix product C = A. B of two n x n matrices A and B. Then, for i, j=1, 2, ..., n, we compute

$$c_{ij} \sum_{k=1}^{n} a_i k \bullet b_{kj} \qquad (4)$$

Observe that if we make the substitutions

$l^{(m-1)} \rightarrow a,$

$w \rightarrow b,$

$l^{(m)} \rightarrow c,$

$\min \rightarrow +,$

$+ \rightarrow \cdot$

in equation (.2), we obtain equation (.4). Thus, if we make these changes to EXTEND-SHORTEST-PATHS and also replace ∞ (the identity for min) by 0(the identity for +), we obtain the straightforward $\Theta(n^3)$ -time procedure for matrix multiplication:

MATRIX-MULTIPLY(A, B)

```
n ← rows[A]
let C be an n x n matrix
for i ←1 to n
do for j ← 1 to n
do c_ij ← 0
for k ← 1 to n
do c_ij ← c_ij + ai_k • b_kj
return C
```

Returning to the all-pairs shortest-paths problem, we compute the shortest-path weights by extending shortest paths edge by edge. Letting $A \bullet B$ denote the matrix "product" returned by EXTEND-SHORTEST-PATHS (A, B), we compute the sequence of $n - 1$ matrices

$$L^{(1)} = L^{(0)} \bullet W = W$$
$$L^{(2)} = L^{(1)} \bullet W = W2$$
$$L^{(3)} = L^{(2)} \bullet W = W3$$
$$L^{(n-1)} = L^{(n-2)} , W = W^{n-1} .$$

As we argued above, the matrix $L^{(n-1)} = W^{n-1}$ contains the shortest-path weights. The following procedure computes this sequence in $\Theta(n^4)$ time.

SLOW-ALL-PAIRS-SHORTEST-PATHS (W)

```
n ← rows[W]
L(i) ← W
for m ← 2 to n-1
do L(m) ←EXTEND -SHORTEST-PATHS(L(in-1), W)
return L(n-1)
```

Figure shows a graph and the matrices $L^{(m)}$ computed by the procedure SLOW-ALL-PAIRS-SHORTEST-PATHS.

3.2 IMPROVING THE RUNNING TIME

Our goal, however, is not to compute *all* the $L^{(m)}$ matrices: we are interested only in matrix $L^{(n-1)}$. Recall that in the absence of negative-weight cycles, equation (.3) implies $L^{(m)} = L^{(n-1)}$ for all integers $m \geq n - 1$. Just as traditional matrix multiplication is associative, so is matrix multiplication defined by the EXTEND-SHORTEST-PATHS procedure . Therefore, we can compute $L^{(n-1)}$ with only [lg(n – 1)1 matrix products by computing the sequence

$$L^{(1)} = \begin{vmatrix} 0 & 3 & 8 & \infty & -4 \\ \infty & 0 & \infty & 1 & 7 \\ \infty & 4 & 0 & \infty & \infty \\ 2 & \infty & -5 & 0 & \infty \\ \infty & \infty & \infty & 6 & \infty \end{vmatrix}$$

$$L^{(2)} = \begin{vmatrix} 0 & 3 & 8 & 2 & -4 \\ 3 & 0 & -4 & 1 & 7 \\ \infty & 4 & 0 & 5 & 11 \\ 2 & -1 & -5 & 0 & -2 \\ 8 & \infty & 1 & 6 & 0 \end{vmatrix}$$

$$L^{(3)} = \begin{vmatrix} 0 & 3 & -3 & 2 & -4 \\ 3 & 0 & -4 & 1 & -1 \\ 7 & 4 & 0 & 5 & 11 \\ 2 & -1 & -5 & 0 & -2 \\ 8 & 5 & 1 & 6 & 0 \end{vmatrix}$$

$$L^{(4)} = \begin{vmatrix} 0 & 1 & -3 & 2 & -4 \\ 3 & 0 & -4 & 1 & -1 \\ 7 & 4 & 0 & 5 & 3 \\ 2 & -1 & -5 & 0 & -2 \\ 8 & 5 & 1 & 6 & 0 \end{vmatrix}$$

$L^{(1)} = W,$

$L^{(2)} = W^2 = W.W,$

$L^{(4)} = w^4 = w2.\ _{W}2$

$L^{(8)} = W^8 = W^4 \cdot W^4,$

$\mathbf{L}^{(2\lceil \lg(n-1) \rceil)} = \mathbf{W}^{(2\lceil \lg(n-1) \rceil)} = \mathbf{W}^{(2\lceil \lg(n-1) \rceil)-1} . \mathbf{W}^{(2\lceil \lg(n-1) \rceil)-1}$

Since $2^{(\lceil \lg(n-1) \rceil)} \geq \mathbf{n} - 1$, the final product $\mathbf{L}^{(2\lceil \lg(n-1) \rceil)}$ is equal to $L^{(n-1)}$.

The following procedure computes the above sequence of matrices by using this technique of ***repeated squaring.***

FASTER-ALL -PAIRS -S HORTEST-PATHS (W)

```
n ← rows[W]
L(1) ← W
m ← 1
while m< n- 1
```

```
5    do L^(2m) ← EXTEND-SHORTEST-PATHS (L^(m), L^(m))
6    m ← 2m
7    return L^(m)
```

In each iteration of the **while** loop of lines 4-6, we compute $L^{(2m)} = (L^{(m)})^2$ starting with $m = 1$. At the end of each iteration, we double the value of m. The final iteration computes $L^{(n-1)}$ by actually computing $L^{(2m)}$ for some $n - 1 \le 2m < 2n - 2$. By equation (.3), $L^{(2m)} = L^{(n-1)}$. The next time the test in line 4 is performed, m has been doubled, so now $m \ge n - 1$, the test fails, and the procedure returns the last matrix it computed.

The running time of FASTER-ALL-PAIRS-SHORTEST-PATHS is $\Theta(n^3 \lg n)$ since each of the $\lceil \lg(n-1) \rceil$ matrix products takes $\Theta(n^3)$ time. Observe that the code is tight, containing no elaborate data structures, and the constant hidden in the Θ-notation is therefore small.

3.3 FLOYD-WARSHALL ALGORITHM

In this section, we shall use a different dynamic-programming formulation to solve the all-pairs shortest-paths problem on a directed graph $G = (V, E)$. The resulting algorithm, known as the ***Floyd-Warshall algorithm***, runs in $\Theta(V^3)$ time. As before, negative-weight edges may be present, but we assume that there are no negative-weight cycles. As in Section .1, we shall follow the dynamic programming process to develop the algorithm. After studying the resulting algorithm, we shall present a similar method for finding the transitive closure of a directed graph.

The structure of a shortest path

In the Floyd-Warshall algorithm, we use a different characterization of the structure of a shortest path than we used in the matrix-multiplication-based all-pairs algorithms. The algorithm considers the "intermediate" vertices of a shortest path, where an ***intermediate*** vertex of a simple path $p = (v_1, v_2, \ldots, v_l)$ is any vertex of p other than v_1 or v_l, that is, any vertex in the set $\{v_2, v_3, \ldots, v_{l-1}\}$.

The Floyd-Warshall algorithm is based on the following observation. Under our assumption that the vertices of G are $V = \{1, 2, \ldots, n\}$, let us consider a subset $\{1, 2, \ldots, k\}$ of vertices for some k. For any pair of vertices $i, j \in V$, consider all paths from i to j whose intermediate vertices are all drawn from $\{1, 2, \ldots, k\}$, and let p be a minimum-weight path from among them. (Path p is simple.) The FloydWarshall algorithm exploits a relationship between path p and shortest paths from i to j with all intermediate vertices in the set $\{1, 2, \ldots, k - 1\}$. The relationship depends on whether or not k is an intermediate vertex of path p.

- If k is not an intermediate vertex of path p, then all intermediate vertices of path p are in the set $\{1, 2, \ldots, k - 1\}$. Thus, a shortest path from vertex i to vertex j with all intermediate vertices in the set $\{1, 2, \ldots, k - 1\}$ is also a shortest path from i to j with all intermediate vertices in the set $\{1, 2, \ldots, k\}$.
- If k is an intermediate vertex of path p, then we break p down into $i \sim k \sim j$ as shown in Figure . By Lemma .1, p_1 is a shortest path from i to k with

all intermediate vertices in the set {1, 2, .. . , k}. Because vertex k is not an intermediate vertex of path p_1, we see that p, is a shortest path from i to k with all intermediate vertices in the set {1, 2, ..., k - 1}. Similarly, p_2 is a shortest path from vertex k to vertex j with all intermtdiate vertices in the set {1,2,...,k-1}.

A recursive solution to the all-pairs shortest-paths problem

Based on the above observations, we define a recursive formulation of shortest-path estimates that is different from the one in Section .1. Let d_{ij} be the weight of a shortest path from vertex i to vertex j for which all intermediate vertices are in the set { 1, 2, ..., k}. When $k = 0$, a path from vertex i to vertex j with no intermediate vertex numbered higher than 0 has no intermediate vertices at all. Such a path has at most one edge, and hence $d_{ij}^{(0)} = w_{ij}$. A recursive definition following the above discussion is given by

$$d_{ij}^{(k)} = \begin{cases} w_{ij} & \text{if } k = 0 \\ \min(d_{ij}^{(k-1)} d_{ij}^{(k-1} + d_{kj}^{(k-1)} & \text{if } k \geq 1 \end{cases}$$

Because for any path, all intermediate vertices are in the set {1, 2, . . . , n}, the matrix $D^{(n)} = (d_{ij}^{(n)})$ gives the. final answer: $d_{ij}^{(n)} = \delta(i, j)$ for all $i, j \in V$.

Computing the shortest-path weights bottom up

Based on recurrence (.5), the following bottom-up procedure can be used to compute the values $d_{ij}^{(k)}$ in order of increasing values of k. Its input is an $n \times n$ matrix W defined as in equation (.1). The procedure returns the matrix $D^{(n)}$ of shortest-path weights.

```
FLOYD-WARSHALL(W)
1.   n ← rows[W]
2.   D(0) ← W
3.   for k ← 1 to n
4.   for i ← 1 to n
5.   do for j ← 1 to n
6.   do dij(k) ← min (dij(k-1), dik(k-1) + dik(k-1))
7.   return D(n)
```

The running time of the Floyd-Warshll algorithm is determined by the triply nested for loops of lines 3–6. because each execution of line 6 takes o(1) time, the algorithm of time $\Theta(n^3)$. As in the final algorithm the code is tight, with no elaborate data structures, and so the constant hidden in the 0-notation is small. Thus, the Floyd-Warshall algorithm is quite practical for even moderate-sized input graphs.

$$D^{(0)} = \begin{vmatrix} 0 & 3 & 8 & \infty & -4 \\ \infty & 0 & \infty & 1 & 7 \\ \infty & 4 & 0 & \infty & \infty \\ 2 & \infty & -5 & 0 & \infty \\ \infty & \infty & \infty & 6 & 0 \end{vmatrix} \qquad \Pi^{(0)} = \begin{vmatrix} \text{NIL} & 1 & 1 & \text{NIL} & 1 \\ \text{NIL} & \text{NIL} & \text{NIL} & 2 & 2 \\ \text{NIL} & 3 & \text{NIL} & \text{NIL} & \text{NIL} \\ 4 & \text{NIL} & 4 & \text{NIL} & \text{NIL} \\ \text{NIL} & \text{NIL} & \text{NIL} & 5 & \text{NIL} \end{vmatrix}$$

$$D^{(1)} = \begin{vmatrix} 0 & 3 & 8 & \infty & -4 \\ \infty & 0 & \infty & 1 & 7 \\ \infty & 4 & 0 & \infty & \infty \\ 2 & \infty & -5 & 0 & -2 \\ \infty & \infty & \infty & 6 & 0 \end{vmatrix} \qquad \Pi^{(0)} = \begin{vmatrix} \text{NIL} & 1 & 1 & \text{NIL} & 1 \\ \text{NIL} & \text{NIL} & \text{NIL} & 2 & 2 \\ \text{NIL} & 3 & \text{NIL} & \text{NIL} & \text{NIL} \\ 4 & 1 & 4 & \text{NIL} & 1 \\ \text{NIL} & \text{NIL} & \text{NIL} & 5 & \text{NIL} \end{vmatrix}$$

$$D^{(2)} = \begin{vmatrix} 0 & 3 & 8 & 4 & -4 \\ \infty & 0 & \infty & 1 & 7 \\ \infty & 4 & 0 & 5 & -2 \\ 2 & 5 & -5 & 0 & -2 \\ \infty & \infty & \infty & 6 & 0 \end{vmatrix} \qquad \Pi^{(0)} = \begin{vmatrix} \text{NIL} & 1 & 1 & 2 & 1 \\ \text{NIL} & \text{NIL} & \text{NIL} & 2 & 2 \\ \text{NIL} & 3 & \text{NIL} & 2 & 2 \\ 4 & 1 & 4 & \text{NIL} & 1 \\ \text{NIL} & \text{NIL} & \text{NIL} & 5 & \text{NIL} \end{vmatrix}$$

$$D^{(3)} = \begin{vmatrix} 0 & 3 & 8 & 4 & -4 \\ \infty & 0 & \infty & 1 & 7 \\ \infty & 4 & 0 & 5 & 11 \\ 2 & -1 & -5 & 0 & -2 \\ \infty & \infty & \infty & 6 & 0 \end{vmatrix} \qquad \Pi^{(3)} = \begin{vmatrix} \text{NIL} & 1 & 1 & 2 & 1 \\ \text{NIL} & \text{NIL} & \text{NIL} & 2 & 2 \\ \text{NIL} & 3 & \text{NIL} & 2 & 2 \\ 4 & 3 & 4 & \text{NIL} & 1 \\ \text{NIL} & \text{NIL} & \text{NIL} & 5 & \text{NIL} \end{vmatrix}$$

$$D^{(4)} = \begin{vmatrix} 0 & 3 & -1 & 4 & -4 \\ 3 & 0 & -4 & 1 & -1 \\ 7 & 44 & 0 & 5 & 3 \\ 2 & -1 & -5 & 0 & -2 \\ 8 & 5 & 1 & 6 & 0 \end{vmatrix} \qquad \Pi^{(4)} = \begin{vmatrix} \text{NIL} & 1 & 4 & 2 & 1 \\ 4 & \text{NIL} & 4 & 2 & 1 \\ 4 & 3 & \text{NIL} & 2 & 1 \\ 4 & 3 & 4 & \text{NIL} & 1 \\ 4 & 3 & 4 & 5 & \text{NIL} \end{vmatrix}$$

$$D^{(5)} = \begin{vmatrix} 0 & 1 & -3 & 2 & -4 \\ 3 & 0 & -4 & 1 & -1 \\ 7 & 4 & 0 & 5 & 3 \\ 2 & -1 & -5 & 0 & -2 \\ 8 & 5 & 1 & 6 & 0 \end{vmatrix} \qquad \Pi^{(4)} = \begin{vmatrix} \text{NIL} & 3 & 4 & 5 & 1 \\ 4 & \text{NIL} & 4 & 2 & 1 \\ 4 & 3 & \text{NIL} & 2 & 1 \\ 4 & 3 & 4 & \text{NIL} & 1 \\ 4 & 3 & 4 & 5 & \text{NIL} \end{vmatrix}$$

Constructing a shortest path

There are a variety *of* different methods for constructing shortest paths in the FloydWarshall algorithm. One way is to compute the matrix D *of* shortest-path weights and then construct the predecessor matrix II from the *D* matrix. This method can be implemented to run in $O(n^3)$ time . Given the predecessor matrix Π, the PRINT-ALL-PAIRS-SHORTEST-PATH procedure can be used to print the vertices on a given shortest path.

We can compute the predecessor matrix Π "on-line" just as the Floyd-Warshall algorithm computes the matrices $D^{(k)}$. Specifically, we compute a sequence *of* matrices $\Pi^{(o)}$, $\Pi^{(1)}$, ..., $\Pi^{(n)}$, where $\Pi = \Pi^{(n)}$ and $\pi_{ij}^{(k)}$ is defined to be the predecessor *of* vertex *j* on a shortest path from vertex i with all intermediate vertices in the set {1, 2,..., *k*}.

We can give a recursive formulation *of* $\pi_{ij}^{(k)}$. When *k = 0*, a shortest path from *i* to *j* has no intermediate vertices at all. Thus,

$$\pi_{IJ}^{(K)} = \begin{cases} \text{NIL if } i=j \text{ or } w_{ij} = \infty \\ i \ \text{ if } i \neq j \text{ and } w_{ij} < \infty \end{cases} \tag{6}$$

For $k \geq 1$, *if* we take the path *i ~ k~ j*, where $k \neq j$, then the predecessor of *j* we choose is the same as the predecessor *of j* we chose on a shortest path from *k* with all intermediate vertices in the set {1, 2, ... , *k* – 1}. Otherwise, we choose the same predecessor *of j* that we chose on a shortest path from i with all intermediate vertices in the set (1, 2, . . . , k - 1}. Formally, for $k \geq 1$,

$$\pi_{IJ}^{(K)} = \begin{cases} \pi_{ij}^{(k-1)} \ \text{ of } d_{ij}^{(k-1)} \leq d_{ij}^{(k-1)} + d_{kj}(k-1) \\ \pi_{kj}^{(k-1)} \ \text{ if } d_{ij}^{(k-1)} > d_{ij}^{(k-1)} + d_{kj}^{(k-1)} \end{cases}$$

We leave the incorporation *of* the $\Pi^{(k)}$ matrix computations into the FLOYD-WARSHALL procedure as shows the sequence of $\Pi^{(k)}$ matrices that the resulting algorithm computes for *the graph of Figure . The exercise also asks for the more difficult task *of* proving that the predecessor subgraph $G_{\pi,j}$ is a shortest-paths tree with root *i*.

Transitive closure of a directed graph

Given a directed graph G = *(V, E)* with vertex set V=*{1, 2, ... , n}*, we may wish to find out whether there is a path in G from *i* to *j* for all vertex pairs i, $j \in V$. The ***transitive closure of*** G is defined as the graph G* =*(V, E*)*, where

E*={(i , j) : there is a path from vertex *i* to vertex *j* in G}.

One way to compute the transitive closure of a graph in $O(n^3)$ time is to assign a weight of 1 to each edge of *E* and run the Floyd-Warshall algorithm. If there is a path from vertex *i* to vertex *j*, we get $d_{ij} < n$. Otherwise, we get $dij = \infty$There is another, similar way to compute the transitive closure of *G* in $\Theta(n^3)$ time that can save time and space in practice. This method involves substitution of the logical operations $\vee$ (logical OR) and $\wedge$ (logical AND) for the arithmetic operations min and + in the Floyd-Warshall algorithm. For i, *j*, *k* = *1*, *2*, ..., n, we define $t_{ij}^{(k)}$ to be 1 if there exists a path in graph G from vertex i to vertex *j* with all intermediate vertices in the set {1, 2, ..., ***k***}, and 0 otherwise. We construct the transitive closure *G*_(V , E*)* by putting edge *(i, j)* into *E** if and only if $t_{ij}^{(n)} = 1$. A recursive definition of $t_{ij}^{(k)}$, analogous t to recurrene is,

$$t_{ij}^{(o)} = \begin{cases} 0 \text{ if } \neq j \text{ and } (i,j) \notin E \\ 1 \text{ if } = j \text{ and } (i,j) \in E \end{cases}$$

and for $k \geq 1$

$$t_{ij}^{(k)} = t_{ij}^{(k-1)} \vee (t_{ik}^{(k)} \wedge t_{kj}^{(k)})$$

As in the Floyd-Warshall algorithm, we compute the matrices $T(k) = t_{ij}^{(k)}$ in order of increasing k.

```
TRANSITIVE-CLOSURE (G)
n ← |V [G]|
for i ← 1 to n
do for j ← 1 to n
do if i = j or (i, j) ∈ E[G]
then t_ij^(0) ← 1
else t_ij^(k) ← 0
for k ← 1 to n
do for i ← 1 to n
do for j ← 1 to n
do t_ij^(k) ← t_ij^(k-1) ∨ (t_ik^(k) ∧ t_kj^(k))
return T^(n)
```

The matrices $T^{(k)}$ computed by the TRANSITIVE-CLOSURE procedure on a sample graph. The TRANSITIVE-CLOSURE procedure, like the FloydWarshall algorithm, runs in $8(n^3)$ time. On some computers, though, logical operations on single-bit values execute faster than arithmetic operations on integer words of data. Moreover, because the direct transitive-closure atgorithm uses only boolean values rather than integer values, its space requirement is less than the Floyd-Warshall algorithm's by a factor corresponding to the size of a word of computer storage.

REVIEW QUESTIONS

1. What are the methods of finding shortest paths between all pairs of vertices in a graph?
2. Explain the all-pairs-shortest-path algorithm in detail
3. How shortest path and shortest paths and matrix multiplication are related.
4. Explain recursive solution to the all-pairs shortest-paths problem.
5. How the running time can be improved using shortest path algorithm.
6. Explain the working and usage of Floyd-Warshall algorithm in details.
7. What are the variants of shortest path problems?
8. What is the optimal substructure of a shortest path?

CHAPTER 4

DIJKSTRA'S ALGORITHM

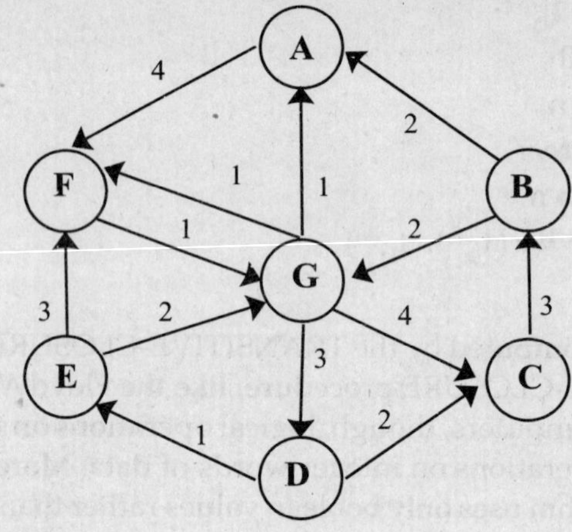

4.1 INTRODUCTION

Dijkstra's algorithm solves the single-source shortest-paths problem on a weighted, directed graph G = *(V, E)* for the case in which all edge weights are nonnegative. In this section, therefore, we assume that ω(u, v) ≥ 0 for each edge (u, v) E *E. As* we shall see, with a good implementation, the running time of Dijkstra's algorithm is lower than that of the Bellman-Ford algorithm.

Dijkstra's algorithm maintains a set S of vertices whose final shortest-path weights from the source s have already been determined. The algorithm repeatedly selects the vertex u ∈ *V* - S with the minimum shortest-path estimate, adds *u* to S, and relaxes all edges leaving u. In the following implementation, we use a min-priority queue Q of vertices, keyed by their d values.

```
DIJKSTRA(G, w, s)
INITIALIZE-SINGLE-SOURCE(G, s)
S ←θ
Q ← V [G]
    while Q ≠ 0
    do u← EXTRACT-MIN(Q)
    S←SU {u}
for each vertex v E Adj[u]
do RELAX(u, v, ω)
```

Dijkstra's algorithm relaxes edges as shown in Figure. Line 1 performs the usual initialization of d and π values, and line 2 initializes the set S to the empty set. The algorithm maintains the invariant that Q = V - S at the start of each iteration of the **while** loop of lines 4-8. Line 3 initializes the min-priority queue Q to contain all the vertices in V; since S = θ at that time, the invariant is true after line 3. Each time through the **while** loop of lines 4-8, a vertex u is extracted from Q = V - S and added to set S, thereby maintaining the invariant. (The first time through this loop, u = s.) Vertex u, therefore, has the smallest shortest-path estimate of any vertex in V - S. Then, lines 7-8 relax each edge (u, v) leaving u, thus updating the estimate $d[v]$ and the predecessor π[v] if the shortest path to v can be improved by going through u. Observe that vertices are never inserted into Q after line 3 and that each vertex is extracted from Q and added to S exactly once, so that the **while** loop of lines 4-8 iterates exactly |V| times.

Because Dijkstra's algorithm always chooses the "lightest" or "closest" vertex in V-S to add to set S, we say that it uses a greedy strategy. Greedy strategies are presented in detail, but you need not have read that chapter to understand Dijkstra's algorithm. Greedy strategies do not always yield optimal results in general, but as the following theorem and its corollary show, Dijkstra's ' algorithm does indeed compute shortest paths. The key is to show that each time a vertex u is added to set S, we have $d[u] = \delta(s, u)$.

4.2 THEOREM (CORRECTNESS OF DI1KSTRA'S ALGORITHM)

Dijkstra's algorithm, run on a weighted, directed graph G = (V, E) with non-negative weight function w and source s, terminates with $d[u] = \delta(s, u)$ for all vertices u ∈ V.

Proof We use the following loop invariant:

At the start of each iteration of the while loop of lines 4-8, $d[v] = \delta(s, v)$ for each vertex v ∈ S.

It suffices to show for each vertex u ∈ V, we have $d[u] = \delta(s, u)$ at the time when u is added to set S. Once we show that $d[u] = \delta(s, u)$, we rely on the upper-bound property to show that the equality holds at all times thereafter.

Initialization: Initially, S = θ, and so the invariant is trivially true.

Maintenance: We wish to show that in each iteration, $d[u] = \delta(s, u)$ for the vertex added to set S. For the purpose of contradiction, let u be the first vertex for which $d[u] \neq \delta(s, u)$ when it is added to set S. We shall focus our attention on the situation at the beginning of the iteration of the **while** loop in which u is added to S and derive the contradiction that $d[u] = \delta(s, u)$ at that time by examining a shortest path from s to u. We must have $u \neq$ s because s is the first vertex added to set S and $d[s] = \delta(s, s) = 0$ at that time. Because $u \neq s$, .we also have that $S \neq \theta$ just before u is added to S. There must be some path from s to u, for otherwise $d[u] = \delta(s, u) = \infty$ by the no-path property, which would violate our assumption that $d[u] \neq S(s, u)$. Because there is at least one path, there is a shortest path p from s to u. Prior to adding u to S, path p connects a vertex in S, namely s, to a vertex in V- S, namely u. Let us consider the first vertex y along p such that y ∈ V- S, and let x ∈ S be y's predecessor. Thus, path p can be decomposed as s~ x~ y~. u. (Either of paths p_1 or p_2 may have no edges.). We claim that $d[y] = \delta(s, y)$ when u is added to S. To prove this claim. observe that x ∈ S.

Then, because u is chosen as the first vertex for which $d[u] \neq \delta(s, u)$ when it is added to S, we had $d[x] = \delta(s, x)$ when x was added to S. Edge (x, y) was relaxed at that time, so the claim follows from the convergence property.

We can now obtain a contradiction to prove that $d[u] = \delta(s, u)$. Because y occurs before u on a shortest path from s to u and all edge weights are non–negative (notably those on path p_2), we have $S(s, y) \leq S(s, u)$, and thus

$d[Y] = \delta(s. Y)$

$\leq$ **S(s, u)**

$\leq$ **d[u]** (by the upper-bound property) .

But because both vertices u and y were in V –S when u was chosen in line 5, we have $d[u] \leq d[y]$. Thus, the two inequalities are in fact equalities, giving

$$d[y] = \delta(s, y) = \delta(s, u) = d[u] .$$

Consequently, $d[u] = \delta(s, u)$, which contradicts our choice of u. We conclude that $d[u] = \delta(s, u)$ when u is added to S, and that this equality is maintained at all times thereafter.

Termination: At termination, Q = θ which, along with our earlier invariant that $Q = V$- S, implies that S= V. Thus, $d[u] = \delta(s, u)$ for all vertices $u \in V$.

4.3 COROLLARY

If we run Dijkstra's algorithm on a weighted, directed graph G = $(V,$ E) with non–negative weight function w and source s, then at termination, the predecessor sub graph G_π is a shortest-paths tree rooted at s.

Proof Immediate from Theorem and the predecessor-sub graph property.

Analysis

How fast is Dijkstra's algorithm? It maintains the min-priority queue Q by calling three priority-queue operations: INSERT (implicit in line 3), EXTRACT-MIN (line 5), and DECREASE-KEY (implicit in RELAX, which is called in line 8). INSERT is invoked once per vertex, as is EXTRACT-MIN. Because each vertex $v \in V$, is added to set S exactly once, each edge in the adjacency list *Adj[U]* is examined in the for loop of lines 7-8 exactly once during the course of the algorithm. Since the total number of edges in all the adjacency lists is $|E|$, there are a total of $|E|$ iterations of this for loop, and thus a total of at most $|E|$ DECREASE-KEY operations. (Observe once again that we are using aggregate analysis.)

The running time of Dijkstra's algorithm depends on how the min-priority queue is implemented. Consider first the case in which we maintain the min-priority queue by taking advantage of the vertices being numbered 1to$|V|$ We simply store d[v] in the vth entry of an array. Each INSERT and DECREASE-KEY operation takes O(1) time, and each EXTRACT-MIN operation -takes O(V) time (since we have to search through the entire array), for a total time of $O(V^2+E) = O(V^2)$.

If the graph is sufficiently sparse-in particular, E= $o(V^2/\lg V)$-it is practical to implement the min-priority queue with a binary min-heap. (As discussed in an important implementation detail is that vertices arid corresponding heap elements must maintain handles to each other.) Each EXTRACT-MIN operation then takes time $O(\lg V)$. As before, there are| V | such operations. The time to build the binary min-heap is $O(V)$. Each DECREASE-KEY operation takes time O(lg V), and there are still at most | E | such operations. The total running time is therefore $O((V + E) \lg V)$, which is $O(E \lg V)$ if all vertices are reachable from the source. This running time is an improvement over the straightforward $O(V^2)$ time implementation if E = $o(V^2/\lg V)$.

We can in fact achieve a running time of $O(V \lg V + E)$ by implementing the min-priority queue with a Fibonacci heap. The amortized cost of each of the | V | EXTRACT-MIN operations is $O(\lg V)$, and each DECREASEKEY call, of which there are at most | E |, takes only O(1) amortized time. Historically, the development of Fibonacci heaps was motivated by the observation that in Dijkstra's algorithm there are typically mapy more DECREASE-KEY calls than EXTRACT-MIN calls, so any method of reducing the amortized time of each DECREASE-KEY operation to $o(\lg V)$ without increasing the amortized time of EXTRACT-MIN would yield an asymptotically faster implementation than with binary heaps.

Dijkstra's algorithm bears some similarity to both breadth-first search) and Prim's algorithm for computing minimum spaipning trees . It is like breadth-first search in that set S corresponds to the set of black vertices in a breadth-first search; just as vertices in S have their final shortest-path weights, so do black vertices in a breadth-first search have their correct breadthfirst distances. Dijkstra's algorithm is like Prim's algorithm in that both algorithms use a min-priority queue to find the "lightest" vertex outside a given set (the set S in Dijkstra's algorithm and the tree being grown in Prim's algorithm), add this vertex into the set, and adjust the weights of the remaining vertices outside the set accordingly.

4.4 DIFFERENCE CONSTRAINTS AND SHORTEST PATHS

Studies the general linear-programming problem, in which we wish to optimize a linear function subject to a set of linear inequalities. In this section, we investigate a special case of linear programming that can be reduced to finding shortest paths from a single source. The single-source shortest-paths problem that results can then be solved using the Bellman-Ford algorithm, thereby also solving the linear-programming problem.

Linear programming

In the general ***linear programming problem,*** weare given an m x n matrix A, an m-vector b, and an n-vector c. We wish to find a vector x of n elements that maximizes the ***objective function*** $\Sigma_{i=1} c_i x_i$ subject to the m constraints given by $Ax \leq b$.

Although the simplex algorithm, which is the focus does not always run in time polynomial in the size of its input, there are other linearprogramming algorithms that do run in polynomial time. There are several reasons that it is important to understand the setup of linear-programming problems. First, knowing that a given problem can be cast as a polynomial-sized linearprogramming problem immediately means that there is a polynomial-time algorithm for the problem. Second, there are many special cases of linear programming for which faster algorithms exist. For example, as shown in this section, the singlesource shortest-paths problem is a special case of linear programming. Other problems that can be cast as linear programming include the single-pair shortest-path problem and the maximum-flow problem.

Sometimes we don't really care about the objective function; we just wish to find any ***feasible solution,*** that is, any vector x that satisfies $Ax \leq b$, or to determine that no feasible solution exists. We shall focus on one such ***feasibility problem.***

Systems of difference constraints

In *a system of difference constraints,* each row of the linear-programming matrix A contains one 1 and one -1, and all other entries of A are 0. Thus, the constraints given by $Ax \leq b$ are a"set of m **difference *constraints*** involving *n* unknowns, in which each constraint is a simple linear inequality of the form

$$x_j - x_i < b_{k'}$$

where l <u>≤*i*, *j*</u> <nancil <u>≤*k* ≤*m*.</u>

For example, consider the problem of finding the 5-vector $x=(x_i)$ that satisfies

$$\begin{pmatrix} 1 & -1 & 0 & 0 & 0 \\ 1 & 0 & 0 & 0 & -1 \\ 0 & 1 & 0 & 0 & -1 \\ -1 & 0 & 1 & 0 & 0 \\ -1 & 0 & 0 & 1 & 0 \\ 0 & 0 & -1 & 1 & 0 \\ 0 & 0 & -1 & 0 & 1 \\ 0 & 0 & 0 & -1 & 1 \end{pmatrix} \begin{pmatrix} x_1 \\ x_2 \\ x_3 \\ x_4 \\ x_5 \end{pmatrix} \begin{pmatrix} 0 \\ -1 \\ 1 \\ 5 \\ 4 \\ -1 \\ -3 \\ -3 \end{pmatrix}$$

This problem is equivalent to finding the unknowns x_i for i= 1, 2,...,5, such that the following 8 difference constraints are satisfied:

$x_1 - x_2 \leq 0,$

$x_1 - x_5 \leq -1,$

$x_2 - x_5 \leq 1,$

$x_3 - x_1 \leq 5,$

$x_4 - x_1 \leq 4,$

$x_4 - x_3 \leq -1,$

$x_5 - x_3 \leq -3,$

$x_5 - x_4 \leq -3,$

One solution to this problem is x =(-5, -3, 0, -1, -4), as can be verified directly by checking each inequality. In fact, there is more than one solution to this problem. Another is $x' = (0, 2, 5, 4, 1)$. These two solutions are related: each component of x' is 5 larger than the corresponding component of x. This fact is not mere coincidence.

Lemma

Let $x=(x_1, x_2, ..., xn)$ be a solution to a system $Ax \le b$ of difference constraints, and let d be any constant. Then $x+ d=(x_i +d, x_2 +d, ..., x_n +d)$ *is* a solution to $Ax \le b$ as well.

Proof For each x_i and x_j, we have $(x_j + d)-(x_i + d) = x_j - x_i$. Thus, if x satisfies $Ax \le b$, so does $x + d$.

Systems of difference constraints occur in many different applications. For example, the unknowns x_i may be times at which events are to occur. Each constraint can be viewed as stating that there must be at least a certain amount of time, or at most a certain amount of time, between two events. Perhaps the events are jobs to be performed during the assembly of a product. If we apply an adhesive that takes 2 hours to set at time x_i and we have to wait until it sets to install a part at time x2, then we have the constraint that $x_2 \ge x_1 + 2$ or, equivalently, that $x_1 - x_2 \le -2$. Alternatively, we might require that the part be installed after the adhesive has been applied but no later than the time that the adhesive has set halfway. In this case, we get the pair of constraints $x_2 \ge x_1$ and $x_2 < x_1 + 1$ or, equivalently, $x_1 - x_2 \le 0$ and $x_2 - x_1 \le 1$.

4.5 CONSTRAINT GRAPH

It is beneficial to interpret systems of difference constraints from a graph-theoretic point of view. The idea is that in a system $Ax \le b$ of difference constraints, the m x n linear-programming matrix A can be viewed as the transpose of an incidence matrix for a graph with n vertices and m edges. Each vertex v_i in the graph, for i = 1, 2, ..., n, corresponds to one of the n unknown variables x_i. Each directed edge in the graph corresponds to one of the m inequalities involving two unknowns.

More formally, given a system $Ax \le b$ of difference constraints, the corresponding constraint graph is a weighted, directed graph G=(V, E), where

$$V = \{v_0, v_1, \ldots, v_n\}$$

and

$$E=\{(v_i, v_j): x_j - x_i \le b_k \text{ is a constraint}\}$$

$$\cup \{(v_o, v_r)> (v_o, V_2), (v_o, v_3), \ldots, (v_o, v_n)\}.$$

The additional vertex v_o is incorporated, as we shall see shortly, to guarantee that every other vertex is reachable from it. Thus, the vertex set V consists of a vertex v_i for each unknown x_i, plus an additional vertex v_o. The edge set E contains an edge for each difference constraint, plus an edge (v_o, v_i) for each unknown x_i. If $x_j - x_j \le b_k$ is a difference constraint, then the weight of edge (v_i, v_j) is $w(u_i, v_j) = b_k$. The weight of each edge leaving v_o is 0. The constraint graph for the system of difference constraints.

The following theorem shows that we can find a solution to a system of difference constraints by finding shortest-path weights in the corresponding constraint graph.

4.6 THEOREM

Given a system $Ax \leq b$ of difference constraints, let $G = (V, E)$ be the corresponding constraint graph. If G contains no negative-weight cycles, then

$$x=(\delta(v_o, v_i), \delta(v_o, v_2, \delta(v_o, v_3), ..., \delta(v_o, v_n))$$

is a feasible solution for the system. If G contains a negative-weight cycle, them there is no feasible solution for the system.

Proof We first show that if the constraint graph contains no negative-weight cycles, then equation gives a feasible solution. Consider any **edge** $(V_i, v_j) \in E$. By the triangle inequality, $\delta(v_o, v_j) \leq \delta(v_o, v_i) + w(v_i, v_j)$ *or.* equivalently, $\delta(v_o, v_j) - \delta(v_o, v_i) <\_ w(v_i, v_j)$. Thus, letting $xi = \delta(v_o, v_i)$ **and** $x_j = \delta(vo, v_j)$ satisfies the difference constraint $x_j - xi \leq w(v_i, v_j)$ that corresponds to edge (v_i, v_j).

Now we show that if the constraint graph contains a negative-weight cycle, then the system of difference constraints has no feasible solution. Without loss of generality, let the negative-weight cycle be c= $(v_1, v_2 ... v_k)$, where $v_1 = v_j$.. (The vertex vo cannot be on cycle c, because it has no entering edges.) Cycle c, corresponds to the following difference constraints:

$$x_2 - x_1 \leq w(v_1, v_2),$$
$$x_3 - x_2 \leq w(v_2, v_3),$$
$$x_k - x_{k-1} \leq w(v_{k-1}, v_k),$$
$$x_1 - x_k \leq w(v_k, v_1),$$

Suppose that there is a solution for x satisfying each of these k inequalities. This solution must also satisfy the inequality that results when we sum the k inequalities together. If we sum the left-hand sides, each unknown x_i is added in once and subtracted out once, so that the left-hand side of the sum is 0. The right-hand side sums to w(c), and thus we obtain $0 \leq w(c)$. But since c is a negative-weight cycle, $w(c) < 0$, and we obtain the contradiction that $0 \leq w(c) < 0$.

Solving Systems of Difference Constraints

Theorem tells us that we can use the Bellman-Ford algorithm to solve a system of difference constraints. Because there are edges from the source vertex v_o to all other vertices in the constraint graph, any negative-weight cycle in the constraint graph is reachable from v_o. If the Bellman-Ford algorithm returns TRUE, then the shortest-path weights give a feasible solution to the system. In Figure 24.8, for example, the shortest-path weights provide the feasible solution x=(-5, -3, 0, -1, -4), and by Lemma x=(d - 5, d-3, d, d-1, d- 4) is also a feasible solution for any constant d. If the Bellman-Ford algorithm returns FALSE, there is no feasible solution to the system of difference constraints.

A system of difference constraints with m constraints on n unknowns produces a graph with $n+ 1$ vertices and $n+m$ edges. Thus, using the Bellman-Ford algorithm, we can solve the system in $O((n+l)(n+m)) = O(n^2 +nm)$ time. that asks you to modify the algorithm to run in $O(nm)$ time, even if m is much less then n.

REVIEW QUESTIONS

1. Explain Di1kstra's algorithm in details.
2. Prove: Dijkstra's algorithm, run on a weighted, directed graph G = *(V, E)* with non-negative weight function w and source s, terminates with $d[u] = \delta(s, u)$ for all vertices $u \in V$.
3. Prove: If we run Dijkstra's algorithm on a weighted, directed graph G = (V, E) with non–negative weight function w and source s, then at termination, the predecessor sub graph G_π is a shortest-paths tree rooted at s
4. What is linear programming? Explain in details
5. What is constraint graph? Prove: Given a system $Ax \le b$ of difference constraints, let *G = (V, E)* be the corresponding constraint graph. If G contains no negative-weight cycles, then $x=(\delta(v_o, v_i), \delta(v_o, v_2, \delta(v_o, v_3), ...,\delta(v_o, v_n))$ is a feasible solution for the system. If G contains a negative-weight cycle, then there is no feasible solution for the system.

UNIT 4

MINIMUM-COST SPANNING TREES

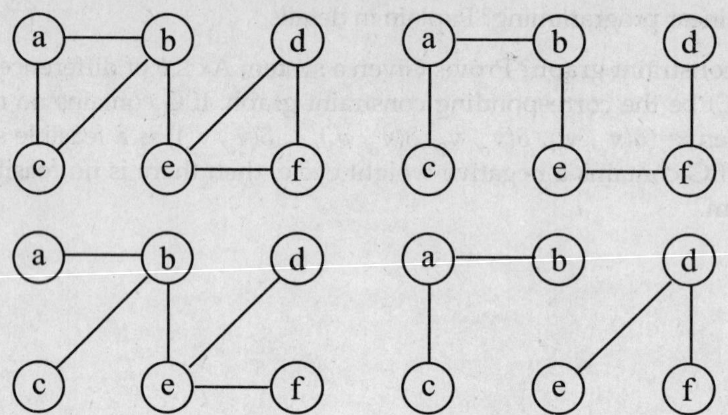

5.1 INTRODUCTION

Let G = *(V, E)* be an undirected connected graph. A subgraph t=*(V, E')* of G is a ***spanning tree*** of G if it is a tree.

For example Figure 1 shows the complete graph on four nodes together with three of its spanning trees.

Spanning trees have many applications. For example, they can be used to obtain an independent set of circuit equations for an electric network. First, a spanning tree for the electric network is obtained. Let *B* be the set of network edges not in the spanning tree. Adding an edge from *B* to the spanning tree creates a cycle.

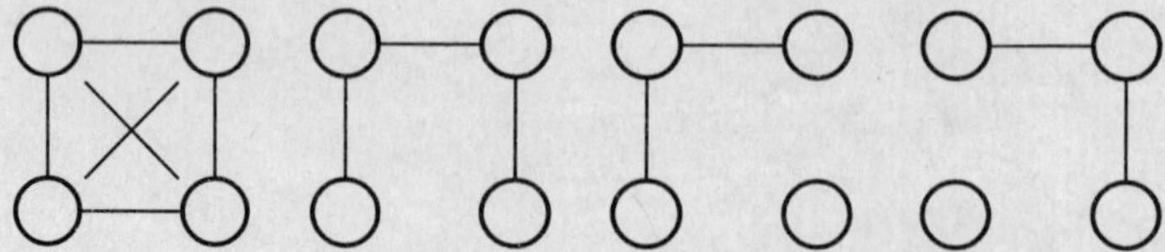

Figure 1. An undirected graph and three of its spanning trees

We apply Kirchoff's second law on each cycle to obtain a circuit equation. The cycles obtain in this way are independent (i.e., none of these cycles can be obtained by taking a linear combination of the remaining cycles) as each contains an edge from B that is not contained in any other cycle. Hence, the circuit equations so obtained are also independent. In fact, it can be shown that the cycles obtained by introducing the edges of B one at a time into the resulting spanning tree form a cycle basis, and so all other cycles in the graph can be constructed by taking a linear combination of the cycles in the basis.

Another application of spanning trees arises from the property that a spanning tree is a minimal subgraph G′ of G such that V(G′) = *V(G)* and G's connected. (A minimal subgraph is one with the fewest number of edges.) Any connected graph. with n vertices must have at least n–1 edges and all connected graphs-with n – 1 edges are trees. If the, nodes of G represent cities and the edges represent possible communication links connecting two cities then the minimum number of links needed to connect the n cities is n – 1. The spanning trees of G represent all feasible choices.

In practical situations, the edges have weights assigned to them. These weights may represent. The cost of construction, the length of the link, and so on. Given such a weighted graph, one would then wish to select cities to have minimum total cost or minimum total length. In either case the links selected have to form a tree (assuming all weights are positive). If this is not so, then the selection of links contains a cycle. Removal of any one of the links on this cycle results in a link selection of less cost connecting all cities. We are therefore interested in finding a spanning tree of G with minimum cost. (The cost of a spanning tree is the sum of the costs of the edges in that tree.) Figure 2 shows a graph and one of its minimum-cost spanning trees. Since the identification of a minimum-cost spanning tree involves the selection of a sub set of the edges, this problem fits the subset paradigm

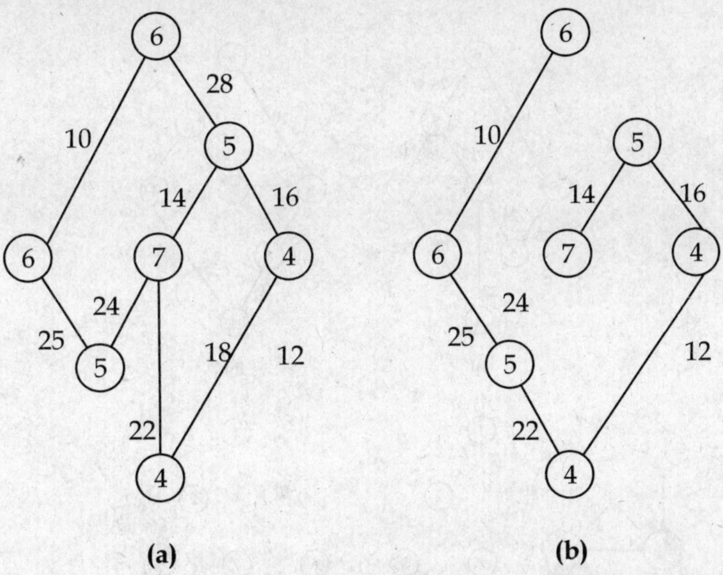

Figure 2. A graph and its minimum cost spanning tree

5.2 PRIM'S ALGORITHM

A greedy method to obtain a minimum-cost spanning tree builds this tree edge by edge. The next edge to include is chosen according to some. optimization criterion. The simplest such criterion is to choose an edge that results in a minimum increase in the sum the costs of the edges. So for included. There are two possible ways to interpret this criterion. In the first, the set of edges so far selected form a tree, Thus, if A is the set of edges selected so far, then *A* forms a, tree. The next edge (u,v), to be included in *A* is a minimum-cost edge not in A with the property that A U{(u, v) } is also a tree. This selection criterion results in a minimum-cost spanning tree. The corresponding algorithm is known as Prim's algorithm.

Working of Prim's method

The working of Prim's Algorithm on the graph of figure 2 can be explained as below. It has a minimum cost of 99.

Having seen how Prim's method works, let us obtain a pseudocode algorithm to find a minimum-cost spanning tree using this method. The algorithm will start with a tree that includes only a minimum-cost edge of G. Then, edges are added to this tree one by one. The next edge (i, j) to be added is such that *i* is a vertex already included in the tree, j is a vertex not yet included, and the cost of (i, j), ***cost[i, j]***, is minimum among all edges *(k, 1)* such that vertex *k* is in the tree and vertex l is not in the tree. To determine this edge (i, j) efficiently, we associate with each vertex j not-yet included in the tree a value near(j]. The value ***near[j]*** is a vertex in the tree such that coat[j, near[j]] is minimum among all choices for near[j]. We define near[j] = 0 for all vertices j that are already in the tree.

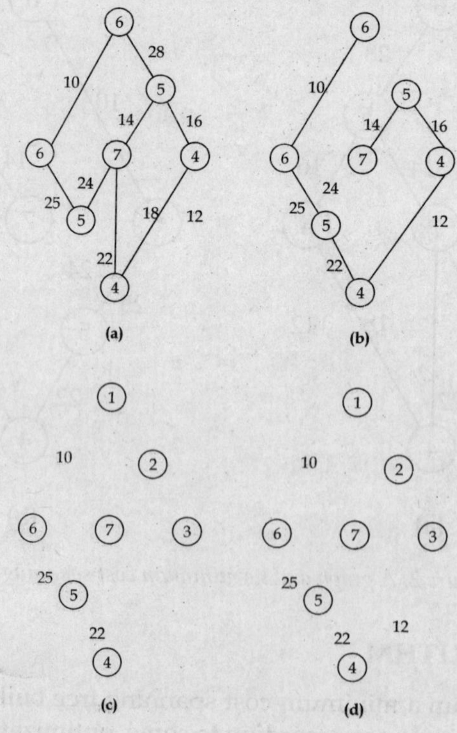

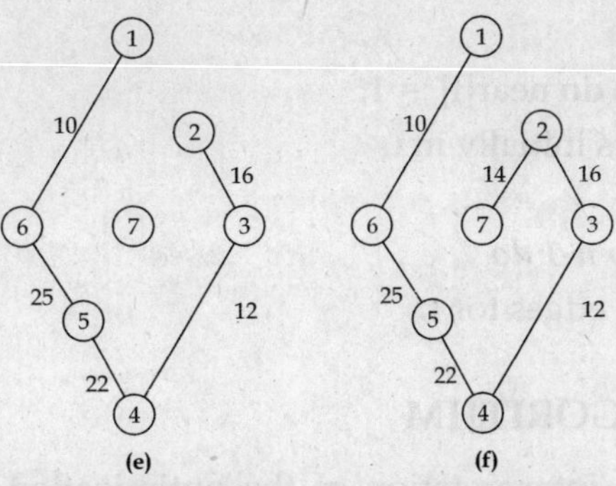

Figure 3. Stages in Prim's algorithm

The next edge to include is defined by the vertex *j* such that *near[j]* ≠ *0* (j not already in the tree) and cost [j,near[j]] is minimum

In function Prim (Algorithm 1), line 9 selects a minimum-cost edge. Lines 10 to 15 initialize the variables so as to represent a tree comprising only the edge (k, 1). In the for loop of line 16 the remainder of the spanning tree is built up edge by edge. Lines 18 and 19 select (j, near[j]) as the next edge to include. Lines 23 to 25 update near[ ].

The time required by algorithm Prim-is $O(n^2)$, where *n* is the number of vertices in the graph G. To see this, note that line 9 takes O(| E |) time and line 10 takes Θ(1) time. The for loop of line 12 takes ***O(n)*** time. Lines 18 and 19 and the for loop of line 23 require ***O(n)*** time. So, each iteration of the for loop of line 16 takes ***O(n)*** time. The total time for the for loop of line 16 is therefore $\boldsymbol{O(n^2)}$. Hence, Prim runs in $\boldsymbol{O(n^2)}$ time.

If we store the nodes not yet included in the tree as a red-black tree lines 18 and 19 take O(log n) time. Note that a red-black tree supports the following operations in ***O(logn)*** time: insert, delete (an arbitrary element), find-min, and search (for an arbitrary element). The for loop of line 23 has to examine only the nodes adjacent to j. Thus its overall frequency is *O(| E|)*. Updating in lines 24 and 25 also takes O(log n) time (since an update can be done using a delete and an insertion into the red-black tree). Thus the overall run time is ***O((n + I*** | E|) log n) .

The algorithm can be speeded a bit by making the observation that a minimum-cost spanning tree includes for each vertex v a minimum-cost edge incident to v. To see this, suppose *t is* a minimum-cost spanning tree for G= *(V, E)*. Let *v* be any vertex in *t*. Let *(v, w)* be an edge with minimum cost among all edges incident to *v*. Assume that *(v, w)* ∉ *E(t)* and *cost[v, w]* < *cost[v, x]* for all edges *(v, x)* ∈ *E(t)*. The inclusion of *(v, w)* into *t* creates a unique cycle. This cycle must include an edge *(v, x), x≠ w*. Removing (v, *x*) from *E(t) U{(v, w)}* breaks this cycle without disconnecting the graph *(V, E(t) U{(v, w)})*. Hence, *(V, E(t) U{(v, w)} -{(v, x)})* is also a spanning tree. Since *cost[v, w]* < *cost[v, x]*, this spanning tree has lower cost than *t*. This contradicts the assumption that ***t*** is a minimum-cost spanning tree of G. So, t includes minimum-cost edges as stated above.

From this observation it follows that we can start the algorithm with a tree consisting of any arbitrary vertex and no edge. Then edges can be added one, by one. The changes needed are to lines 9 to 17. These lines can be replaced by the lines

```
mincost := 0;
for i := 2 to n do near[i] := 1;
// Vertex 1 is initially in t.
near[1] := 0;
-16 for i:=l to n-1 do
{// Find n- I edges for t,
```

5.3 KRUSKAL'S ALGORITHM

There, is second possible interpretation of the optimization criteria mentioned earlier in which the edges of the graph are considered in nondecreasing order of cost. This interpretation is that the set ***t*** of edges so far selected for the spanning tree be such that it is possible to complete ***t*** into a tree. Thus ***t*** may not be a tree at all stages in the algorithm. In fact, it will generally only be a forest since the set of edges ***t*** can be completed into a tree if there are no cycles in t. This method is due to Kruskal.

```
Algorithm Prim(E, cost, n, t)
// E is the set of edges in G. cost[1 : n, l: n] is the cost
// adjacency matrix of an n vertex graph such that cost[i, j] is
// either a positive real number or ∞ if no edge (i, j) exists.
// A minimum spanning tree is computed and stored as a set of
// edges in the array t[1 : n - 1,1 : 2]. (t[i, l], t[i, 2]) is an edge in
// the minimum-cost spanning tree. The final cost is returned.
{
Let (k, 1) be an edge of minimum cost in 'E;
mincost := cost[k, l];
t[1, 1] := k; t[1, 2] := 1;
for i:= 1 to n do // Initialize near.
if (cost[i, 1] < cost[i, k]) then near[i] := 1;
else near[i] := k;
near[k] := near[l] := 0;
for i:= 2 to n - 1 do
{// Find n - 2 additional edges for t.
Let j be an index such that near[j] ≠ 0 and
cost[j, near[j]] is minimum;
t[j,1] := j; t[i, 2] := near[j];
mincost := mincost + cost[j, near[j]];
near[j] := 0;
for k:= 1 to n do // Update near[ ].
if (near[k] ≠ 0) and (cost[k, near[k]] > cost[k, j]))
then near[k] := j;
}
return mincost;
}
```

Algorithm 1: Prim's minimum-cost spanning tree algorithm

For example Consider the graph of Figure 1(a). We begin with no edges selected. Figure 3(a) shows the current graph with no edges selected. Edge (1, 6) is the first edge considered. It is included in the spanning tree being built. This yields the graph of Figure 3(b). Next, the edge (3,4) is selected and included in the tree (Figure 3(c)). The next edge to be considered is (2, 7). Its inclusion in the tree being built does not create a cycle, so we get the graph of Figure 3(d). Edge (2,3) is considered next and included in the tree Figure 3(e). Of the edges not yet considered, (7,4) has the least cost. It is considered next. Its inclusion in the tree results in a cycle, so this edge is discarded. Edge (5,4) is the next edge to be added to the tree being built. This results in the configuration of Figure 3(f). The next edge to be considered is the edge (7, 5). It is discarded, as its inclusion creates a cycle. Finally, edge (6,5) is considered and included in the tree being built. This completes the spanning tree. The resulting tree has cost 99.

On the other hand Kruskal's method is written out more formally in Algorithm 2. Initially *E* is the set of all edges in G. The only functions we wish to perform on this set are (1) determine an edge with minimum cost (line 4) and (2) delete this edge (line 5). Both these functions can be performed efficiently if the edges- in *E* are maintained as a sorted sequential list. It is not essential to sort all the edges so long as the next edge for line 4 call be determined easily. If the edges are maintained as a minheap, then the next edge to consider can be obtained in O(log| E| ,) time. The construction of the heap itself takes O(| E|) time.

To be able to perform step 6 efficiently, the vertices in G should be grouped together in such a way that one can easily determine whether the vertices *v* and *w* are already connected by the earlier selection of edges. If they are, then the edge *(v, w)* is to be discarded. If they are not, then (*v*, w) is to be added to t. One possible grouping is to place all vertices in the same connected component of t into a set.(all connected components of t will also be trees). Then, two vertices *v* and *w* are connected in t if they are in the same set. For example, when the edge (2,6) is to be considered, the sets are 11, 2}, {3, 4, 6}, and {5}. Vertices 2 and 6 are in different sets so these sets are combined to give {1,2,3,4,6} and {5}. The next edge to be considered is (l,4). Since vertices 1 and 4 are in the same set, the edge is rejected. The edge (3,5) connects vertices in different sets and results in the final spanning tree. The computing time is, therefore, determined by the time for lines 4 and 5, which in the worst case is O(| E| log | E|).

If the representations discussed above are used, then the pseudocode of Algorithm 3 results. In line 6 an initial heap of edges is constructed. In line 7 each vertex is to a distinct set (and hence to a distinct tree). The set t is the set of edges to be included in the minimum-cost spanning tree and *i* is the number of edges in *t*. The set *t* can be represented as a sequential list using a two-dimensional array t[1 : n-1,1 : 2]. Edge (u, v) can be added to *t* by the assignments t[i, 1] := u ; and *t[i, 2]* := v;. In the while loop of line 10, edges are removed from the heap one by one in nondecreasing order of cost. Line 14 determines the sets containing u and *v*. If $j \neq$ k, then vertices u and v are in different sets (and so in different trees) and edge (u, v) is included into t. The sets containing u and v are combined (line 20). If u = v, the edge (u, v) is discarded as its inclusion into t would create a cycle. Line 23 determines whether a spanning tree was found. It follows that $i \neq$ n - *1* iff the graph

G is not connected. One can verify that the computing time is O(| E| + log | E |), where E is the edge set of G.

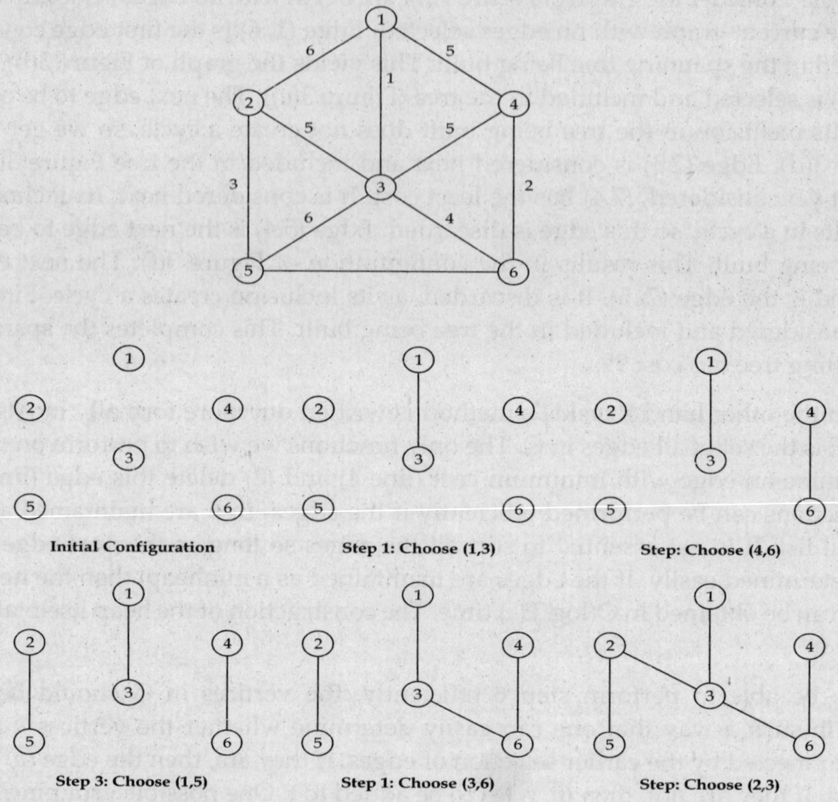

Theorem . Kruskal's algorithm generates a minimum-cost spanning tree for every connected undirected graph G.

Proof: Let G be any undirected connected graph. Let ***t*** be the spanning tree for G generated by Kruskal's algorithm. Let ***t'*** be a minimum-cost spanning tree for G. We show that both *t* and *t'* have the same cost.

Let ***E(t)*** and **E(t')** respectively be the edges in *t* and *t'*. If *n* is the number of vertices in G, then both *t* and *t'* have n – *1* edges. If *E(t)* = *E(t')*, then *t* is clearly of minimum cost. If *E(t)* ≠ *E(t')*, then let *q* be a minimum-cost edge such that q ∈ *E(t)* and q ∈ (t'). Clearly, such a *q* must exist. The inclusion of *q* into *t'* creates a unique cycle. Let q, e_1, e_2, ..., e_k be this unique cycle. At least one of the *ei's*, 1≤ i≤_ k, is not in *E(t)* as otherwise *t* would also contain the cycle *q, e1 , e2, _ .., ek*. Let e_j be an edge on this cycle such that *ej* ∉ *E(t)*. If *ej* is of lower cost than q, then Krusks,l's algorithm will consider e_j before *q* and include *ej* into t. to se this, note that all edges in E(t0 of cost less then the of q are also in E(t) and do not form a cycle with *ej*. So cost(*ej*) ≥ cost(q).

Now, reconsider the graph with edge set *E(t) U{q}*. Removal of any edge on the cycle *q*, e_1, e_2, ..., *ek* will leave behind a tree t". In particular, if we delete the edge ej, then the resulting tree *t"* will have a cost no more than the cost of *t'* (*as cost(*e_j*) ≥ cost(e)*). Hence, t" is also a minimum-cost tree.

By repeatedly using the transformation described above, tree t′ can be transformed into the spanning tree t without any increase in cost. Hence, *t* is a minimum-cost spanning tree.

```
t:= θ;
while ((t has less than n – 1 edges) and′ (E ≠ 0)) do
{
Choose an edge (v, w) from E of lowest cost;
Delete (v, w) from E;
if (v, w) does not create a cycle in t then add (v, w) to t;
else discard (v, w);
}
```

Algorithm 2: Early form of Kruskal's minimum-cost spanning tree

Below is the algorithm due to Kruskal.

```
Algorithm Kruskal(E, cost, n, t)
// E is the set of edges in G. G has n vertices. cost[u, v] is the
// cost of edge (u, v). t is the set of edges in the minimum-cost
// spanning tree. The final cost is returned.
{
Construct a heap out of the edge costs using Heapify;
for i:= 1 to n do parent[i] := –1;
// Each vertex is in a different set.
i := 0; mincost := ∞;
while ((i < n – 1) and (heap not empty)) do
{
Delete a minimum cost edge (u, v) from the heap
and reheapify using Adjust;
j := Find(u); k:= Find(v);
if ( j≠ k) then
{
i:=i,+1;
t[i, 1] := u; t[i, 2] := v;
mincost := mincost + cost[u, v];
Union(j, k);
}
}
if (i ≠ n – 1) then write ("No spanning tree");
else return mincost;
}
```

Algorithm 3: Kruskal's algorithm

REVIEW QUESTIONS

1. What are minimum-cost spanning trees? Explain with examples.
2. Explain the Prim's Algorithm in details.
3. Explain Kruskal's Algorithm in details.
4. Explain with examples the construction stages in Kruskal's algorithm.

UNIT 5

RANDOMIZATION, STRING AND AMORTIZED ANALYSIS

CHAPTER 1

STRING MATCHING

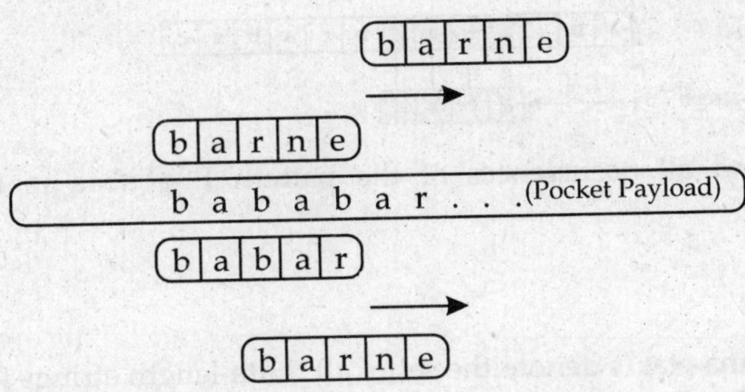

1.1 INTRODUCTION

Finding all occurrences of a pattern in a text is a problem that arises most frequently in text-editing programs. Typically, the text is a document being edited, and the pattern searched for is a particular word supplied by the user. Efficient algorithms for this problem can greatly aid the responsiveness of the text-editing program. String-matching algorithms are also used to search for particular patterns in DNA sequences in medical science.

We formalize the ***string-matching problem*** as follows. We assume that the text is an array $T[1 \,..\, n]$ of length n and that the pattern is an array $P[1 \,..\, m]$ of length m. We further assume that the elements of P and T are characters drawn from a finite alphabet Σ. For example, we may have $\Sigma = \{0, 1\}$ or $\Sigma = \{a, b, \ldots, z\}$. The character arrays P and T are often called ***strings*** of characters.

We say that pattern P ***occurs with shift s*** in text T (or, equivalently, that pattern P ***occurs beginning at position s + 1*** in text T) if $0 \le s \le n - m$ and $T[s + 1 \,..\, s + m] = P[1 \,..\, m]$ (that is, if $T[s + j] = P[j]$, for $1 \le j \le m$). If P occurs with shift s in T, then we call s a ***valid shift***; otherwise, we call s an ***invalid shift***. The string-matching problem is the problem of finding all valid shifts with which a given pattern P occurs in a given text T.

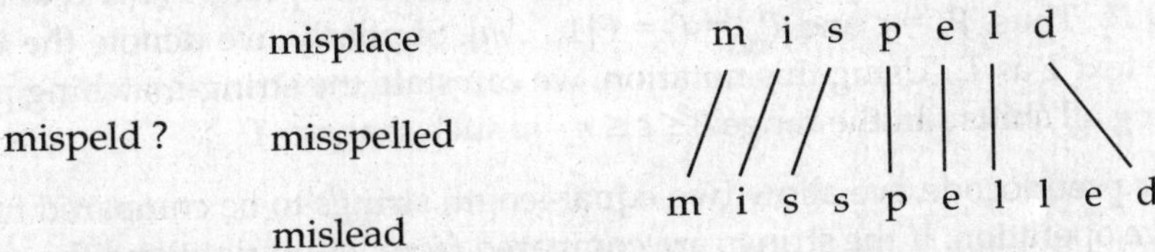

This chapter is organized in following way: we review the naive brute-force algorithm for the string-matching problem, which has worst-case running time

$O((n - m + 1)m)$, then we presents an interesting string-matching algorithm, due to Rabin and Karp. This algorithm also has worst-case running time $O((n - m + 1)m)$, but it works much better on average and in practice. It also generalizes nicely to other pattern-matching problems. Next we describes a string-matching algorithm that begins by constructing a finite automaton specifically designed to search for occurrences of the given pattern P in a text. This algorithm runs in time $O(n + m\ |\Sigma|)$. The similar but much cleverer Knuth-Morris-Pratt (or KMP) algorithm is presented ; the KMP algorithm runs in time $O(n + m)$. Finally we describes an algorithm due to Boyer and Moore that is often the best practical choice, although its worst-case running time (like that of the Rabin-Karp algorithm) is no better than that of the naive string-matching algorithm.

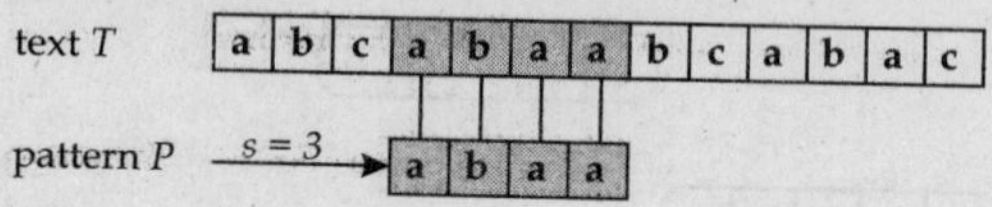

The goal is to find all occurrences of the pattern P = abaa in the text T = abcabaabcabac.

Basic Terminology

We shall let Σ^* (read "sigma-star") denote the set of all finite-length strings formed using characters from the alphabet Σ. In this chapter, we consider only finite-length strings. The zero-length ***empty string***, denoted ε, also belongs to Σ^*. The length of a string x is denoted $|x|$. The ***concatenation*** of two strings x and y, denoted xy, has length $|x| + |y|$ and consists of the characters from x followed by the characters from y.

We say that a string w is a ***prefix*** of a string x, denoted $w \subset x$, if $x = wy$ for some string $y \in \Sigma^*$. Note that if $w \subset x$, then $|w| \leq |x|$. Similarly, we say that a string w is a ***suffix*** of a string x, denoted $w \supset x$, if $x = wy$ for some $y \in \Sigma^*$. It follows from $w \supset x$ that $|w| \leq |x|$. The empty string ε is both a suffix and a prefix of every string. For example, we have ab $\subset$ abcca and cca $\subset$ abcca. It is useful to note that for any strings x and y and any character a, we have $x \supset y$ if and only if $xa \supset ya$. Also note that $\subset$ and $\supset$ are transitive relations. The following lemma will be useful later.

Lemma 1

Suppose that x, y, and z are strings such that $x \supset z$ *and* $y \supset z$. If $|x| \leq |y|$, then $x \supset y$. If $|x| \geq |y|$, then $y \supset x$. If $|x| = |y|$, then $x = y$.

Proof.

For brevity of notation, we shall denote the k-character prefix $P[1 \,..\, k]$ of the pattern $P[1 \,..\, m]$ by P_k. Thus, $P_0 = \varepsilon$ and $P_m = P = P[1 \,..\, m]$. Similarly, we denote the k-character prefix of the text T as T_k. Using this notation, we can state the string-matching problem as that of finding all shifts s in the range $0 \leq s \leq n - m$ such that $p \supset T_{s-m}$.

In our pseudocode, we allow two equal-length strings to be compared for equality as a primitive operation. If the strings are compared from left to right and the comparison stops when a mismatch is discovered, we assume that the time taken by such a test is a linear function of the number of matching characters discovered. To be precise, the test "x

= y" is assumed to take time $\Theta(t + 1)$, where t is the length of the longest string z such that $z \subset x$ and $z \subset$).

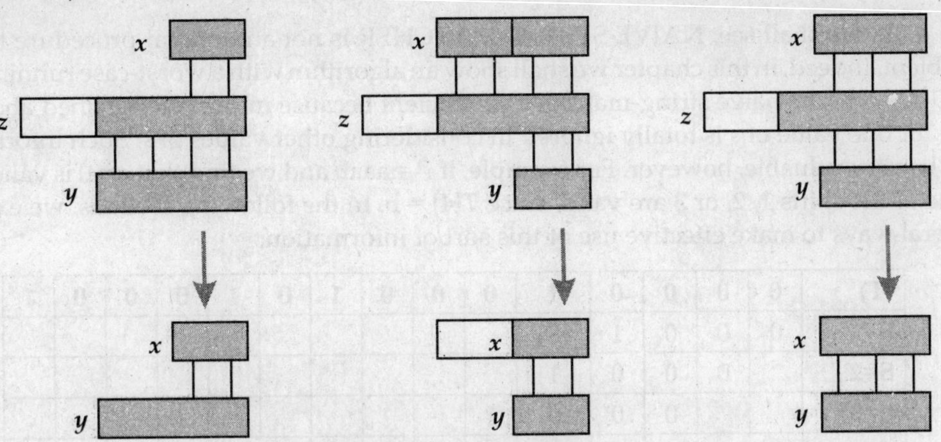

Figure: A graphical proof of Lemma 1.

1.2 NAIVE STRING-MATCHING ALGORITHM

The naive algorithm finds all valid shifts using a loop that checks the condition $P[1 \mathinner{..} m] = T[s + 1 \mathinner{..} s + m]$ for each of the $n - m + 1$ possible values of s.

```
NAIVE-STRING-MATCHER(T, P)
1   n ← length[T]
2   m ← length[P]
3   for s ← 0 to n - m
4   do if P[1 . . m] = T[s + 1 . . s + m]
5   then print "Pattern occurs with shift" s
```

The naive string-matching procedure can be interpreted graphically as sliding a "template" containing the pattern over the text, noting for which shifts all of the characters on the template equal the corresponding characters in the text, as illustrated in Figure . The **for** loop beginning on line 3 considers each possible shift explicitly. The test on line 4 determines whether the current shift is valid or not; this test involves an implicit loop to check corresponding character positions until all positions match successfully or a mismatch is found. Line 5 prints out each valid shift s.

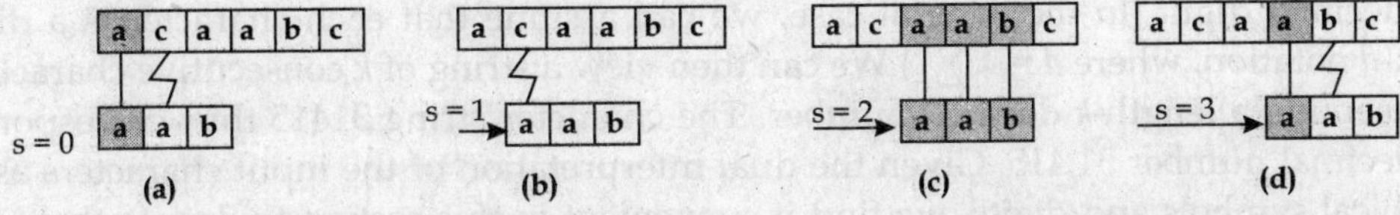

Figure The operation of the naive string matcher for the pattern P = **aab and the text T = acaabc.**

NAIVE-STRING-MATCHER takes time $\Theta((n - m + 1)m)$ in the worst case. For example, consider the text string a^n (a string of n a's) and the pattern a^m. For each of the $n - m + 1$ possible values of the shift s, the implicit loop on line 4 to compare corresponding characters must execute m times to validate the shift. The worst-case running time is thus $\Theta((n - m + 1)m)$, which is $\Theta(n^2)$ if $m = \lfloor n/2 \rfloor$.

As we shall see, NAIVE-STRING-MATCHER is not an optimal procedure for this problem. Indeed, in this chapter we shall show an algorithm with a worst-case running time of $O(n + m)$. The naive string-matcher is inefficient because information gained about the text for one value of s is totally ignored in considering other values of s. Such information can be very valuable, however. For example, if P = aaab and we find that $s = 0$ is valid, then none of the shifts 1, 2, or 3 are valid, since $T[4]$ = b. In the following sections, we examine several ways to make effective use of this sort of information.

(T)	**0**	**0**	**0**	**0**	**1**	**0**	**0**	**0**	**1**	**0**	**1**	**0**	**0**	**0**	**1**
S=1	0	0	0	1	(P)										
S=2		0	0	0	1										
S=3			0	0	0	1									
S=4				0	0	0	1								
S=5					0	0	0	1							
S=6						0	0	0	1						
S=7							0	0	0	1					
S=8								0	0	0	1				
S=9									0	0	0	1			
S=10										0	0	0	1		
S=11											0	0	0	1	
S=12												0	0	0	1

1.3 THE RABIN-KARP ALGORITHM

Rabin and Karp have proposed a string-matching algorithm that performs well in practice and that also generalizes to other algorithms for related problems, such as two-dimensional pattern matching. The worst-case running time of the Rabin-Karp algorithm is $O((n - m + 1)m)$, but it has a good average-case running time.

This algorithm makes use of elementary number-theoretic notions such as the equivalence of two numbers modulo a third number.

For expository purposes, let us assume that $\Sigma = \{0, 1, 2, \ldots, 9\}$, so that each character is a decimal digit. (In the general case, we can assume that each character is a digit in radix-d notation, where $d = |\Sigma|$) We can then view a string of k consecutive characters as representing a length-k decimal number. The character string 31415 thus corresponds to the decimal number 31,415. Given the dual interpretation of the input characters as both graphical symbols and digits, we find it convenient in this section to denote them as we would digits, in our standard text font.

Given a pattern $P[1 \,..\, m]$, we let p denote its corresponding decimal value. In a similar manner, given a text $T[1 \,..\, n]$, we let t_s denote the decimal value of the length-m substring $T[s + 1 \,..\, s + m]$, for $s = 0, 1, \ldots, n - m$. Certainly, $t_s = p$ if and only if $T[s + 1 \,..\, s +$

$m] = P[1 \,..\, m]$; thus, s is a valid shift if and only if $t_s = p$. If we could compute p in time $O(m)$ and all of the t_i values in a total of $O(n)$ time, then we could determine all valid shifts s in time $O(n)$ by comparing p with each of the t_s's. (For the moment, let's not worry about the possibility that p and the t_s's might be very large numbers.)

We can compute p in time $O(m)$ using Horner's rule

$$p = P[m] + 10\,(P[m-1] + 10(P[m-2] + \ldots + 10(P[2] + 10P[1])\ldots)).$$

The value t_0 can be similarly computed from $T[1 \,..\, m]$ in time $O(m)$.

To compute the remaining values $t_1, t_2, \ldots, t_{n-m}$ in time $O(n - m)$, it suffices to observe that t_{s+1} can be computed from t_s in constant time, since

$$t_{s+1} = 10(t_s - 10^{m-1}T[s+1]) + T[s+m+1].$$

For example, if $m = 5$ and $t_s = 31415$, then we wish to remove the high-order digit $T[s + 1] = 3$ and bring in the new low-order digit (suppose it is $T[s + 5 + 1] = 2$) to obtain

$$t_{s+1} = 10(31415 - 10000.3) + 2$$
$$= 14152\,.$$

Subtracting 10^m-1 $T[s+1]$ removes the high-order digit from t_s, multiplying the result by 10 shifts the number left one position, and adding $T[s + m + 1]$ brings in the appropriate low-order digit. If the constant 10^m-1 is precomputed (which can be done in time $O(1\text{g } m)$), then each execution of equation takes a constant number of arithmetic operations. Thus, p and $t_0, t_1, \ldots, t_n$-m can all be computed in time $O(n + m)$, and we can find all occurrences of the pattern $P[1 \,..\, m]$ in the text $T[1 \,..\, n]$ in time $O(n + m)$.

The only difficulty with this procedure is that p and t_s may be too large to work with conveniently. If P contains m characters, then assuming that each arithmetic operation on p (which is m digits long) takes "constant time" is unreasonable. Fortunately, there is a simple cure for this problem, as shown in Figure 34.4 : compute p and the t_s's modulo a suitable modulus q. Since the computation of p, t_0, and the recurrence can all be performed modulo q, we see that p and all the t_s's can be computed modulo q in time $O(n + m)$. The modulus q is typically chosen as a prime such that $10q$ just fits within one computer word, which allows all of the necessary computations to be performed with single-precision arithmetic.

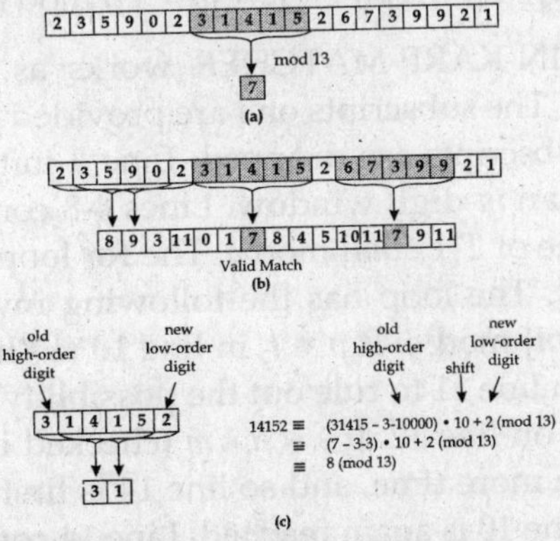

Figure: The Rabin-Karp algorithm. Each character is a decimal digit, and we compute values modulo 13.

In general, with a d-ary alphabet $\{0, 1, \ldots, d - 1\}$, we choose q so that $d\,q$ fits within a computer word and adjust the recurrence equation (34.1) to work modulo q, so that it becomes

$$t_{s+1} = (d(t_s - T[s + 1]h) + T[s + m + 1]) \bmod q,$$

where $h \in d^{m-1} \pmod q$ is the value of the digit "1" in the high-order position of an m-digit text window.

The ointment of working modulo q now contains a fly, however, since $t_s \equiv p \pmod q$ does not imply that $t_s = p$. On the other hand, if ts $\neq$ p (mod q), then we definitely have that $t_s \neq p$, so that shift s is invalid. We can thus use the test $t_s \equiv p \pmod q$ as a fast heuristic test to rule out invalid shifts s. Any shift s for which $t_s \equiv p \pmod q$ must be tested further to see if s is really valid or we just have a ***spurious hit***. This testing can be done by explicitly checking the condition $P[1 \,..\, m] = T[s + 1 \,..\, s + m]$. If q is large enough, then we can hope that spurious hits occur infrequently enough that the cost of the extra checking is low.

The following procedure makes these ideas precise. The inputs to the procedure are the text T, the pattern P, the radix d to use (which is typically taken to be $|\Sigma|$), and the prime q to use.

```
RABIN-KARP-MATCHER(T, P, d, q)
1    n ← length[T]
2    m ← length[P]
3    h ← d^(m-1) mod q
4    p ← 0
5    t_0 ← 0
6    for i ← 1 to m
7    do p ← (dp + P[i]) mod q
8    t_0 ← (dt_0 + T[i]) mod q
9    for s ← 0 to n - m
10   do if p = t_s
11   then if P[1 . . m] = T[s + 1 . . s + m]
12   then "Pattern occurs with shift" s
13   if s < n - m
14   then t_(s+1) ← (d(t_s - T[s + 1]h) + T[s + m + 1]) mod q
```

The procedure RABIN-KARP-MATCHER works as follows. All characters are interpreted as radix-d digits. The subscripts on t are provided only for clarity; the program works correctly if all the subscripts are dropped. Line 3 initializes h to the value of the high-order digit position of an m-digit window. Lines 4-8 compute p as the value of $P[1 \,..\, m] \bmod q$ and t_0 as the value of $T[1 \,..\, m] \bmod q$. The **for** loop beginning on line 9 iterates through all possible shifts s. The loop has the following invariant: whenever line 10 is executed, $t_s = T[s + 1 \,..\, s + m] \bmod q$. If $p = t_s$ in line 10 (a "hit"), then we check to see if $P[1 \,..\, m] = T[s + 1 \,..\, s + m]$ in line 11 to rule out the possibility of a spurious hit. Any valid shifts found are printed out on line 12. If $s < n - m$ (checked in line 13), then the **for** loop is to be executed at least one more time, and so line 14 is first executed to ensure that the loop invariant holds when line 10 is again reached. Line 14 computes the value of $t_{s+1} \bmod q$ from the value of $t_s \bmod q$ in constant time using equation.

The running time of RABIN-KARP-MATCHER is $\Theta((n - m + 1)m)$ in the worst case, since (like the naive string-matching algorithm) the Rabin-Karp algorithm explicitly verifies every valid shift. If $P = a^m$ and $T = a^n$, then the verifications take time $\Theta((n - m + 1)m)$, since each of the $n - m + 1$ possible shifts is valid. (Note also that the computation of d^{m-1} mod q on line 3 and the loop on lines 6-8 take time $O(m) = O((n - m + 1)m)$.)

1.4 STRING MATCHING WITH FINITE AUTOMATA

Many string-matching algorithms build a finite automaton that scans the text string T for all occurrences of the pattern P. This section presents a method for building such an automaton. These string-matching automata are very efficient: they examine each text character *exactly once,* taking constant time per text character. The time used—after the automaton is built—is therefore $\Theta(n)$. The time to build the automaton, however, can be large if Σ is large. We begin this section with the definition of a finite automaton. We then examine a special string-matching automaton and show how it can be used to find occurrences of a pattern in a text. This discussion includes details on how to simulate the behavior of a string-matching automaton on a given text. Finally, we shall show how to construct the string-matching automaton for a given input pattern.

Finite automata

A ***finite automaton*** M is a 5-tuple $(Q, q_0, A, \Sigma, \delta)$, where

Q is a finite set of **states,**

$q_0 \in Q$ is the **start state,**

$A \subseteq Q$ is a distinguished set of **accepting states,**

Σ is a finite **input alphabet,**

δ is a function from $Q \times \Sigma$ into Q, called the **transition function** of M.

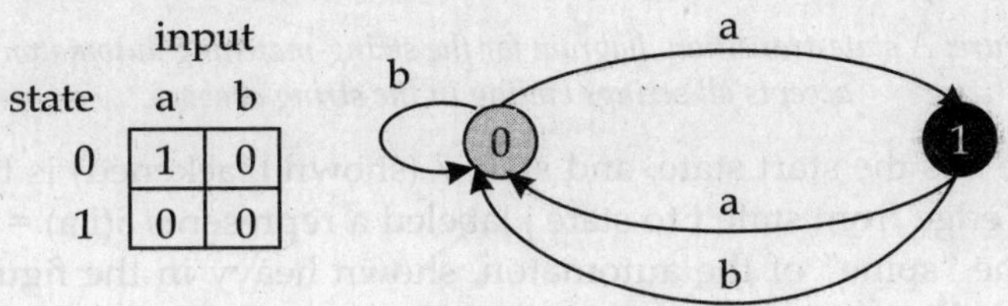

state	input a	input b
0	1	0
1	0	0

Figure: A simple two-state finite automaton .

The finite automaton begins in state q_0 and reads the characters of its input string one at a time. If the automaton is in state q and reads input character a, it moves ("makes a transition") from state q to state $\delta(q, a)$. Whenever its current state q is a member of A, the machine M is said to have *accepted* the string read so far. An input that is not accepted is said to be *rejected.*

A finite automaton M induces a function ø, called the ***final-state function,*** from Σ^* to Q such that ø(w) is the state M ends up in after scanning the string w. Thus, M accepts a string w if and only if ø$(w) \in A$. The function ø is defined by the recursive relation

$$ø(\delta) = qo ,$$

$$ø(wa) = δ(ø(w), a) \text{ for } w \in \Sigma^*, a \in \Sigma.$$

1.5 STRING-MATCHING AUTOMATA

There is a string-matching automaton for every pattern *P*; this automaton must be constructed from the pattern in a preprocessing step before it can be used to search the text string. Figure illustrates this construction for the pattern *P* = ababaca. From now on, we shall assume that *P* is a given fixed pattern string; for brevity, we shall not indicate the dependence upon *P* in our notation.

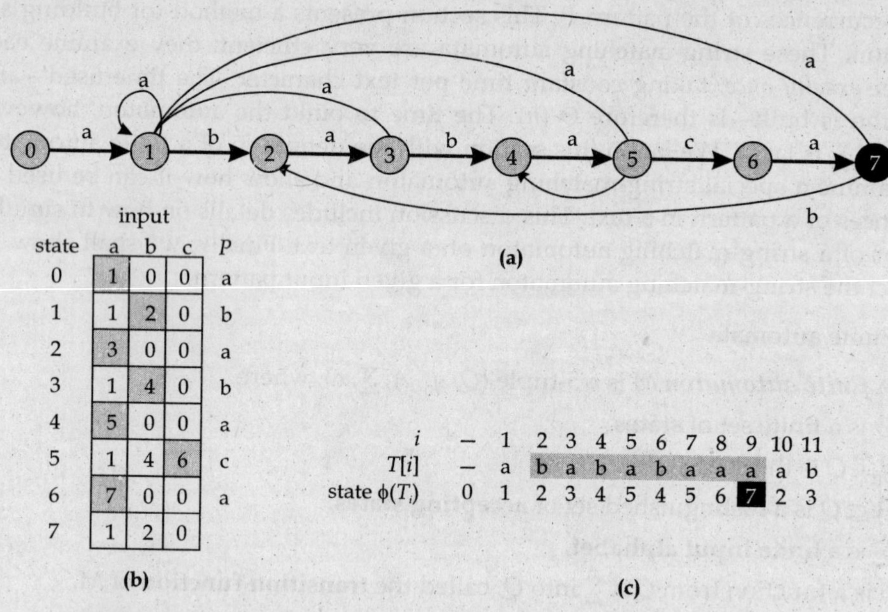

input

state	a	b	c	P
0	1	0	0	a
1	1	2	0	b
2	3	0	0	a
3	1	4	0	b
4	5	0	0	a
5	1	4	6	c
6	7	0	0	a
7	1	2	0	

(b)

i	—	1	2	3	4	5	6	7	8	9	10	11
$T[i]$	—	a	b	a	b	a	b	a	a	a	a	b
state $\phi(T_i)$	0	1	2	3	4	5	4	5	6	7	2	3

(c)

Figure: A state-transition diagram for the string-matching automaton that accepts all strings ending in the string ababaca.

Here State 0 is the start state, and state 7 (shown blackened) is the only accepting state. A directed edge from state i to state j labeled a represents δ(i,a) = j. The right-going edges forming the "spine" of the automaton, shown heavy in the figure, correspond to successful matches between pattern and input characters. The left-going edges correspond to failing matches. Some edges corresponding to failing matches are not shown; by convention, if a state i has no outgoing edge labeled a for some a $\in \Sigma$, then δ (i,a) = 0. (b) The corresponding transition function δ, and the pattern string P = ababaca. The entries corresponding to successful matches between pattern and input characters are shown shaded. (c) The operation of the automaton on the text T = abababacaba. Under each text character T[i] is given the state ø(T_i) the automaton is in after processing the prefix T_i. One occurrence of the pattern is found, ending in position 9.

In order to specify the string-matching automaton corresponding to a given pattern *P*[1 . . *m*], we first define an auxiliary function Σ, called the ***suffix function*** corresponding to *P*. The function Σ is a mapping from Σ^* to {0, 1, . . . , *m*} such that Σ (*x*) is the length of the longest prefix of *P* that is a suffix of *x*:

$$\phi(x) = \max\{k : p_k \sqsupset x\}$$

The suffix function $\sum$is well defined since the empty string $P_0 = \varepsilon$ is a suffix of every string. As examples, for the pattern P = ab, we have $\sum(\varepsilon) = 0$, $\sum$(ccaca) = 1, and $\sum$(ccab) = 2. For a pattern P of length m, we have $\sum(x) = m$ if and only if $P \sqsupset x$. It follows from the definition of the suffix function that if $x \sqsupset y$, then $\sum(x) \leq \sum(y)$.

We define the string-matching automaton corresponding to a given pattern P[1 . . m] as follows.

- The state set Q is {0, 1, . . . , m}. The start state q_0 is state 0, and state m is the only accepting state.
- The transition function δ is defined by the following equation, for any state q and character a:

$$\delta\,(q, a) = \sum\,(P_q a)\,.$$

Here is an intuitive rationale for defining δ(q, a) = $\sum(P_q a)$. The machine maintains as an invariant of its operation that

$$\Phi(T_i) = \sum(T_i)\;;$$

1.6 KNUTH-MORRIS-PRATT ALGORITHM

We now present a linear-time string-matching algorithm due to Knuth, Morris, and Pratt. Their algorithm achieves a $\Theta(n + m)$ running time by avoiding the computation of the transition function δ altogether, and it does the pattern matching using just an auxiliary function π[1 . . m] precomputed from the pattern in time $O(m)$. The array π allows the transition function δ to be computed efficiently (in an amortized sense) "on the fly" as needed. Roughly speaking, for any state q = 0, 1, . . . , m,and any character $a \in \sum$, the value $\pi[q]$ contains the information that is independent of a and is needed to compute $\delta\,(q, a)$. (This remark will be clarified shortly.) Since the array π has only m entries, whereas δ has $O(m\ |\sum|)$ entries, we save a factor of $\sum$ in the preprocessing by computing π rather than δ.

The prefix function for a pattern

The prefix function for a pattern encapsulates knowledge about how the pattern matches against shifts of itself. This information can be used to avoid testing useless shifts in the naive pattern-matching algorithm or to avoid the pre-computation of δ for a string-matching automaton.

Consider the operation of the naive string matcher. Figure below shows a particular shift s of a template containing the pattern P = ababaca against a text T. For this example, q = 5 of the characters have matched successfully, but the 6th pattern character fails to match the corresponding text character. The information that q characters have matched successfully determines the corresponding text characters. Knowing these q text characters allows us to determine immediately that certain shifts are invalid. In the example of the figure, the shift s + 1 is necessarily invalid, since the first pattern character, an a, would be aligned with a text character that is known to match with the second pattern character, a b. The shift s + 2 shown in part (b) of the figure, however, aligns the first three pattern characters with three text characters that must necessarily match. In general, it is useful to know the answer to the following question:

Given that pattern characters $P[1\,..\,q]$ match text characters $T[s + 1\,..\,s + q]$, what is the least shift $s' > s$ such that

$$P[1\,..\,k] = T[s'\,1\,..\,s'\,k],$$

where $s' + k = s + q$?

Such a shift s' is the first shift greater than s that is not necessarily invalid due to our knowledge of $T[s + 1\,..\,s + q]$. In the best case, we have that $s' = s + q$, and shifts $s + 1, s + 2, \ldots, s + q - 1$ are all immediately ruled out. In any case, at the new shift s' we don't need to compare the first k characters of P with the corresponding characters of T, since we are guaranteed that

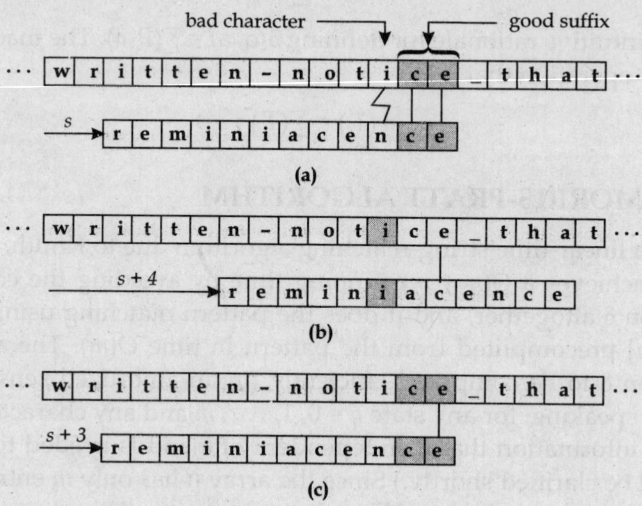

Figure: The prefix function π. (a) The pattern P = ababaca is aligned with a text T so that the first q = 5 characters match. Matching characters, shown shaded, are connected by vertical lines. (b) Using only our knowledge of the 5 matched characters, we can deduce that a shift of s + 1 is invalid, but that a shift of s' = s + 2 is consistent with everything we know about the text and therefore is potentially valid. (c) The useful information for such deductions can be precomputed by comparing the pattern with itself. Here, we see that the longest prefix of P that is also a suffix of P_5 is P_3. This infomation is precomputed and represented in the array π, so that π[5] = 3. Given that q characters have matched successfully at shift s, the next potentially valid shift is at s' = s + (q - π[q]).

We formalize the precomputation required as follows. Given a pattern $P[1\,..\,m]$, the ***prefix function*** for the pattern P is the function π: $\{1, 2, \ldots, m\} \rightarrow \{0, 1, \ldots, m - 1\}$ such that

$$\pi[q] = \max\{k : k < q \text{ and } P_k \supset P_q\}$$

That is, $\pi[q]$ is the length of the longest prefix of P that is a proper suffix of P_q.

The Knuth-Morris-Pratt matching algorithm is given in pseudocode below as the procedure KMP-MATCHER. It is mostly modeled after FINITE-AUTOMATON-MATCHER, as we shall see. KMP-MATCHER calls the auxiliary procedure COMPUTE-PREFIX-FUNCTION to compute π.

```
KMP-MATCHER(T, P)
n ← length[T]
m ← length[P]
π ← COMPUTE-PREFIX-FUNCTION(P)
q ← 0
for i ← 1 to n
do while q > 0 and P[q + 1] ≠ T[i]
do q ← π [q]
if P[q + 1] = T[i]
then q ← q + 1
if q = m
then print "Pattern occurs with shift" i - m
q ← π [q]
```

```
COMPUTE-PREFIX-FUNCTION(P)
1   m ← length[P]
2   π [1] ← 0
3   k ← 0
4   for q ← 2 to m
5   do while k > 0 and P[k + 1 ≠ P[q]
6   do k ← π [k]
7   if P[k + 1] = P[q]
8   then k ← k + 1
9   π [q] ← k
10  return π
```

We begin with an analysis of the running times of these procedures. Proving these procedures correct will be more complicated.

Analysis

We know the running time of COMPUTE-PREFIX-FUNCTION is O(m), using an amortized analysis . We associate a potential of k with the current state k of the algorithm. This potential has an initial value of 0, by line 3. Line 6 decreases k whenever it is executed, since π[k] < k. Since π [k] ≥ 0 for all k, however, k can never become negative. The only other line that affects k is line 8, which increases k by at most one during each execution of the for loop body. Since k < q upon entering the for loop, and since q is incremented in each iteration of the for loop body, k < q always holds. (This justifies the claim that π [q] < q as well, by line 9.) We can pay for each execution of the while loop body on line 6 with the corresponding decrease in the potential function, since π [k] < k. Line 8 increases the potential function by at most one, so that the amortized cost of the loop body on lines 5-9 is O(1). Since the number of outer-loop iterations is O(m), and since the final potential function is at least as great as the initial potential function, the total actual worst-case running time of COMPUTE-PREFIX-FUNCTION is O(m).

The Knuth-Morris-Pratt algorithm runs in time O(m + n). The call of COMPUTE-PREFIX-FUNCTION takes O(m) time as we have just seen, and a similar amortized analysis, using the value of q as the potential function, shows that the remainder of KMP-MATCHER takes O(n) time.

Compared to FINITE-AUTOMATON-MATCHER, by using π rather than δ, we have reduced the time for preprocessing the pattern from O(m |∑|) to O(m), while keeping the actual matching time bounded by O(m + n).

1.7 THE BOYER-MOORE ALGORITHM

If the pattern P is relatively long and the alphabet ∑ is reasonably large, then an algorithm due to Robert S. Boyer and J. Strother Moore is likely to be the most efficient string-matching algorithm.

```
BOYER-MOORE-MATCHER(T, P, ∑)
1    n ← length[T]
2    m ← length[P]
3    Λ ← COMPUTE-LAST-OCCURRENCE-FUNCTION(P, m, ∑)
4    γ ← COMPUTE-GOOD-SUFFIX-FUNCTION(P, m)
5    s ← 0
6    while s ≤ n - m
7    do j ← m
8    while j > 0 and P[j] = T[s + j]
9    do j ← j - 1
10   if j = 0
11   then print "Pattern occurs at shift" s
12   s ← s + γ [0]
13   else s ← s + max(γ [j], j - Λ [T[s + j]])
```

Aside from the mysterious-looking Λ's and γ's, this program looks remarkably like the naive string-matching algorithm. Indeed, suppose we comment out lines 3-4 and replace the updating of s on lines 12-13 with simple incrementations as follows:

```
12   s ← s + 1
13   else s ← s + 1
```

The modified program now acts exactly like the naive string matcher: the **while** loop beginning on line 6 considers each of the $n - m + 1$ possible shifts s in turn, and the **while** loop beginning on line 8 tests the condition $P[1 \,..\, m] = T[s + 1 \,..\, s + m]$ by comparing $P[j]$ with $T[s + j]$ for $j = m, m - 1, \ldots, 1$. If the loop terminates with $j = 0$, a valid shift s has been found, and line 11 prints out the value of s. At this level, the only remarkable features of the Boyer-Moore algorithm are that it compares the pattern against the text *from right to left* and that it increases the shift s on lines 12-13 by a value that is not necessarily 1.

The Boyer-Moore algorithm incorporates two heuristics that allow it to avoid much of the work that our previous string-matching algorithms performed. These heuristics are so effective that they often allow the algorithm to skip altogether the examination of many text characters. These heuristics, known as the "bad-character heuristic" and the "good-suffix heuristic," are illustrated in Figure below. They can be viewed as operating independently in parallel. When a mismatch occurs, each heuristic proposes an amount by which s can safely be increased without missing a valid shift. The Boyer-Moore algorithm chooses the larger amount and increases s by that amount: when line 13 is reached after a mismatch, the bad-character heuristic proposes increasing s by $j - \Lambda[T[s + j]]$, and the good-suffix heuristic proposes increasing s by $\gamma[j]$.

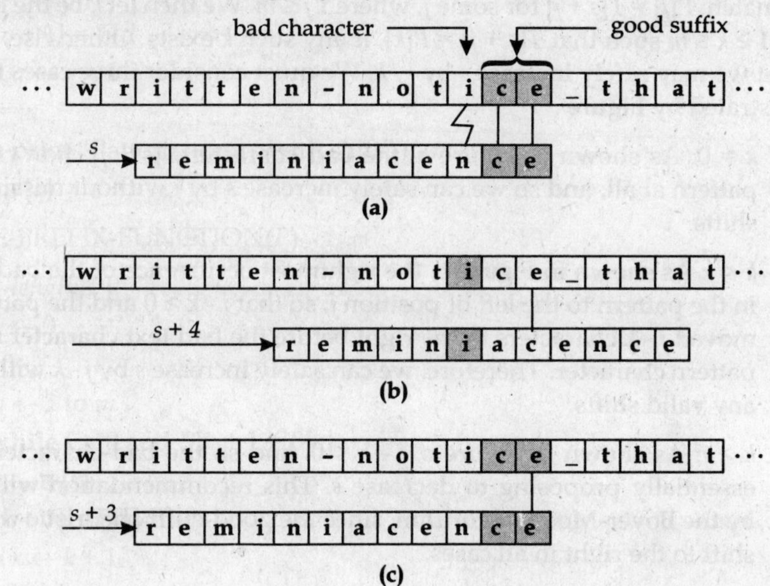

Figure : An illustration of the Boyer-Moore heuristics. (a) Matching the pattern reminiscence against a text by comparing characters in a right-to-left manner. The shift s is invalid; although a "good suffix" ce of the pattern matched correctly against the corresponding characters in the text (matching characters are shown shaded), the "bad character" i, which didn't match the corresponding character n in the pattern, was discovered in the text. (b) The bad-character heuristic proposes moving the pattern to the right, if possible, by the amount that guarantees that the bad text character will match the rightmost occurrence of the bad character in the pattern. In this example, moving the pattern 4 positions to the right causes the bad text character i in the text to match the rightmost i in the pattern, at position 6. If the bad character doesn't occur in the pattern, then the pattern may be moved completely past the bad character in the text. If the rightmost occurrence of the bad character in the pattern is to the right of the current bad character position, then this heuristic makes no proposal. (c) With the good-suffix heuristic, the pattern is moved to the right by the least amount that guarantees that any pattern characters that align with the good suffix ce previously found in the text will match those suffix characters. In this example, moving the pattern 3 positions to the right satisfies this condition. Since the good-suffix heuristic proposes a movement of 3 positions, which is smaller than the 4-position proposal of the bad-character heuristic, the Boyer-Moore algorithm increases the shift by 4.

1.8 THE BAD-CHARACTER HEURISTIC

When a mismatch occurs, the bad-character heuristic uses information about where the bad text character T[s + j] occurs in the pattern (if it occurs at all) to propose a new shift. In the best case, the mismatch occurs on the first comparison (P[m] ≠T[s + m]) and the bad character T[s + m] does not occur in the pattern at all. (Imagine searching for am in the text string bn.) In this case, we can increase the shift s by m, since any shift smaller than s + m will align some pattern character against the bad character, causing a mismatch. If the best case occurs repeatedly, the Boyer-Moore algorithm examines only a fraction 1/m of the text characters, since each text character examined yields a mismatch, thus causing s to increase by m. This best-case behavior illustrates the power of matching right-to-left instead of left-to-right.

In general, the ***bad-character heuristic*** works as follows. Suppose we have just found a mismatch: $P[j] \neq T[s + j]$ for some j, where $1 j \leq m$. We then let k be the largest index in the range $1 \geq k \leq m$ such that $T[s + j] = P[k]$, if any such k exists. Otherwise, we let $k = 0$. We claim that we may safely increase s by $j - k$. We must consider three cases to prove this claim, as illustrated by Figure .

- $k = 0$: As shown in Figure a, the bad character $T[s + j]$ didn't occur in the pattern at all, and so we can safely increase s by j without missing any valid shifts.

- $k < j$: As shown in Figure b, the rightmost occurrence of the bad character is in the pattern to the left of position j, so that $j - k > 0$ and the pattern must be moved $j - k$ characters to the right before the bad text character matches any pattern character. Therefore, we can safely increase s by $j - k$ without missing any valid shifts.

- $k > j$: As shown in Figure c, $j - k < 0$, and so the bad-character heuristic is essentially proposing to decrease s. This recommendation will be ignored by the Boyer-Moore algorithm, since the good-suffix heuristic will propose a shift to the right in all cases.

The following simple program defines Λ [a] to be the index of the rightmost position in the pattern at which character a occurs, for each a ∈ ∑. If a does not occur in the pattern, then Λ [a] is set to 0. We call Λ the last-occurrence function for the pattern. With this definition, the expression j - Λ [T[s + j]] on line 13 of BOYER-MOORE MATCHER implements the bad-character heuristic. (Since j - Λ [T[s + j]] is negative if the rightmost occurrence of the bad character T[s + j] in the pattern is to the right of position j, we rely on the positivity of γ [j], proposed by the good-suffix heuristic, to ensure that the algorithm makes progress at each step.)

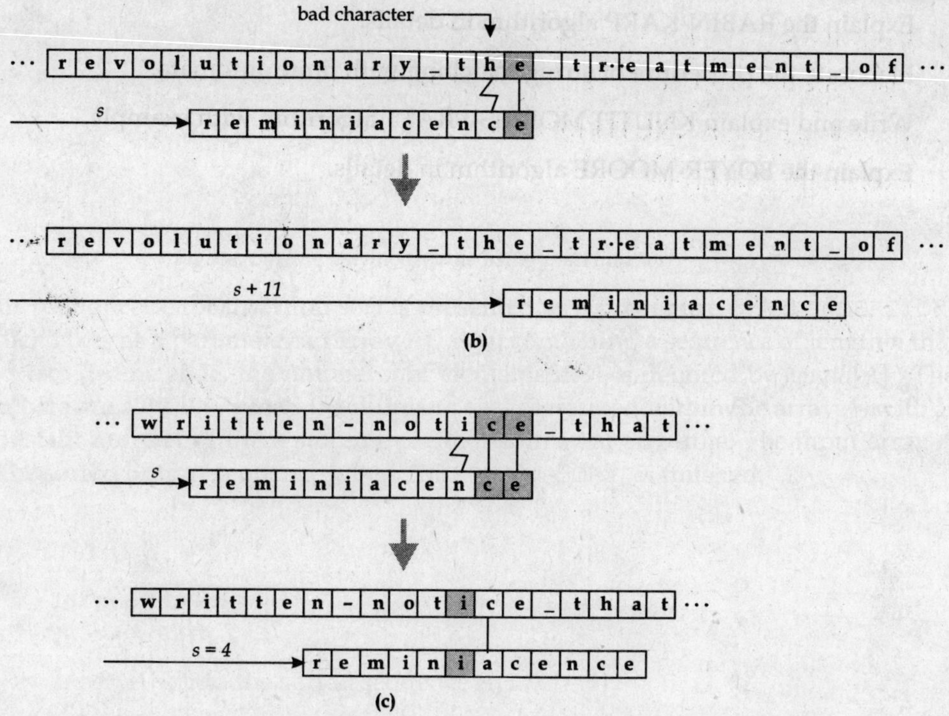

Figure : The cases of the bad-character heuristic. (a) The bad character h occurs nowhere in the pattern, and so the pattern can be advanced j = 11 characters until it has passed over the bad character. (b) The rightmost occurrence of the bad character in the pattern is at position k < j, and so the pattern can be advanced j - k characters. Since j = 10 and k = 6 for the bad character i, the pattern can be advanced 4 positions until the i's line up. (c) The rightmost occurrence of the bad character in the pattern is at position k > j. In this example, j = 10 and k = 12 for the bad character e. The bad-character heuristic proposes a negative shift, which is ignored.

COMPUTE-LAST-OCCURRENCE-FUNCTION(P, m, Σ)

```
for each character a ∈ Σ
do Λ [a] = 0
for j ← 1 to m
do Λ [P[j]] ← j
return Λ
```

The running time of procedure COMPUTE-LAST-OCCURRENCE-FUNCTION is $O(|\Sigma| + m)$.

REVIEW QUESTIONS

1. What is string-matching problem? Explain in details.
2. Prove: suppose that x, y, and z are strings such that $x \supset$ and $y \supset z$. if $|x| \leq |y|$, then $x \supset y$. if $|x| \geq |y|$, then $y \supset x$. if $|x| = |y|$, then $x = y$.
3. Elaborate the working of naive string-matching algorithm.

4. Explain the RABIN-KARP algorithm in details.
5. Elaborate the procedure of string matching with finite automata.
6. Write and explain KNUTH-MORRIS-PRATT algorithm with example.
7. Explain the BOYER-MOORE algorithm in details.

CHAPTER 2

RANDOMIZATION

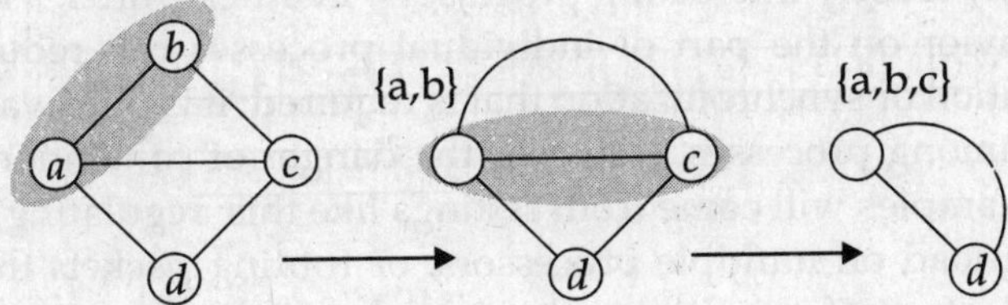

2.1 INTRODUCTION

The idea that a process can be "random" is not a new one; we can trace the notion far back into the history of human thought . Subjects like geometry and logic have been treated mathematically for several thousand years, the mathematical study of probability is surprisingly young; the first known attempts to seriously formalize it came about in the 1600s.

Randomization and probabilistic analysis are themes that cut across many areas of computer science, including algorithm design, and when one thinks about random processes in the context of computation, it is usually in one of two distinct ways. One view is to consider the world as behaving randomly: One can consider traditional algorithms that confront randomly generated input. This approach is often termed *average-case analysis*, since we are studying the behavior of an algorithm on an "average" input (subject to some underlying random process), rather than a worst-case input.

A second view is to consider algorithms that behave randomly: The world provides the same worst-case input as always, but we allow our algorithm to make random decisions as it processes the input. Thus the role of randomization in this approach is purely internal to the algorithm and does not require new assumptions about the nature of the input. It is this notion of a *randomized algorithm* that we will be considering in this chapter.

Why might it be useful to design an algorithm that is allowed to make random decisions? A first answer would be to observe that by allowing randomization, we've made our underlying model more powerful. Efficient deterministic algorithms that always yield the correct answer are a special case of efficient randomized algorithms that only need to yield the correct answer with high probability; they are also a special case of randomized algorithms that are always correct, and run efficiently *in expectation*.

Even in a worst-case world, an algorithm that does its own "internal" randomization may be able to offset certain worst-case phenomena. So problems that may not have been solvable by efficient deterministic algorithms may still be amenable to randomized algorithms.

But this is not the whole story, and in fact we'll be looking at randomized algorithms for a number of problems where there exist comparably efficient deterministic algorithms. Even in such situations, a randomized approach often exhibits considerable power for further reasons: It may be conceptually much simpler; or it may allow the algorithm to function while maintaining very little internal state or memory of the past. The advantages of randomization seem to increase further as one considers larger computer systems and networks, with many loosely interacting processes—in other words, a *distributed sys- tem.* Here random behavior on the part of individual processes can reduce the amount of explicit communication or synchronization that is required; it is often valuable as a tool for *symmetry-breaking* among processes, reducing the danger of contention and "hot spots." A number of our examples will come from settings like this: regulating access to a shared resource, balancing load on multiple processors, or routing packets through a network. Even a small level of comfort with randomized heuristics can give one considerable leverage in thinking about large systems.

2.2 A FIRST APPLICATION: CONTENTION RESOLUTION

Let us begin with a first application of randomized algorithms contention resolution in a distributed system—that illustrates the general style of analysis.

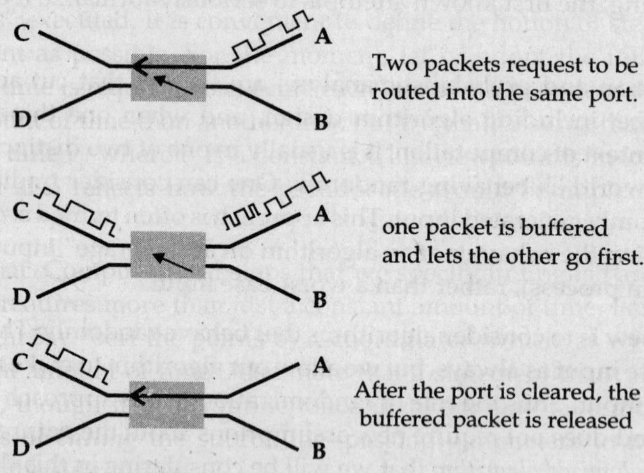

Fig: An example of contention resolution

We will be using for many of the algorithms that follow. In particular, it is a chance to work through some basic manipulations involving *events* and their probabilities, analyzing intersections of events using *independence* as well as unions of events using a simple *Union Bound.* For the sake of completeness, we give a brief summary of these concepts in the final section of this chapter

The Problem

Suppose we have n processes $P1, P2, \ldots, Pn$, each competing for access to a single shared database. We imagine time as being divided into discrete *rounds*. The database has the property that it can be accessed by at most one process in a single round; if two or more processes attempt to access it simultaneously, then all processes are "locked out" for the duration of that round. So, while each process wants to access the database as often as possible, it's pointless for all of them to try accessing it in every round; then everyone will be perpetually locked out. What's needed is a way to divide up the rounds among the processes in an equitable fashion, so that all processes get through to the database on a regular basis.

If it is easy for the processes to communicate with one another, then one can imagine all sorts of direct means for resolving the contention. But suppose that the processes can't communicate with one another at all; how then can they work out a protocol under which they manage to "take turns" in accessing the database?

Designing a Randomized Algorithm

Randomization provides a natural protocol for this problem, which we can specify simply as follows. For some number $p > 0$ that we'll determine shortly, each process will attempt to access the database in each round with probability p, independently of the decisions of the other processes. So, if exactly one process decides to make the attempt in a given round, it will succeed; if two or more try, then they will all be locked out; and if none try, then the round is in a sense "wasted." This type of strategy, in which each of a set of identical processes randomizes its behavior, is the core of the *symmetry- breaking* paradigm that we mentioned initially: If all the processes operated in lockstep, repeatedly trying to access the database at the same time, there'd be no progress; but by randomizing, they "smooth out" the contention.

Analyzing the Algorithm

As with many applications of randomization, the algorithm in this case is extremely simple to state; the interesting issue is to analyze its performance.

Defining Some Basic Events When confronted with a probabilistic system like this, a good first step is to write down some basic events and think about their probabilities. Here's a first event to consider. For a given process Pi and a given round t, let A[i, t] denote the event that Pi attempts to access the database in round t. We know that each process attempts an access in each round with probability p, so the probability of this event, for any i and t, is Pr A[i, t] = p. For every event, there is also a *complementary event*, indicating that the event did not occur; here we have the complementary event A[i, t] that Pi does not attempt to access the database in round t, with probability

$$\Pr[\,A[i,t]\,] = 1 - \Pr[\,A[i,t]\,] = 1 - p.$$

Our real concern is whether a process *succeeds* in accessing the database in a given round. Let S[i, t] denote this event. Clearly, the process Pi must attempt an access in round t in order to succeed. Indeed, succeeding is equivalent to the following: Process Pi attempts to access the database in round *t*, and each other process *does not* attempt to access the database in round *t*. Thus S[*i, t*] is equal to the intersection of the event A[*i, t*] with all the complementary events

A[*j* , *t*], for *j*! = *i*:

$$S[i,t]=A[i,t]\cap\left(\bigcap_{j\neq i}\overline{A[j,t]}\right)$$

All the events in this intersection are independent, by the definition of the contention-resolution protocol. Thus, to get the probability of S[*i, t*], we can multiply the probabilities of all the events in the intersection:

$$\Pr[S(i,t)]=\Pr[A(i,t)]\cdot\prod_{j\neq i}\Pr\left[\overline{A(j,t)}\right]=p(1-p)^{n-1}$$

We now have a nice, closed-form expression for the probability that *Pi* succeeds in accessing the database in round *t*; we can now ask how to set *p* so that this success probability is maximized. Observe first that the success probability is 0 for the extreme cases *p* = 0 and *p* = 1 (these correspond to the extreme case in which processes never bother attempting, and the opposite extreme case in which every process tries accessing the database in every round, so that everyone is locked out). The function *f* (*p*) = *p*(1 − *p*) *n*−1 is positive for values of *p* strictly between 0 and 1, and its derivative *f* (*p*) = (1 − *p*)*n*−1 − (*n* − 1)*p*(1 − *p*)*n*−2 has a single zero at the value *p* = 1/*n*, where the maximum is achieved. Thus we can maximize the success probability by setting *p* = 1/*n*. (Notice that *p* = 1/*n* is a natural intuitive choice as well, if one wants exactly one process to attempt an access in any round.)

When we set *p* = 1/*n*, we get

$$\Pr[S(i,t)]=\frac{1}{n}\left(1-\frac{1}{n}\right)^{n-1}$$

Waiting for a Particular Process to Succeed Let's consider this protocol with the optimal value *p* = 1/*n* for the access probability. Suppose we are interested in how long it will take process *Pi* to succeed in accessing the database at least once. We see from the earlier calculation that the probability of its succeeding in any one round is not very good, if *n* is reasonably large. How about if we consider multiple rounds?

Let F[*i, t*] denote the "failure event" that process *Pi* does not succeed in *any* of the rounds 1 through *t*. This is clearly just the intersection of the complementary events S[*i, r*] for *r* = 1, 2, ... , *t*. Moreover, since each of these events is independent, we can compute the probability of F[*i, t*] by multiplication:

$$\Pr[S(i,t)]=\Pr\left[\bigcap_{r=1}\overline{S[i,r]}\right]-\left[1-\frac{1}{n}\left(1-\frac{1}{n}\right)^{n-1}\right]^{r}$$

Waiting for All Processes to Get Through Finally, we're in a position to ask the question that was implicit in the overall setup: How many rounds must elapse before there's a high probability that all processes will have succeeded in accessing the database at least once?

To address this, we say that the protocol *fails* after *t* rounds if some process has not yet succeeded in accessing the database. Let F*t* denote the event that the protocol fails after *t* rounds; the goal is to find a reasonably small value of *t* for which Pr F*t* is small.

The event F*t* occurs if and only if one of the events F[*i*, *t*] occurs; so we can write

$$F_t = \bigcup_{i=1}^{n} F[i,t]$$

Previously, we considered intersections of independent events, which were very simple to work with; here, by contrast, we have a union of events that are not independent. Probabilities of unions like this can be very hard to compute exactly, and in many settings it is enough to analyze them using a simple *Union Bound*, which says that the probability of a union of events is upper-bounded by the sum of their individual probabilities.

2.3 FINDING THE GLOBAL MINIMM CUT

Randomization naturally suggested itself in the previous example, since we were assuming a model with many processes that could not directly commu- nicate. We now look at a problem on graphs for which a randomized approach comes as somewhat more of a surprise, since it is a problem for which perfectly reasonable deterministic algorithms exist as well.

The Problem

Given an undirected graph *G* = (*V* , *E*), we define a *cut* of *G* to be a partition of *V* into two non-empty sets *A* and *B*. Earlier, when we looked at network flows, we worked with the closely related definition of an *s-t cut*: there, given a directed graph *G* = (*V* , *E*) with distinguished source and sink nodes *s* and *t*, an *s-t cut* was defined to be a partition of *V* into sets *A* and *B* such that *s* ε *A* and *t* ∈ *B*. Our definition now is slightly different, since the underlying graph is now undirected and there is no source or sink.

For a cut (*A, B*) in an undirected graph *G*, the *size* of (*A, B*) is the number of edges with one end in *A* and the other in *B*. A *global minimum cut* (or "global min-cut" for short) is a cut of minimum size. The term *global* here is meant to connote that any cut of the graph is allowed; there is no source or sink. Thus the global min-cut is a natural "robustness" parameter; it is the smallest number of edges whose deletion disconnects the graph. We first check that network flow techniques are indeed sufficient to find a global min-cut.

There is a polynomial-time algorithm to find a global min-cut in an undirected graph G.

Proof. We start from the similarity between cuts in undirected graphs and *s-t* cuts in directed graphs, and with the fact that we know how to find the latter optimally.

So given an undirected graph *G* = (*V* , *E*), we need to transform it so that there are directed edges and there is a source and sink. We first replace every undirected edge *e* = (*u* , *v*) *E* with two oppositely oriented directed edges, *e* = (*u* , *v*) and *e* = (*v* , *u*), each of capacity 1. Let G denote the resulting directed graph.

Now suppose we pick two arbitrary nodes *s*, *t* ε *V* , and find the minimum *s-t* cut in G . It is easy to check that if (A, B) is this minimum cut in G , then (A, B) is also a cut of minimum size in G *among all those that separate s from t*. But we know that the global min-cut in G must separate s from *something,* since both sides A and B are nonempty, and s belongs to only one of them. So we fix any $s \varepsilon V$ and compute the minimum s-t cut in G for every other node $t \varepsilon V-\{s\}$. This is $n-1$ directed minimum-cut computations, and the best among these will be global minimum cut.

The algorithm gives the strong impression that finding a global min-cut in an undirected graph is in some sense a *harder* problem than finding a minimum s-t cut in a flow network, as we had to invoke a subroutine for the latter problem $n-1$ times in our method for solving the former. But it turns out that this is just an illusion. A sequence of increasingly simple algorithms in the late 1980s and early 1990s showed that global min-cuts in undirected graphs could actually be computed just as efficiently as s-t cuts or even more so, and by techniques that didn't require augmenting paths or even a notion of flow. The high point of this line of work came with David Karger's discovery in 1992 of the Contraction Algorithm, a randomized method that is qualitatively simpler than all previous algorithms for global min-cuts. Indeed, it is sufficiently simple that, on a first impression, it is very hard to believe that it actually works.

Designing the Algorithm

Here we describe the Contraction Algorithm in its simplest form. This version, while it runs in polynomial time, is not among the most efficient algorithms for global min-cuts. However, subsequent optimizations to the algorithm have given it a much better running time.

The Contraction Algorithm works with a connected *multigraph* $G = (V, E)$; this is an undirected graph that is allowed to have multiple "parallel" edges between the same pair of nodes. It begins by choosing an edge $e = (u, v)$ of G uniformly at random and *contracting* it, as shown in Figure.1. This means we produce a new graph G in which u and v have been identified into a single new node w; all other nodes keep their identity. Edges that had one end equal to u and the other equal to v are deleted from G . Each other edge e is preserved in G , but if one of its ends was equal to u or v, then this end is updated to be equal to the new node w. Note that, even if G had at most one edge between any two nodes, G may end up with parallel edges.

The Contraction Algorithm then continues recursively on G , choosing an edge uniformly at random and contracting it. As these recursive calls proceed, the constituent vertices of G should be viewed as *supernodes*: Each supernode w corresponds to the subset $S(w) \varepsilon V$ that has been "swallowed up" in the contractions that produced w. The algorithm terminates when it reaches a graph G that has only two supernodes $v1$ and $v2$ (presumably with a number of parallel edges between them). Each of these super-nodes vi has a corresponding subset $S(vi) \varepsilon V$ consisting of the nodes that have been contracted into it, and these two sets $S(v1)$ and $S(v2)$ form a partition of V . We output $(S(v1), S(v2))$ as the cut found by the algorithm.

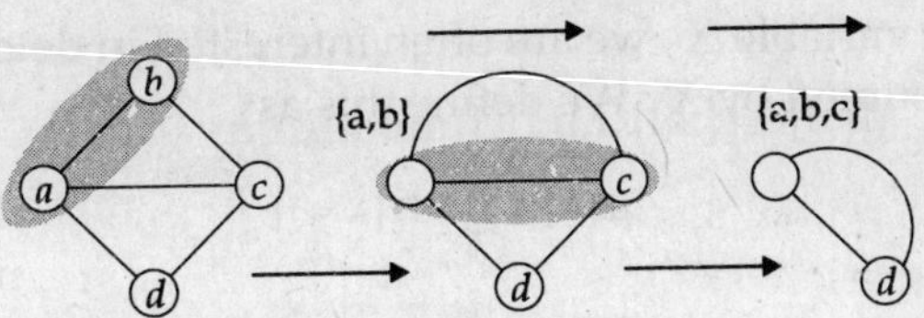

Figure .1 The Contraction Algorithm applied to a four-node input graph.

The Contraction Algorithm applied to a multigraph $G = (V, E)$:

For each node v, we will record the set $S(v)$ of nodes that have been contracted into v Initially $S(v) = \{v\}$ for each v

If G has two nodes $v1$ and $v2$, then return the cut $(S(v1), S(v2))$

Else choose an edge $e = (u, v)$ of G uniformly at random

Let G be the graph resulting from the contraction of e, with a new node zuv replacing u and v

Define

$$S(Zuv)–S(u) \cup S(v)$$

Apply the Contraction Algorithm recursively to G End if

Analyzing the Algorithm

The algorithm is making random choices, so there is some probability that it will succeed in finding a global min-cut and some probability that it won't. One might imagine at first that the probability of success is exponentially small. After all, there are exponentially many possible cuts of G; what's favoring the minimum cut in the process? But we'll show first that, in fact, the success probability is only polynomially small. It will then follow that by running the algorithm a polynomial number of times and returning the best cut found in any run, we can actually produce a global min-cut with high probability.

2.4 Random Variables and Their Expectations

Thus far our analysis of randomized algorithms and processes has been based on identifying certain "bad events" and bounding their probabilities. This is a qualitative type of analysis, in the sense that the algorithm either succeeds or it doesn't. A more quantitative style of analysis would consider certain parameters associated with the behavior of the algorithm—for example, its running time, or the quality of the solution it produces—and seek to determine the *expected* size of these parameters over the random choices made by the algorithm. In order to make such analysis possible, we need the fundamental notion of a *random variable.*

Given a probability space, a random variable X is a function from the underlying sample space to the natural numbers, such that for each natural number j, the set X $-1(j)$ of all sample points taking the value j is an event. Thus we can write Pr [X = j] as loose shorthand for Pr X $-1(j)$; it is because we can ask about X's probability of taking a given value that we think of it as a "random variable."

Given a random variable X, we are often interested in determining its *expectation*— the "average value" assumed by X. We define this as

$$E[X] = \sum_{j=0}^{\infty} J \cdot \Pr[X = j]$$

declaring this to have the value ∞ if the sum diverges. Thus, for example, if X takes each of the values in {1, 2, ... , n} with probability $1/n$, then

$$E[X] = 1(1/n) + 2(1/n) + \ldots + n(1/n) = n+1/n = (n+1)/$$

Example:

Waiting for a First Success

Here's a more useful example, in which we see how an appropriate random variable lets us talk about something like the "running time" of a simple random process. Suppose we have a coin that comes up heads with probability $p > 0$, and tails with probability $1 - p$. Different flips of the coin have independent outcomes. If we flip the coin until we first get a heads, what's the expected number of flips we will perform? To answer this, we let X denote the random variable equal to the number of flips performed. For $j > 0$, we have $\Pr[X = j] = (1 - p)j-1p$: in order for the process to take exactly j steps, the first $j - 1$ flips must come up tails, and the jth must come up heads. Now, applying the definition, we have

$$E[X] = \sum_{j=0}^{\infty} J \cdot \Pr[X = j] = \sum_{j=1}^{\infty} j(1-p)^{j-1} p = \frac{p}{1-p} \sum_{j=1}^{\infty} j(1-p)^{j}$$

$$= \frac{p}{1-p} \cdot \frac{(1-p)}{p^2} = \frac{1}{p}$$

Linearity of Expectation

We broke events down into unions of much simpler events, and worked with the probabilities of these simpler events. This is a powerful technique when working with random variables as well, and it is based on the principle of *linearity of expectation.*

Linearity of Expectation. *Given two random variables X and Y defined over the same probability space, we can define X + Y to be the random variable equal to X (ω) + Y (ω) on a sample point ω. For any X and Y, we have*

$$E[X + Y] = E[X] + E[Y].$$

We omit the proof, which is not difficult. As a result, if we need to compute the expectation of a complicated random variable X, we can first write it as a sum of simpler random variables $X = X1 + X2 + \ldots + Xn$, compute each $E\ Xi$, and then determine $E[X] = E\ Xi$. We now look at some examples of this principle in action.

Example

Collecting Coupons

Before moving on to more sophisticated applications, let's consider one more basic example in which linearity of expectation provides significant leverage.

Suppose that a certain brand of cereal includes a free coupon in each box. There are n different types of coupons. As a regular consumer of this brand, how many boxes do you expect to buy before finally getting a coupon of each type?

Clearly, at least n boxes are needed; but it would be sort of surprising if you actually had all n types of coupons by the time you'd bought n boxes. As you collect more and more different types, it will get less and less likely that a new box has a type of coupon you haven't seen before. Once you have $n - 1$ of the n different types, there's only a probability of $1/n$ that a new box has the missing type you need.

Here's a way to work out the expected time exactly. Let X be the random variable equal to the number of boxes you buy until you first have a coupon of each type. As in our previous examples, this is a reasonably complicated random variable to think about, and we'd like to write it as a sum of simpler random variables. To think about this, let's consider the following natural idea: The coupon-collecting process *makes progress* whenever you buy a box of cereal containing a type of coupon you haven't seen before. Thus the goal of the process is really to make progress n times. Now, at a given point in time, what is the probability that you make progress in the next step? This depends on how many different types of coupons you already have. If you have j types, then the probability of making progress in the next step is $(n - j)/n$: Of the n types of coupons, $n - j$ allow you to make progress. Since the probability varies depending on the number of different types of coupons we have, this suggests a natural way to break down X into simpler random variables, as follows.

Let's say that the coupon-collecting process is in *phase* j when you've already collected j different types of coupons and are waiting to get a new type. When you see a new type of coupon, phase j ends and phase $j + 1$ begins. Thus we start in phase 0, and the whole process is done at the end of phase $n - 1$. Let Xj be the random variable equal to the number of steps you spend in phase j. Then X = X0 + X1 + ... + $Xn-1$, and so it is enough to work out $E\ Xj$ for each j.

$$E\ Xj = n/(n - j).$$

Proof. In each step of phase j, the phase ends immediately if and only if the coupon you get next is one of the $n - j$ types you haven't seen before. Thus, in phase j, you are really just waiting for an event of probability $(n - j)/n$ to occur, and so, the expected length of phase j is $E\ Xj = n/(n - j)$.

Using this, linearity of expectation gives us the overall expected time.

The expected time before all n types of coupons are collected is

$$E\,[X] = nH\,(n) = (n \log n).$$

Proof. By linearity of expectation, we have

$$E[X] = \sum_{j=0}^{n-1} E[X_j] = \sum_{j=0}^{n-1} \frac{n}{n-j} = n\sum_{i=0}^{n-1} \frac{1}{n-j} = n\sum_{i-1}^{n} \frac{1}{i} = nH(n)$$

we know this is asymptotically equal to $\Theta(nlog\ n)$

Once $n - 1$ of the n types of coupons are collected, you expect to buy n more boxes of cereal before you see the final type. In the meantime, you keep getting coupons you've already seen before, and you might conclude that this final type is "the rare one." But in fact it's just as likely as all the others; it's simply that the final one, whichever it turns out to be, is likely to take a long time to get.

A Final Definition: Conditional Expectation

We now discuss one final, very useful notion concerning random variables that will come up in some of the subsequent analyses. Just as one can define the conditional probability of one event given another, one can analogously define the expectation of a random variable conditioned on a certain event. Suppose we have a random variable X and an event E of positive probability. Then we define the *conditional expectation* of X , given E, to be the expected value of X computed only over the part of the sample space corresponding to E. We denote this quantity by $E[X \mid E]$. This simply involves replacing the probabilities Pr $[X = j]$ in the definition of the expectation with conditional probabilities:

$$E[X \mid \varepsilon] = \sum_{j=0}^{\infty} j \cdot \Pr[X = j \mid \varepsilon]$$

2.5 A RANDOMIZED APPROXIMATION ALGORITHM FOR MAX 3-SAT

In the previous section, we saw a number of ways in which linearity of expectation can be used to analyze a randomized process. We now describe an application of this idea to the design of an approximation algorithm. The problem we consider is a variation of the 3-SAT Problem, and we will see that one consequence of our randomized approximation algorithm is a surprisingly strong general statement about 3-SAT that on its surface seems to have nothing to do with either algorithms or randomization.

The Problem

When we studied NP-completeness, a core problem was 3-SAT: Given a set of clauses $C1$, ... , Ck, each of length 3, over a set of variables $X = \{x1, \ldots, xn\}$, does there exist a satisfying truth assignment?

Intuitively, we can imagine such a problem arising in a system that tries to decide the truth or falsehood of statements about the world (the variables $\{xi\}$), given pieces of information that relate them to one another (the clauses $\{Cj\}$). Now the world is a fairly contradictory place, and if our system gathers enough information, it could well end up with a set of clauses that has no satisfying truth assignment.

A natural approach, if we can't find a truth assignment that satisfies all clauses, is to turn the 3-SAT instance into an optimization problem: Given the set of input clauses $C1$, ... , Ck, find a truth assignment that satisfies *as many as possible*. We'll call this the *Maximum 3-Satisfiability Problem* (or *MAX 3-SAT* for short). Of course, this is an NP-hard optimization problem, since it's NP-complete to decide whether the maximum number of simultaneously satisfiable clauses is equal to k.

2.6 RANDOMIZED DIVIDE AND CONQUER: MEDIAN-FINDING AND QUICKSORT

We've done the divide-and-conquer paradigm for designing algorithms at various earlier points in the book. Divide and conquer often works well in conjunction with randomization, and we illustrate this by giving divide-and- conquer algorithms for two fundamental problems: computing the median of n numbers, and sorting. In each case, the "divide" step is performed using randomization; consequently, we will use expectations of random variables to analyze the time spent on recursive calls.

The Problem: Finding the Median

Suppose we are given a set of n numbers $S = \{a1, a2, \dots, an\}$. Their *median* is the number that would be in the middle position if we were to sort them. There's an annoying technical difficulty if n is even, since then there is no "middle position"; thus we define things precisely as follows: The median of $S = \{a1, a2, \dots, an\}$ is equal to the kth largest element in S, where $k = (n + 1)/2$ if n is odd, and $k = n/2$ if n is even. In what follows, we'll assume for the sake of simplicity that all the numbers are distinct. Without this assumption, the problem becomes notationally more complicated, but no new ideas are brought into play.

It is clearly easy to compute the median in time $O(n \log n)$ if we simply sort the numbers first. But if one begins thinking about the problem, it's far from clear why sorting is *necessary* for computing the median, or even why $(n \log n)$ time is necessary. In fact, we'll show how a simple randomized approach, based on divide-and-conquer, yields an expected running time of $O(n)$.

Designing the Algorithm

A Generic Algorithm Based on Splitters The first key step toward gettingan expected linear running time is to move from median-finding to the more general problem of *selection*. Given a set of n numbers S and a number k between 1 and n, consider the function Select(S, k) that returns the kth largest element in S. As special cases, Select includes the problem of finding the median of S via Select$(S, n/2)$ or Select$(S, (n + 1)/2)$; it also includes the easier problems of finding the minimum (Select$(S, 1)$) and the maximum (Select(S, n)). Our goal is to design an algorithm that implements Select so that it runs in expected time $O(n)$.

The basic structure of the algorithm implementing Select is as follows. We choose an element $a_i \in S$, the "splitter," and form the sets $S- = \{aj : aj < ai\}$ and $S+ = \{aj : aj > ai\}$. We can then determine which of $S-$ or $S+$ contains the kth largest element, and iterate only on this one. Without specifying yet how we plan to choose the splitter, here's a more concrete description of how we form the two sets and iterate.

Select(S,k):
Choose a splitter $a_i \in S$, For each element aj of S Put aj in $S-$ if $aj < ai$
Put aj in $S+$ if $aj > ai$
Endfor
If $|S-| = k - 1$ then
The splitter ai was in fact the desired answer

Else if $|S-| \geq k$ then
The kth largest element lies in $S-$
Recursively call *Select(S− , k)*
Else suppose $|S-| = < k - 1$
The kth largest element lies in $S+$
Recursively call *Select(S+ , k − 1 −)*
Endif

Observe that the algorithm is always called recursively on a strictly smaller set, so it must terminate. Also, observe that if $|S| = 1$, then we must have $k = 1$, and indeed the single element in S will be returned by the algorithm. Finally, from the choice of which recursive call to make, it's clear by induction that the right answer will be returned when $|S| > 1$ as well.

Choosing a Good Splitter Now let's consider ho w the running time of Select depends on the way we choose the splitter. Assuming we can select a splitter in linear time, the rest of the algorithm takes linear time plus the time for the recursive call. But how is the running time of the recursive call affected by the choice of the splitter? Essentially, it's important that the splitter significantly reduce the size of the set being considered, so that we don't keep making passes through large sets of numbers many times. So a good choice of splitter should produce sets $S-$ and $S+$ that are approximately equal in size.

For example, if we could always choose the median as the splitter, then we could show a linear bound on the running time as follows. Let cn be the running time for Select, not counting the time for the recursive call. Then, with medians as splitters, the running time $T(n)$ would be bounded by the recurrence $T(n) \leq T(n/2) + cn$. It has the solution $T(n) = O(n)$.

Of course, hoping to be able to use the median as the splitter is rather circular, since the median is what we want to compute in the first place! But, in fact, one can show that any "well-centered" element can serve as a good splitter: If we had a way to choose splitters *ai* such that there were at least εn elements both larger and smaller than *ai*, for any fixed constant $\varepsilon > 0$, then the size of the sets in the recursive call would shrink by a factor of at least $(1 - \varepsilon)$ each time. Thus the running time $T(n)$ would be bounded by the recurrence $T(n) \leq T((1 - \varepsilon)n) + cn$. The same argument that showed the previous recurrence had the solution $T(n) = O(n)$ can be used here: If we unroll this recurrence for any $\varepsilon > 0$, we get

$$T(n) \leq cn + c(n-1) + c(n-2) + \ldots = \frac{cn(n+1)}{2} = \Theta(n^2)$$

Random Splitters Choosing a "well-centered" splitter, in the sense we have just defined, is certainly similar in flavor to our original problem of choosing the median; but the situation is really not so bad, since *any* well-centered splitter will do.

Thus we will implement the as-yet-unspecified step of selecting a splitter using the following simple rule:

Choose a splitter *ai* ε *S* uniformly at random

The intuition here is very natural: since a fairly large fraction of the elements are reasonably well-centered, we will be likely to end up with a good splitter simply by choosing an element at random.

The analysis of the running time with a random splitter is based on this idea; we expect the size of the set under consideration to go down by a fixed constant fraction every iteration, so we should get a convergent series and hence a linear bound as previously. We now show how to make this precise.

Analyzing the Algorithm

We'll say that the algorithm is in *phase j* when the size of the set under consideration is at most *n*(3/4)*j* but greater than *n*(3/4)*j*+1. Let's try to bound the expected time spent by the algorithm in phase *j*. In a given iteration of the algorithm, we say that an element of the set under consideration is *central* if at least a quarter of the elements are smaller than it and at least a quarter of the elements are larger than it.

Now observe that if a central element is chosen as a splitter, then at least a quarter of the set will be thrown away, the set will shrink by a factor of 3 or better, and the current phase will come to an end. Moreover, half of all the elements in the set are central, and so the probability that our random choice of splitter produces a central element is 1 . Hence, by our simple waiting-time bound the expected number of iterations before a central element is found is 2; and so the expected number of iterations spent in phase *j*, for any *j*, is at most 2.

This is pretty much all we need for the analysis. Let *X* be a random variable equal to the number of steps taken by the algorithm. We can write it as the sum X = X0 + X1 + X2 + .. ., where *Xj* is the expected number of steps spent by the algorithm in phase .*j*

$$E[X] = \sum_j E[X_j] \leq \sum_j 2cn \leq \left(\frac{3}{4}\right)^j = 2cn \sum_j \left(\frac{3}{4}\right)^j \leq 6cn$$

The expected running time of Select(*n, k*) *is O*(*n*).

A Second Application: Quicksort

The randomized divide-and-conquer technique we used to find the median is also the basis of the sorting algorithm Quicksort. As before, we choose a splitter for the input set *S*, and separate *S* into the elements below the splitter value and those above it. The difference is that, rather than looking for the median on just one side of the splitter, we sort both sides recursively and glue the two sorted pieces together (with the splitter in between) to produce the overall output. Also, we need to explicitly include a base case for the recursive code: we only use recursion on sets of size at least 4. A complete description of Quicksort is as follows.

Quicksort(*S*):
If $|S| \leq 3$ then
Sort *S*
Output the sorted list
Else

Choose a splitter *ai belonging S* uniformly at random
For each element *aj* of *S*
Put *aj* in *S*− if *aj* < *ai*
Put *aj* in *S*+ if *aj* > *ai*
Endfor
Recursively call Quicksort(*S*−) and Quicksort(*S*+)
Output the sorted set *S*−, then *ai*, then the sorted set *S*+
Endif

As with median-finding, the worst-case running time of this method is not so good. If we always select the smallest element as a splitter, then the running time $T(n)$ on n-element sets satisfies the same recurrence as before:

$T(n) \leq T(n-1) + cn$, and so we end up with a time bound of $T(n) = (n2)$.

In fact, this is the worst-case running time for Quicksort.

On the positive side, if the splitters selected happened to be the medians of the sets at each iteration, then we get the recurrence $T(n) \leq 2T(n/2) + cn$, which arose frequently in the divide-and-conquer analyses ; the running time in this lucky case is $O(n \log n)$.

Here we are concerned with the *expected running time*; we will show that this can be bounded by $O(n \log n)$, almost as good as in the best case when the splitters are perfectly centered. Our analysis of Quicksort will closely follow the analysis of median-finding. Just as in the Select procedure that we used for median-finding, the crucial definition is that of a *central splitter* —one that divides the set so that each side contains at least a quarter of the elements. (As we discussed earlier, it is enough for the analysis that each side contains at least some fixed constant fraction of the elements; the use of a quarter here is chosen for convenience.) The idea is that a random choice is likely to lead to a central splitter, and central splitters work well. In the case of sorting, a central splitter divides the problem into two considerably smaller subproblems.

To simplify the presentation, we will slightly modify the algorithm so that it only issues its recursive calls when it finds a central splitter. Essentially, this modified algorithm differs from Quicksort in that it prefers to throw away an "off-center" splitter and try again; Quicksort, by contrast, launches the recursive calls even with an off-center splitter, and at least benefits from the work already done in splitting *S*. The point is that the expected running time of this modified algorithm can be analyzed very simply, by direct analogy with our analysis for median-finding. With a bit more work, a very similar but somewhat more involved analysis can also be done for the original Quicksort algorithm as well; however, we will not describe this analysis here.

Modified Quicksort(*S*):

If $|S| \leq 3$ then
Sort *S*
Output the sorted list
Endif
Else

While no central splitter has been found
Choose a splitter *ai belonging S* uniformly at random
For each element *aj* of *S* Put *aj* in *S*− if *aj* < *ai* Put *aj* in *S*+ if *aj* > *ai*
Endfor
If |*S*−| ≥ |*S*|/4 and |*S*+| ≥ |*S*|/4 then
ai is a central splitter
Endif
Endwhile
Recursively call Quicksort(*S*−) and Quicksort(*S*+)
Output the sorted set *S*−, then *ai*, then the sorted set *S*+
Endif

Consider a subproblem for some set *S*. Each iteration of the While loop selects a possible splitter *ai* and spends $O(|S|)$ time splitting the set and deciding if *ai* is central. Earlier we argued that the number of iterations needed until we find a central splitter is at most 2. This gives us the following statement.

The expected running time for the algorithm on a set S, excluding the time spent on recursive calls, is $O(|S|)$.

The expected running time of Modified Quicksort *is* $O(n \log n)$.

We considered this modified version of Quicksort to simplify the analy- sis. Coming back to the original Quicksort, our intuition suggests that the expected running time is no worse than in the modified algorithm, as accept- ing the noncentral splitters helps a bit with sorting, even if it does not help as much as when a central splitter is chosen. As mentioned earlier, one can in fact make this intuition precise, leading to an $O(n \log n)$ expected time bound for the original Quicksort algorithm; we will not go into the details of this here.

REVIEW QUESTIONS

1. Define the term randomization. What are its benefits.?
2. What are applications of randomization?
3. Explain modified version of quicksort. Use randomization.
4. What is randomized divide and conquer.?
5. Explain the process of randomization?

UNIT 5

CHAPTER 3

AMORTIZED ANALYSIS OF DATA STRUCTURE

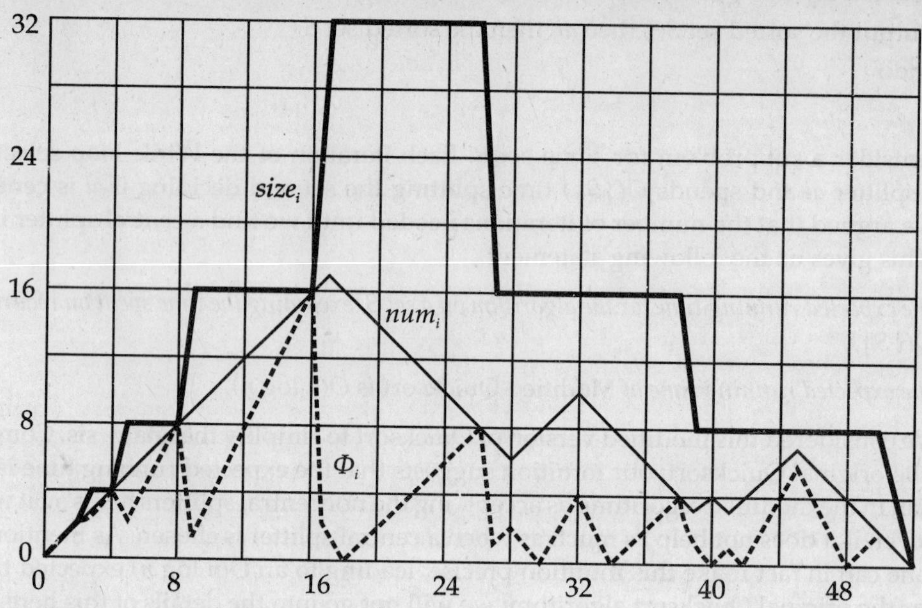

3.1 INTRODUCTION

Auppose you have a data structure such that every time you do a sequence of n operations starting from the empty structure, the total time is O(n) (worst-case over all possible sequences of n operations).`

This is almost as good as having a data structure with O(1) worst case time per operation.

In fact it is exactly as good if the data structure is used only within an algorithm.

We say that a data structure has operations running in amortized time T (·), if every time we do n operations the total running time is O(nT (n)).

This is the "aggregate method" approach to the definition of amortized complexity. It does not allow to differentiate the complexity of more or less efficient operations.

More General Definition

In general, say that you have implemented operations op1; :: : ; opi., You can say that they have, respectively, amortized running time t1();::: ; ti() if for any sequence of operations, where you are doing in total n1 applications of op1, n2 applications of op2 etc. the total time is at most

$$n1t1(n)+ n2t2(n)+ \cdots + niti(n)$$

where n = n1 + ::: ni.

3.2 USES OF AMORTIZED ANALYSIS

Typically a data structure allows efficient find and find-min operations when it has a nice structure . But it is hard to maintain a nice structure when insert and delete operations are allowed.

If the data structure is allowed to be a mess (a linked list) then insert is easy (also delete if you have a pointer), but find and find-min are hard.

Good worst-case efficient data structures are a compromise.

They do have a structure, so find is efficient, and it is not too rigid, so insert and delete are efficient.

If we can use amortized analysis, we can think of a data structure that we allow to grow into a bit of a mess for a little while, but we periodically tidy it up.

Even if each tidying up takes a lot of time, provided that they occur sparsely, one can still prove good amortized upper bounds.

3.3 IMPLEMENTING A STACK WITH A VECTOR

Consider the standard implementation of a stack.

We have a vector V [1;::: ; k] and a pointer p 2 f0;::: ; kg. To push an element a we increase p and put a in V [p].

To pop an element we read V [p] and then decrease p. When p > k we are in trouble.

Heuristic

When the stack is full, a reasonable heuristic is to allocate a new vector twice bigger, and then copy all the elements in the new vector (and free the memory of the old one). This costs O(k) time.

Suppose initially we create the empty stack using a vector of size one.

What is amortized time of operations?

Suppose we do n operations. Each pop is O(1) time in the worst case. We have to account for the push operations.

Let N be the final size of the vector. The last time the vector was doubled, there were more than N=2 elements in the stack. At no time there were more than n elements. Then N 2n.

If we start from vector of size 1, we end with vector of size N , we did a create-and-copy operation to go to size 2, 4, . . . , N.

(Note that N is a power of two.)

When we create a new vector of size 2i, the time isc2i, where c is some constant.

So the total time for n operations is O(n) for the pop, O(n) for the creations, and O(n) for the push after creations. Constant amortized time. The heuristic makes sense.

Suppose we want to maintain a counter.

The counter is initially zero. Each inc operation increases its value by 1.

The implementation must be able to work with an unbounded number of increases.

3.4 BIG INTEGER

We represent the counter as a linked list of bits. We start with the least significant bit.

Initially, length-zero list containing only a zero.

Move a pointer from the beginning of the list.

If the pointer is on a 1, change to 0 and move on. If the pointer is on a 0, change to 1 and stop.

If the pointer reaches the end of the list create a new digit and put 1.

Running time

Worst case: when the value of the counter is of the form n = 2k − 1, inc takes O(k) = O(log n) time.

Amortized analysis: when we do n applications of inc, half of the times we just do one step; 1/4 of the times we need two steps, . . .

The total running time is a big-Oh of

= n + n=2+ n=4+ n=8+ n=16 + ::: + n=2k + ::: +1 < 2n

So the amortized time of inc is O(1)

3.5 QUEUE WITH TWO STACKS

Let's see how to implement a queue by using two stacks as a black box.

We have stacks A and B. We can execute operations push and pop. We want to use A and B to implement a queue supporting operations insert and remove.

Implementation

insert(x): push(x; A).

remove():

– if B is not empty, return x = pop(B).

– if B is empty, then repeat the following until A is empty:

x = pop(A); push(x; B). Finally, return x = pop(B).

Correctness is clear(?), worst-case running time is O(n), where n is the size of A at the time an unfortunate remove is executed.

Amortized Analysis

We want to prove that insert has amortized running time 3 and remove has amortized running time 1. (i.e. we want to show that after n1 insert and n2 remove, we have done no more than 3n1 + n2 elementary operations)

Potential Method

At any time, we associate to the data structure (A; B) a non-negative integer value $\Phi(A; B)$ that we call the potential.

We want a definition satisfying the following properties:

1. The potential is always 0, and it is zero for the empty data structure.
2. The actual cost of each operation is (at most) equal to its claimed amortized running time plus the difference between the potential before the operation and potential after the operation.

Our Case

We define the potential as twice the number of elements in A. We want to prove the definition satisfies properties 1 and 2. 1 is clear, have to prove 2.

Consider insert: its actual cost is 1, and it increases the potential by 2. Its claimed amortized running time is 3, we are OK.

Consider remove: if B is not empty, then the cost is 1, the potential stays the same, the claimed amortized running time is 1, we are fine.

If B is not empty, the cost is 1 + twice the number of elements of A, the potential goes down by a factor of twice the elements of A, the claimed amortized running time is 1, OK.

Then . . .

This gives a proof that the claimed amortized running times are true.

Suppose we do a sequence of n operations, having claimed amortized running times a1;::: ; an. Let the potential be initially p0 = 0 and then p1; p2;::: ; pn.

The actual running time (by property 2) is at most

(a1 + p0 − p1)+ (a2 + p1 − p2)+ ⋯ + (an + pn−1 − pn)

= a1 + ::: + an + p0 − pn a1 + ::: + an

General method.

We define a data structure and implement operators.

We attach a potential function to each instance of the data structure and a cost to each operator.

We prove that properties 1 and 2 hold, and this gives a proof that the costs are actually the amortized running times of the operators.

In practice, we define the potential so that property 1 is true, and then we set the amortized time of an operator as the worst case of the expression actual running time + old potential - new potential

This guarantees that property 2 is true.

3.6 BINOMIAL HEAPS

Claim: if delete-min is not allowed, then the insert operator takes O(1) amortized time.

Recall that insert(x; H) is the special case of union where we take the union of a binomial heap H (say of size n) with a "singleton" binomial heap made only by x.

Also recall that the trees in H are in 1-1 correspondence with the 1s in the binary representation of n. insert performs a sequence of tree-unions, each one taking constant time.

The running time of insert is proportional to the running time of inc applied to a counter whose value is n.

In the same way inc uses O(1) amortized time (if no decrease operation is allowed), the same is true for insert.

Possible Improvements

It would be trivial to implement find-min in O(1) time.

We can implement insert in O(1) amortized time even when delete − min is allowed.

Define the potential of a Binomial Heap to be (a suitable constant times) the number of trees.

Under this definition, insert takes constant amortized time.

Also delete-min is still having a logarithmic cost.

So does union (one has to consider the sum of the potentials of the two initial heaps).

So our amortized bounds are O(1) for find-min and insert, and logarithmic for decrease-key, union and delete-min.

With Fibonacci Heaps we can do everything in O(1) amortized except delete-min.

Note that it is impossible (with comparison-based implementations) to do both insert and delete-min in o(log n) amortized time, otherwise we could sort in o(n log n) time.

REVIEW QUESTIONS

1. Define amortized analysis of data structures.
2. What are the Uses of Amortized Analysis.
3. Explain the procedure of
4. Implementing a Stack with a Vector.
5. Queue with two Stacks
6. Explain the amortized analysis of Binomial Heaps.